Invitation to Mathematics

L. Carey Bolster
Supervisor of Mathematics
Baltimore County Public Schools
Towson, Maryland

Warren Crown
Assistant Professor of Mathematics Education
Rutgers University
New Brunswick, New Jersey

Mary Montgomery Lindquist
Professor of Mathematics Education
National College of Education
Evanston, Illinois

Charles McNerney
Professor of Mathematics
University of Northern Colorado
Greeley, Colorado

William Nibbelink
Professor and Chairman
Elementary Education
University of Iowa
Iowa City, Iowa

Glenn Prigge
Professor of Mathematics
University of North Dakota
Grand Forks, North Dakota

Cathy Rahlfs
Math Consultant
Region IV Education Service Center
Houston, Texas

David Robitaille
Head, Department of Mathematics
and Science Education
University of British Columbia
Vancouver, British Columbia, Canada

James Schultz
Associate Professor of Mathematics
The Ohio State University
Columbus, Ohio

Jane Swafford
Professor of Mathematics
Northern Michigan University
Marquette, Michigan

Irvin Vance
Professor of Mathematical Sciences
New Mexico State University
Las Cruces, New Mexico

James Wilson
Professor of Mathematics Education
University of Georgia
Athens, Georgia

Robert Wisner
Professor of Mathematical Sciences
New Mexico State University
Las Cruces, New Mexico

Scott, Foresman and Company

Editorial Offices: Glenview, Illinois

Regional Offices: Palo Alto, California •
Tucker, Georgia • Glenview, Illinois •
Oakland, New Jersey • Dallas, Texas

Advisors

Robert Hamada
Supervisor of Mathematics
Los Angeles Unified School District
Los Angeles, California

Viggo Hansen
Professor, Mathematics Education
California State University
Northridge, California

David E. Williams
Assistant Director
Division of Education
School District of Philadelphia
Philadelphia, Pennsylvania

Teacher Consultants for Grade 8

Alicia Rogerio
Christen Junior High School
2001 Santa Maria Streets
Laredo, Texas

Judy Takaya
Fleming Junior High School
25424 Walnut Street
Lomita, California

Acknowledgments

Data on pages 67, 74, and 75 from NUTRITIVE VALUE OF AMERICAN FOODS (published by United States Department of Agriculture, 1975). Data on pages 188 and 189 courtesy of the Lake County, Illinois, Heart Association.

For permission to reproduce photographs on the following pages, acknowledgment is made to:

Cover photo Chuck O'Rear/West Light   **6–7** FOCUS WEST   **40** Courtesy of 3M, St. Paul, Minn.   **56** Courtesy the Moore School of Electrical Engineering   **142–143** Ray Hillstrom Photography   **144–145** © Norma Morrison/RAY HILLSTROM STOCK PHOTOGRAPHY   **154–155** Eric Carle/SHOSTAL ASSOCIATES   **173** R. Burda/ALPHA/FPG   **186–187** Lee Boltin   **280** © Marjorie Pickens   **324** bottom Eric Carle/SHOSTAL ASSOCIATES   **324** bottom right & **325** Tom Morton/SHOSTAL ASSOCIATES   **336–337** California Institute of Technology   **350–351** Ray Hillstrom Photography   **352–353** The Bettmann Archive, Inc.   **364** © Al Grotell, 1980   **368** Jeff Rotman **375** Courtesy California Institute of Technology & Carnegie Institute, Washington, D.C.

Editorial development, design, art and photography by: Scott, Foresman staff; Norman Perman, Inc.; Diane Kavelaras, Teubner & Associates

Bautzmann, Roland; Bleck, Catherine; Bruce Wood Studio; Criswell, Ron; Duggan, Lee; Enriquez, Mary Ann; German, Kathleen E.; Giancarlo, Jennifer; Graham, Bill; Kalyniuk, Jerry; Kazu; Keeling, Robert; Moch, Paul; Moody, Roy; Musgrave, Steve; Nelson, Fred; Nelson, Kris; Rawson, Jon; Simmons, Bob; Signorino, Slug; Singleton, Earl; Wickart, Mark; Zielinski, John

ISBN: 0-673-22508-9

950 miles
212 passengers
201,400 passenger miles

Number Patterns

A. Students at Mendota Junior High School can buy school sweatshirts for $12. There is a handling charge of $1 for each order. Maria wrote and ran a computer program to show the costs.

SHIRTS	DOLLARS
1	13 ⟩ + 12
2	25 ⟩ + 12
3	37 ⟩ + 12
4	49 ⟩ + 12
5	61 ⟩ + 12
6	73

Each difference is 12.
Each number is 12 more than the number before it.

B. Find a pattern and list the next five numbers.

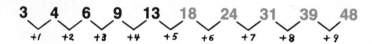

3 4 6 9 13 18 24 31 39 48
 +1 +2 +3 +4 +5 +6 +7 +8 +9

Each difference is 1 more than the difference before it. Continue this pattern.

Try Find a pattern and list the next five numbers.

a. 100, 99, 97, 94, 90, . . .

b. 25, 30, 29, 34, 33, . . .

Practice Find a pattern and list the next five numbers.

1. 5, 10, 15, 20, 25, . . .

2. 9, 16, 23, 30, 37, . . .

3. 51, 48, 45, 42, 39, . . .

4. 100, 94, 88, 82, 76, . . .

5. 0, 2, 6, 12, 20, . . .

6. 4, 5, 7, 10, 14, . . .

7. 999, 998, 996, 993, 989, . . .

8. 70, 68, 64, 62, 58, . . .

9. 14, 9, 14, 9, 14, . . .

10. 1, 11, 10, 20, 19, . . .

11. 1, 3, 2, 4, 3, . . .

12. 500, 450, 458, 408, 416, . . .

13. 1, 8, 22, 43, 71, . . .

14. 50, 54, 62, 74, 90, . . .

★15. 1, 1, 2, 3, 5, 8, . . .

★16. 1, 3, 9, 27, 81, . . .

```
10 REM SWEATSHIRT PROGRAM
20 PRINT "SHIRTS    DOLLARS"
30 FOR SHIRTS=1 TO 10
40 LET DOLLARS = SHIRTS*12+1
50 PRINT SHIRTS,DOLLARS
60 NEXT SHIRTS
70 END
```

Apply   Solve each problem.

17. Complete Maria's list to show the costs of 7, 8, 9, and 10 sweatshirts.

18. Phil noticed a pattern in the numbers that label the statements in Maria's program. What is the pattern?

19. Make a list to show the cost of up to 8 T-shirts that cost $5 each.

20. Make a list to show the cost of up to 10 diskettes at $4 each, plus a $2 handling charge for each order.

A. 103,985 people attended a football game at the Rose Bowl. How would a newspaper headline show this number rounded to the nearest thousand?

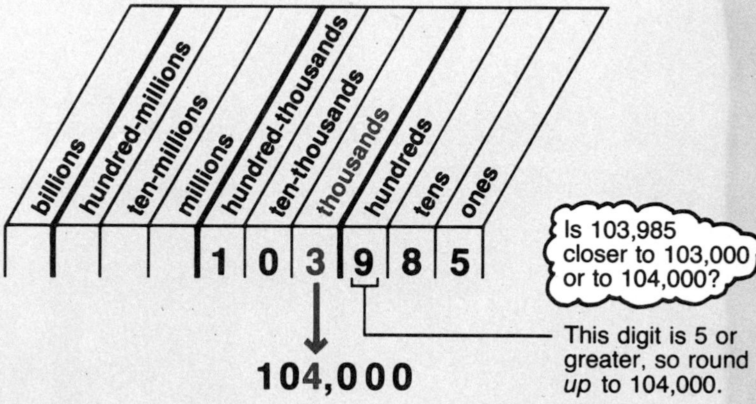

billions | hundred-millions | ten-millions | millions | hundred-thousands | ten-thousands | thousands | hundreds | tens | ones

| | | | 1 | 0 | 3 | 9 | 8 | 5 |

Is 103,985 closer to 103,000 or to 104,000?

104,000

This digit is 5 or greater, so round *up* to 104,000.

The headline would show 103,985 as 104,000.

B. Round 7,099,876 to the nearest million.

7,099,876

Closer to 7,000,000 or to 8,000,000?

This digit is less than 5, so round *down* to 7,000,000.

7,000,000

When rounding, look at the digit to the right of the digit to be rounded.
If it is 5 or greater, round up.
If it is less than 5, round down.

c. *Expanded form*
100,000 + 3,000 + 900 + 80 + 5

Standard form
103,985

Try

a. Round 317 to the nearest hundred.

b. Round 5,722 to the nearest ten-thousand.

c. Write 45,290 in expanded form.

Practice Round to the nearest hundred.

1. 406   **2.** 500   **3.** 1,233   **4.** 1,907   **5.** 8,854   **6.** 57,435

Round to the nearest thousand.

7. 6,570   **8.** 329,004   **9.** 5,699,935   **10.** 872

Round to the nearest hundred-thousand.

11. 814,783   **12.** 4,950,000   **13.** 3,000,800   **14.** 94,619

Round to the nearest million.

15. 8,321,000   **16.** 13,597,222   **17.** 9,999,999   **18.** 681,837

Write each number in expanded form.

19. 213   **20.** 321   **21.** 44,444   **22.** 9,502,050

Apply Round the seating capacity of each stadium as directed.

University	Capacity of stadium	Round to the nearest		
		ten-thousand	thousand	hundred
Northern Illinois	30,233	**23.**	**24.**	**25.**
Notre Dame	59,075	**26.**	**27.**	**28.**
Yale	70,874	**29.**	**30.**	**31.**
Nebraska	76,000	**32.**	**33.**	**34.**
Michigan	104,000	**35.**	**36.**	**37.**

★38. To the nearest thousand, the attendance at a football game was 58,000 people. What is the greatest number of people that could have attended? What is the least number?

Estimating Sums and Differences

A. The attendance for two football games in Los Angeles was 52,649 and 39,460. Estimate the total attendance for these games.

Round the numbers to the same place.
Then add.

52,649 + 39,460

50,000 + 40,000 = 90,000

52,649 + 39,460 ≈ 90,000   The symbol "≈" means "is approximately equal to."

The total attendance was about 90,000 people.

B. Estimate 46,525 − 7,900.

Round the numbers to the same place.
Then subtract.

46,525 − 7,900

47,000 − 8,000 = 39,000

46,525 − 7,900 ≈ 39,000

Discuss When might you need only an estimate, rather than an exact answer?

Try *Estimation* To estimate the answer, first round the numbers to the same place.

a. 498 + 553

b. 8,155 − 2,380

c. 358 + 1,720

d. 692,047 − 41,402

Practice _Estimation_ To estimate the answer, first round the numbers to the same place.

1. 245 + 781

2. 356 + 404

3. 711 − 232

4. 524 − 379

5. 775 + 1,326

6. 697 + 1,851

7. 4,710 − 230

8. 3,640 − 210

9. 7,215 + 2,734

10. 5,501 + 4,099

11. 8,910 − 3,651

12. 6,130 − 1,998

13. 17,234 + 72,541

14. 36,215 + 52,179

15. 26,400 − 11,095

16. 47,800 − 23,105

17. 308,744 + 409,321

18. 269,112 + 852,615

19. 714,618 − 68,502

20. 589,214 − 51,463

★21. 36,853 + 61,391 + 45,610

★22. 8,007 + 295 + 3,748

Find two numbers, each of which rounds to 8,000 and whose sum rounds to

★23. 15,000.

★24. 16,000.

★25. 17,000.

Apply _Estimation_ Solve each problem.

26. Monday's attendance at a baseball game was 27,842. Tuesday's attendance was 19,246. Estimate the total attendance.

27. Friday's attendance of 31,014 was 9,871 more than Thursday's attendance. About how many people attended the game on Thursday?

Adding and Subtracting Whole Numbers

A. Riverfront Stadium in Cincinnati seats 59,754 for football and 52,392 for baseball. How many more people does it seat for football?

Find 59,754 − 52,392.

```
    6 15
  59,7̸5̸4
− 5 2,3 9 2
   7,3 6 2
```
Align the numbers. Subtract, beginning with the ones column.

Estimate:
```
  60,000
− 52,000
   8,000
```

Riverfront Stadium seats 7,362 more people for football.

B. Find 49,756 + 3,871 + 50,430.

```
  1 2 1
  4 9,7 5 6
     3,8 7 1
+  5 0,4 3 0
  1 0 4,0 5 7
```
Align the numbers. Add, beginning with the ones column.

Estimate:
```
   50,000
    4,000
+  50,000
  104,000
```

Try   Add or subtract.

a. 7,094 + 8,257

b. 6,239 − 3,177

c. 52 + 800 + 846

d. 4,300 − 615

Practice   Add or subtract.

1. 756 + 142	**2.** 418 + 351	**3.** 6,679 + 2,175	**4.** 5,227 + 3,293
5. 738 62 + 500	**6.** 567 800 + 33	**7.** 5,177 859 + 7	**8.** 7,239 675 + 8

9. 1,278 + 9,044

10. 76,013 + 14,298

11. 153,789 + 68,214

12. 39,153 + 205,817

13. 5,055 + 9,318 + 2,748

14. 10,043 + 28,650 + 45,333

15. 17,097 + 1,690 + 3,191 + 400

16. 16,483 + 1,084 + 7,280 + 92

17. 4,005 + 17 + 1,888 + 607 + 10,000

18. 1,732 + 505 + 19 + 3,008 + 266

19.	742	20.	961	21.	7,028	22.	6,036
	− 337		− 258		− 2,698		− 4,876

23.	5,600	24.	8,200	25.	37,003	26.	10,256
	− 847		− 642		− 5,414		− 7,159

27. 7,235 − 5,876   28. 5,072 − 2,438

29. 3,647 − 515   30. 9,065 − 706

31. 2,000,000 − 6,967   32. 5,000,000 − 7,098

Apply For each stadium, find the difference in the two seating capacities. Then find the totals.

Stadium	Football seating	Baseball seating	Difference
Riverfront	59,754	52,392	7,362
Candlestick	61,115	58,000	**33.**
Kingdome	64,752	59,438	**34.**
Veterans'	71,464	65,454	**35.**
Total	**36.**	**37.**	**38.**

★39. Describe another way to do Problem 38.

Multiply or divide.

1. 4 × 5

2. 6 × 9

3. 36 ÷ 4

4. 20 ÷ 4

5. 81 ÷ 9

6. 7 × 4

7. 3 × 8

8. 72 ÷ 9

9. 63 ÷ 7

10. 9 × 7

11. 72 ÷ 8

12. 56 ÷ 8

13. 8 × 7

14. 21 ÷ 7

15. 48 ÷ 6

16. 8 × 6

17. 45 ÷ 9

18. 9 × 5

19. 18 ÷ 3

20. 2 × 6

Estimating Products

A. *Career* Earl Graves, an airplane mechanic, maintains some jumbo jets that can carry 47,000 gallons of fuel. Estimate how far Earl could travel in his own car on this much gasoline if his car gets 31 miles per gallon.

Estimate 47,000 × 31.

47,000 × 31   Round each number so that only the first digit is not zero.

50,000 × 30 = 1,500,000

5 × 3   4 zeros + 1 zero

47,000 × 31 ≈ 1,500,000

Earl could travel about 1,500,000 miles.

B. 47,000 × 31 can also be written with parentheses.

47,000(31)

(47,000)31

(47,000)(31)

Try *Estimation* Round each number so that only the first digit is not zero. Then estimate the product.

a. 876 × 324

b. 45(3,561)

Practice *Estimation* Round each number so that only the first digit is not zero. Then estimate the product.

1. 379 × 413   **2.** 824 × 563   **3.** 283 × 775   **4.** 310 × 525

5. 3,156(4,875)   **6.** 2,734(4,269)   **7.** 2,337(9,281)   **8.** 7,902(2,504)

9. (736)92   **10.** (597)16   **11.** (7,603)(45)   **12.** (2,560)(64)

13. 43,566(46)   **14.** 16,009(83)   **15.** 75(20,575)   **16.** 22(23,456)

★17. 34 × 94 × 64   **★18.** (35)(95)(65)   **★19.** 100(647)(88)

Apply *Estimation* Solve each problem.

20. If a jet uses 2,401 gallons of fuel per hour, about how much fuel will it use in 18 hours?

21. A car that gets 28 miles per gallon has a 19-gallon gas tank. About how far can it go on one tank of gasoline?

Multiplying Whole Numbers

One passenger traveling one mile is called one *passenger mile*. A jumbo jet carried 332 passengers a distance of 1,970 miles. How many passenger miles did this flight represent?

Find 332 × 1,970.

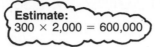

Estimate:
300 × 2,000 = 600,000

```
   1,970
 ×   332
   3 9 4 0     ← 2 × 1,970
 5 9 1 0 0     ← 30 × 1,970
5 9 1 0 0 0    ← 300 × 1,970
6 5 4,0 4 0
```

This flight represented 654,040 passenger miles.

Try Multiply.

a. 834
  ×   7

b. (953)508

c. 34(51)(89)

Practice Multiply.

1.	2.	3.	4.	5.	6.
39	70	255	906	50	30
× 6	× 8	× 4	× 7	× 90	× 80

7.	8.	9.	10.	11.	12.
82	43	696	407	651	977
× 76	× 49	× 72	× 65	× 831	× 203

13. 8(29)

14. 5(62)

15. 9(700)

16. 4(779)

17. 40(98)

18. 70(82)

19. 45(43)

20. 87(31)

21. (63)290

22. (14)603

23. (27)555

24. (15)2,900

25. 46(2,984)

26. 89(4,705)

27. 300(927)

28. 241(606)

29. (733)(833)

30. (676)(1,982)

31. (914)(2,065)

32. (495)(7,208)

33. 23 × 49 × 56

34. (82)(79)(48)

35. 85(75)(45)

12

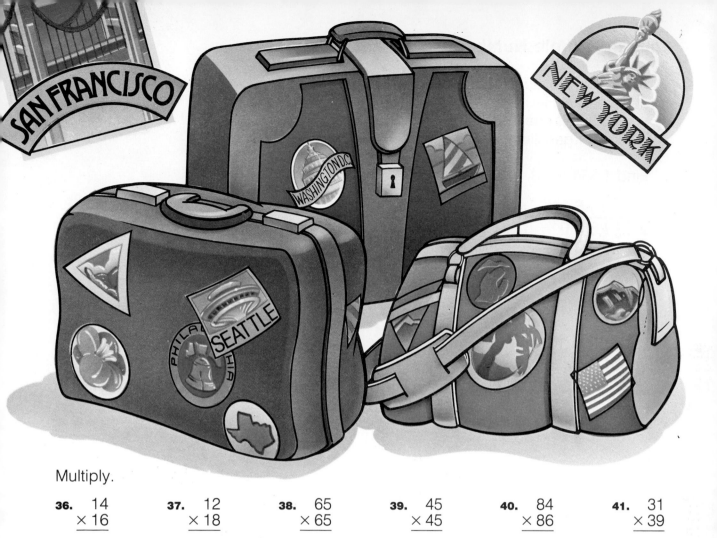

Multiply.

36. $\begin{array}{r} 14 \\ \times 16 \\ \hline \end{array}$ **37.** $\begin{array}{r} 12 \\ \times 18 \\ \hline \end{array}$ **38.** $\begin{array}{r} 65 \\ \times 65 \\ \hline \end{array}$ **39.** $\begin{array}{r} 45 \\ \times 45 \\ \hline \end{array}$ **40.** $\begin{array}{r} 84 \\ \times 86 \\ \hline \end{array}$ **41.** $\begin{array}{r} 31 \\ \times 39 \\ \hline \end{array}$

★42. In Exercises 36–41, what is special about the ones digits of the factors? the tens digits of the factors?

★43. Describe an easy way to find each product above.

Apply   Solve each problem.

44. An airplane flew 1,900 miles with 131 passengers. How many passenger miles is this?

45. A group of 75 people flew from Tampa, Florida, to San Antonio, Texas, a distance of 980 miles. How many passenger miles is this?

46. In two flights, a jet plane logged 40,000 passenger miles and 35,618 passenger miles. What is the difference in the number of passenger miles?

★47. Which flight represents more passenger miles, a 1,034-mile flight with 280 people or a 900-mile flight with 313 people?

Dividing Whole Numbers

A. Mary Bujan's vacation trip will cover 1,650 miles. Her car gets 28 miles per gallon. If she drives, how many gallons of gasoline will she use?

Find 1,650 ÷ 28.

```
        5
28)1,6 5 0
   1 4 0
     2 5
```

Divide.
THINK Round 28 to 30.
How many 3s in 16? 5

Multiply.
Subtract and compare.
25 < 28

```
      58 R26
28)1,6 5 0
   1 4 0↓
     2 5 0
     2 2 4
         2 6
```

Bring down.
Divide.
Multiply.
Subtract and compare.

The remainder is 26.

The remainder is nearly as large as the divisor. Ms. Bujan will use nearly 59 gallons of gasoline.

Check
```
        58   ← Quotient
      × 28   ← Divisor
       464
     1,160
     1,624
   +    26   ← Remainder
     1,650   ← Dividend
```

B. You can use a bar to show division. 40,297 ÷ 53 can be written as $\frac{40,297}{53}$.

Find $\frac{40,297}{53}$.

```
        8
53)40,2 9 7
    4 2 4
```

Divide.

Multiply.
424 > 402, so 8 is too big.

```
       7 6
53)40,2 9 7
    3 7 1↓
      3 1 9
      3 1 8
          1
```

Try 7.
Multiply.
Subtract and compare.
Bring down.
Divide.
Multiply.
Subtract and compare.

```
      760 R17
53)40,2 9 7
    3 7 1│
      3 1 9│
      3 1 8↓
          1 7
```

Bring down.
Divide.

14

Try Divide.

a. $6\overline{)559}$

b. $31\overline{)744}$

c. $29{,}586 \div 59$

d. $\dfrac{13{,}096}{425}$

Practice Divide.

1. $8\overline{)433}$

2. $9\overline{)645}$

3. $7\overline{)924}$

4. $5\overline{)2{,}029}$

5. $4\overline{)3{,}623}$

6. $32\overline{)711}$

7. $29\overline{)847}$

8. $55\overline{)504}$

9. $68\overline{)4{,}896}$

10. $92\overline{)4{,}876}$

11. $825 \div 5$

12. $389 \div 6$

13. $1{,}801 \div 3$

14. $2{,}402 \div 8$

15. $1{,}225 \div 27$

16. $8{,}082 \div 58$

17. $15{,}526 \div 33$

18. $25{,}900 \div 35$

19. $\dfrac{20{,}513}{81}$

20. $\dfrac{6{,}680}{72}$

21. $\dfrac{685}{187}$

22. $\dfrac{921}{215}$

23. $\dfrac{5{,}400}{528}$

24. $\dfrac{3{,}627}{910}$

25. $\dfrac{13{,}763}{623}$

26. $\dfrac{159{,}598}{390}$

Find each missing number.

★**27.** $37\overline{)\rule{2em}{0.8em}}$ 207 R30

★**28.** $\rule{2em}{0.8em}\overline{)5{,}005}$ 73 R41

Apply Solve each problem.

29. By airplane, Ms. Bujan could travel the 1,650 miles in 3 hours. How many miles per hour is this?

30. If Ms. Bujan can drive at an average of 50 miles per hour, how many hours of driving time should she allow for the 1,650 miles?

★**31.** If Ms. Bujan drives, she will allow $82 for gasoline, $50 for meals, and $105 for lodging. If she flies, her air fare will be $275 and the taxicab ride to the airport will be $10. Which set of expenses is less, driving or flying? How much less?

Problem Solving: Choose the Operation

Read   Read the problem. What facts are given? What is the question?

A bird called the Indian chimney swift can fly 195 miles per hour (mph). A jet airplane can fly 585 mph. The plane is how many times as fast as the bird?

Plan   What can you do to solve the problem?

Divide to find how many groups of 195 there are in 585. Find 585 ÷ 195.

Solve   Do the work.

$$
\begin{array}{r}
3 \\
195\overline{)585} \\
585 \\
\hline
0
\end{array}
$$

Answer   Give the answer.

The plane is 3 times as fast as the bird.

Look Back   Read the question. Does the answer make sense?

The numbers used are very close to 200 and 600. Since 600 ÷ 200 = 3, the answer seems reasonable.

16

Try Tell which operation to use. Then find the answer.

a. What is the difference in the speeds of the jet flying 585 mph and the chimney swift flying 195 mph?

b. Orville and Wilbur Wright made their first two flights on December 17, 1903. They flew 120 feet and 852 feet. What was the total distance flown?

Apply Tell which operation to use to solve the problem.

1. A flight from Vancouver, British Columbia, to Montreal, Quebec, takes ▓▓ hours if the pilot flies at an average speed of ● mph. How far apart are the cities?

2. What is the difference in speeds of a jumbo jet flying ▓▓ mph and a helicopter flying ● mph?

Tell which operation to use. Then find the answer.

3. The Wright brothers' final flight lasted about 60 seconds. This is about how many times as long as the first flight, which lasted 12 seconds?

4. Orville and Wilbur Wright's first flight covered 120 feet. This distance is how much shorter than a jet that is 231 feet long?

5. During migration, geese may fly 12 hours a day at a speed of 65 mph. At this rate, how far can they fly in one day?

6. What is the difference in speeds of a hawk diving 500 mph and a bird flying 25 mph?

One airline has two flights each day from Chicago to Los Angeles.
The early flight can carry 396 passengers on a jumbo jet.
The late flight can carry 137 people on a regular jet.
Use this information for Problems 7–10.

7. How many passengers can be flown to Los Angeles each day on these two flights?

8. The jumbo jet can carry how many more passengers than the regular jet?

9. How many passengers can travel on the early flight during one year? (Use 1 year = 365 days.)

*10. How many regular jets would be needed to carry the same number of passengers as one jumbo jet?

Practice: Computing with Whole Numbers

Find each answer.

1. $\begin{array}{r} 416 \\ +892 \\ \hline \end{array}$
2. $\begin{array}{r} 1,520 \\ -\ \ 587 \\ \hline \end{array}$
3. $\begin{array}{r} 59,089 \\ -21,602 \\ \hline \end{array}$
4. $\begin{array}{r} 8,648 \\ +2,903 \\ \hline \end{array}$
5. $\begin{array}{r} 16,342 \\ -\ 7,916 \\ \hline \end{array}$
6. $\begin{array}{r} 74,391 \\ +80,002 \\ \hline \end{array}$

7. $\begin{array}{r} 37,487 \\ +21,602 \\ \hline \end{array}$
8. $\begin{array}{r} 933 \\ +587 \\ \hline \end{array}$
9. $\begin{array}{r} 1,308 \\ -\ \ 416 \\ \hline \end{array}$
10. $\begin{array}{r} 4,300 \\ -\ \ 827 \\ \hline \end{array}$
11. $\begin{array}{r} 7,916 \\ +8,426 \\ \hline \end{array}$
12. $\begin{array}{r} 11,551 \\ -\ 2,903 \\ \hline \end{array}$

13. $\begin{array}{r} 23 \\ 47 \\ +59 \\ \hline \end{array}$
14. $\begin{array}{r} 1,294 \\ 7 \\ +\ \ 241 \\ \hline \end{array}$
15. $\begin{array}{r} 2,168 \\ 4,910 \\ +7,732 \\ \hline \end{array}$
16. $\begin{array}{r} 21,005 \\ 6,365 \\ +\ \ \ \ \ 23 \\ \hline \end{array}$
17. $\begin{array}{r} 8,011 \\ 1,939 \\ +1,876 \\ \hline \end{array}$
18. $\begin{array}{r} 1,000 \\ 47,846 \\ +\ \ \ \ 923 \\ \hline \end{array}$

19. $\begin{array}{r} 463 \\ \times 192 \\ \hline \end{array}$
20. $7\overline{)362}$
21. $\begin{array}{r} 405 \\ \times\ \ \ 9 \\ \hline \end{array}$
22. $\begin{array}{r} 88 \\ \times 82 \\ \hline \end{array}$
23. $21\overline{)946}$
24. $17\overline{)3,000}$

25. $5\overline{)4,513}$
26. $\begin{array}{r} 85 \\ \times\ \ 6 \\ \hline \end{array}$
27. $\begin{array}{r} 97 \\ \times 30 \\ \hline \end{array}$
28. $42\overline{)924}$
29. $\begin{array}{r} 14 \\ \times 78 \\ \hline \end{array}$
30. $681\overline{)1,445}$

31. $825\overline{)62,509}$
32. $\begin{array}{r} 175 \\ \times\ \ 24 \\ \hline \end{array}$
33. $9\overline{)812}$
34. $322\overline{)2,420}$

35. $\begin{array}{r} 806 \\ \times\ \ 31 \\ \hline \end{array}$
36. $458\overline{)159,384}$
37. $\begin{array}{r} 727 \\ \times 503 \\ \hline \end{array}$
38. $66\overline{)39,204}$

39. $6,000 - 459$
40. 320×8
41. $9\overline{)4,578}$

42. $51\overline{)4,475}$
43. $608 + 994$
44. 209×628

45. $2,732 - 2,598$
46. $782\overline{)234,605}$
47. 93×97

48. $4\overline{)963}$
49. 575×425
50. $3,146 + 81,492$

51. $96\overline{)30,816}$
52. $63,166 - 48,566$
53. 716×40

54. $18 + 635 + 93 + 1,976$
55. $8,000,000 - 231,642$

Apply Solve each problem.

56. A jet airliner flying 595 mph is traveling how many times as fast as a helicopter that is flying 85 mph?

57. An automobile has a 15-gallon gas tank. If the car gets 32 miles per gallon, how far can it go on one tank of gas?

58. In the last three working days, a flight attendant has logged 1,450 miles, 2,026 miles, and 1,779 miles. How many miles has he traveled in all?

59. If 112,200 passenger miles were recorded on a 600-mile flight, how many passengers were on this flight?

60. _Estimation_ If a jet uses 1,900 gallons of fuel per hour, about how much fuel does it use in 11 hours of flying?

61. The football stadium at the University of Iowa holds 60,000 people. If ticket sales for an upcoming game with Ohio State are 55,914, how many tickets are still available?

COMPUTER

BASIC: PRINT Statements

The computer recognizes these symbols of operation.

+ add   * multiply
− subtract   / divide

The PRINT statement causes the computer to print what is between quotation marks, or the answers to calculations. The following is a program written in BASIC. The program statements are executed in order of the line numbers from least to greatest.

This is printed.

```
10 PRINT "HELLO"    HELLO
20 PRINT 36+18      54
30 PRINT 36/3       12
40 END
```

Tell what would be printed for each of the following programs.

1.
```
10 PRINT "THE PRODUCT IS"
20 PRINT 58*27
30 END
```

2.
```
10 PRINT 432-189
20 PRINT 777-54
30 END
```

3.
```
10 PRINT "WHAT'S THE
   DIFFERENCE?"
20 PRINT 9015-2763
30 END
```

4.
```
40 END
20 PRINT 75-25
10 PRINT 75+25
30 PRINT 75/25
```

Divisibility

A. It takes the earth a little more than 365 days to orbit the sun, so periodically an extra day is added to the calendar to create a *leap year*. If you divide the date of any leap year by 4, the remainder is 0. This means that the dates of leap years are *divisible* by 4.

The following work shows that the number 1,992 is divisible by 4, but that 2,005 is not.

```
     498              501 R1
4)1,992           4)2,005
  1 6               2 0
   39                005
   36                  4
   32                  1
   32
    0
```

Sometimes you can use a divisibility test instead of doing the actual division.

A whole number is divisible by	if
2	its *ones digit* is 0, 2, 4, 6, or 8.
3	the *sum of its digits* is divisible by 3.
4	the *number formed by its last two digits* is divisible by 4.
5	its *ones digit* is 0 or 5.
9	the *sum of its digits* is divisible by 9.
10	its *ones digit* is 0.

B. Apply the divisibility tests to the number 1,770.

Ones digit: 0   1,770 is divisible by 2, 5, and 10.

Sum of digits: 15   1,770 is divisible by 3 but not by 9.

Number formed by last two digits: 70   1,770 is not divisible by 4.

Try Apply the divisibility tests to these numbers.

a. 2,052 **b.** 12,345 **c.** 29

Practice Copy and complete this table.

				Divisible by			
	Number	2	3	4	5	9	10
	1,770	√	√		√		√
1.	450						
2.	5,128						
3.	1,000						
4.	9,855						
5.	389						
6.	1,945						
7.	73,440						
8.	88,389						
9.	346,512						
10.	5,096,997						

★11. Can you find a number divisible by 4 that is not divisible by 2?

★12. Can you find a number divisible by 2 and 3 that is not divisible by 6?

★13. List all the numbers less than 50 that are divisible by 2 and 6 but not by 12.

★14. Find the least number divisible by 2, 5, and 9.

★15. Develop a test for divisibility by 8.

★16. Develop a test for divisibility by 11.

Prime and Composite Numbers

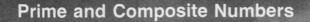

Between now and the year 2030, Finlay's comet should pass by Earth in the years that are divisible by 7. 1995 is one of those years.

Since 1,995 is divisible by 7, we say that 7 is a *divisor*, or *factor*, of 1,995. Some other factors of 1,995 are 285, 1, and 1,995 itself.

```
      285
  7) 1,995
     14
     ──
      59
      56
      ──
       35
       35
       ──
        0 ← Remainder of 0
             means 1,995 is
             divisible by 7.
```

A. How many factors does 13 have?

$$13 = 1 \times 13$$

13 has two factors: 1 and 13.

A **prime number** is a whole number with only two distinct factors, 1 and itself. 13 is prime.

The first six prime numbers are 2, 3, 5, 7, 11, and 13.

B. How many factors does 36 have?

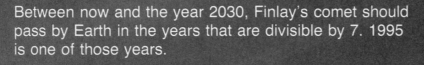

36 has nine factors: 1, 2, 3, 4, 6, 9, 12, 18, and 36.

A **composite number** is a whole number with more than two factors. 36 and 1,995 are composite.

The numbers 0 and 1 are considered neither prime nor composite, but every whole number greater than 1 is either prime or composite.

Try Tell whether each number is prime or composite.
If it is composite, list all of its factors.

a. 4   **b.** 17   **c.** 60

Practice Tell whether each number is prime or composite.
If it is composite, list all of its factors.

1. 10   **2.** 18   **3.** 29   **4.** 39   **5.** 49   **6.** 57   **7.** 83

8. 96   **9.** 100   **10.** 103   **11.** 123   **12.** 127   **13.** 143   **14.** 361

★15. 592   **★16.** 593   **★17.** 447   **★18.** 527   **★19.** 1,995

20. List all the prime numbers that are less than 50.

21. **Twin primes** are two prime numbers that differ by 2, such as 11 and 13.
List all the twin primes that are less than 50.

★22. Recall that numbers divisible by 2 are **even numbers**.
Why is 2 the only even number that is prime?

★23. Name five consecutive numbers that are composite.

Apply

★24. In what years between now and 2030 should Finlay's comet pass by
Earth? Can any of these dates be prime numbers? Why?

Prime Factorization

A. In the last lesson, 1,995 was shown to be a composite number. Any composite number can be written as the product of prime numbers.

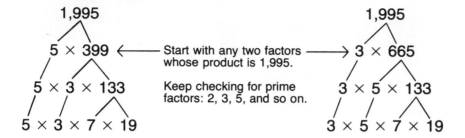

The *prime factorization* of 1,995 is 3 × 5 × 7 × 19.

Each arrangement shown above is a *factor tree*. No matter how you start a factor tree for a number, the bottom row will always contain the same factors.

Except for the order of factors, any composite number has just one prime factorization.

B. Use the prime factorization of 90 to list all of its factors.

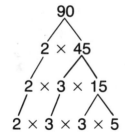

The factors of 90 are:

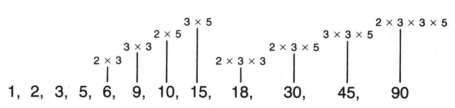

C. 3 × 3 can be written 3^2. 3^2 is read "three squared." The *exponent*, 2, tells you that 3 is a factor two times. 3^2, or 9, is the second *power* of 3.

8 × 8 × 8	8^3	"eight to the third power" or "eight cubed"
2 × 2 × 2 × 2	2^4	"two to the fourth power"

The prime factorization of 90 written with exponents is:

$2 × 3^2 × 5$

Try Show two factor trees for each number.

a. 36   **b.** 105

Write the prime factorization of each number.
Use exponents when you can.

c. 42   **d.** 80   **e.** 117

f. Use the prime factorization of 42 to list
all of its factors.

Practice Show two factor trees for each number.

1. 24   **2.** 66   **3.** 210   **4.** 255

Write the prime factorization of each number.
Use exponents when you can.

5. 14   **6.** 15   **7.** 28   **8.** 33

9. 70   **10.** 80   **11.** 325   **12.** 100

13. 162   **14.** 255   **15.** 291   **16.** 1,000

★17. 32,400   **★18.** 165,375   **★19.** 189,728

Write the prime factorization of each number
and list all of its factors.

20. 8   **21.** 12   **22.** 44   **23.** 125

24. 84   **25.** 96   **★26.** 891   **★27.** 1,275

Apply

28. Show the factor tree for 1,995 that starts
with 7 × 285.

★29. Write the next three numbers in this
sequence of numbers.

2, 6, 30, 210, 2,310, ▧, ▧, ▧

Tell what to do to
get a pattern of
"empty"
alternating with
"full."

You may handle
only one glass.

Greatest Common Factor

A. Eighth graders at Ardmore School are making banners with a border design of squares. What is the largest square that can be used on a 20-inch by 28-inch banner?

Both 20 and 28 must be divisible by the side measure of the square. List the factors of 20 and 28.

20: 1, 2, 4, 5, 10, 20

28: 1, 2, 4, 7, 14, 28
Common factors

The *greatest common factor* (GCF) of 20 and 28 is 4.

The largest square that can be used is a 4-inch square.

Discuss How many 4-inch squares would be placed on the 20-inch side? on the 28-inch side?

B. Instead of listing factors, you can decide what the GCF is by using prime factorization. Find the GCF of 84 and 56.

$$84 = 2 \times 2 \times 3 \times 7$$
$$56 = 2 \times 2 \times 2 \times 7$$

Count the fewest times that a prime factor appears in both numbers.

The GCF of 84 and 56 is $2 \times 2 \times 7$, or 28.

Try List the common factors of

a. 55 and 40.   **b.** 16 and 9.

Find the GCF of

c. 36 and 90.   **d.** 27 and 16.

Practice   List the common factors of each pair of numbers.

1. 8 and 10
2. 12 and 9
3. 16 and 24
4. 35 and 25

5. 8 and 9
6. 7 and 21
7. 72 and 63
8. 24 and 60

Find the GCF of each pair of numbers.

9. 15 and 9
10. 18 and 10
11. 60 and 18
12. 42 and 24

13. 3 and 8
14. 5 and 9
15. 48 and 60
16. 39 and 52

17. 25 and 5
18. 36 and 56
19. 65 and 195
20. 27 and 99

Find the common factors and the GCF of each triple of numbers.

★21. 32, 64, and 80
★22. 135, 81, and 27
★23. 194, 132, and 298

Apply   Solve each problem.

24. What is the largest square that could be used on the border of a banner that is 40 inches by 55 inches?

25. According to Example A on page 26, what other squares could be used on the 20-inch by 28-inch banner?

26. What size of square would always fit, as long as the dimensions of a banner are whole numbers?

★27. For the border of a 27-inch by 36-inch banner, why might you not use the square that is represented by the GCF of 27 and 36? Draw a sketch on graph paper to support your answer.

★28. How many 4-inch squares will be needed for the border of the 20-inch by 28-inch banner?

Least Common Multiple

A. The Ardmore School banners will be stored in boxes that are either 6 inches or 9 inches high. To save space, the building superintendent plans to adjust some wall shelves so that groups of either size box will fit exactly. What is the closest that two shelves can be?

The distance has to be a number that is divisible by both 6 and 9. The number has to be a *common multiple* of 6 and 9.

Multiples of

6:   6, 12, 18, 24, 30, 36, 42, . . .

9:   9, 18, 27, 36, 45, . . .

The *least common multiple* of 6 and 9 is 18.

Two shelves can be as close as 18 inches.

B. Use prime factorization to find the least common multiple (LCM) of 84 and 56.

$$84 = 2 \times 2 \quad \times \boxed{3} \quad \boxed{7}$$
$$56 = \boxed{2 \times 2 \times 2} \quad \times 7$$

Count the most times that a prime factor appears in either number.

The LCM of 84 and 56 is $2 \times 2 \times 2 \times 3 \times 7$, or 168.

Try List the first five multiples of

a. 8.   **b.** 12.   **c.** 17.

List the first three common multiples of

d. 15 and 25.   **e.** 8 and 32.

f. Use prime factorization to find the LCM of 36 and 120.

Practice List the first five multiples of each number.

1. 5 **2.** 9 **3.** 11 **4.** 16

5. 20 **6.** 27 **7.** 36 **8.** 48

For each pair of numbers, list the first three common multiples.

9. 4 and 6 **10.** 9 and 12 **11.** 15 and 10

12. 5 and 8 **13.** 3 and 2 **14.** 5 and 25

15. 4 and 16 **16.** 30 and 12 **17.** 49 and 21

Use prime factorization to find the LCM of each pair of numbers.

18. 100 and 40 **19.** 39 and 26 **20.** 20 and 21

21. 36 and 27 **22.** 44 and 45 **23.** 51 and 33

24. 28 and 30 **25.** 24 and 26 **26.** 14 and 15

Find the LCM of each triple of numbers.

★27. 35, 14, and 49 **★28.** 300, 180, and 120

Apply Solve each problem.

29. What is the least distance between two shelves that can fit groups of 3-inch boxes and 4-inch boxes exactly?

30. What is the least distance between two shelves that can fit groups of 8-inch boxes and 5-inch boxes exactly?

★31. What is true of two numbers if their GCF and their LCM are equal?

To get multiples on your calculator, use repeated addition. Your calculator should display the first three multiples of 7 when you press either

7 [+] [=] [=]

or 7 [+] [+] [=] [=]

or 7 [+] 7 [+] 7 [+]

Use your calculator to list the first seven multiples of:

1. 12 **2.** 15

3. 18 **4.** 51

5. 85 **6.** 119

Use your lists from Exercises 1–6 to find the LCM of:

7. 12 and 18

8. 18 and 15

9. 51 and 85

10. 51 and 119

11. 119 and 85

Problem Solving: Find a Pattern

Read   *Career* James and Rosita are computer programmers
in their city's planning department. Trying to find
errors, or *bugs*, in a program can take a long time,
especially if the program contains many *decision
statements*. Each single statement is either true or
false, which creates two paths in a flow chart. How
many paths are in a program that has 4 decision
statements?

Plan   Determine the number of paths that result from one
statement, two statements, and three statements. Look
for a pattern between number of statements and
number of paths.

Solve

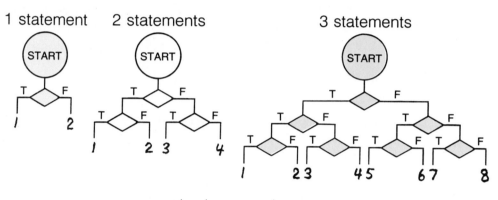

Number of statements	1	2	3
Number of paths	2	4, or 2^2	8, or 2^3

According to this pattern, 4 should correspond to 2^4.
2^4 is $2 \times 2 \times 2 \times 2$, or 16.

Answer   A computer program with 4 decision statements
has 16 paths.

Look Back   Make a diagram that shows 4 decision statements.
Count the paths to see if there are 16.

Try   Solve the problem.

a. A printout shows that the city's population has been
changing yearly, from 100,000 to 103,000 to
106,000. If this trend continues, what should be the
next population figure?

30

Apply Solve each problem. Use the pattern on page 30 or look for another pattern.

1. Rosita has a program that has 10 decision statements. How many paths does it have?

2. One program has fewer than 30 paths. What is the greatest number of decision statements it could have?

3. James said he would like to be paid weekly at the rate of $3, $9, $27, and so on. At this rate, how much would he receive for the eighth week?

4. In contrast to James's rate, Rosita decided that she would *not* want to be paid weekly at the rate of $3, $6, $9, and so on. How much would she receive the eighth week at this rate?

5. The number of employees in the planning department has gone from 23 to 19 to 15. If this trend were to continue, what would be the next number in this pattern?

6. Rosita's son drew a family tree. He showed his parents in the first row and his grandparents in the second row. How many great-great-grandparents did he have?

*7. Rosita checked a program with 6 decision statements. She found a bug in the 50th path she checked. How many paths still have to be checked?

*8. James attended a computer conference. Pascal, the cab driver, offered to drive James without charge from the hotel (*H*) to the conference (*C*) if James knew how many different routes there are between the two points. (Pascal drives only north or east.) James said there were 20. Did he have to pay?

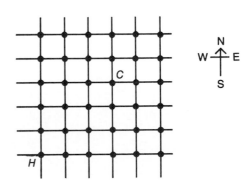

Chapter 1 Test

Find a pattern and list the next five numbers.

1. 86, 82, 78, 74, 70, . . .

2. 1, 6, 4, 9, 7, . . .

3. Write 3,642 in expanded form.

Round 4,903,479 to the nearest

4. thousand.   5. million.

Estimate each sum or difference. For each exercise, first round the numbers to the same place.

6. 7,145 − 583   7. 12,923 + 26,737

Add or subtract.

8. 715,394
  + 142,655

9. 4,522
  − 876

Round each factor so that only the first digit is not zero. Then estimate each product.

10. (18)235   11. 824(419)

Multiply.

12. 65
   × 32

13. 744
   × 805

14. 2,381
    ×   53

Divide.

15. 56)‾8,392

16. $\dfrac{16,487}{212}$

Write which operation to use. Then find the answer.

17. A car is traveling at an average speed of 50 mph. How far will it go in 4 hours?

18. A post office sold 382 stamps in the morning and 491 in the afternoon. How many more stamps were sold in the afternoon?

For each number, write which of these numbers it is divisible by: 2, 3, 4, 5, 9, or 10.

19. 321   20. 1,755

Write whether each number is prime or composite. If it is composite, list all of its factors.

21. 52   22. 37

Write the prime factorization of each number. Use exponents when you can.

23. 30   24. 56

25. List the common factors of 18 and 27.

26. What is the GCF of 16 and 36?

27. What is the LCM of 15 and 20?

Solve this problem.

28. A city's population has been changing yearly, from 250,000 to 235,000 to 220,000. If this trend continues, what should be the next population figure?

CHALLENGE

The Fibonacci Sequence

One of the number patterns in the first lesson of this chapter bears the nickname of a thirteenth-century mathematician, Leonardo of Pisa. The pattern is the *Fibonacci sequence*. Fibonacci numbers have many kinds of applications, from seashells to building design to family trees for drone bees.

1, 1, 2, 3, 5, 8, 13, . . .

1. How is a Fibonacci number related to the two numbers just before it?

2. Write the first 15 Fibonacci numbers. Label their positions 1 through 15.

3. What are the positions of the Fibonacci numbers that are divisible by 2?

4. Would you expect 2 to divide the eighteenth Fibonacci number? the twenty-fifth number?

5. Without extending your list, describe the first six Fibonacci numbers that should be divisible by 3.

6. Two whole numbers whose greatest common factor is 1 are called *relatively prime*. What is the GCF of any two consecutive Fibonacci numbers?

7. A female bee has both parents, but the male drone bee has only a mother. Sketch the family tree of the male bee to show how many great-great-great-grandparents he has. How does your diagram show Fibonacci numbers?

MAINTENANCE

Find each answer.

1. 742
    − 595

2. 3,083
    − 1,991

3. 6,005
    −   247

4. 68,000
    − 59,514

5. 32,111
    − 4,711

6. 25,340
    − 13,879

7. 707
    + 514

8. 249
    + 730

9. 8,035
    +   485

10. 3,990
       87
    +   453

11.   29
      629
    + 8,029

12. 53,279
    + 46,721

13. 400
    × 53

14. 988
    ×   6

15. 49
    × 47

16. 5,004
    ×   92

17. 258
    × 619

18. 7,540
    ×   237

19. 6)4,117

20. 52)3,665

21. 37)7,700

22. 724)67,332

23. 71 × 39

24. 503 − 196

25. 9,745 ÷ 8

26. 40,270 ÷ 60

27. 42 × 970

28. 67 + 380 + 3,272

29. 9,000 − 4,288

30. 5,035 ÷ 95

31. 777 − 389

32. 17,003 + 439

33. 8,145 ÷ 27

34. 2,905 × 8

35. 685 × 925

36. 5,075 − 847

37. 160,678 ÷ 322

38. 6,000,000 − 652,073

39. 2,000 + 15 + 7,643 + 95

Solve each problem.

40. San Francisco's Candlestick Park has 58,000 seats for baseball. Riverfront Stadium in Cincinnati has 52,392. How many more seats does Candlestick Park have?

41. A sportscaster reported Sunday attendance at the ball park last month as 28,005, 25,647, 17,338, and 25,995. What was the total attendance?

42. _Estimation_ If a truck has been using 21 gallons of gasoline per day, about how much gasoline would it use in 210 days?

43. A small jet that is flying 192 miles per hour (mph) is traveling how many times as fast as a blimp flying 16 mph?

Equations and
Graphs

$625 for each horn

$3n = 1{,}875$

Order of Operations

Jenny

$12 + 18 \times 5 - 2$

$30 \times 5 - 2$

$150 - 2$

148

Tricia

$12 + 18 \times 5 - 2$

$12 + 90 - 2$

$102 - 2$

100

ABE

$12 + 18 \times 5 - 2$

30×3

90

A. Not all three answers above can be correct. We need some rules for computing. When there are no parentheses, use this *standard order of operations*:

1. *Multiply as indicated by exponents.*
2. *Multiply and divide from left to right.*
3. *Add and subtract from left to right.*

Tricia used the standard order.
$12 + 18 \times 5 - 2 = 100$

$$4 + \frac{9(10-2)^2}{6^2}$$

$$4 + \frac{9(8)^2}{6^2}$$

B. If an expression contains any parentheses or division bars, use these guidelines:

Compute inside parentheses first, using standard order.

$$4 + \frac{9(64)}{36}$$

Compute above and below the division bars, using standard order, before you divide.

$$4 + \frac{576}{36}$$

Do the remaining computation, using standard order.

$$4 + 16$$

$$20$$

36

Try Compute each answer.

a. $10 + 6 \div 2$ **b.** $13 - 3^2$ **c.** $11 - (6 + 2)$

d. $(7 + 8)5$ **e.** $\dfrac{12 - 8}{4}$ **f.** $\dfrac{6(4 + 5)}{3}$

Practice Compute each answer.

1. $2 + 3 \times 4$ **2.** $4 + 15 \div 3$

3. $10 \div 2 - 2$ **4.** $10 - 4 + 1$

5. $9 + 4 - 2$ **6.** $12 \div 2 \times 5$

7. $13 + 3 - 40 \div 4$ **8.** $100 \times 3 \div 6 + 4 - 4$

9. $5 + 5 - 5 \times 5 \div 5$ **10.** $3(8) - 7$

11. $65 + 2(10)$ **12.** $(5)9 \div 3$

13. $17(10 - 7)$ **14.** $17 - (10 - 7)$ **15.** $17 - 10 - 7$ **16.** $(17 - 10) - 7$

17. $10 - 2^2$ **18.** $4 + 5^2$ **19.** $(10 - 2)^2$ **20.** $(4 + 5)^2$

21. $\dfrac{14 + 6}{2}$ **22.** $\dfrac{2 + 3 \times 4}{5 + 2 - 0}$ **23.** $\dfrac{8(2 + 9)}{4}$ **24.** $\dfrac{(9 - 3)7}{6}$

25. $\dfrac{5(6 - 1)}{20 + 5}$ **26.** $\dfrac{(3 - 1)12}{(7 - 6)8}$ **27.** $\dfrac{6^2 + 8^2}{40 - 30}$ **28.** $\dfrac{(3 + 3)^2}{3^2 + 3^2}$

29. $7 + \dfrac{6}{2}$ **30.** $12 - \dfrac{5}{5}$ **31.** $\dfrac{20(2)}{10} + 1$ **32.** $\dfrac{81}{3(3)} - 3$

33. $5 + \dfrac{16(2)}{4^2}$ **34.** $\dfrac{6^2}{(1)2} - 2$ **35.** $\dfrac{1(1 - 1)}{6(5 + 4)} + 9$ **36.** $\dfrac{6(14 - 7)}{7(1 + 5)} - 1$

Choice Properties Now Available

Offer a chance to make your work easier if used before you apply the rules of standard order.

Commutative Properties of Addition and Multiplication

The order of numbers can be changed without changing the sum or product.

$3 + 29 = 29 + 3$

$8 \times 9 = 9 \times 8$

Associative Properties of Addition and Multiplication

The grouping of numbers can be changed without changing the sum or product.

$(6 + 1) + 9 = 6 + (1 + 9)$

$(3 \times 25) \times 4 = 3 \times (25 \times 4)$

Distributive Property of Multiplication over Addition

$3(70 + 4) = 3(70) + 3(4)$

$3(74) = 3(70) + 3(4)$

Property of 1 for Multiplication

The product of 1 and a number is that number.

$589 \times 1 = 589$

Properties of 0 for Addition and Multiplication

The sum of 0 and a number is that number.

$589 + 0 = 589$

The product of 0 and a number is 0.

$589 \times 0 = 0$

Try Find each missing number. Then name the property.

a. $13 \times 70 = \blacksquare \times 13$ **b.** $25 + \blacksquare = 25$ **c.** $6(56) + 6(44) = 6(56 + \blacksquare)$

Compute. Use the properties when you can.

d. $(32 \times 8) \times 5$ **e.** $(6 - 5)872$ **f.** $98 + (2 + 59)$

Practice Find each missing number. Then name the property.

1. $(9 + 20) + 80 = 9 + (20 + \blacksquare)$ **2.** $16(\blacksquare) = 0$ **3.** $25 + 8 = \blacksquare + 25$

4. $4(115) = 4(\blacksquare) + 4(15)$ **★5.** $25 \times (76 \times 4) = 76 \times (4 \times \blacksquare)$

Compute. Use the properties when you can.

6. 92×1 **7.** $0 + 58$ **8.** $2 + (8 + 5)$

9. $5(20 + 7)$ **10.** $6 + 17 + 3 + 4$ **11.** $13(60) + 13(40)$

12. $(47 + 25) + 75$ **13.** $(16)(48)(0)$ **14.** $(42)5 + (58)5$

15. $(11 \times 5) \times 2$ **16.** $11 + 34 + 0 + 66$ **17.** $(60)(25)(3 - 3)$

18. $4(96 - 86)$ **19.** $(4 - 3)279$ **20.** $(3)(70)(1)(3 - 2)$

21. $7(5) + 7(6) + 7(9)$ **22.** $16 - 7 + 7$ **23.** $44 + 10 - 10$

24. $3 \times \dfrac{10}{10}$ **25.** $\dfrac{3(8)}{3}$ **26.** $\left(\dfrac{54}{18}\right)18$

Apply Solve each problem.

27. Tim bought 7 bags of map tacks for 79¢ each and 3 packs of string for 79¢ each. How much money did he spend?

28. Mrs. Seng bought packages of paper for 59¢, 59¢, and 99¢, but she returned the 99¢ package. How much did she spend?

Evaluating Expressions

A. Louise's computer stores each letter of the alphabet as some arrangement of 8 binary digits, or *bits*. The expression 8c tells how many bits are used to store a word with c letters. The **variable** c represents any whole number.

To find the number of bits in a 9-letter word, *evaluate* 8c when c is 9.

8c

8(9)   Substitute 9 for c.

72   Multiply.

B. Evaluate 3(21 − d) when d is 5.

3(21 − d)

3(21 − 5)   Substitute 5 for d.

3(16)   Subtract inside the parentheses.

48   Multiply.

c. Evaluate $\dfrac{r + s}{r}$ when r = 8 and s = 16.

$$\frac{r + s}{r}$$

$$\frac{8 + 16}{8}$$ Substitute 8 for r in both places. Substitute 16 for s.

$$\frac{24}{8}$$ Add above the division bar.

3   Divide.

Try   Evaluate each expression when
p = 4 and n = 3.

a. $p + 5$ **b.** $2pn$ **c.** $\dfrac{p + n}{p - n}$ **d.** $(p - 1)4$

40

Practice Evaluate each expression when $f = 9$.

1. $f + 2$ 　　　　**2.** $f - 3$ 　　　　**3.** $6f$

4. $8f$ 　　　　**5.** $8f - 2f$ 　　　　**6.** $2f + 3f$

7. $2f + 5$ 　　　　**8.** $2(f + 5)$ 　　　　**9.** $f - 7 + 7$

10. $3 + f - 3$ 　　　**11.** $\dfrac{10f}{10}$ 　　　**12.** $\left(\dfrac{f}{9}\right)9$

Evaluate $3(k + 1)$ when k is:

13. 0 　　**14.** 1 　　**15.** 50 　　**16.** 99 　　**17.** 200

Evaluate $\dfrac{(r - 5)2}{7}$ when r is:

18. 5 　　**19.** 12 　　**20.** 19 　　**21.** 40 　　**22.** 215

Evaluate each expression when $h = 5$ and $m = 2$.

23. $h + m$ 　　　　**24.** $h - m$ 　　　　**25.** hm

26. $2hm$ 　　　　**27.** $h(h + 8)$ 　　　　**28.** $h(m - 1)$

29. $(2 - m)7$ 　　　**30.** $(h + 3)m$ 　　　**31.** $\dfrac{2h}{5m}$

32. $\dfrac{10m}{h}$ 　　　★**33.** m^3 　　　★**34.** $\dfrac{h^2}{h}$

Look for a pattern in the 0s and 1s.

Write the rest of this computer code for the letters K through Z.

```
A 01000001
B 01000010
C 01000011
D 01000100
E 01000101
F 01000110
G 01000111
H 01001000
I 01001001
J 01001010
```

Apply Solve each problem.

Some computers use 65,000 bits to produce one second of music. The expression $65{,}000s$ describes how many bits are needed to produce s seconds of music. How many bits are needed for

35. background music for a 15-second commercial?

36. a popular song that is 200 seconds long?

★**37.** a 20-minute section of a symphony?

Writing Expressions

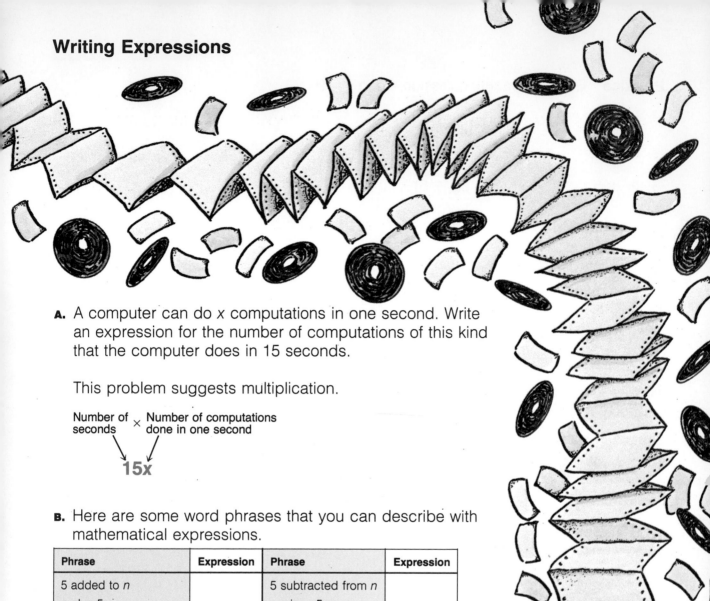

A. A computer can do *x* computations in one second. Write an expression for the number of computations of this kind that the computer does in 15 seconds.

This problem suggests multiplication.

Number of seconds × Number of computations done in one second

15x

B. Here are some word phrases that you can describe with mathematical expressions.

Phrase	Expression	Phrase	Expression
5 added to *n* *n* plus 5 the sum of *n* and 5 the total of *n* and 5 5 more than *n* *n* increased by 5	$n + 5$	5 subtracted from *n* *n* minus 5 5 fewer than *n* 5 less than *n* *n* decreased by 5	$n - 5$
n multiplied by 5 5 multiplied by *n* 5 times *n* the product of 5 and *n*	$5n$	*n* divided by 5 the quotient *n* divided by 5	$\frac{n}{5}$ or $n \div 5$

Try Write a mathematical expression for each phrase.

a. *s* divided by 18

b. 8 minus *t*

c. *t* decreased by 8

d. The sum of w^2 and 11

42

Practice   Write a mathematical expression for each phrase.

1. m increased by 31

2. 16 less than b

3. 4 subtracted from p

4. 3 minus r

5. 6 times f^3

6. s multiplied by 2

7. t divided by 6

8. The sum of x and 1

9. The total of k and 6

10. u divided by 12

11. The product of a and b

12. 10 decreased by y^3

13. b added to c^2

14. The product of 6 and y

15. 4 divided by n

16. 6 divided by n

17. x less than 3

18. 4 less than cd

Apply   Write a mathematical expression for each problem.

19. If a computer can do c computations in one second, how many computations of this kind can it do in 60 seconds?

20. Lidia has 10 dollars more than she needs to buy a computer game that costs g dollars. How much money does she have?

21. Ann's program goes through a loop 1 less than n times. How many times is this?

22. Scott's monitor displays 40 characters per line. How many lines are needed for c characters?

★23. Mrs. Garcia bought 4 diskettes for d dollars each and an instruction manual for f dollars. How much did these items cost?

Solving Addition and Subtraction Equations

A. A certain symphony orchestra has 100 members. Besides the people in the string section, there are 16 people in the woodwind section, 11 in brass, and 5 in percussion. How many people are there in the string section?

Let s be the number of people in the string section. Then $s + (16 + 11 + 5)$ expresses the total number, and so does 100.

String section +   Other sections   = Total number

$s + (16 + 11 + 5) = 100$	Solve this equation.
$s + 32 = 100$	Rewrite $(16 + 11 + 5)$ as 32. *32 is added* to s.
$s + 32 - 32 = 100 - 32$	To find s and to keep the equality, *subtract 32* from both sides of the equation.
$s = 68$	

There are 68 people in the string section.

Check $s + (16 + 11 + 5) = 100$
$$s + 32 = 100$$
$$68 + 32 \stackrel{?}{=} 100$$
$$100 = 100$$

B. Solve the equation $x - 18 = 27$.

$$x - 18 = 27 \qquad \text{\textit{18 is subtracted from x.}}$$

$$x - 18 + 18 = 27 + 18 \qquad \text{To find } x \text{ and to keep the equality, \textit{add 18} to both sides.}$$

$$x = 45$$

Try   Solve each equation.

a. $29 = m - 15$

b. $18 + x = 46$

c. $90 = y + 15 + 3$

Practice Solve each equation.

1. $k + 7 = 34$

2. $w + 806 = 909$

3. $x - 81 = 53$

4. $y - 9 = 48$

5. $61 = h - 4$

6. $109 = n - 17$

7. $193 = t - 81$

8. $117 = z - 86$

9. $8 + q = 93$

10. $12 + g = 231$

11. $216 = 63 + r$

12. $56 = 11 + s$

13. $y + 8 + 5 = 41$

14. $r + 8 + 2 = 50$

15. $65 = a + 1 + 2 + 3$

16. $42 = b + 2 + 2 + 2$

17. $10 + 56 + q = 66$

18. $7 + 0 + s = 16$

★19. $20 - x = 15$

★20. $31 - p = 14$

★21. $7 - j = 11 - 7$

Apply Solve each problem.

22. Wolfgang Mozart wrote 41 symphonies. Franz Joseph Haydn wrote 104. How many more symphonies did Haydn write? (HINT: $41 + s = 104$)

23. Mozart lived only 35 years, but Haydn lived 77 years. How many more years did Haydn live? (HINT: $77 - 35 = n$)

24. The orchestra's schedule includes concerts in November, 9 concerts in December, and 8 concerts in January, for a total of 25. How many November concerts will there be? (HINT: $c + 9 + 8 = 25$)

★25. There are 42 violinists and cellists in the orchestra. There are 26 more violinists than cellists. How many cellists are there? (HINT: $42 = c + c + 26$)

Solving Multiplication and Division Equations

A. In a music contest next month, 15 trombone soloists are to perform during 120 minutes. How much time can be allowed for each soloist?

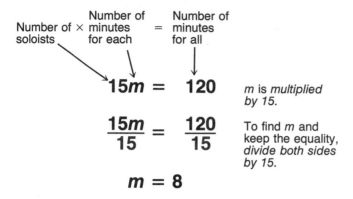

Number of soloists × Number of minutes for each = Number of minutes for all

$$15m = 120$$ *m* is *multiplied by 15.*

$$\frac{15m}{15} = \frac{120}{15}$$ To find *m* and keep the equality, *divide both sides by 15.*

$$m = 8$$

8 minutes can be allowed for each soloist.

Check $15m = 120$

$$15(8) \stackrel{?}{=} 120$$

$$120 = 120$$

B. Solve the equation $\frac{x}{7} = 24$.

$$\frac{x}{7} = 24$$ *x* is *divided by 7.*

$$\frac{x}{7}(7) = 24(7)$$ To find *x* and to keep the equality, *multiply by 7.*

$$x = 168$$

Try   Solve each equation.

a. $92 = 4d$ **b.** $3 = \frac{r}{17}$

Practice   Solve each equation.

1. $9t = 108$

2. $6r = 198$

3. $91 = 7x$

4. $91 = 13y$

5. $\dfrac{w}{17} = 11$

6. $\dfrac{c}{9} = 18$

7. $38 = \dfrac{a}{5}$

8. $12 = \dfrac{x}{4}$

9. $14p = 196$

10. $3b = 51$

11. $\dfrac{x}{6} = 66$

12. $\dfrac{y}{8} = 808$

13. $9q = 9$

14. $67 = 67s$

15. $n = 8(56)$

16. $m = \dfrac{114}{3}$

17. $1 = \dfrac{u}{7}$

18. $\dfrac{r}{30} = 1$

19. $3m = 114$

20. $7(1) = u$

21. $30(1) = r$

22. $x + 37 = 60$

23. $y - 20 = 60$

Apply   Solve each problem.

24. Ms. Hirata, the band director at Lyons School, has allowed 48 minutes for auditioning 6 flutists. How much time can she allow each flutist? (HINT: $48 = 6n$)

25. During the contest, 48 clarinetists will have 6 minutes each to perform. How long will all of these performances take? (HINT: $48(6) = n$)

26. Last year the contestants from Lyons School won 5 gold medals and 8 silver medals and some bronze medals. They won 25 medals in all. How many of the medals were bronze? (HINT: $5 + 8 + b = 25$)

27. Mr. Confare bought a used trumpet for $225. This amount was 3 times what he paid for a guitar. How much did he pay for the guitar? (HINT: $225 = 3g$)

Problem Solving: Write an Equation

Read   *Career* Martin Kjelson is a marine biologist. During a twelve-day period, he collected 180 samples of fish and plants and placed them in holding tanks. On the average, how many samples did he collect each day?

Plan   Write an equation that uses a letter for the number collected each day.

$$\underset{\text{of days}}{\text{Number}} \times \underset{\text{each day}}{\text{Number collected}} = \underset{\text{collected}}{\text{Number}}$$

$$12d = 180$$

Solve   Divide both sides of the equation by 12.

$$12d = 180$$

$$\frac{12d}{12} = \frac{180}{12}$$

$$d = 15$$

Answer   Dr. Kjelson collected an average of 15 samples each day.

Look Back $12(15) = 180$ The answer checks.

Discuss What is another equation you could write for this problem?

Try Write an equation. Then find the answer.

a. A number x divided by 8 is 14.

b. Sixty of the 180 samples that Dr. Kjelson collected were plants, and the others were fish. How many fish did he collect?

Apply Write an equation. Then find the answer.

1. t divided by 408 is 17.

2. 17 less than t is 408.

3. 17 less than 408 is t.

4. t added to 17 is 408.

5. The 120 fish were butterfly fish and 48 angelfish. How many butterfly fish were collected?

6. The 60 plants collected were algae and 15 samples of eelgrass. How many plants were algae?

7. Temperature readings of the water were taken every 14 days for 224 days. How many readings were taken?

8. The water in the tanks was changed every 16 days during the 224 days. How many times was the water changed?

9. A group of fish was divided into 15 equal groups. There were 92 fish per group. How many fish were there to begin with?

★10. For one experiment, 3 plants are needed for each fish. What is the greatest number of fish that can be used in a group of 246 plants and 97 fish?

Practice: Expressions and Equations

Evaluate each expression when a is 8 and b is 9.

1. $a + 4$

2. $a - 4$

3. $4a$

4. $\dfrac{a}{4}$

5. $4b + 11$

6. $3b - 2$

7. $2b - 1$

8. $3b + 5$

9. $4(b + 11)$

10. $3(b - 2)$

11. $2(b - 1)$

12. $3(b + 5)$

13. $a + b$

14. b^2

15. ab

16. ba

17. $\dfrac{a + 10}{b}$

18. $\dfrac{b + 7}{a}$

19. $\dfrac{10a}{2(b - a)}$

20. $\dfrac{b + a}{b - a}$

Evaluate $\dfrac{(r - 3)r}{6}$ when r is:

21. 6

22. 3

23. 15

24. 21

25. 33

26. 18

Write a mathematical expression for each phrase.

27. c divided by 8

28. g increased by 1

29. The product of x and y

30. v minus 120

31. 81 fewer than h

32. The sum of 2 and x

33. 3 times y

34. 64 divided by x

35. The total of e and 5

36. w plus 726

37. g decreased by 1

38. k multiplied by 99

39. x divided by 64

40. 100 less than y

41. y less than 100

Solve each equation.

42. $a + 13 = 130$

43. $b - 13 = 130$

44. $13c = 130$

45. $\dfrac{d}{13} = 130$

46. $9 = \dfrac{e}{2}$

47. $45 = \dfrac{n}{5}$

48. $82 = g - 53$

49. $37m = 0$

50. $101 = 21 + f$

51. $i + 2 + 5 = 16$

52. $21 = t + 4 + 10$

53. $80 = x - 7$

54. $j - 5 = 31$

55. $10r = 10$

56. $q + 42 = 42$

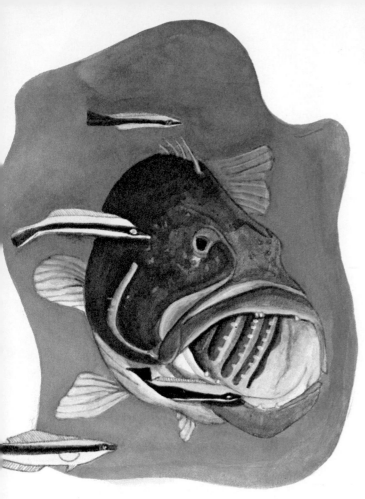

MAINTENANCE

Round 85,284 to the

1. nearest ten.

2. nearest hundred.

3. nearest thousand.

4. nearest ten-thousand.

Estimation Estimate each answer. First round each number so that only the first digit is not zero.

5. 79 × 93

6. 54 × 39

7. 92 − 58

8. 802 + 917

9. 814 × 203

10. 281 × 178

11. 486 − 211

12. 892 × 591

13. 51,893 + 12,186

14. 68,401 − 19,012

Estimation Estimate each answer. First round both numbers to the same place.

15. 219 + 63

16. 694 − 51

17. 591 − 32

18. 27 + 449

19. 578 + 4,259

20. 8,366 − 728

21. 1,503 − 954

22. 5,924 + 776

23. 11,981 + 4,263

24. 29,005 − 1,367

Solve each problem.

57. The fish collection at the city aquarium was reduced to 2,161 when 219 fish died. How many fish were there to begin with?

58. There are 29 girls in the marching band, which has 62 members in all. How many members are boys?

59. How much does one microcomputer cost if 8 microcomputers are bought for $3,160?

*60. The school choir has twice as many girls as boys. How many of the 54 choir members are boys?

Solving Two-Step Equations

A. The air pressure on a person at sea level is called 1 *atmosphere*. The pressure in the ocean increases 1 additional atmosphere for every 33 feet of depth. At what depth is the pressure equal to 3 atmospheres?

Pressure at sea level	+	Pressure in *d* feet of water	=	Total pressure

$$1 + \frac{d}{33} = 3$$

$$1 + \frac{d}{33} - 1 = 3 - 1$$

1 is added to $\frac{d}{33}$, so subtract 1 from each side.

$$\frac{d}{33} = 2$$

$$33\left(\frac{d}{33}\right) = 33(2)$$

d is divided by 33, so multiply both sides by 33.

$$d = 66$$

The pressure is 3 atmospheres at 66 feet.

B. Solve $43 = 5r - 2$.

$$43 = 5r - 2$$

$$43 + 2 = 5r - 2 + 2$$

$$45 = 5r$$

$$\frac{45}{5} = \frac{5r}{5}$$

$$9 = r$$

Check $\quad 1 + \frac{d}{33} = 3$

$$1 + \frac{66}{33} \stackrel{?}{=} 3$$

$$1 + 2 \stackrel{?}{=} 3$$

$$3 = 3$$

Try Solve each equation.

a. $6a + 3 = 21$

b. $\frac{5x}{7} = 10$

Practice Solve each equation.

1. $\frac{x}{2} + 7 = 51$

2. $190 = \frac{u}{3} + 100$

3. $\frac{c}{8} - 16 = 4$

4. $8 = \frac{d}{7} - 3$

5. $4r + 13 = 45$

6. $50 = 4f + 6$

7. $3a + 28 = 178$

8. $76 = 8h + 12$

9. $6w - 9 = 3$

10. $8 = 11n - 3$

11. $17r - 34 = 187$

12. $153 = 17w - 51$

13. $\frac{2x}{3} = 18$

14. $36 = \frac{4m}{3}$

15. $\frac{10c}{6} = 5$

16. $14 = \frac{7t}{2}$

★17. $\frac{2d}{5} + 32 = 54$

★18. $\frac{4x}{7} - 89 = 91$

Apply Solve each problem.

19. At what depth is the pressure on a diver 5 atmospheres? (HINT: $1 + \frac{d}{33} = 5$)

20. How many atmospheres of pressure are there at a depth of 330 feet? (HINT: $1 + \frac{330}{33} = a$)

★21. *Estimation* Scuba divers usually do not dive more than about 160 feet. Estimate the pressure at this depth.

On many calculators you can solve

$4r + 13 = 41$

by pressing:

41 ⊟ 13 ⊜ ⊘ 4 ⊜

To solve

$\frac{w}{5} - 29 = 67,$

you would press:

67 ⊞ 29 ⊜ ⊗ 5 ⊜

Solve these equations with your calculator. Check your answers.

1. $12x + 14 = 218$

2. $57x + 369 = 5,670$

3. $\frac{x}{4} + 13 = 27$

4. $\frac{x}{123} + 852 = 889$

5. $8x - 35 = 189$

6. $91x - 2 = 5,367$

7. $\frac{x}{6} - 40 = 59$

8. $\frac{x}{24} - 16 = 944$

Locating Points with Ordered Pairs

Different computers need different instructions for drawing graphs and pictures, but all the methods are based on the ideas of René Descartes. About 350 years ago, this French mathematician showed one way to describe points with numbers.

A. Two number lines called *axes* are used. The axes meet at the *origin*. They separate the plane into four sections called *quadrants*.

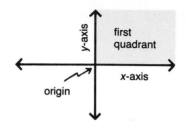

B. Any point in the plane can be located by an ordered pair of numbers, called the *coordinates* of the point.

The coordinates of the origin are (0, 0). What point is at (5, 3)?

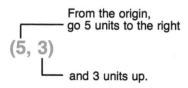

From the origin, go 5 units to the right

(5, 3)

and 3 units up.

Point *L* is at (5, 3).

c. What are the coordinates of points *J* and *S*?

Point *J*:   (3, 5)

Point *S*:   (0, 2)

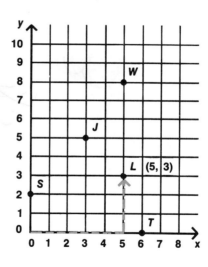

Try   Use the graph above for Exercises a and b.

a. What point is at (6, 0)?

b. Give the coordinates of point *W*.

c. Draw an *x*-axis and a *y*-axis on grid paper. Graph these points and label them with their coordinates:

(4, 1)   (1, 4)   (7, 0)   (0, 3)   (2, 2)

Practice Use this graph with Exercises 1–9.

What point is at

1. (2, 5)?   **2.** (4, 4)?   **3.** (8, 0)?

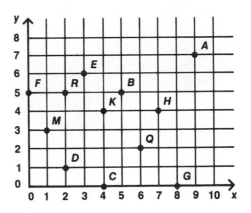

Give the coordinates of:

4. A   **5.** B   **6.** C

7. D   **8.** E   **9.** F

Draw the x-axis and the y-axis on grid paper.
Graph these points and label them with the ordered pairs.

10. (1, 1)   **11.** (3, 3)   **12.** (6, 4)   **13.** (4, 6)   **14.** (7, 0)   **15.** (0, 7)

Apply Copy the computer terms that begin and end at these points.

	Begin	End
16.	(5, 8)	(7, 8)
17.	(2, 7)	(4, 7)
18.	(1, 0)	(8, 0)
19.	(2, 8)	(2, 2)
20.	(1, 7)	(1, 4)
21.	(0, 6)	(0, 1)
22.	(8, 8)	(5, 5)
23.	(8, 1)	(1, 1)
24.	(2, 2)	(8, 2)
25.	(4, 8)	(4, 6)

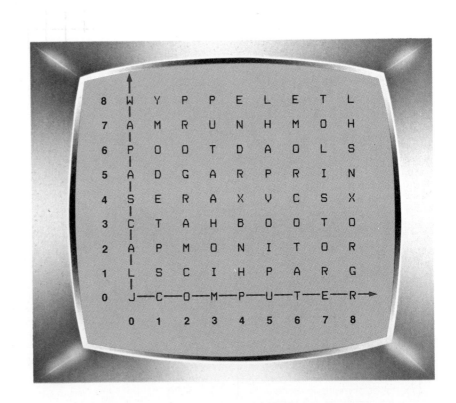

Reading Graphs

A. ENIAC, the first electronic computer, was developed in the 1940s. This *line graph* shows how fast ENIAC could multiply. How many multiplications could it do in 6 minutes?

Find 6 on the *x*-axis. Go up to the graph and over to the *y*-axis. 300 is the number on the *y*-axis.

In 6 minutes, ENIAC could do 300 multiplications.

B. Read the graph to find the coordinates of points *J*, *K*, and *L*. Arrange them in a table.

J (1, 50)   *K* (2, 100)   *L* (6, 300)

Time (minutes)	1	2	6
Number of multiplications	50	100	300

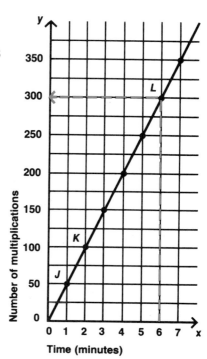

56

Try Use the graph on page 56.

a. How long did it take ENIAC to do 200 multiplications?

b. Complete this table.

Time (minutes)	0	1	2	3			
Number of multiplications					200	250	350

Practice By the 1950s, some computers were working at the rate shown by this line graph.

How long did it take to perform each number of calculations?

1. 600   **2.** 1,800   **3.** 2,400

How many calculations were done during the time given?

4. 2 minutes   **5.** 4 minutes

6. 1 minute   **7.** 6 minutes

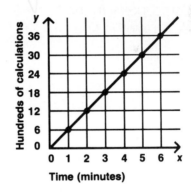
Time (minutes)

Complete this table.

Time (minutes)	0	**8.**	**9.**	3	6	**12.**
Hundreds of calculations	0	6	12	**10.**	**11.**	30

13. This graph shows the rates of work of a 1970s computer. Rate I is how many calculations per minute?

14. After how many minutes did the rate change?

*15. How many calculations were done while the computer performed at Rate II?

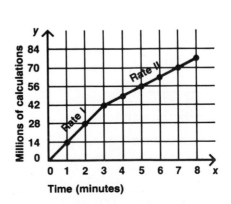
Time (minutes)

Graphing Equations

A. Traci's horse Shadow trots at about 10 feet per second. The distance he travels is expressed by this equation.

To graph the equation, first make a table of ordered pairs.

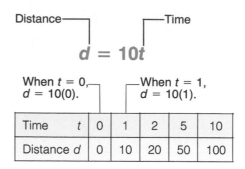

Distance─┐   ┌─Time

$$d = 10t$$

When $t = 0$, $d = 10(0)$.   When $t = 1$, $d = 10(1)$.

Time t	0	1	2	5	10
Distance d	0	10	20	50	100

Label a pair of axes t and d.
The t-axis has to include 0 through 10.
The d-axis has to include 0 through 100.
Use the ordered pairs in the table to graph points. Draw the line.

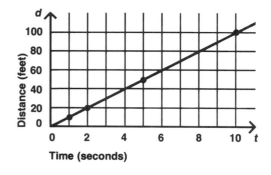

B. Graph the equation $c = 2n + 1$.

When $n = 0$, $c = 2(0) + 1$.

n	0	1	2	3
c	1	3	5	7

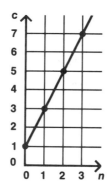

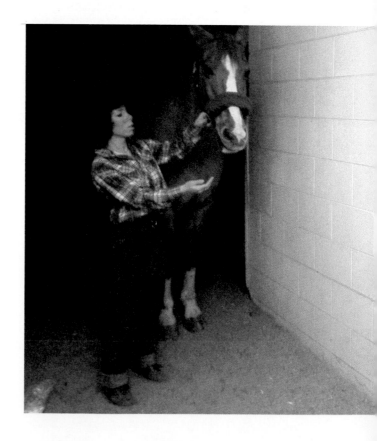

Try Complete this table and graph the equation $F = 3m + 5$.

m	0	1	2	3	4
F	5	8			

Practice Complete each table. Then graph each equation.

1. $d = 5t$

t	0	1	2	3	4
d	0	5			

2. $q = 32p$

p	0	1	2	5	10
q	0	32			

3. $b = a + 7$

a	0	1	2	5	10
b	7	8			

4. $y = 2x + 3$

x	0	10	20	30	40
y	3	23			

5. $h = 50 + 4g$

g	0	1	2	3	4
h	50	54			

6. Graph these three equations on the same grid. Label each line with its equation.

$y = x$ $y = x + 3$ $y = x + 5$

Apply Solve the problem.

7. Suppose Shadow was 20 feet from the barn when he started to trot at 10 feet per second. Graph $d = 10t + 20$ to show his distance from the barn at 0 seconds, 1 second, 5 seconds, and 10 seconds.

Hexadecimal Numbers

Some computers use hexadecimal numbers, base 16, to reduce the amount of symbols needed to write numbers.

These are the numbers from 1 to 30 in base 16.

1	1_{16}	11	B_{16}	21	15_{16}
2	2_{16}	12	C_{16}	22	16_{16}
3	3_{16}	13	D_{16}	23	17_{16}
4	4_{16}	14	E_{16}	24	18_{16}
5	5_{16}	15	F_{16}	25	19_{16}
6	6_{16}	16	10_{16}	26	$1A_{16}$
7	7_{16}	17	11_{16}	27	$1B_{16}$
8	8_{16}	18	12_{16}	28	$1C_{16}$
9	9_{16}	19	13_{16}	29	$1D_{16}$
10	A_{16}	20	14_{16}	30	$1E_{16}$

In base 16, the number 10_{16} means one 16 and zero 1s.

To convert the number $1A3_{16}$ to a decimal number, multiply each digit by its place value and then add.

$(1 \times 16^2) + (A \times 16) + (3 \times 1) =$
$(1 \times 256) + (10 \times 16) + (3 \times 1) =$
$256 + 160 + 3 = 419_{10}$

1. Write the numbers from 31 to 50 in base 16.

Write each of the following base 16 numbers as decimal numbers.

2. 55_{16} **3.** $C7_{16}$ **4.** $8D_{16}$

5. $20E_{16}$ **6.** $4B5_{16}$ **7.** $7A24_{16}$

Problem Solving: Use a Graph

Read   Suppose a lion is running 15 meters per second and a zebra is running 5 meters per second. If the zebra has a head start of 70 meters, how long is it before the lion overtakes the zebra?

Plan   Make a table of ordered pairs for both running rates. Make a graph and read it to answer the question.

Solve

Seconds	0	1	2	3	4
Meters (Zebra)	70	75	80	85	90
Meters (Lion)	0	15	30	45	60

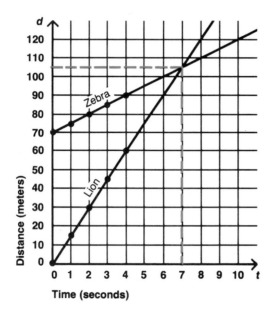

The lines appear to intersect at (7, 105).

Answer   The lion overtakes the zebra in 7 seconds.

Look Back   After 7 seconds, the lion has run 7(15), or 105, meters. The zebra has run 7(5) + 70, or 105, meters. The lion has overcome the zebra's 70-meter advantage.

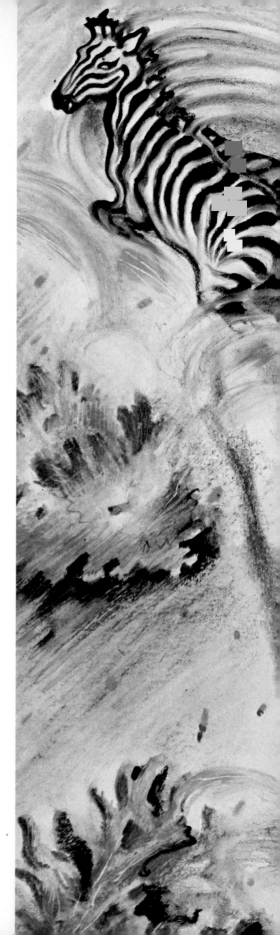

60

Try Make a graph to solve the problem. Use the information from the example on page 60.

a. In how many seconds would the lion overtake the zebra if the zebra had a head start of 50 meters?

Apply Solve Problems 1 and 2 by reading the graph on page 60.

1. How far does the lion run in 6 seconds?

2. How long does it take the lion to run 75 meters?

Suppose that a fox is running 10 meters per second and a rabbit is running 5 meters per second.

3. Make a table to show how far a fox can run in 0, 1, 2, and 3 seconds.

4. Repeat Problem 3 for the rabbit.

5. If the rabbit has a 25-meter head start, in how many seconds should the fox catch it?
(HINT: Adjust the table from Problem 4.)

Make a graph to solve each problem.

6. A dog and a cat are 30 meters apart. If the dog starts to run away at 7 meters per second and the cat chases it, running 10 meters per second, in how many seconds should the cat catch the dog?

7. *Estimation* A giant tortoise can travel about 8 centimeters per second. A garden snail can travel about 1 centimeter per second. About how long would it take the tortoise to catch up with the snail if the snail starts 1 meter ahead?
(1 meter = 100 centimeters)

Problem Solving: Write a Problem

PUPPIES
POODLES $95
TERRIERS $39
COLLIES $125

BIRDS
PARROTS $159
PARAKEETS $32

CATS
SIAMESE $80
ANGORA $55

WHITE RATS $1

ASSORTED SNAKES $15 PER FOOT

A. Pablo wrote a subtraction problem about cats.

A Siamese cat costs $80 and an Angora cat costs $55. How much more does the Siamese cat cost?

B. Write a problem about parakeets and division.

If Amy and her sister buy a parakeet for $32 and split the cost, how much will each girl pay?

Discuss Make up a multiplication problem about cats.

Try Use the information in the advertising signs.

a. Write your own addition problem about puppies.

62

Apply Use the information in the advertising signs.
Write your own problem about

1. goldfish and multiplication.

2. birds and subtraction.

3. dogs and addition.

4. snakes and multiplication.

5. the total cost of one poster and one tarantula.

6. the change received when paying for a dozen goldfish.

7. division.

8. multiplication.

★9. multiplication, addition, and subtraction.

★10. Solve the problems you wrote.

Chapter 2 Test

Compute each answer.

1. $8 \div 2 - 1$ **2.** $3(5) - 4$

Find the missing number. Then name the property.

3. $27 \times$ ▓ $= 27$

Evaluate each expression when $g = 10$.

4. $5g$ **5.** $g - 6$

Write a mathematical expression for each phrase.

6. 4 less than t **7.** r divided by 2

Solve each equation.

8. $b + 9 = 32$ **9.** $50 = m - 12$

10. $\frac{h}{4} = 16$ **11.** $6k = 102$

12. $\frac{n}{3} + 6 = 16$

Write an equation. Then find the answer.

13. 15 less than 45 is n.

14. Olga practiced the harp 2 hours a day for 6 days. How many hours did she practice in all?

15. What point is at (4, 3)?

16. Give the coordinates of point A.

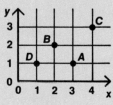

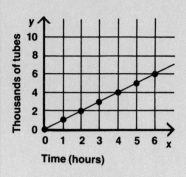

Time (hours)

17. This graph shows the rate at which a machine produces tubes of toothpaste. How many tubes are made in 4 hours?

18. Complete the table. Then make a graph.

$t = 2s$

s	0	1	2	3	4
t	0	2			

Solve this problem by making and reading a graph.

19. A cheetah runs 20 meters per second and an antelope runs 15 meters per second. If the antelope has a head start of 20 meters, how long is it before the cheetah overtakes the antelope?

20. Dog leashes cost $4, and feeding dishes cost $2 and $5. Write a problem about leashes and multiplication.

CHALLENGE

Èquations with Squares

If air resistance is ignored, the number of feet an object falls in t seconds is given by the formula $h = 16t^2$. How far does an object fall in 3 seconds?

$h = 16t^2$

$h = 16(3^2)$ Substitute 3 for t.

$h = 16(9)$ 3^2 means 3×3.

$h = 144$

The object falls 144 feet.

How far does an object fall in

1. 1 second?   2. 10 seconds?   3. 60 seconds?

How long would it take an object to fall

4. 64 feet?   5. 100 feet?   6. 400 feet?

7. Graph $h = 16t^2$ for at least six values of t from 0 through 30.

8. Use your graph to estimate how long it takes an object to fall 1,000 feet.

9. Brian launched a model rocket for science class. Its height in feet after t seconds is given by the formula $h = 160t - 16t^2$. Graph this equation.

10. After how many seconds did the rocket reach its maximum height? What was the maximum height?

MAINTENANCE

Find each answer.

1. $\begin{array}{r} 800 \\ -590 \\ \hline \end{array}$ 2. $\begin{array}{r} 93 \\ \times 64 \\ \hline \end{array}$ 3. $\begin{array}{r} 231 \\ +596 \\ \hline \end{array}$ 4. $28\overline{)588}$ 5. $\begin{array}{r} 58 \\ \times 7 \\ \hline \end{array}$ 6. $8\overline{)7,208}$

7. $\begin{array}{r} 926 \\ -423 \\ \hline \end{array}$ 8. $\begin{array}{r} 84 \\ 29 \\ 56 \\ +27 \\ \hline \end{array}$ 9. $\begin{array}{r} 706 \\ \times 20 \\ \hline \end{array}$ 10. $\begin{array}{r} 5,123 \\ 2,249 \\ +8,434 \\ \hline \end{array}$ 11. $7\overline{)826}$ 12. $\begin{array}{r} 10,000 \\ -241 \\ \hline \end{array}$

13. $8 \times 4 \times 7 \times 9$ 14. $8,492 - 6,218$ 15. $35,577 \div 59$

16. $\dfrac{100,000}{125}$ 17. $28 + 390 + 51 + 0 + 62$

Use standard order of operations to find each answer.

18. $86 + 57 - 23$ 19. $81 + 28(15)$ 20. $3(3) + 4(4)$

Solve each problem.

21. How many days old was John on his thirteenth birthday?
(1 year = 365 days)

22. How many months old was John on his thirteenth birthday?
(1 year = 12 months)

23. Jill was born on New Year's Day of 1971. On which New Year's Day will she be 65 years old?

24. Adela was born in 1968. In which year will she celebrate her 21st birthday?

25. Mr. Ortiz had 6 candles on his birthday cake for his 72nd birthday last week. Each candle represented how many years?

26. The Rosens, a family of four, added their ages and got a sum of 96. What was the average age?

27. Thomas Jefferson was born in April of 1743 and died in July of 1826. How old was he when he died?

28. John Kennedy was born in May of 1917 and died in November of 1963. How old was he when he died?

Decimals

Whole orange:
1.3 g protein
0.3 g fat

Reading and Writing Decimals

Career Diane Tamura is a public health official. She studies tiny animals that live in fresh water. Some of those animals are shown here, magnified 100 times.

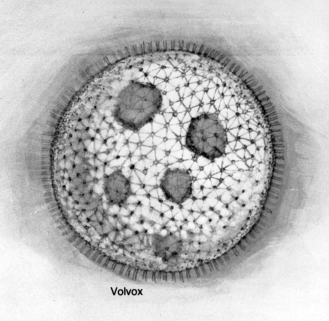

Volvox

A. A volvox is actually about *583 ten-thousandths* of a centimeter in diameter. This number can be written as a fraction with a denominator of 10,000.

$$\frac{583}{10,000}$$

The place-value chart for whole numbers can be extended to show a number like 583 ten-thousandths as a *decimal*.

millions	hundred-thousands	ten-thousands	thousands	hundreds	tens	ones	tenths	hundredths	thousandths	ten-thousandths	hundred-thousandths	millionths
						0	0	5	8	3		

0.0583

five hundred eighty-three ten-thousandths

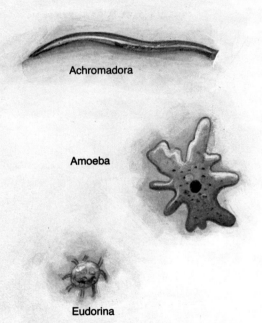

Achromadora

Amoeba

Eudorina

B. The decimal for twenty-one and three hundred six millionths is 21.000306.

C. In 8.107953, the 5 means 5 hundred-thousandths.

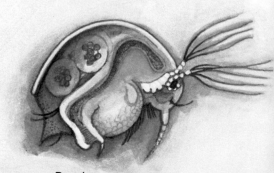

Bosmina

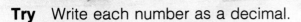

Try   Write each number as a decimal.

a. Forty-five hundred-thousandths

b. $\frac{37}{1,000}$

c. Write 4.1007 in words.

d. Tell what the 9 means in 7.3291.

Practice   Write each number as a decimal.

1. $\frac{8}{10}$
2. $\frac{395}{1,000}$
3. $\frac{6}{100}$
4. $\frac{784}{10,000}$
5. $\frac{2,965}{100,000}$

6. Fifty-three hundredths

7. Nine and seventeen thousandths

8. Ninety-eight ten-thousandths

9. Thirty-five and three tenths

10. Four hundred-thousandths

11. Eight and seven ten-thousandths

12. Two hundred fifty-one millionths

13. Sixty-one and sixty-one millionths

Tell what the 4 means in each number.

14. 8.3704
15. 4.00816
16. 67.4135

17. 0.783004
18. 512.994
19. 8,249.0

Write each decimal in words.

20. 0.34
21. 2.85
22. 47.8

23. 41.008
24. 0.0022
25. 0.00009

Apply   For each problem, give the answer.

26. An amoeba is about 0.03 centimeters long. Write this number as a fraction.

27. A bosmina is about $\frac{4}{100}$ of a centimeter long. Write this number as a decimal.

28. An achromadora is about 0.0005 meter long. Write this number in words.

Comparing and Ordering Decimals

A. Compare the length of a coldoda and the thickness of a human hair.

Compare 0.055 and 0.06.

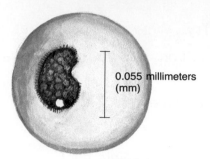

0.055 millimeters (mm)

Coldoda
magnified 300 times

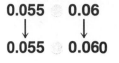
Write the numbers with the same number of decimal places. 0.06 = 0.060

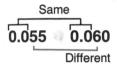
Compare the digits from left to right. 5 is less than 6. 0.055 is less than 0.060.

0.055 < 0.060   "<" means "is less than."

0.055 < 0.06

0.06 > 0.055   ">" means "is greater than."

0.06 mm

Human hair
magnified 300 times

The length of the coldoda is less than the thickness of a human hair. The thickness of a human hair is more than the length of a coldoda.

B. List 5.3, 5.275, 5, and 5.037 in order from least to greatest.

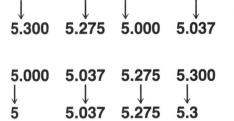

Write the numbers with the same number of decimal places.

Compare the digits from left to right. Write the numbers in order.

c. 5.037 is one number *between* 5 and 5.3 because 5 < 5.037 and 5.037 < 5.3. Name three other numbers between 5 and 5.3.

Three possibilities are 5.01, 5.2, and 5.25.

Try

a. Use <, >, or = to compare 3.8 and 3.808.

b. Write an equal decimal for 6 in hundredths.

c. List 3.01, 3, 3.017, and 3.1 in order from least to greatest.

d. Give three numbers that are between 5.9 and 6.1.

70

Practice For each number, write an equal decimal in hundredths.

1. 0.7   **2.** 3.8   **3.** 4.760   **4.** 8   **5.** 0.030   **6.** 1.000

For each number, write an equal decimal in thousandths.

7. 6.93   **8.** 14   **9.** 4.20   **10.** 0.6810   **11.** 0.9   **12.** 100

Use <, >, or = to compare the numbers.

13. 0.54 ● 0.44   **14.** 0.632 ● 0.631   **15.** 0.2467 ● 0.3467

16. 0.8351 ● 0.8361   **17.** 0.136 ● 0.1306   **18.** 0.483 ● 0.484

19. 0.478 ● 0.478   **20.** 37.34 ● 37.35   **21.** 0.41115 ● 0.411

22. 0.0024 ● 0.003   **23.** 3.4 ● 3.4000   **24.** 0.2358 ● 0.23581

Write the numbers in order from least to greatest.

25. 4.62 6.42 4.26   **26.** 0.247 0.24 0.2704   **27.** 0.3186 0.3286 0.33

28. 0.018 0.014 0.18 0.01   **29.** 3.03 3.303 3.033 3.330

Give 3 numbers between each pair of numbers.

30. 3.4 and 3.8   **31.** 1 and 1.4   **32.** 5 and 6   **33.** 0.67 and 0.68

★34. Write the least number in thousandths that is between 0 and 1 and that uses the digits 9, 3, 2, and 0 one time.

Apply A human hair is about 0.06 mm wide. Tell whether each measurement given is greater than or less than 0.06 mm.

35.
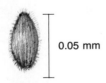
0.05 mm

Glaucoma

36.
0.065 mm

Gymnodinium

37.
0.057 mm

Peridinium

Rounding Decimals

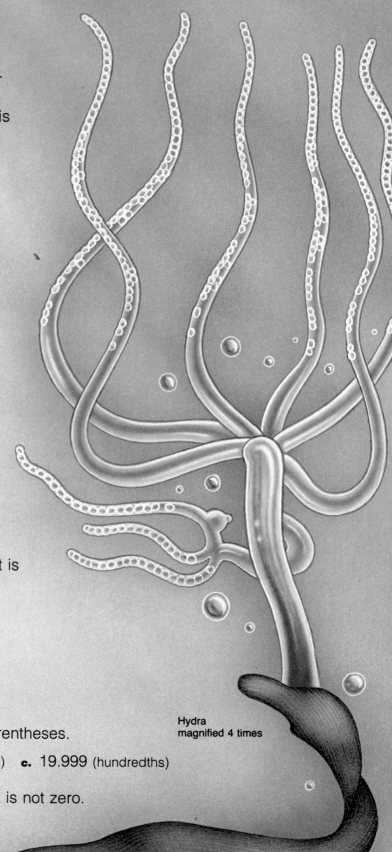

A. The hydra is a common fresh-water animal whose overall length may reach 50.8 millimeters (mm). What is its length to the nearest millimeter?

Round 50.8 to the nearest one.

Decimals are rounded as whole numbers are.

Ones place — Greater than 5, so round *up*.

50.8

51

A hydra is about 51 mm long.

B. Round 4.952 to the nearest tenth.

Tenths place — Equal to 5, so round *up*.

4.952

5.0

C. Round 0.0243 so that only one digit is not zero.

First nonzero digit — Less than 5, so round *down*.

0.0243

0.02

Hydra
magnified 4 times

Try Round to the place shown in parentheses.

a. 0.03942 (thousandths) **b.** 0.958 (ones) **c.** 19.999 (hundredths)

d. Round 2.8075 so that only one digit is not zero.

Practice Round each number to the place shown in parentheses.

1. 8.817 (ones) 2. 71.009 (ones) 3. 4.562 (tenths)

4. 3.119 (tenths) 5. 6.052 (hundredths) 6. 4.243 (hundredths)

7. 0.2374 (thousandths) 8. 48.0556 (thousandths) 9. 0.93 (ones)

10. 0.0008 (thousandths) 11. 424.427 (tenths) 12. 9.502 (hundredths)

13. 0.595 (hundredths) 14. 39.9199 (thousandths) 15. 199.7 (ones)

16. 1.003 (hundredths) 17. 3.987 (tenths) 18. 0.9999 (thousandths)

19. 0.444444 (hundred-thousandths) 20. 4.0002377 (millionths)

21. 16.13435 (ten-thousandths) 22. 0.000999 (hundred-thousandths)

Round so that only one digit is not zero.

23. 21.327 24. 0.0612 25. 7.005 26. 341.93 27. 2,781.4

28. 0.122299 29. 0.00025 30. 0.15038 31. 0.985 32. 99.7

Apply Each of the animals shown below is magnified 80 times.

33. A synura is actually about 0.0254 mm long. Round this number to the nearest thousandth.

34. A rotaria is actually about 0.901 mm long. Round this number to the nearest hundredth.

35. An amoeba is actually about 0.294 mm long. Round this number to the nearest tenth.

★36. To the nearest millimeter, a trilobus is about 1 mm long. Give 5 measures that can each be rounded to 1 mm.

* Synura

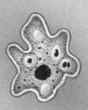

Amoeba

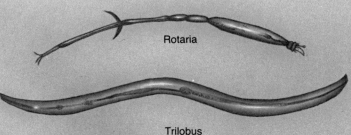

Rotaria

Trilobus

Adding and Subtracting Decimals

A. The amount of sodium in Larry's breakfast is given in this list. Find the total amount of sodium.

Eggs	0.28 grams (g)
Sausages	1.1 g
Toast and butter	0.245 g
Orange juice	0.001 g

Find 0.28 + 1.1 + 0.245 + 0.001.

$$
\begin{array}{r}
\overset{1}{}0.28 \\
1.1 \\
0.245 \\
+\,0.001 \\
\hline
1.626
\end{array}
$$

Line up the decimal points. Then add.

The total amount of sodium is 1.626 grams.

B. How much more sodium could Larry consume today and stay within a limit of 2 grams?

Find 2 − 1.626.

$$
\begin{array}{r}
\overset{9\ \ 9}{\underset{}{1\ \cancel{10}\cancel{10}\,10}} \\
2.\cancel{0}\cancel{0}\cancel{0} \\
-\,1.626 \\
\hline
0.374
\end{array}
$$

Line up the decimal points. Write 2 as 2.000 so that you can subtract. Then subtract.

Larry can consume 0.374 more grams of sodium.

Try Add or subtract.

a. 1.25 + 4.581

b. 32.4 − 7.653

c. 21.47 + 0.3 + 6 + 0.004

Practice Add or subtract.

1. $\begin{array}{r} 1.041 \\ +7.379 \end{array}$
2. $\begin{array}{r} 3.452 \\ +8.41 \end{array}$
3. $\begin{array}{r} 17 \\ +11.286 \end{array}$
4. $\begin{array}{r} 6.575 \\ -2.82 \end{array}$
5. $\begin{array}{r} 29.000 \\ -0.914 \end{array}$
6. $\begin{array}{r} 21.7 \\ -0.359 \end{array}$

7. 21.793 + 11.215
8. 8.3 + 6.99
9. 12.97 + 28

10. 76.32 − 16.81
11. 34.88 − 14.12
12. 6.427 − 3.316

13. 47 + 23.41
14. 8.4 − 2.69
15. 40.813 − 27.38

16. 26 + 48.602
17. 36 − 7.82
18. 1.3812 − 0.79

19. 0.71 − 0.4983
20. 0.8 − 0.73127
21. 75 − 0.0322

22. 0.243 + 7.61 + 11 + 3.2
23. 3.8 + 11.72 + 0.865 + 7

Apply Solve each problem.

24. A raw hamburger patty contains about 0.065 g of sodium, while a deluxe hamburger sandwich may contain 1.2 g. How much more sodium is in the sandwich?

25. A serving of popcorn contains 0.005 g of sodium. If butter adds 0.116 g of sodium and salt adds 0.5 g, how much sodium is in a serving of popcorn with butter and salt?

Estimating Sums and Differences

lemons
12¢ ea.

oranges
4 lb. 77¢

delicious apples
3 lb. 99¢

watermelon
$2.99 ea.

bananas
32¢ per lb.

A. The Nizers estimated the amount they spent for fruit. They rounded each price to the nearest 10 cents (tenth of a dollar) and added the rounded numbers.

Oranges	$0.77	→	0.8 0
Apples	$0.99	→	1.0 0
Cantaloupe	$0.49	→	0.5 0
Lemon	$0.12	→	+ 0.1 0
			2.4 0

An estimate of the total is $2.40.

B. Estimate 3.946 − 0.7. First round the numbers to the same place.

$$3.946 \rightarrow 3.9$$
$$- 0.7 \rightarrow - 0.7$$
$$3.2$$

$3.946 - 0.7 \approx 3.2$

Try *Estimation* Estimate each sum or difference.

a. Round each number to the nearest one.

$18.53 - 13.89$

b. Round each number to the nearest tenth.

$5.682 + 4.275 + 0.731$

c. Round both numbers to the same place.

$4.3 + 1.73$

Practice _Estimation_ Estimate each sum or difference. First round each number to the nearest one.

1. 14.76 − 8.21

2. 25.01 + 6.84

3. 61.6 − 36.7

4. 41.25 + 35.85

First round each number to the nearest tenth.

5. 0.34 + 0.89 + 0.49

6. 2.316 − 1.684

7. 0.18 + 0.24 + 0.28

8. 17.92 − 7.88

First round each number to the nearest hundredth.

9. 4.038 + 2.715

10. 0.6123 + 14.000

11. 28.213 − 14.011

12. 45.119 − 0.062

First round the numbers to the same place.

13. 3.0416 + 2.73

14. 0.653 + 0.9 + 0.41

15. 6.8441 − 1.07

16. 27.2 − 0.6357

17. 0.0148 + 0.005

18. 15.3671 − 8

Apply _Estimation_ Use the prices on pages 76–77. Estimate each total cost by first rounding each price to the nearest 10 cents. Remember, _lb._ means _pounds_.

19. 5 lb. grapefruit
    1 lb. green grapes
    4 lb. oranges
    3 lb. apples

20. 4 lb. oranges
    1 watermelon
    3 lb. apples
    1 lemon

★21. 2 lb. bananas
    3 lemons
    3 cantaloupes

★22. 9 lb. apples
    4 lemons
    4 cantaloupes

Problem Solving: Too Much or Too Little Information

```
    BIG VALUE SUPERMARKET

01/19/84    11:25    105 207

2% Milk            1.68
Doz Lg Eggs        0.96
Cottage Cheese     1.19
Meat               1.39
Corn Flakes        1.45
Noodles            0.87
Grocery            1.55
Grocery            4.99  TX
Salad dressing     0.85
Paper toweling     0.66  TX
Shampoo            2.19  TX
Meat              14.27
Meat               4.55
Rye bread          0.73
Dinner rolls       1.12
Produce            0.82
Produce            0.37

     Subtotal     39.64
          Tax      0.47

     Total        40.11
```

A. Read In many areas not all grocery items are taxed. Use the register tape at the left and find the total of the taxable items. These items are coded with the letters TX.

Plan The register tape gives more information than you need. Select only those items listed with the code TX. Find their total cost.

Find 4.99 + 0.66 + 2.19.

Solve

$$\begin{array}{r} 4.99 \\ 0.66 \\ +\,2.19 \\ \hline 7.84 \end{array}$$

Answer The total cost of the taxable items is $7.84.

Look Back An estimate of the cost is 5 + 1 + 2, or 8, dollars. The answer is reasonable.

B. Read This register tape is for Debbie's purchases. How much change did Debbie receive when she paid the bill?

Plan You know the amount of the bill, but you do not know how much money Debbie gave the clerk. There is not enough information given to solve the problem.

Discuss Reword the problem in Example B so that it can be solved.

78

Try If not enough information is given, write *too little information*. Otherwise, solve the problem.

a. Mrs. Kelly bought a large bottle of apple juice and two medium-sized bottles. How many liters of juice did she buy?

b. Mr. Serrano also bought 3 bottles of apple juice. What did he pay for the juice?

WASHINGTON VALLEY
APPLE JUICE
SMALL (1.42 L) $1.35
MEDIUM (1.89 L) $1.75
LARGE (3.78 L) $3.29

Apply If not enough information is given, write *too little information*. Otherwise, solve the problem. For Problems 1–5, use the register tape on page 78. For Problems 6 and 7, use the apple juice advertisement.

1. How much did Debbie spend on meat items?

2. How much did Debbie spend on milk, eggs, and cottage cheese?

3. Debbie gave the clerk $45. How much change did she receive?

4. Debbie paid $4.55 for ground beef. How many kilograms did she buy?

5. Debbie's monthly food budget is $150. How much of this has she spent this month?

6. How much more does a large bottle of apple juice cost than a small bottle?

7. How much more juice is in the large bottle?

8. A 3-kilogram bag of potatoes costs 99¢. What is the cost per kilogram?

9. For a dozen, large eggs cost $0.96, medium eggs cost $0.84, and small eggs cost $0.72. What is the difference in the prices of a dozen large eggs and a dozen small eggs?

10. Chicken is on sale for $0.98 a kilogram for whole chickens and $1.30 a kilogram for cut-up chicken. What is the savings over the regular price on 3 kilograms of cut-up chicken?

11. A 4-kilogram bag of oranges costs $2.28. What is the price per orange?

★12. Rewrite each problem with too little information so that you can solve the problem. Then solve the problems you wrote.

Multiplying Decimals

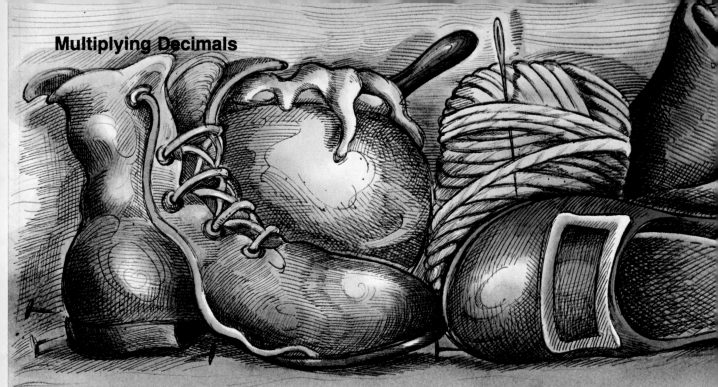

In the early 1800s, the American government put a tariff, or tax, on imported shoes to make them more expensive than locally made shoes.

A. Before the tariff, certain imported shoes sold for $1.50. What was the total income from the sale of 12 pairs of shoes?

Find 12 × 1.50.

```
  1.5 0  ← 2 decimal places
×   1 2  ← 0 decimal places
  3 0 0
1 5 0 0
1 8.0 0  ← 2 decimal places
```

The total income was $18.00.

To multiply decimals, first multiply as with whole numbers. Then count the total number of decimal places in the factors. Show that number of decimal places in the product.

B. Find 0.3 × 0.019.

```
0.0 1 9  ← 3 decimal places
×    0.3  ← 1 decimal place
0.0 0 5 7  ← To show 4 decimal places,
             write 2 extra zeros.
```

c. Find (0.65)(4.012).

```
    4.0 1 2  ← 3 decimal places
×     0.6 5  ← 2 decimal places
    2 0 0 6 0
  2 4 0 7 2 0
  2.6 0 7 8 0, or 2.6 0 7 8
```

Try Multiply.

a. 3.4 × 8

b. (0.004)(0.005)

c. 1.3 × 0.021

d. $(0.76)^2$

Practice Multiply.

1. $\begin{array}{r} 1.25 \\ \times\ \ \ 4 \\ \hline \end{array}$

2. $\begin{array}{r} 0.03 \\ \times\ \ 33 \\ \hline \end{array}$

3. $\begin{array}{r} 0.021 \\ \times\ 0.06 \\ \hline \end{array}$

4. $\begin{array}{r} 0.058 \\ \times\ 0.12 \\ \hline \end{array}$

5. $\begin{array}{r} 12.01 \\ \times\ 0.0025 \\ \hline \end{array}$

6. 4.3×0.08

7. 6.4×0.9

8. 5.13×3.2

9. 8.28×7.5

10. $(3.7)^2$

11. $(0.08)^2$

12. $(0.015)^2$

13. $(16.2)^2$

14. $(53.91)(100)$

15. $(264.8)(10)$

16. $(10.012)(4)$

17. $(20.301)(3)$

18. $(0.0063)(0.0005)$

19. $(1.7)(1.2)(0.03)$

20. $(0.66)(0.5)(0.002)$

Place a decimal point in each factor so that the answer is correct. Do each exercise four different ways.

★21. $273(400) = 109.2$

★22. $125(184) = 23$

★23. $14(63)(5) = 44.1$

Apply Solve each problem.

24. In 1800, an American shoe company sold 385 pairs of shoes for $1.75 per pair. What was the total income from the sale of these shoes?

★25. The year after the tariff was put on imported shoes, the same company sold 925 pairs of shoes. Find the profit on these shoes if each pair cost $1.25 to make. (Profit = Income − Expenses)

Estimating Products

A. In 1890, the average cost of a pound of potatoes was $0.016. In 1980, the cost was 12 times as much. Estimate the cost of a pound of potatoes in 1980.

Estimate 12 × 0.016.

12 × 0.016

Round each factor so that only one digit is not zero. Then multiply.

10 × 0.02 = 0.2

12 × 0.016 ≈ 0.2

In 1980, potatoes cost about $0.20 a pound.

B. Estimate 0.683(0.08).

0.683(0.08)

0.7 × 0.08 = 0.056

0.683(0.08) ≈ 0.056

Try *Estimation* Estimate each product.

a. 475 × 0.42　　**b.** 0.002 × 0.542　　**c.** 12.4(9.5)

Practice *Estimation* Estimate each product.

1. 3.7 × 4.7　　　**2.** 4.07 × 3.2　　　**3.** 5.6 × 7.8

4. 57.8 × 9.03　　**5.** 20.05 × 36　　　**6.** 54 × 0.6

7. 3.07 × 0.089　　**8.** 0.288 × 2.15　　**9.** 0.9 × 562

10. 2.506(0.05)　　**11.** 0.524(3.8)　　**12.** 4.71(0.035)

13. 0.056(1.05)　　**14.** 0.23(5.97)　　**15.** 0.018(4.1)

16. (0.016)0.5　　**17.** (0.125)0.3　　**18.** (0.2)0.132

19. $0.8 \times 15.7 \times 2.09$　　**20.** $0.6 \times 0.23 \times 11$

21. $1.55 \times 27 \times 0.031$　　**22.** $27.5 \times 0.2 \times 1.36$

23. $7.8 \times 0.094 \times 0.22$　　**24.** $0.053 \times 0.2 \times 0.06$

Each estimated product was found after each factor was rounded to one nonzero digit. Give four different numbers that could replace n.

★25. $0.837n \approx 0.0032$　　**★26.** $n \times 12.6771 \approx 0.5$

Apply　Solve each problem.

27. *Estimation* In 1900, the average price of a dozen eggs was $0.207. Estimate the income derived from the sale of 200 dozen eggs.

28. *Estimation* In 1980, the average price of a dozen eggs was $0.844. Estimate the income derived from the sale of 200 dozen eggs.

29. *Estimation* In 1890, sugar cost $0.069 a pound. Estimate the cost of 50 pounds of sugar.

30. In 1920, butter cost an average of $0.552 a pound. In 1980, the price was $1.878 a pound. What is the difference in these prices?

MAINTENANCE

Solve each equation.

1. $r - 41 = 80$　　**2.** $t + 16 = 54$　　**3.** $27 + n = 55$

4. $93 = d - 28$　　**5.** $5m = 20$　　**6.** $64 = 4x$

7. $15n = 345$　　**8.** $4r + 1 = 45$　　**9.** $6w - 23 = 61$

10. $\dfrac{b}{5} = 14$　　**11.** $\dfrac{k}{4} + 2 = 3$　　**12.** $\dfrac{4x}{7} = 8$

Dividing a Decimal by a Whole Number

A. In the 1850s, a beginning railroad construction worker might have earned $10.80 for a 60-hour work week. How much is this per hour?

Find 10.80 ÷ 60.

$$60 \overline{)10.80}$$

Place the decimal point in the quotient directly above the decimal point in the dividend.

```
    0.1 8
60)1 0.8 0
   6 0
   ───
   4 8 0
   4 8 0
   ─────
       0
```

Then divide the same way you divide whole numbers.

This amount is $0.18 per hour.

Check   Estimate the product of 60 and 0.18.

60 × 0.18
   ↓   ↓
60 × 0.2 = 12.0

12 is close to 10.80, so the answer is reasonable.

B. Find 0.75 ÷ 4.

```
   0.1 8 7 5
4)0.7 5 0 0
  4
  ─
  3 5
  3 2
  ───
    3 0
    2 8
    ───
      2 0
      2 0
      ───
        0
```

Write zeros in the dividend so that you can finish dividing.

c. Find 0.9125 ÷ 125.

```
      0.0 0 7 3
125)0.9 1 2 5
    8 7 5
    ─────
      3 7 5
      3 7 5
      ─────
          0
```

There are no 125s in 9 or in 91, so write zeros above the 9 and the 1. Continue to divide.

Try   Divide.

a. $6\overline{)0.75}$

b. $\dfrac{0.4}{16}$

c. _**Estimation**_ Estimate to decide if the quotient in 385 ÷ 45 = 0.73 is reasonable. Write *yes* or *no*.

Practice Divide.

1. $12\overline{)78}$
2. $15\overline{)111}$
3. $24\overline{)18}$
4. $32\overline{)8}$

5. $47\overline{)24.91}$
6. $33\overline{)15.18}$
7. $58\overline{)0.348}$
8. $79\overline{)0.316}$

9. $24\overline{)87.36}$
10. $62\overline{)117.18}$
11. $46\overline{)16.1}$
12. $25\overline{)21.5}$

13. $10\overline{)437.6}$
14. $100\overline{)627.6}$
15. $51\overline{)3,223.2}$
16. $23\overline{)2,148.2}$

17. $0.768 \div 32$
18. $0.972 \div 27$
19. $0.068 \div 16$
20. $0.0874 \div 23$

21. $0.3 \div 25$
22. $0.6 \div 48$
23. $2.352 \div 42$
24. $32.096 \div 8$

25. $\dfrac{2}{25}$
26. $\dfrac{3}{75}$
27. $\dfrac{15.009}{3}$
28. $\dfrac{24.072}{12}$

Estimation Estimate to decide if each quotient is reasonable. Write _yes_ or _no_.

29. $1.05 \div 7 = 1.5$
30. $29.16 \div 27 = 1.08$
31. $3.36 \div 48 = 0.7$

32. $53.04 \div 136 = 0.39$
33. $8.4 \div 15 = 0.56$
34. $737.2 \div 388 = 0.19$

Apply Solve each problem.

35. In the 1850s, a railroad official might have earned $1,950 a year. How much is this per week? Use 52 weeks for 1 year.

36. _Estimation_ At a salary of $10.80 per week, estimate how much the beginning railroad worker earned in 52 weeks.

Multiplying and Dividing by Powers of 10

A. One *gas unit* of heating gas is 100 cubic feet. In April the Schaefers used 84 gas units. How many cubic feet is this?

Find 84 × 100.

```
    84
 × 100
 8,400
```

Here is another way to multiply.

100 × 84 = 8,400.

2 zeros   2 places to the right

This amount is 8,400 cubic feet.

To multiply by a power of 10 (numbers like 10, 100, 1,000, and so on), move the decimal point as many places to the right as there are zeros in the power of 10.

B. One *kilowatt* of electricity is 1,000 watts. The Schaefers' television set uses about 2.9 watts per minute. How many kilowatts does it use per minute?

Find 2.9 ÷ 1,000.

```
        0.0029
1,000)2.9000
```

Here is another way to divide.

2.9 ÷ 1,000 = 0.0029

3 zeros   3 places to the left

The television set uses about 0.0029 kilowatts per minute.

To divide by a power of 10, move the decimal point as many places to the left as there are zeros in the power of 10.

Try   Multiply or divide.

a. 1,000 × 37   **b.** 10 × 0.45   **c.** 682 ÷ 10   **d.** 0.02 ÷ 100

Practice   Multiply or divide.

1. 456×100　　**2.** $38 \times 10,000$　　**3.** $1,000 \times 0.061$　　**4.** $0.96 \times 100,000$

5. 10×2.4　　**6.** 4.5×100　　**7.** $0.003 \times 1,000$　　**8.** 0.00874×10

9. $519 \div 10$　　**10.** $4.7 \div 100$　　**11.** $0.06 \div 1,000$　　**12.** $9.5 \div 10,000$

13. $0.3417 \div 100$　　**14.** $0.002 \div 100$　　**15.** $5,000 \div 1,000$　　**16.** $3 \div 1,000,000$

Multiply 3.4 by each number.

17. 10　　**18.** 100　　**19.** 1,000　　**20.** 10,000　　**21.** 100,000

Divide 3.4 by each number.

22. 10　　**23.** 100　　**24.** 1,000　　**25.** 10,000　　**26.** 100,000

Apply　Solve each problem. Use the information on page 86 for Problems 27–30.

27. 97 gas units = ▧ cubic feet

28. 5,300 cubic feet = ▧ gas units

29. 564 watts = ▧ kilowatts

30. 7.8 kilowatts = ▧ watts

31. The Schaefers' gas bill for 100 days was $427.95. What was the average daily cost?

★32. One *kilowatt-hour* is 1,000 watts used for 1 hour. How many kilowatt-hours are used by a 75-watt stereo running for 108.5 hours?

Dividing by a Decimal

Career Jerry Schollian is an energy auditor. He shows people how to fix up their homes to save energy and money. The *payback* in years on an improvement is the cost of the improvement divided by the annual savings in utility bills.

A. Adding more insulation to the Novaks' attic would cost $256.50. The payback would be 7.5 years. What would be the annual savings in the heating bill?

Find 256.50 ÷ 7.5.

$$7.5\overline{)256\overset{.}{5}0}$$

The divisor must be a whole number. Multiply both the divisor and the dividend by 10. Place the decimal point in the answer.

$$
\begin{array}{r}
3\,4.2 \\
7.5\overline{)256\,5.0} \\
225 \\
\hline
3\,1\,5 \\
3\,0\,0 \\
\hline
1\,5\,0 \\
1\,5\,0 \\
\hline
0
\end{array}
$$

Divide 2,565.0 by 75.

The annual savings would be $34.20.

B. Find 9.67 ÷ 2.8 to the nearest tenth.

Divide until the quotient is in hundredths. Round to the nearest tenth.

$$
\begin{array}{r}
3.4\,5 \approx 3.5 \\
2.8\overline{)96.7\,0} \\
84 \\
\hline
1\,2\,7 \\
1\,1\,2 \\
\hline
1\,5\,0 \\
1\,4\,0 \\
\hline
1\,0
\end{array}
$$

Try

a. Find $\dfrac{52.5}{0.025}$.

b. Find 7.091 ÷ 35 to the nearest hundredth.

Practice   Divide.

1. $0.02\overline{)0.7}$

2. $0.06\overline{)1.5}$

3. $4.52\overline{)3.616}$

4. $5.05\overline{)25.25}$

5. $3.4\overline{)19.72}$

6. $7.3\overline{)33.58}$

7. $2.8\overline{)0.14}$

8. $5.5\overline{)0.44}$

9. $0.06\overline{)18}$

10. $0.09\overline{)54}$

11. $0.004\overline{)3.2}$

12. $0.007\overline{)0.28}$

Divide. Round the quotient to the nearest tenth.

13. $215 \div 0.3$

14. $4.62 \div 0.09$

15. $7 \div 0.581$

16. $\dfrac{7.47}{4.6}$

17. $\dfrac{0.656}{2.3}$

18. $\dfrac{9}{0.924}$

Divide. Round the quotient to the nearest hundredth.

19. $51.2 \div 0.6$

20. $6.78 \div 0.8$

21. $4 \div 0.277$

22. $\dfrac{2.9}{0.37}$

23. $\dfrac{5.3}{8.7}$

24. $\dfrac{5}{0.604}$

Apply   Solve each problem. If necessary, round the answer to the nearest tenth.

25. New storm windows would cost the Novaks $1,230, with an annual savings in heating bills of $89. What would be the payback?

26. If the Novaks have their windows caulked for $125, the payback will be 0.8 year. What will be the annual savings?

27. The cost of the new storm windows would be cut in half if the Novaks put in the windows themselves. How much of the $1,230 would they save by doing this work themselves?

CALCULATOR

One month the Novaks used 582 kilowatt-hours (kW·h) of electricity. Their bill was based on these charges.

Minimum charge: $4.02

Energy charge per kilowatt-hour:
0–500 kW·h $0.08002
Over 500 kW·h $0.05571

Computations are rounded to the nearest cent.

Minimum charge: $4.02

Energy charge:
500 × 0.08002   40.01
82 × 0.05571   4.57
                   _____
Total $48.60

For each amount of electricity, find the total bill. Use the rates listed above.

1. 500 kW·h

2. 458 kW·h

3. 625 kW·h

4. 596 kW·h

5. 713 kW·h

6. 1,085 kW·h

Practice: Computing with Decimals

What would you have to do if Thomas Edison hadn't invented the lightbulb?

Compute. To answer the riddle, replace each answer at the bottom of the page with the letter it matches.

1. 5×0.2 **I**

2. $18.6 - 3.6$ **A**

3. $3.9 \div 1.3$ **T**

4. $16 + 4.8$ **L**

5. $5.6 - 1.28$ **C**

6. 0.3×0.4 **V**

7. $7.5 \div 0.25$ **E**

8. $17.9 + 6.41$ **G**

9. $10 \div 0.1$ **A**

10. $3.6 \div 1,000$ **I**

11. 2.8×0.02 **E**

12. $45 - 12.78$ **T**

13. $4.78 + 1.9 + 0.8$ **I**

14. 0.006×100 **T**

15. $0.1 \div 0.01$ **E**

16. 0.231×100 **H**

17. $37.8 + 4.158$ **Y**

18. 0.37×56 **D**

19. $0.453 - 0.08$ **W**

20. 5.04×10 **L**

21. $0.275 + 0.3126$ **C**

22. $0.0051 \div 0.03$ **N**

23. 0.2×0.04 **O**

24. $5.85 \div 9$ **N**

25. $8.76 + 286$ **B**

26. $3 - 0.15$ **S**

27. $1 - 0.3214$ **L**

28. $0.217 + 1.6 + 38$ **H**

0.373	100	32.22	0.5876	23.1

0.6	30	0.6786	0.056	0.12	0.0036	2.85	1	0.008	0.17

294.76	41.958

4.32	15	0.65	20.72	50.4	10	20.8	7.48	24.31	39.817	3

Apply Solve each problem.

29. The Tabors bought extra insulation for their attic and installed it themselves for $239.50. A contractor would have charged $175 more. How much would a contractor have charged?

30. _Estimation_ At a cost of $0.09375 per kilowatt-hour, estimate the cost of 394 kilowatt-hours of electricity.

31. The width of a human hair is about 0.06 millimeters (mm). How many hairs placed side by side would be 1 centimeter, or 10 mm, wide? Round to the nearest whole number.

32. A protein molecule is actually 0.000009 mm long. How long would it appear under a microscope that magnifies 1,000 times?

33. Under a microscope that magnifies 1,000 times, a small grain of sand is 25 mm long. What is the actual length of this grain of sand?

34. In 1980, the retail price of a dozen eggs was $0.844. Of this, the farmer received $0.51. What is the difference between the amount the farmer received and the retail price?

COMPUTER

BASIC: INPUT and LET Statements

In this program, an INPUT statement is used to enter numbers. While the computer is running, a ? will appear on the screen when the computer reads INPUT. The computer will wait until two numbers are typed in. Line 30 is a LET statement. A LET statement puts a number into a memory location to be used later in the program. In line 40, a semicolon is used so that more than one item will print on the same line.

```
10 PRINT "GIVE TWO NUMBERS"
20 INPUT A,B
30 LET S=A+B
40 PRINT "SUM = ";S
50 END
```

When 8.23 is entered for A and 3.47 for B, this is printed.

```
GIVE TWO NUMBERS
? 8.23,3.47          ⟵——— Separate input
SUM = 11.7                    numbers with
                              commas.
```

Tell what is printed for the program above when the following are entered.

1. 23.08 for A and 16.724 for B

2. 3.2 for A and 0.085 for B

3. Tell what is printed for the following program.

```
10 LET X=7.48
20 LET Y=3.4
30 PRINT "PRODUCT = ";X*Y
40 END
```

Solving Equations with Decimals

A. *Career* Mrs. Breeker is a part-time cook in the Woodlawn School cafeteria. Her specialty is tacos. She works 4.5 hours a day, 13.5 hours a week. How many days per week does Mrs. Breeker work?

$$\underset{\text{of days}}{\text{Number}} \times \underset{\text{hours a day}}{\text{Number of}} = \underset{\text{of hours}}{\text{Total number}}$$

$$n \times 4.5 = 13.5$$

$$4.5n = 13.5 \qquad \text{\textit{n} is multiplied by 4.5.}$$

$$\frac{4.5n}{4.5} = \frac{13.5}{4.5} \qquad \begin{array}{l}\text{To find \textit{n} and to keep the}\\ \text{equality, divide both sides by 4.5.}\end{array}$$

$$n = 3$$

Mrs. Breeker works 3 days per week.

B. Solve $0.5x + 6.6 = 10.6$.

$$0.5x + 6.6 = 10.6$$

$$0.5x + 6.6 - 6.6 = 10.6 - 6.6$$

$$0.5x = 4$$

$$\frac{0.5x}{0.5} = \frac{4}{0.5}$$

$$x = 8$$

Try Solve each equation.

a. $1.5 = 3r - 4.8$

b. $\dfrac{m}{0.3} = 2.4$

Practice Solve each equation.

1. $x + 3.7 = 6.8$

2. $25.7 = a + 3.8$

3. $n - 4.9 = 5.7$

4. $v - 2 = 4.1$

5. $3m = 27.9$

6. $36.8 = 4r$

7. $5 + 9 + y = 18.6$

8. $3.76 = x - 5.26$

9. $4.8z = 29.76$

10. $t - 8.06 = 19.4$

11. $62.8 + b = 102.2$

12. $8.5r = 2.924$

13. $x + 9.1 + 8.6 = 20$

14. $5.8c = 56.84$

15. $28.31 + 2.8 = y$

16. $k = 33.86 - 4.8$

17. $\dfrac{x}{12} = 27.6$

18. $\dfrac{f}{24} = 0.05$

19. $10.71 = \dfrac{t}{5.1}$

20. $7.5 = \dfrac{h}{2.6}$

★21. $0.4m + 1.6 = 4.4$

★22. $0.3d - 1.8 = 2.4$

Apply Solve each problem.

23. One week, Mrs. Breeker worked 17 hours at the cafeteria instead of 13.5. How many extra hours did she work that week? (HINT: $13.5 + n = 17$)

24. At $4.50 per hour, how many hours does Mrs. Breeker have to work to earn $90? (HINT: $4.50x = 90$)

Problem Solving: Write an Equation

Career Dorothy Walker is the manager of the food service company that runs the Woodlawn School cafeteria. Her computer printouts often show prices and quantities given to three or four decimal places.

Read   The food service pays $0.046 for a hamburger roll. How many were ordered if the total bill was $11.50?

Plan   Write an equation. Let n be the number of hamburger rolls.

Number of items × Cost per item = Total cost

$$n \quad \times \quad 0.046 \quad = \quad 11.50$$

Solve
$$\frac{0.046n}{0.046} = \frac{11.50}{0.046}$$

$$n = 250$$

Answer   250 hamburger rolls were ordered.

Look Back   Substitute 250 for n in the equation. The answer checks.

$$(250)0.046 \stackrel{?}{=} 11.50$$

$$11.50 = 11.50$$

Discuss What is another equation you could write for this problem?

Try Write an equation. Then find the answer.

a. 4.158 is 14.6 less than a number x. Find the number.

b. One meal features tacos. The cook has 38.75 pounds of ground beef, but she needs 70 pounds in all. How much more meat does she need?

Apply Write an equation. Then find the answer.

1. The product of a number t and 2.6 is 1.82.

2. 8.7 subtracted from a number c is 0.714.

3. How many packages of cheese crackers did Ms. Walker buy at $0.141 each if the total bill was $8.46?

4. The cook used 56 pounds of ground beef to make spaghetti for 280 students. What was the average amount of meat in each serving?

5. For one lunch, Ms. Walker made fruit punch. If she served 4.5 gallons and 1.2 gallons were left, how much had she made?

6. Ms. Walker spent $37.50 for milk, $8.75 for butter, and the remainder of $75 for eggs. How much did she spend for eggs?

7. When ordered in bulk, a carton of 48 ice-cream sandwiches costs $5.76. What is the cost of one sandwich?

8. If one hot-dog bun costs $0.045, how many hot-dog buns are in a package that costs $0.54?

CHALLENGE

Use any combination of addition, subtraction, multiplication, and division.

1. Write 100 by using exactly four 9s.

2. Write 1,000 by using exactly eight 8s.

Chapter 3 Test

1. Write 5.203 in words.

2. What does the 6 mean in the number 0.786?

3. Write $\frac{3}{100}$ as a decimal.

Use >, <, or = to compare these numbers.

4. 0.342 ● 0.329   5. 2.7 ● 2.70

6. Write the numbers in order from least to greatest.

   0.16   0.2   0.1604

Round each number to the place shown in parentheses.

7. 3.452 (tenths)   8. 17.718 (ones)

9. 0.97344 (ten-thousandths)

Add or subtract.

10. 12 + 0.57   11. 6.5 − 4.82

12. 1.385 + 3.25827

Estimate each sum or difference. First round the numbers to the same place.

13. 2.159 + 3.2   14. 17.1 − 0.9129

Multiply.

15. 4.2 × 1.25   16. $(0.04)^2$

Estimate each product.

17. 7.9 × 5.3   18. 2.86(0.08)

Multiply or divide.

19. 1,000 × 0.018   20. 3.6 ÷ 100

Divide.

21. $43\overline{)9.46}$ 22. 0.585 ÷ 5

23. $2.4\overline{)1.728}$ 24. $\dfrac{3.5}{0.175}$

Divide. Round the quotient to the nearest hundredth.

25. $0.3\overline{)4.06}$

Solve this equation.

26. $k - 2.6 = 8.7$

If not enough information is given, write *too little information*. Otherwise, solve the problem.

27. A 10-kilogram bag of potatoes costs $3.50. What is the cost per kilogram?

28. Leroy gave the bookstore clerk $20. How much change did he receive?

Write an equation for each problem. Then find the answer.

29. At $5.50 an hour, how many hours does Ms. Chen have to work to earn $88?

30. Isabel jogged 4.25 miles. Shauna jogged 3.5 miles. How much farther did Isabel jog?

CHALLENGE

Patterns in Multiplication and Division

Replace each ● with > or <.

1. 2×3 ● 2 2×3 ● 3

2. 0.2×3 ● 0.2 0.2×3 ● 3

3. 2×0.3 ● 2 2×0.3 ● 0.3

4. 0.2×0.3 ● 0.2 0.2×0.3 ● 0.3

5. When is the product of two numbers greater than either factor?

6. When is the product greater than one factor and less than the other?

7. When is the product less than either factor?

Replace each ● with > or <.

8. $10 \div 2$ ● 10

9. $10 \div 0.2$ ● 10

10. $0.6 \div 3$ ● 0.6

11. $0.6 \div 0.3$ ● 0.6

12. When is the quotient of two numbers less than the dividend?

13. When is the quotient greater than the dividend?

When n in $0.4 \times n$ is replaced with any number between 0 and 1, the product is less than 0.4. Describe the product $0.7 \times k$ when k is replaced with

14. any number greater than 1.

15. any number between 0 and 1.

Describe $3.4 \div y$ when y is replaced with

16. any number between 0 and 1.

17. any number greater than 1.

Describe the number that replaces q in each of the following.

18. $0.72 \div q = 0.72$

19. $0.72 \div q < 0.72$

20. $0.72 \div q > 0.72$

Describe the number that replaces r in each of the following.

21. $r \times 4.2 < 4.2$

22. $r \times 4.2 > 4.2$

23. $r \times 4.2 = 4.2$

MAINTENANCE

Write the prime factorization of each number.
Use exponents when you can.

1. 8　　　**2.** 15　　　**3.** 28　　　**4.** 24　　　**5.** 54　　　**6.** 60

7. 72　　　**8.** 125　　　**9.** 147　　　**10.** 99　　　**11.** 10　　　**12.** 100

Find the GCF of each pair of numbers.

13. 6 and 9　　　**14.** 4 and 20　　　**15.** 14 and 21　　　**16.** 5 and 35

17. 7 and 18　　　**18.** 24 and 10　　　**19.** 72 and 81　　　**20.** 36 and 16

Find the LCM of each pair of numbers.

21. 7 and 14　　　**22.** 12 and 9　　　**23.** 2 and 5　　　**24.** 30 and 6

25. 4 and 9　　　**26.** 3 and 13　　　**27.** 8 and 10　　　**28.** 30 and 24

Solve each problem.

29. It is about 2,565 air miles from New York City to San Francisco. What average speed is necessary to make the trip in 6 hours?

30. The normal precipitation in northern Florida is 54.47 inches per year. In southern Florida it is 39.99 inches. What is the difference in these amounts?

31. _Estimation_ In 1982, there were 10,260,570 bound volumes in the Harvard University library. If the average width of the books was 0.03 meter, estimate how much shelf space was needed for these books.

32. If Raul's car averages 28.5 miles per gallon, about how many gallons will he use in a 1,729-mile trip from Chicago to Phoenix? Round your answer to the nearest gallon.

33. A human lives an average of 73.6 years, while a dog lives an average of only 12 years. How many times as long as a dog's life span is a human's life span? Round your answer to the nearest tenth.

34. A catalog is 4.5 centimeters thick. It contains 960 sheets of paper. To the nearest thousandth, what is the thickness of one sheet of paper?

98

Cumulative Test, Chapters 1–3

Give the letter for the correct answer.

1. Round 14,389,267 to the nearest hundred-thousand.

  A 14,000,000
  B 14,400,000
  C 14,389,000
  D 14,390,000

2. Subtract.

$$5{,}028$$
$$-\,3{,}142$$

  A 1,986
  B 1,886
  C 2,166
  D 2,886

3. Multiply.

17(435)

  A 3,480
  B 7,165
  C 3,240
  D 7,395

4. Divide.

$2{,}351 \div 21$

  A 111 R20
  B 121
  C 100 R9
  D 110 R1

5. Choose the operation that should be used to solve this problem. Then solve the problem.

In 1912, the record speed for an airplane was 161 km/h. In 1931, the record was 655 km/h. How many kilometers per hour faster was the 1931 record?

  A Addition: 816 km/h
  B Multiplication: 105,455 km/h
  C Subtraction: 494 km/h
  D Division: 4 km/h

6. What is the greatest common factor of 36 and 27?

  A 3   **B** 12   **C** 6   **D** 9

7. Evaluate $3k + 2k$ when $k = 5$.

  A 25   **B** 10   **C** 1   **D** 15

8. Which mathematical expression means the product of f and g?

  A $f + g$ **C** $f - g$

  B fg **D** $\dfrac{f}{g}$

9. Solve the equation.

$93 = m - 40$

  A 53   **C** 133
  B 43   **D** 143

10. Solve the equation.

$\dfrac{c}{4} = 24$

  A 20   **C** 28
  B 6   **D** 96

11. Choose the equation that should be used to solve this problem. Then solve the problem.

A computer monitor displays 80 characters per line. How many characters are displayed in 15 lines?

A $15x = 80; x = 5.3$

B $\frac{x}{80} = 15; x = 1,200$

C $x - 80 = 15; x = 95$

D $x + 15 = 80; x = 65$

12. Solve the equation.

$3h + 15 = 45$

A 10   **B** 20   **C** 15   **D** 0

13. What does the 5 mean in 3.1582?

A 5 tenths
B 5 ones
C 5 thousandths
D 5 hundredths

14. Which numbers are written in order from least to greatest?

A 0.1   0.02   0.025
B 0.1   0.025   0.02
C 0.02   0.025   0.1
D 0.025   0.02   0.1

15. Round 32.4637 to the nearest tenth.

A 32.5   **C** 32.46
B 32   **D** 30

16. Add.

$3.157 + 1.9$

A 4.1057
B 5.057
C 3.176
D 4.166

17. Solve the problem. If there is not enough information given, mark "Too little information."

A 2-kilogram bag of apples is on sale, reduced from $2.50 to $1.88. What is the cost of one apple?

A $0.62
B $0.09
C $0.25
D Too little information

18. Multiply.

$(0.06)^2$

A 0.036
B 0.0036
C 0.36
D 3.6

19. Divide.

$45\overline{)2.25}$

A 0.5
B 5
C 0.05
D 0.005

20. Divide.

$7.2\overline{)16.56}$

A 0.23
B 23
C 2.3
D 0.023

Fractions

Diameter:

$\dfrac{3}{125}$ **in.**

Equal Fractions

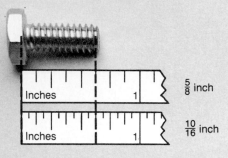

5/8 inch

10/16 inch

A. John Aoki replaced a rusty bolt on his motocross bike. It measured $\frac{5}{8}$, or $\frac{10}{16}$, inch. $\frac{5}{8}$ and $\frac{10}{16}$ are *equal fractions*.

To find equal fractions, you can multiply or divide both the numerator and the denominator of a fraction by the same nonzero number.

$$\overset{5 \times 2}{\frac{5}{8}} = \frac{10}{16} \quad \underset{8 \times 2}{}$$

$$\overset{10 \div 2}{\frac{10}{16}} = \frac{5}{8} \quad \underset{16 \div 2}{}$$

B. Find the missing numbers.

$$\frac{2}{3} = \frac{10}{\text{▦}} \qquad \frac{24}{30} = \frac{\text{▦}}{5}$$

$$\overset{2 \times 5}{\frac{2}{3}} = \frac{10}{15} \quad \underset{3 \times 5}{}$$

$$\overset{24 \div 6}{\frac{24}{30}} = \frac{4}{5} \quad \underset{30 \div 6}{}$$

C. A fraction is in *lowest terms* when 1 is the only whole number that divides both the numerator and the denominator.

Write $\frac{12}{20}$ in lowest terms.

$$\overset{12 \div 4}{\frac{12}{20}} = \frac{3}{5} \quad \underset{20 \div 4}{}$$

Divide the numerator and the denominator by their greatest common factor (GCF). 4 is the GCF of 12 and 20.

$\frac{12}{20}$ in lowest terms is $\frac{3}{5}$.

Discuss Without determining the greatest common factor, how can you write $\frac{12}{20}$ in lowest terms? When is a fraction equal to 0? Equal to 1?

Try Give each missing number.

a. $\frac{3}{4} = \frac{24}{\blacksquare}$ b. $\frac{16}{48} = \frac{\blacksquare}{3}$

Write each fraction in lowest terms.

c. $\frac{9}{15}$ d. $\frac{8}{32}$ e. $\frac{17}{20}$

Practice Give each missing number.

1. $\frac{2}{5} = \frac{\blacksquare}{40}$
2. $\frac{7}{10} = \frac{\blacksquare}{100}$
3. $\frac{6}{7} = \frac{54}{\blacksquare}$
4. $\frac{7}{12} = \frac{42}{\blacksquare}$
5. $\frac{56}{64} = \frac{\blacksquare}{8}$

6. $\frac{12}{48} = \frac{1}{\blacksquare}$
7. $\frac{45}{60} = \frac{9}{\blacksquare}$
8. $\frac{12}{32} = \frac{\blacksquare}{16}$
9. $\frac{0}{18} = \frac{\blacksquare}{36}$
10. $\frac{1}{9} = \frac{9}{\blacksquare}$

11. $\frac{8}{21} = \frac{40}{\blacksquare}$
12. $\frac{34}{85} = \frac{\blacksquare}{5}$
13. $\frac{25}{15} = \frac{5}{\blacksquare}$
14. $\frac{12}{8} = \frac{\blacksquare}{2}$
15. $\frac{5}{4} = \frac{\blacksquare}{100}$

16. $\frac{7}{8} = \frac{\blacksquare}{16} = \frac{\blacksquare}{24} = \frac{28}{\blacksquare}$
17. $\frac{3}{10} = \frac{\blacksquare}{20} = \frac{9}{\blacksquare} = \frac{12}{\blacksquare}$

Write each fraction in lowest terms.

18. $\frac{18}{48}$
19. $\frac{14}{49}$
20. $\frac{14}{24}$
21. $\frac{15}{16}$
22. $\frac{90}{210}$
23. $\frac{55}{80}$
24. $\frac{17}{24}$

25. $\frac{24}{40}$
26. $\frac{33}{88}$
27. $\frac{50}{125}$
28. $\frac{26}{100}$
29. $\frac{60}{120}$
30. $\frac{17}{51}$
31. $\frac{19}{95}$

Apply For each problem, write the answer as a fraction in lowest terms.

32. John has 40 bolts in his toolbox. 12 of them are brass. What fraction of the bolts are brass?

33. There are 60 washers in John's toolbox. 48 of them are zinc-plated. What fraction of the washers are zinc-plated?

34. Using the ruler shown, give 3 equal measures for the length of the bolt pictured.

★35. John has a bolt less than 1 inch long. Using a ruler like the one shown in Problem 34, he was able to give the bolt's length with 4 different denominators. How long is the bolt?

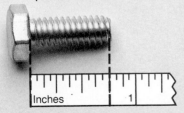

Comparing and Ordering Fractions

A. John used a socket wrench to tighten a bolt on his motocross bike. He tried a $\frac{13}{16}$-inch socket, but it was too small. Is a $\frac{7}{8}$-inch socket larger?

Compare $\frac{13}{16}$ and $\frac{7}{8}$.

$\frac{13}{16}$ ● $\frac{7}{8}$ Write the fractions with a *common denominator.*

$\downarrow$ $\downarrow$ 16 is the *least common denominator.*

$\frac{13}{16}$ ● $\frac{14}{16}$

$\frac{13}{16} < \frac{14}{16}$ Compare the numerators.

$\downarrow$ $\downarrow$

$\frac{13}{16} < \frac{7}{8}$

$\frac{7}{8} > \frac{13}{16}$ Since $\frac{13}{16} < \frac{7}{8}$, $\frac{7}{8} > \frac{13}{16}$.

The $\frac{7}{8}$-inch socket is larger than the $\frac{13}{16}$-inch socket.

B. Write $\frac{1}{4}$, $\frac{1}{3}$, and $\frac{1}{6}$ in order from least to greatest.

$\frac{1}{4}$ $\frac{1}{3}$ $\frac{1}{6}$ Write the fractions with a common denominator.

$\downarrow$ $\downarrow$ $\downarrow$

$\frac{3}{12}$ $\frac{4}{12}$ $\frac{2}{12}$

$\frac{2}{12}$ $\frac{3}{12}$ $\frac{4}{12}$ Order the numerators.

$\downarrow$ $\downarrow$ $\downarrow$

$\frac{1}{6}$ $\frac{1}{4}$ $\frac{1}{3}$

Try Compare these fractions. Use <, >, or =.

a. $\frac{4}{9} \bullet \frac{2}{9}$ **b.** $\frac{7}{12} \bullet \frac{3}{4}$ **c.** $\frac{1}{6} \bullet \frac{3}{8}$ **d.** $\frac{16}{20} \bullet \frac{4}{5}$

e. List $\frac{5}{6}$, $\frac{4}{5}$, and $\frac{7}{10}$ in order from least to greatest.

Practice Compare these fractions. Use <, >, or =.

1. $\frac{6}{7} \bullet \frac{4}{7}$ **2.** $\frac{19}{32} \bullet \frac{21}{32}$ **3.** $\frac{4}{8} \bullet \frac{16}{32}$ **4.** $\frac{2}{3} \bullet \frac{3}{4}$ **5.** $\frac{5}{6} \bullet \frac{4}{9}$

6. $\frac{9}{15} \bullet \frac{3}{5}$ **7.** $\frac{4}{5} \bullet \frac{9}{10}$ **8.** $\frac{3}{4} \bullet \frac{11}{16}$ **9.** $\frac{5}{8} \bullet \frac{2}{9}$ **10.** $\frac{2}{7} \bullet \frac{1}{6}$

11. $\frac{1}{4} \bullet \frac{1}{5}$ **12.** $\frac{7}{9} \bullet \frac{7}{8}$ **13.** $\frac{5}{16} \bullet \frac{21}{64}$ **14.** $\frac{29}{32} \bullet \frac{7}{8}$ **15.** $\frac{8}{15} \bullet \frac{1}{2}$

List the fractions in order from least to greatest.

16. $\frac{1}{3}$ $\frac{3}{4}$ $\frac{1}{2}$ **17.** $\frac{2}{5}$ $\frac{1}{4}$ $\frac{3}{10}$ **18.** $\frac{1}{16}$ $\frac{1}{8}$ $\frac{1}{4}$ **19.** $\frac{4}{5}$ $\frac{6}{15}$ $\frac{13}{15}$

20. $\frac{5}{32}$ $\frac{3}{16}$ $\frac{1}{8}$ **21.** $\frac{2}{3}$ $\frac{4}{5}$ $\frac{7}{10}$ **22.** $\frac{1}{3}$ $\frac{3}{8}$ $\frac{5}{12}$ **23.** $\frac{7}{8}$ $\frac{7}{10}$ $\frac{7}{12}$

Apply Solve each problem.

24. Which socket is larger?

$\frac{9}{16}$ in. $\frac{3}{8}$ in.

25. Which socket is smaller?

$\frac{3}{4}$ in. $\frac{11}{16}$ in.

★26. John has these sockets for his socket wrench. Arrange them from smallest to largest.

$\frac{13}{16}$ in. $\frac{1}{2}$ in. $\frac{11}{16}$ in. $\frac{3}{8}$ in. $\frac{3}{4}$ in. $\frac{5}{8}$ in. $\frac{7}{16}$ in. $\frac{9}{16}$ in.

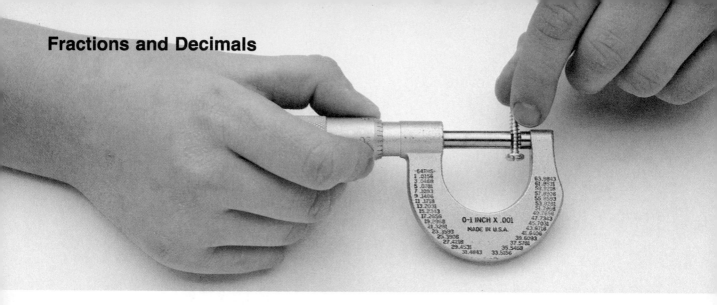

Fractions and Decimals

A. A *micrometer* is a tool used to make very precise measurements. This micrometer gives measures to the nearest thousandth of an inch.

one thousandth $= \frac{1}{1000} = 0.001$

B. Write 0.34 as a fraction in lowest terms.

$$0.34 = \frac{34}{100} = \frac{17}{50}$$

C. Divide to write $\frac{1}{6}$ as a decimal.

$$\begin{array}{r} 0.1\,6\,6\,6 \\ 6\overline{)1.0\,0\,0\,0} \\ 6 \\ \hline 4\,0 \\ 3\,6 \\ \hline 4\,0 \\ 3\,6 \\ \hline 4\,0 \\ 3\,6 \\ \hline 4 \end{array}$$

Write zeros in the dividend and divide.

If you continue dividing, the remainder will always be 4. There will never be a remainder of 0. The digit 6 will repeat in the quotient.

$\frac{1}{6} = 0.1666 \ldots$

0.1666 . . . is a *repeating decimal*. The repeating digit or group of digits is the *repetend*. A repeating decimal is written with a bar over the repetend.

$\frac{1}{6} = 0.1\overline{6}$

D. Divide to write $\frac{3}{8}$ as a decimal.

$$\begin{array}{r} 0.3\,7\,5 \\ 8\overline{)3.0\,0\,0} \\ 2\,4 \\ \hline 6\,0 \\ 5\,6 \\ \hline 4\,0 \\ 4\,0 \\ \hline 0 \end{array}$$

Write zeros in the dividend and divide.

This time there is a remainder of 0.

$\frac{3}{8} = 0.375$

0.375 is a *terminating decimal*.

Try

a. Write 0.425 as a fraction in lowest terms.

b. Write $\frac{5}{16}$ as a decimal.

c. Write $\frac{7}{22}$ as a decimal.

Practice Write each decimal as a fraction in lowest terms.

1. 0.3   **2.** 0.38   **3.** 0.048

4. 0.125   **5.** 0.48   **6.** 0.25

Write each fraction as a decimal.

7. $\frac{1}{2}$ **8.** $\frac{5}{8}$ **9.** $\frac{4}{25}$ **10.** $\frac{7}{10}$

11. $\frac{3}{16}$ **12.** $\frac{7}{32}$ **13.** $\frac{4}{9}$ **14.** $\frac{7}{11}$

15. $\frac{5}{12}$ **16.** $\frac{5}{6}$ **17.** $\frac{7}{40}$ **18.** $\frac{2}{3}$

19. $\frac{5}{74}$ **20.** $\frac{7}{200}$ **21.** $\frac{9}{22}$ **22.** $\frac{233}{505}$

Apply Solve each problem.

23. The diameter of a certain drill bit measures 0.032 inch. Write 0.032 as a fraction in lowest terms.

★24. What is the micrometer measure of a $\frac{3}{4}$-inch screw?

★25. Mr. Kowalski has a certain fractional drill bit whose size is given as $\frac{3}{64}$ inch. The size of his No. 56 drill bit is given as 0.0465 inch. Which bit is larger?

CALCULATOR

You can compare fractions by writing them as decimals and then comparing the decimals.

$\frac{13}{16} = 0.8125$

$\frac{8}{9} = 0.\overline{8}$

Since
$0.8125 < 0.8888 \ldots ,$
$\frac{13}{16} < \frac{8}{9}.$

Write each fraction as a decimal. Then compare, using <, >, or =.

1. $\frac{19}{33}$ ● $\frac{7}{12}$

2. $\frac{1}{16}$ ● $\frac{3}{44}$

3. $\frac{3}{20}$ ● $\frac{1}{7}$

4. $\frac{4}{121}$ ● $\frac{3}{80}$

5. $\frac{13}{32}$ ● $\frac{91}{224}$

6. $\frac{44}{97}$ ● $\frac{7}{15}$

7. $\frac{19}{50}$ ● $\frac{6}{17}$

8. $\frac{174}{384}$ ● $\frac{29}{64}$

9. $\frac{312}{325}$ ● $\frac{44}{49}$

10. $\frac{36}{85}$ ● $\frac{37}{86}$

Mixed Numbers and Improper Fractions

A number that has a whole-number part and a fraction part is a *mixed number*.

$$2\frac{1}{2} \qquad 3\frac{3}{4}$$

An *improper fraction* is a fraction whose numerator is equal to or greater than the denominator.

$$\frac{4}{4} \qquad \frac{13}{4}$$

Every improper fraction can be written either as a whole number greater than zero or as a mixed number.

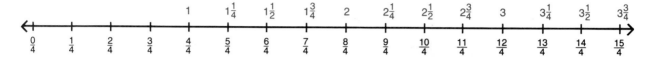

A. Write $5\frac{3}{10}$ as a fraction.

Multiply and add like this.

$$5\frac{3}{10} \qquad \begin{array}{l} 10 \times 5 = 50 \\ 50 + 3 = 53 \end{array}$$

$$5\frac{3}{10} = \frac{53}{10}$$

B. Write 4 as a fraction with 12 as the denominator.

Multiply like this.

$$4 = \frac{4}{1} \overset{4 \times 12}{\underset{1 \times 12}{}} \frac{48}{12}$$

$$4 = \frac{48}{12}$$

C. Write $\frac{20}{6}$ as a whole number or a mixed number.

Divide the numerator by the denominator.

$$\begin{array}{r} 3\frac{2}{6} \leftarrow \text{Remainder} \\ 6\overline{)20} \leftarrow \text{Divisor} \end{array}$$

$$\frac{20}{6} = 3\frac{2}{6}$$

$$3\frac{2}{6} = 3\frac{1}{3} \quad \begin{array}{l} \text{Write the fraction in} \\ \text{lowest terms.} \end{array}$$

D. Compare $2\frac{1}{6}$ and $2\frac{3}{8}$.

$$2\frac{1}{6} \quad \bullet \quad 2\frac{3}{8}$$

The whole numbers are the same. To compare the fractions, write them with a common denominator.

$$2\frac{4}{24} \quad \bullet \quad 2\frac{9}{24}$$

$$2\frac{4}{24} < 2\frac{9}{24}$$

$$2\frac{1}{6} < 2\frac{3}{8}$$

Try

a. Write $10\frac{3}{4}$ as a fraction.

b. Write $\frac{30}{9}$ as a whole number or a mixed number.

c. Compare $9\frac{5}{6}$ and $9\frac{7}{9}$.

d. List $2\frac{2}{3}$, $2\frac{1}{4}$, and $1\frac{3}{4}$ in order from least to greatest.

Practice Write each number as an improper fraction.

1. $9 = \frac{\blacksquare}{1}$ **2.** $6 = \frac{\blacksquare}{10}$ **3.** $5 = \frac{\blacksquare}{2}$ **4.** $15 = \frac{\blacksquare}{1}$ **5.** $10 = \frac{\blacksquare}{4}$ **6.** $1 = \frac{\blacksquare}{16}$

7. $5\frac{2}{3}$ **8.** $1\frac{3}{4}$ **9.** $8\frac{1}{2}$ **10.** $7\frac{5}{8}$ **11.** $4\frac{3}{16}$ **12.** $19\frac{1}{3}$ **13.** $1\frac{4}{7}$

14. $8\frac{7}{16}$ **15.** $15\frac{1}{4}$ **16.** $2\frac{7}{36}$ **17.** $5\frac{9}{10}$ **18.** $12\frac{1}{3}$ **19.** $36\frac{1}{8}$ **20.** $14\frac{5}{6}$

Write each improper fraction as a whole number or a mixed number.

21. $\frac{3}{2}$ **22.** $\frac{20}{5}$ **23.** $\frac{49}{7}$ **24.** $\frac{7}{3}$ **25.** $\frac{27}{1}$ **26.** $\frac{33}{9}$ **27.** $\frac{10}{6}$

28. $\frac{18}{16}$ **29.** $\frac{18}{10}$ **30.** $\frac{16}{16}$ **31.** $\frac{55}{16}$ **32.** $\frac{14}{1}$ **33.** $\frac{8}{8}$ **34.** $\frac{65}{12}$

Compare these numbers. Use $<$, $>$, or $=$.

35. $8\frac{1}{4} \, \bullet \, 8\frac{1}{5}$ **36.** $6\frac{2}{3} \, \bullet \, 6\frac{3}{4}$ **37.** $9\frac{1}{2} \, \bullet \, 9\frac{3}{6}$ **38.** $2\frac{5}{12} \, \bullet \, 2\frac{5}{6}$ **39.** $7\frac{1}{8} \, \bullet \, 6\frac{4}{5}$

40. $2 \, \bullet \, 2\frac{1}{7}$ **41.** $5\frac{4}{9} \, \bullet \, 6$ **42.** $\frac{3}{4} \, \bullet \, 1\frac{1}{2}$ **43.** $4\frac{1}{4} \, \bullet \, \frac{7}{8}$ **44.** $6\frac{4}{10} \, \bullet \, 6\frac{2}{5}$

List the numbers in order from least to greatest.

45. $1\frac{1}{4}$ $1\frac{3}{8}$ $1\frac{1}{6}$ **46.** $7\frac{5}{9}$ $7\frac{1}{3}$ $7\frac{2}{3}$ **47.** $1\frac{1}{8}$ $\frac{1}{2}$ $\frac{9}{16}$ **48.** 8 $7\frac{3}{4}$ $7\frac{7}{8}$

For the fraction $\frac{a}{b}$, what is true about a and b if b is not 0 and if

★49. $\frac{a}{b} = 1$?   **★50.** $\frac{a}{b} < 1$?   **★51.** $\frac{a}{b} > 1$?   **★52.** $\frac{a}{b} = 0$?

Problem Solving: Interpret the Remainder

Read   *Career* Louise Shulman is a motion-picture animator. She draws 24 pictures for each second of viewing time. She drew 156 pictures showing a parrot trying on a hat. How many seconds of viewing time will this scene be?

Plan   Divide the total number of pictures by the number of pictures shown per second.

Solve

$$6\frac{12}{24} = 6\frac{1}{2}$$
$$24\overline{)156}$$
$$\underline{144}$$
$$12$$

Answer   The scene will be $6\frac{1}{2}$ seconds long.

Look Back   Time is often measured in fractions of a second. So it is reasonable to express the remainder in this problem as a fraction.

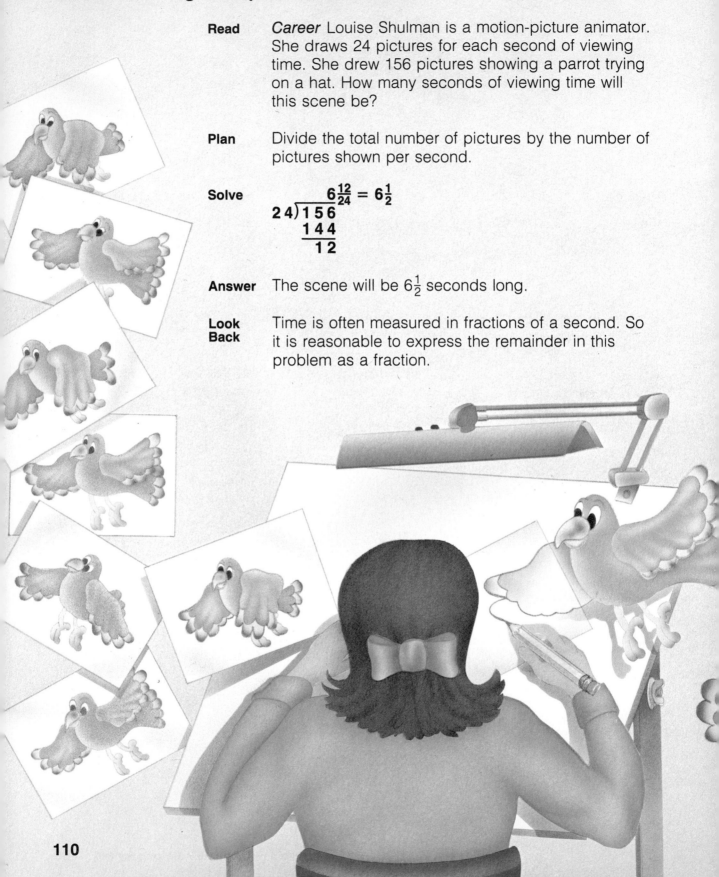

Try Solve each problem.

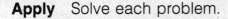

a. Louise drew a 762-picture scene. How many pictures must she cut to fit the scene into 31 seconds? Remember, 24 pictures give 1 second of viewing time.

b. If art paper comes in tablets of 48 sheets each, how many tablets must Louise buy to get 762 sheets?

Apply Solve each problem.

1. Louise's pictures are photographed at a rate of 8 feet of film per hour. How long will it take to photograph 122 feet of film?

2. A one-minute cartoon requires 90 feet of film. What is the viewing time of a cartoon that has 855 feet of film?

3. A small reel holds 900 feet of film. How many reels are needed for 3,100 feet of film?

4. At Louise's studio the animators work four to a room. How many rooms are needed for 30 animators?

5. Louise drew 145 pictures in 8 hours. How many complete pictures can she draw in an hour?

6. Louise drew 732 pictures for a 30-second commercial. How many extra pictures does she have?

7. Louise drew 9,360 pictures for a cartoon. Find the cartoon's viewing time in minutes. (1 minute = 60 seconds)

8. How many 4-minute cartoons can a movie theater show during a 15-minute intermission? (Assume the cartoons are shown without a break.)

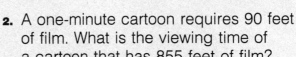

Multiplying Fractions

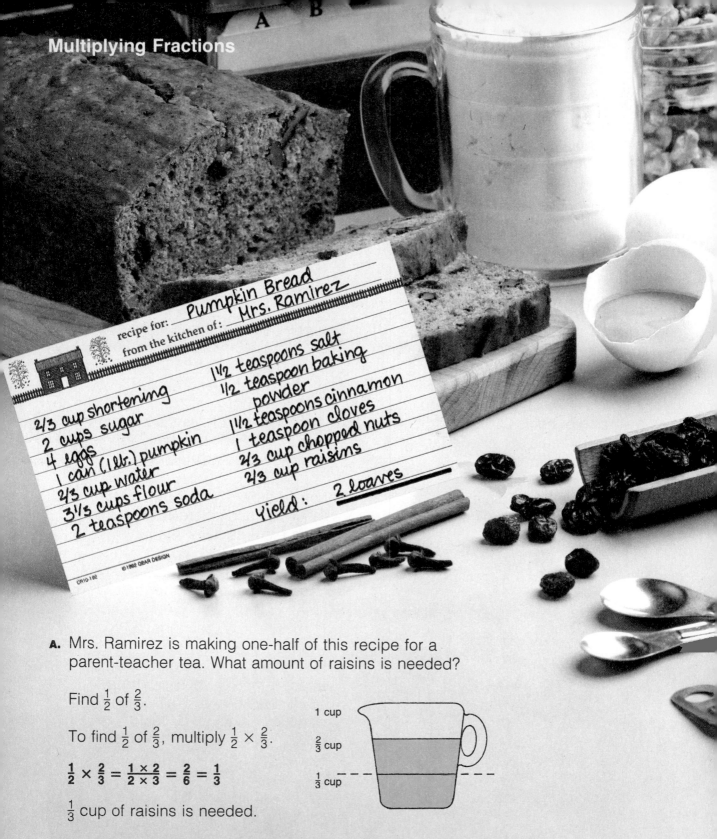

recipe for: Pumpkin Bread
from the kitchen of: Mrs. Ramirez

2/3 cup shortening
2 cups sugar
4 eggs
1 can (1 lb.) pumpkin
2/3 cup water
3⅓ cups flour
2 teaspoons soda

1½ teaspoons salt
½ teaspoon baking powder
1½ teaspoons cinnamon
1 teaspoon cloves
2/3 cup chopped nuts
2/3 cup raisins

Yield: 2 loaves

© 1982 GEAR DESIGN

CR10-192

A. Mrs. Ramirez is making one-half of this recipe for a parent-teacher tea. What amount of raisins is needed?

Find $\frac{1}{2}$ of $\frac{2}{3}$.

To find $\frac{1}{2}$ of $\frac{2}{3}$, multiply $\frac{1}{2} \times \frac{2}{3}$.

$$\frac{1}{2} \times \frac{2}{3} = \frac{1 \times 2}{2 \times 3} = \frac{2}{6} = \frac{1}{3}$$

1 cup

$\frac{2}{3}$ cup

$\frac{1}{3}$ cup

$\frac{1}{3}$ cup of raisins is needed.

To multiply fractions, multiply the numerators and then multiply the denominators.

Whenever possible, divide a numerator and a denominator by a common factor before you multiply.

Try Multiply.

a. $\frac{3}{8} \times \frac{1}{2}$

b. $\frac{3}{4} \times \frac{2}{5}$

c. $12 \times \frac{3}{8}$

d. $\frac{5}{6} \times 12 \times \frac{3}{10}$

B. Find $\frac{3}{4} \times \frac{11}{12}$.

$$\frac{3}{4} \times \frac{11}{12} = \frac{\overset{1}{\cancel{3}} \times 11}{4 \times \underset{4}{\cancel{12}}} = \frac{11}{16}$$

C. Find $\frac{1}{5} \times 10$.

$\frac{1}{5} \times \mathbf{10}$ Write 10 as a fraction.

$$\frac{1}{5} \times \frac{10}{1} = \frac{1 \times \overset{2}{\cancel{10}}}{\underset{1}{\cancel{5}} \times 1} = \frac{2}{1} = 2$$

Practice Multiply.

1. $\frac{1}{2} \times \frac{1}{4}$　　**2.** $\frac{1}{5} \times \frac{3}{10}$　　**3.** $\frac{4}{5} \times \frac{5}{8}$　　**4.** $\frac{2}{3} \times \frac{1}{4}$　　**5.** $\frac{2}{3} \times \frac{3}{4}$　　**6.** $\frac{2}{5} \times \frac{15}{16}$

7. $\frac{3}{8} \times \frac{4}{7}$　　**8.** $\frac{3}{10} \times \frac{5}{14}$　　**9.** $\frac{3}{4} \times 8$　　**10.** $6 \times \frac{1}{3}$　　**11.** $\frac{4}{7} \times 7$　　**12.** $\frac{5}{6} \times \frac{6}{7}$

13. $\frac{3}{16}(5)$　　**14.** $\left(\frac{3}{4}\right)10$　　**15.** $\frac{7}{6}(72)$　　**16.** $\frac{2}{5}\left(\frac{2}{5}\right)$　　**17.** $\left(\frac{1}{6}\right)6$　　**18.** $\frac{3}{5}\left(\frac{5}{3}\right)$

19. $\frac{1}{4} \times \frac{2}{5} \times \frac{5}{6}$　　**20.** $\frac{15}{16} \times \frac{2}{5} \times \frac{3}{4}$　　**21.** $\frac{5}{9} \times \frac{6}{15} \times \frac{3}{4}$　　**22.** $6 \times \frac{3}{8} \times \frac{4}{5}$

23. $\frac{1}{5} \times \frac{3}{8} \times 4$　　**24.** $\frac{3}{4} \times \frac{4}{3} \times 5$　　★**25.** $\left(\frac{1}{2}\right)^3$　　★**26.** $\left(\frac{2}{3}\right)^4$

Apply For each problem, tell how much of each ingredient is needed for one half of the pumpkin bread recipe.

27. Baking powder　　**28.** Cloves　　**29.** Eggs　　**30.** Soda

MAINTENANCE

Find each answer.

1. $4.8 + 5.6$　　**2.** $9.87 - 4.69$　　**3.** 3×2.5　　**4.** 4.7×3.6

5. $17 - 8.44$　　**6.** $35.1 \div 3$　　**7.** $72 \div 4.8$　　**8.** 0.08×0.13

9. $12.96 \div 5.4$　　**10.** $2.85 + 14 + 0.2$　　**11.** $(2.3)(0.05)(1.94)$

Multiplying Mixed Numbers

A. David bought $2\frac{1}{2}$ dozen rolls for a barbecue. How many rolls did he buy? (1 dozen = 12)

Find $2\frac{1}{2} \times 12$.

$2\frac{1}{2} \times 12$ Write each number as a fraction.

$$\frac{5}{2} \times \frac{12}{1} = \frac{5 \times \overset{6}{\cancel{12}}}{\underset{1}{\cancel{2}} \times 1} = \frac{30}{1} = 30$$

He bought 30 rolls.

B. Find $3\frac{2}{3} \times 1\frac{1}{4}$.

$$3\frac{2}{3} \times 1\frac{1}{4} = \frac{11}{3} \times \frac{5}{4} = \frac{11 \times 5}{3 \times 4} = \frac{55}{12} = 4\frac{7}{12}$$

C. Two numbers whose product is 1 are *reciprocals*. $5\frac{1}{3}$ and $\frac{3}{16}$ are reciprocals of each other.

$$5\frac{1}{3} \times \frac{3}{16} = \frac{16}{3} \times \frac{3}{16} = \frac{\overset{1}{\cancel{16}} \times \overset{1}{\cancel{3}}}{\underset{1}{\cancel{3}} \times \underset{1}{\cancel{16}}} = \frac{1}{1} = 1$$

To find the reciprocal of a nonzero number, write the number as a fraction. Then interchange the numerator and the denominator.

Try Multiply.

a. $5\frac{5}{8} \times 40$ **b.** $3\frac{1}{2} \times 4\frac{2}{3}$

Give the reciprocal of each number.

c. $\frac{3}{5}$ **d.** 7   **e.** $4\frac{1}{2}$

Practice Multiply.

1. $1\frac{2}{3} \times 12$

2. $10 \times 4\frac{1}{5}$

3. $2\frac{1}{7} \times 2\frac{1}{3}$

4. $5\frac{1}{3} \times 4\frac{1}{2}$

5. $4\frac{3}{8} \times \frac{1}{7}$

6. $\frac{2}{5} \times 3\frac{3}{4}$

7. $7\frac{1}{2} \times \frac{2}{15}$

8. $2\frac{1}{2} \times 2\frac{1}{2}$

9. $3\frac{1}{7} \times 21$

10. $4\frac{7}{8} \times 6$

11. $13 \times 5\frac{1}{2}$

12. $\frac{3}{20} \times 6\frac{2}{3}$

13. $5\frac{1}{3} \times 6\frac{3}{4}$

14. $4\frac{1}{3} \times 2\frac{2}{3}$

15. $10\frac{2}{3} \times 7\frac{3}{4}$

16. $2\frac{1}{2} \times \frac{3}{5} \times \frac{4}{9}$

17. $3\frac{1}{3} \times \frac{3}{10} \times 6$

18. $\frac{6}{29} \times 4\frac{5}{6} \times \frac{1}{2}$

19. $2\frac{2}{3} \times 1\frac{5}{16} \times 3\frac{1}{7}$

Give the reciprocal of each number.

20. $\frac{1}{3}$

21. $\frac{4}{5}$

22. $1\frac{1}{2}$

23. $7\frac{3}{4}$

24. 1

25. 8

26. $10\frac{1}{4}$

27. $6\frac{4}{5}$

Apply Solve each problem.

28. If there are 4 servings per pound, how many servings are provided by a $4\frac{1}{2}$-pound boneless roast?

29. David allows $\frac{1}{3}$ hour per pound to cook the roast. How long will it take to cook the $4\frac{1}{2}$-pound roast?

★30. A 12-ounce can of frozen juice concentrate is to be mixed with $4\frac{1}{3}$ cans of water. How many ounces of juice will this make?

More Practice Set 47, page 400

115

Dividing Fractions and Mixed Numbers

FRUIT	Pounds of fresh fruit for 1 quart of canned fruit
	$2\frac{1}{2}$
Apples	$1\frac{1}{2}$
Berries	2
Cherries	$2\frac{1}{2}$
Peaches	$2\frac{1}{2}$
Pears	2
Plums	

A. This chart appears in Emily's cookbook. How many quarts of canned peaches can Emily make from 10 pounds of fresh peaches?

Find $10 \div 2\frac{1}{2}$.

You can use a number line to find how many groups of $2\frac{1}{2}$ there are in 10.

$$10 \div 2\frac{1}{2} = 4$$

You can also find the answer by multiplying by the reciprocal of the divisor.

$$10 \div 2\frac{1}{2} = \frac{10}{1} \div \frac{5}{2}$$ Write each number as a fraction.

$$\frac{10}{1} \times \frac{2}{5} = \frac{\overset{2}{\cancel{10}} \times 2}{1 \times \underset{1}{\cancel{5}}} = \frac{4}{1} = 4$$

Emily can make 4 quarts of canned peaches.

Dividing by a number is the same as multiplying by its reciprocal.

B. Find $6\frac{1}{3} \div 8$.

$$6\frac{1}{3} \div 8 = \frac{19}{3} \div \frac{8}{1}$$

$$\frac{19}{3} \times \frac{1}{8} = \frac{19 \times 1}{3 \times 8} = \frac{19}{24}$$

Discuss Use the example below to explain why dividing by a number is the same as multiplying by its reciprocal.

$$\frac{2}{5} \div \frac{3}{4} = \frac{\frac{2}{5}}{\frac{3}{4}} \times \frac{\frac{4}{3}}{\frac{4}{3}} = \frac{\frac{2}{5} \times \frac{4}{3}}{1} = \frac{2}{5} \times \frac{4}{3}$$

Try Divide.

a. $\frac{3}{8} \div \frac{7}{16}$ b. $5 \div \frac{3}{5}$ c. $17\frac{1}{2} \div 1\frac{1}{4}$ d. $6\frac{1}{4} \div 2$

Practice Divide.

1. $\frac{2}{3} \div \frac{5}{6}$ 2. $\frac{3}{16} \div \frac{5}{12}$ 3. $\frac{3}{8} \div \frac{6}{7}$ 4. $\frac{6}{7} \div \frac{3}{8}$ 5. $\frac{1}{2} \div \frac{7}{16}$

6. $\frac{4}{5} \div \frac{2}{9}$ 7. $\frac{3}{7} \div \frac{3}{7}$ 8. $\frac{5}{8} \div 5$ 9. $10 \div 3\frac{1}{3}$ 10. $1\frac{4}{9} \div 1\frac{4}{9}$

11. $\frac{7}{9} \div 7$ 12. $9 \div 2\frac{1}{4}$ 13. $2\frac{1}{2} \div \frac{5}{6}$ 14. $2\frac{3}{16} \div 1\frac{1}{4}$ 15. $\frac{9}{16} \div 3$

16. $6\frac{1}{4} \div 2\frac{1}{2}$ 17. $2\frac{1}{12} \div 3\frac{3}{4}$ 18. $13\frac{1}{3} \div 8$ 19. $4\frac{1}{4} \div 7\frac{7}{8}$

20. $82\frac{1}{2} \div 16\frac{1}{2}$ 21. $58\frac{1}{2} \div 3\frac{1}{4}$ ★22. $\dfrac{\frac{3}{4}}{\frac{2}{3}}$ ★23. $\dfrac{3\frac{1}{8}}{25}$

Apply To solve each problem, refer to the chart on page 116.

24. How many quarts of canned apples can be made from 15 pounds of fresh apples?

25. How many quarts of canned berries can be made from $4\frac{1}{2}$ pounds of fresh berries?

★26. How many full quarts of canned cherries can be made from 9 pounds of fresh cherries?

★27. How many full quarts of canned pears can be made from $26\frac{1}{4}$ pounds of fresh pears?

Adding Fractions

A. Jeff is making turquoise and silver earrings. The length of the silver wire hook is $\frac{7}{16}$ inch. The turquoise bird is $\frac{5}{8}$ inch long. Find the total length of each earring.

$\frac{7}{16}$ inch

$\frac{5}{8}$ inch

Find $\frac{7}{16} + \frac{5}{8}$.

$$\frac{7}{16} = \frac{7}{16}$$ Write the fractions with a common denominator.

$$+ \frac{5}{8} = \frac{10}{16}$$ Add the numerators.

$$\frac{17}{16} = 1\frac{1}{16}$$ Rename the sum.

The earring is $1\frac{1}{16}$ inches long.

B. Find $\frac{2}{3} + \frac{3}{8} + \frac{5}{6}$.

$$\frac{2}{3} = \frac{16}{24}$$ Write the fractions with a common denominator.

$$\frac{3}{8} = \frac{9}{24}$$

$$+ \frac{5}{6} = \frac{20}{24}$$ Add the numerators.

$$\frac{45}{24} = 1\frac{21}{24} = 1\frac{7}{8}$$ Rename the sum. Write it in lowest terms.

Try Add.

a. $\frac{4}{9}$
$+ \frac{8}{9}$

b. $\frac{5}{6} + \frac{1}{4}$

c. $\frac{1}{2} + \frac{9}{10} + \frac{7}{8}$

Practice Add.

1. $\dfrac{5}{12}$
$+\dfrac{1}{12}$

2. $\dfrac{2}{5}$
$+\dfrac{3}{5}$

3. $\dfrac{1}{9}$
$+\dfrac{2}{3}$

4. $\dfrac{1}{4}$
$+\dfrac{15}{16}$

5. $\dfrac{2}{3}$
$+\dfrac{1}{2}$

6. $\dfrac{2}{3}$
$+\dfrac{3}{4}$

7. $\dfrac{5}{6}$
$+\dfrac{1}{6}$

8. $\dfrac{1}{2}$
$+\dfrac{7}{10}$

9. $\dfrac{3}{7}$
$+\dfrac{5}{6}$

10. $\dfrac{3}{4}$
$+\dfrac{1}{18}$

11. $\dfrac{3}{5}$
$+\dfrac{1}{7}$

12. $\dfrac{5}{6}$
$+\dfrac{3}{10}$

13. $\dfrac{3}{4}$
$+\dfrac{4}{9}$

14. $\dfrac{4}{5}$
$+\dfrac{8}{15}$

15. $\dfrac{5}{12} + \dfrac{8}{15}$

16. $\dfrac{1}{8} + \dfrac{1}{10}$

17. $\dfrac{4}{5} + \dfrac{2}{3}$

18. $\dfrac{5}{8} + \dfrac{1}{6}$

19. $\dfrac{1}{2} + \dfrac{5}{9}$

20. $\dfrac{1}{8} + \dfrac{5}{16} + \dfrac{7}{32}$

21. $\dfrac{5}{9} + \dfrac{1}{3} + \dfrac{5}{6}$

22. $\dfrac{9}{10} + \dfrac{7}{8} + \dfrac{3}{5}$

23. $\dfrac{5}{6} + \dfrac{4}{5} + \dfrac{11}{15}$

Apply Solve each problem.

24. Find the width of this bracelet.

$\dfrac{5}{16}$ inch
$\dfrac{5}{16}$ inch

25. Find the length of this pin.

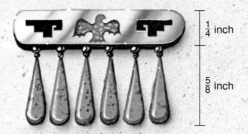

$\dfrac{1}{4}$ inch

$\dfrac{5}{8}$ inch

26. Find the width of this belt buckle.

$\dfrac{3}{8}$ inch

$\dfrac{1}{2}$ inch

$\dfrac{7}{8}$ inch

27. Find the width of this pendant.

$\dfrac{7}{8}$ inch $\dfrac{7}{16}$ inch $\dfrac{7}{8}$ inch

Adding Mixed Numbers

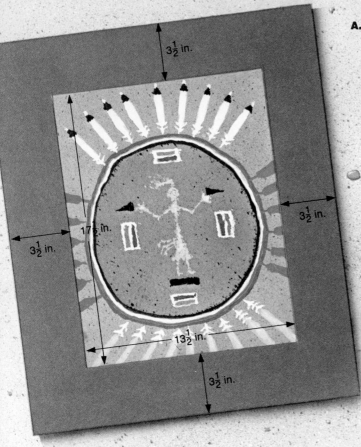

3½ in.

3½ in.

17½ in.

3½ in.

13½ in.

3½ in.

A. Inez wants a $3\frac{1}{2}$-inch mat to border a picture of a sand painting. The opening for the picture needs to be $13\frac{1}{2}$ inches wide. What is the overall width of the mat?

Find $13\frac{1}{2} + 3\frac{1}{2} + 3\frac{1}{2}$.

$$
\begin{array}{r}
13\frac{1}{2} \\
3\frac{1}{2} \\
+\ 3\frac{1}{2} \\
\hline
19\frac{3}{2} = 20\frac{1}{2}
\end{array}
$$

The denominators are the same. Add the fractions. Add the whole numbers. Rename the sum.

$19\frac{3}{2} = 19 + \frac{3}{2}$
$\quad\ = 19 + 1\frac{1}{2}$
$\quad\ = 20\frac{1}{2}$

The overall width of the mat is $20\frac{1}{2}$ inches.

B. Find $5\frac{5}{6} + 3\frac{9}{10}$.

$$5\frac{5}{6} = 5\frac{25}{30}$$

Write the fractions with a common denominator. Add.

$$+3\frac{9}{10} = 3\frac{27}{30}$$

$$8\frac{52}{30} = 9\frac{22}{30} = 9\frac{11}{15}$$

Rename the sum.
Write it in lowest terms.

Try Add.

a. $\begin{array}{r} 2\frac{7}{15} \\ +\ 6\frac{8}{15} \\ \hline \end{array}$

b. $\begin{array}{r} 5\frac{7}{9} \\ +\ 6 \\ \hline \end{array}$

c. $\begin{array}{r} 9\frac{1}{2} \\ +\ \frac{7}{12} \\ \hline \end{array}$

d. $8\frac{1}{4} + 3\frac{7}{10} + 1\frac{3}{5}$

e. $4\frac{5}{6} + 10\frac{4}{9}$

Practice Add.

1. $\begin{array}{r} 2\frac{1}{8} \\ +\ 9\frac{3}{8} \\ \hline \end{array}$

2. $\begin{array}{r} 1\frac{1}{5} \\ +\ 7\frac{4}{5} \\ \hline \end{array}$

3. $\begin{array}{r} 5\frac{5}{9} \\ +\ \frac{4}{9} \\ \hline \end{array}$

4. $\begin{array}{r} 4\frac{2}{3} \\ +\ 7 \\ \hline \end{array}$

5. $\begin{array}{r} 8\frac{3}{5} \\ +\ 3\frac{1}{7} \\ \hline \end{array}$

6. $\begin{array}{r} 5\frac{1}{2} \\ +\ 9\frac{2}{9} \\ \hline \end{array}$

7. $5 + 1\frac{3}{4}$ **8.** $4\frac{1}{2} + 3\frac{1}{6}$ **9.** $7 + \frac{11}{16}$ **10.** $6\frac{3}{5} + 6\frac{2}{5}$ **11.** $2\frac{1}{8} + 9\frac{7}{8}$

12. $11\frac{1}{3} + 2\frac{3}{4}$ **13.** $16\frac{7}{8} + 4\frac{2}{3}$ **14.** $18 + \frac{4}{5}$ **15.** $7\frac{5}{16} + 3\frac{1}{4}$ **16.** $14\frac{5}{36} + 20\frac{17}{18}$

17. $11\frac{4}{5} + \frac{5}{6}$ **18.** $10\frac{5}{8} + 3\frac{5}{6}$ **19.** $6\frac{7}{10} + 5\frac{5}{6}$ **20.** $4\frac{9}{20} + 6\frac{1}{8}$ **21.** $55\frac{1}{12} + 2\frac{11}{12}$

22. $2\frac{1}{8} + 6\frac{7}{8} + 4\frac{5}{8}$ **23.** $3\frac{7}{10} + \frac{9}{10} + 4\frac{3}{10}$ **24.** $5\frac{1}{2} + 7\frac{2}{3} + 4\frac{1}{12}$

25. $4\frac{8}{9} + \frac{7}{9} + 10\frac{2}{3}$ **26.** $18\frac{7}{8} + 1\frac{11}{12} + \frac{5}{6}$ **27.** $2\frac{5}{16} + 7\frac{7}{8} + 12\frac{3}{4}$

Apply   Solve each problem.

28. Find the overall height of the mat in Example A.

29. Gwen wants a $3\frac{3}{4}$-inch mat to border an ink sketch. The opening for the sketch needs to be $18\frac{1}{2}$ inches by 23 inches. Find the overall dimensions of the mat.

★30. Jesse needs two mats with overall dimensions of $17\frac{1}{4}$ inches by $23\frac{1}{2}$ inches and $15\frac{3}{4}$ inches by $11\frac{3}{4}$ inches. Can he cut both mats from a piece of mat board 20 inches by 36 inches?

CHALLENGE

A farmer left 17 horses to his 3 children, Dolly, Ollie, and Molly. The farmer's will stated that Dolly should have $\frac{1}{2}$ of the horses, Ollie should have $\frac{1}{3}$, and Molly should have $\frac{1}{9}$. Since you cannot have $\frac{1}{2}$ of 17 horses, the children borrowed a horse from a neighbor.

Now Dolly took $\frac{1}{2}$ of 18, or 9, horses; Ollie took $\frac{1}{3}$ of 18, or 6, horses; and Molly took $\frac{1}{9}$ of 18, or 2, horses. The extra horse was returned to the neighbor.

Explain what was wrong with the farmer's will.

Clearance 16½ Ft.

Career John Sauble is a truck driver. His truck is $13\frac{1}{4}$ feet high. How much space is there between the top of his truck and an overpass that has a $16\frac{1}{2}$-foot clearance?

Find $16\frac{1}{2} - 13\frac{1}{4}$.

$$16\frac{1}{2} = 16\frac{2}{4}$$
$$-13\frac{1}{4} = 13\frac{1}{4}$$
$$\overline{\phantom{-13\frac{1}{4} = }3\frac{1}{4}}$$

First subtract the fractions. Write them with a common denominator. Subtract the numerators.

Then subtract the whole numbers.

The space between the top of the truck and the overpass is $3\frac{1}{4}$ feet.

Try Subtract.

a. $\frac{5}{8} - \frac{3}{8}$

b. $\frac{2}{3} - \frac{1}{4}$

c. $6\frac{4}{5}$
$-3\frac{1}{2}$

d. $14\frac{1}{3}$
$- 6$

Practice Subtract.

1. $\frac{4}{5} - \frac{1}{5}$

2. $\frac{8}{9} - \frac{4}{9}$

3. $\frac{7}{8} - \frac{3}{16}$

4. $\frac{1}{2} - \frac{1}{3}$

5. $\frac{4}{9} - \frac{1}{6}$

6. $\frac{1}{8}$
$-\frac{1}{12}$

7. $\frac{5}{6}$
$-\frac{3}{8}$

8. $\frac{5}{8}$
$-\frac{1}{10}$

9. $15\frac{6}{7}$
$- 8\frac{3}{7}$

10. $10\frac{9}{10}$
$- 3\frac{1}{10}$

11. $4\frac{11}{12}$
$-1\frac{3}{4}$

12. $12\frac{3}{4}$
$- 5\frac{1}{2}$

13. $9\frac{3}{8}$
-5

14. $26\frac{5}{9}$
$-13\frac{5}{9}$

15. $\frac{9}{10}$
$-\frac{5}{6}$

16. $16\frac{2}{3}$
$-16\frac{7}{16}$

17. $1\frac{7}{12}$
$-\frac{2}{5}$

18. $\frac{5}{6}$
$-\frac{3}{5}$

19. $42\frac{7}{8}$
$-22\frac{7}{8}$

20. $27\frac{15}{16}$
$- 18$

21. $9\frac{2}{3}$
$-9\frac{4}{11}$

22. $9\frac{17}{20}$
$-\frac{4}{5}$

23. $31\frac{7}{8}$
$-14\frac{2}{3}$

Apply Solve each problem.

24. A viaduct has a $17\frac{3}{4}$-foot clearance. How much space is there between the viaduct and a truck that is $14\frac{1}{4}$ feet high?

25. John's truck weighs $3\frac{1}{4}$ tons empty. Fully loaded with produce, the truck weighs $7\frac{1}{2}$ tons. What is the weight of the produce?

26. The weight limit on interstate highways is 10 tons per single axle. A loaded six-wheeler weighs $11\frac{3}{4}$ tons per axle. By how many tons is each axle over the weight limit?

★27. An empty van weighs $1\frac{7}{8}$ tons. The weight limit of a small bridge is $3\frac{1}{2}$ tons. By how many tons is the van under the limit when it carries a $1\frac{1}{4}$-ton load?

Subtracting Mixed Numbers with Renaming

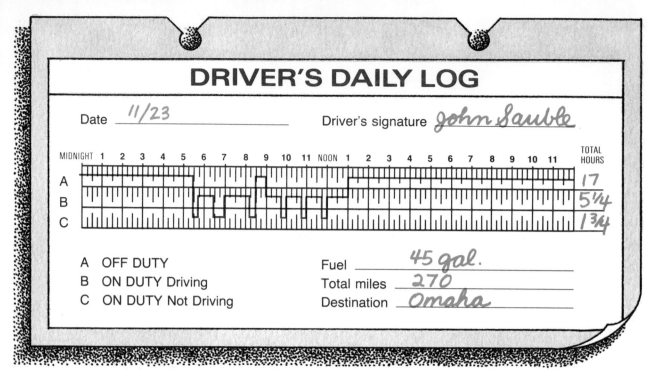

A. For each 24-hour period, John fills out a log. It shows to the nearest quarter hour how much time he spends on duty and off duty. While on duty, how much more time did John spend driving than not driving?

Find $5\frac{1}{4} - 1\frac{3}{4}$.

$$5\frac{1}{4} = 4\frac{5}{4}$$
$$-1\frac{3}{4} = 1\frac{3}{4}$$
$$\overline{\qquad\qquad}$$
$$3\frac{2}{4} = 3\frac{1}{2}$$

$\frac{1}{4} < \frac{3}{4}$, so rename $5\frac{1}{4}$.
$5\frac{1}{4} = 5 + \frac{1}{4}$
$\quad\ = 4\frac{4}{4} + \frac{1}{4}$
$\quad\ = 4\frac{5}{4}$

John spent $3\frac{1}{2}$ hours more driving.

B. Find $12\frac{1}{3} - 7\frac{7}{8}$.

$$12\frac{1}{3} = 12\frac{8}{24} = 11\frac{32}{24}$$
$$-\ 7\frac{7}{8} = \ 7\frac{21}{24} = \ 7\frac{21}{24}$$
$$\overline{\qquad\qquad\qquad\qquad\quad}$$
$$4\frac{11}{24}$$

Write the fractions with a common denominator. Then rename $12\frac{8}{24}$ as $11\frac{32}{24}$.

Try   Subtract.

a. $8\frac{5}{16}$
     $-4\frac{9}{16}$

b. 37
     $-\ 2\frac{3}{8}$

c. $5\frac{1}{6} - 3\frac{4}{5}$

124

Practice   Subtract.

1. $7\frac{1}{6}$
   $-4\frac{5}{6}$

2. $12\frac{2}{5}$
   $-\ 7\frac{4}{5}$

3. $9\frac{1}{3}$
   $-\ \frac{2}{3}$

4. 8
   $-2\frac{3}{4}$

5. 17
   $-\ 8\frac{5}{8}$

6. 47
   $-\ \frac{7}{12}$

7. $39 - \frac{7}{16}$

8. $7\frac{1}{5} - 5\frac{1}{3}$

9. $9\frac{1}{6} - 5\frac{3}{8}$

10. $6\frac{1}{6} - 2\frac{2}{3}$

11. $20\frac{3}{10} - 16\frac{1}{2}$

12. $7\frac{9}{16} - \frac{7}{8}$

13. $10\frac{1}{3} - 6\frac{6}{11}$

14. $14\frac{1}{10} - 9\frac{3}{4}$

15. $32\frac{1}{4} - 18\frac{4}{9}$

16. $47\frac{5}{8} - 20\frac{5}{6}$

17. $18 - 2\frac{11}{12}$

18. $23\frac{3}{10} - 4\frac{5}{12}$

19. $12\frac{17}{20} - 6\frac{7}{8}$

20. $66 - 19\frac{1}{7}$

21. $39\frac{2}{5} - 16\frac{7}{9}$

Apply   Solve each problem.

22. John may work a maximum of 70 hours per week. If he worked $39\frac{1}{4}$ hours at the beginning of the week, how many more hours may he work?

23. On Monday John was on duty for $9\frac{1}{2}$ hours. During that time he drove for $6\frac{3}{4}$ hours. How long was he on duty but not driving?

24. Use the log on page 124. How much more time did John spend off duty than driving?

★25. Use the log on page 124. How many more hours was John off duty than on duty?

Practice: Computing with Fractions

Compare these numbers. Use <, >, or =.

1. $\frac{7}{9}$ ⬤ $\frac{5}{6}$
2. $7\frac{4}{5}$ ⬤ $7\frac{28}{35}$
3. $\frac{3}{16}$ ⬤ $\frac{11}{64}$
4. $3\frac{7}{12}$ ⬤ $3\frac{5}{8}$

Write each decimal as a fraction in lowest terms.

5. 0.41
6. 0.62
7. 0.8
8. 0.175
9. 0.72
10. 0.455

Write each fraction as a decimal.

11. $\frac{3}{5}$
12. $\frac{7}{8}$
13. $\frac{8}{9}$
14. $\frac{793}{1,000}$
15. $\frac{13}{22}$
16. $\frac{40}{101}$

Write each number as an improper fraction.

17. $8 = \frac{\blacksquare}{1}$
18. $4 = \frac{\blacksquare}{12}$
19. $11\frac{1}{4}$
20. $3\frac{5}{16}$
21. $12\frac{2}{3}$
22. $1\frac{9}{10}$

Write each improper fraction as a whole number or a mixed number.

23. $\frac{7}{2}$
24. $\frac{16}{10}$
25. $\frac{27}{12}$
26. $\frac{36}{18}$
27. $\frac{54}{6}$
28. $\frac{58}{8}$

Find each answer.

29. $\frac{2}{3} \times \frac{4}{5}$
30. $\frac{5}{6} + \frac{3}{4}$
31. $1\frac{5}{9} + \frac{2}{3}$
32. $\frac{1}{4} \div \frac{1}{8}$
33. $\frac{19}{32} - \frac{15}{32}$

34. $6\frac{3}{4} \times 6\frac{2}{3}$
35. $\frac{3}{8} \times \frac{5}{9}$
36. $18\frac{7}{8} - 11\frac{7}{16}$
37. $6 \div \frac{2}{3}$
38. $4\frac{5}{9} + 8\frac{1}{6}$

39. $6\frac{7}{20} - 3\frac{3}{5}$
40. $\frac{3}{8} \div \frac{5}{16}$
41. $16 \times 3\frac{5}{8}$
42. $25 - 3\frac{1}{8}$
43. $\frac{6}{7} \div 3$

44. $7\frac{1}{5} + 4\frac{2}{3}$
45. $3\frac{1}{8} \div 3\frac{1}{8}$
46. $27\frac{1}{4} - 18\frac{2}{3}$
47. $10 - \frac{3}{16}$
48. $\frac{3}{7} \times \frac{7}{3}$

49. $\frac{1}{8} + \frac{3}{4} + \frac{7}{12}$
50. $\frac{1}{6} \times \frac{3}{4} \times \frac{5}{6}$
51. $7 \times \frac{4}{9} \times \frac{3}{4}$
52. $\frac{1}{2} + \frac{1}{3} + \frac{1}{4}$

53. $\left(\frac{7}{12}\right)\left(1\frac{5}{7}\right)(4)$
54. $3\frac{2}{5} + 5\frac{1}{6} + 2\frac{2}{3}$
55. $2\frac{7}{8} + 8 + \frac{2}{5}$
56. $\left(2\frac{11}{12}\right)\left(\frac{3}{5}\right)\left(1\frac{7}{9}\right)$

Apply Solve each problem.

57. Mark spent $3\frac{1}{4}$ hours in the morning loading trucks. After lunch he loaded trucks for another $3\frac{1}{2}$ hours. Find the total number of hours Mark spent loading trucks.

58. Mrs. Hart has a $19\frac{1}{2}$-pound turkey in the freezer. If she allows $\frac{3}{4}$ pound per serving, how many servings will the turkey provide?

59. A recipe for cream of mushroom soup calls for $2\frac{1}{4}$ cups of milk. How much milk is needed if the recipe is tripled?

60. Celia shredded 4 cups of cheddar cheese. She used $2\frac{2}{3}$ cups to make a casserole. How much cheese is left?

61. The width of a copper belt buckle is $1\frac{1}{2}$ times the width of the leather belt. The belt is $\frac{3}{4}$ inch wide. Find the width of the buckle.

62. Ruben had a $7\frac{1}{2}$-foot strip of oak lumber. He used $6\frac{3}{4}$ feet of the lumber to make a picture frame. How much lumber was left?

COMPUTER

BASIC: REM Statements

REM statements are remarks in a program. They are used to explain the program to someone reading it. They are ignored by the computer and are not part of the *output*, that which is printed. A REM statement has a line number and can be anywhere in a program.

This program changes a mixed number to an improper fraction.

```
10 REM W IS A WHOLE NUMBER, N IS
NUMERATOR, D IS DENOMINATOR
20 PRINT "GIVE THREE NUMBERS"
30 INPUT W,N,D
40 LET I=W*D+N
50 PRINT I;"/";D
60 END
```

Output

```
GIVE THREE NUMBERS
? 3,2,5
17/5
```

Use the program above to change the following to improper fractions.

1. $2\frac{1}{2}$ 2. $6\frac{2}{3}$ 3. $4\frac{3}{4}$ 4. $9\frac{2}{5}$

5. Write a program using only PRINT statements that will change these improper fractions to whole numbers.
$\frac{10}{5}$ $\frac{20}{4}$ $\frac{15}{3}$ $\frac{16}{4}$ $\frac{18}{2}$

6. Write a program using an INPUT statement that will give the output for Exercise 5.

Solving Equations with Fractions

A. A customer at Flora's Fabrics purchased a full bolt of material plus an additional $17\frac{1}{2}$ yards from a second bolt. A total of $62\frac{1}{4}$ yards was purchased. How much material was on the full bolt?

Yards on full bolt	Yards from second bolt	Yards purchased

$$f \quad + \quad 17\tfrac{1}{2} \quad = \quad 62\tfrac{1}{4}$$

$$f + 17\tfrac{1}{2} - 17\tfrac{1}{2} = 62\tfrac{1}{4} - 17\tfrac{1}{2}$$

$$f = 44\tfrac{3}{4}$$

To find f, subtract $17\frac{1}{2}$ from both sides of the equation.

There were $44\frac{3}{4}$ yards of material on the full bolt.

B. Solve $x - 6\frac{1}{3} = 10\frac{5}{6}$.

$$x - 6\tfrac{1}{3} = 10\tfrac{5}{6}$$

$$x - 6\tfrac{1}{3} + 6\tfrac{1}{3} = 10\tfrac{5}{6} + 6\tfrac{1}{3}$$

$$x = 17\tfrac{1}{6}$$

To find x, add $6\frac{1}{3}$ to both sides of the equation.

If one side of an equation features only a variable multiplied by a number, multiply both sides by the reciprocal of that number.

C. Solve $\frac{2}{3}b = 12$.

$$\frac{2}{3}b = 12$$

$$\left(\tfrac{3}{2}\right)\tfrac{2}{3}b = \left(\tfrac{3}{2}\right)12 \qquad \left(\tfrac{3}{2}\right)\tfrac{2}{3} = 1$$

$$1b = 18$$

$$b = 18 \qquad 1b = b$$

D. Solve $\frac{m}{6} = \frac{4}{5}$.

$$\frac{m}{6} = \frac{4}{5} \qquad \frac{m}{6} = \frac{1 \times m}{6} = \frac{1}{6}m$$

$$\frac{1}{6}m = \frac{4}{5}$$

$$\left(\tfrac{6}{1}\right)\tfrac{1}{6}m = \left(\tfrac{6}{1}\right)\tfrac{4}{5} \qquad \left(\tfrac{6}{1}\right)\tfrac{1}{6} = 1$$

$$1m = \frac{24}{5}$$

$$m = 4\tfrac{4}{5} \qquad 1m = m$$

Try Solve each equation.

a. $5\frac{1}{2} + a = 9\frac{5}{8}$ b. $1\frac{4}{5}n = 27$ c. $\frac{5}{16} = \frac{c}{3}$

Practice Solve each equation.

1. $b + 3\frac{1}{2} = 6$ 2. $c + 8\frac{1}{4} = 12\frac{3}{4}$ 3. $t - 4\frac{1}{8} = 10\frac{3}{16}$

4. $x - 9\frac{7}{8} = 10\frac{3}{8}$ 5. $\frac{5}{6}y = 15$ 6. $\frac{5}{8}n = 4\frac{1}{6}$

7. $\frac{a}{5} = \frac{3}{20}$ 8. $\frac{w}{9} = 4$ 9. $2\frac{1}{3} + d = 11\frac{5}{6}$

10. $7\frac{1}{8} + r = 8\frac{3}{4}$ 11. $\frac{3}{10} + m = \frac{2}{3}$ 12. $s - \frac{4}{9} = \frac{1}{6}$

13. $5\frac{1}{4}b = 1\frac{4}{5}$ 14. $3\frac{1}{4}y = 2\frac{1}{2}$ 15. $7\frac{3}{4} = n + 4\frac{1}{2}$

16. $r - 8\frac{3}{5} = 12$ 17. $w - 4\frac{1}{4} = 7\frac{4}{5}$ 18. $8\frac{5}{8} = c + 4\frac{3}{16}$

19. $\frac{s}{9} = \frac{1}{2}$ 20. $\frac{1}{6}t = 3\frac{2}{3}$ 21. $7m = 3\frac{1}{2}$

22. $7\frac{8}{9} = m + 6\frac{5}{6}$ 23. $\frac{8}{9}n = \frac{8}{9}$ 24. $3\frac{2}{5} = \frac{r}{10}$

25. $d + 3\frac{1}{4} = 3\frac{1}{4}$ 26. $\frac{15}{16} = 5a$ 27. $4\frac{1}{8} = s + \frac{4}{5}$

28. $2\frac{1}{2}y = 2\frac{1}{2}$ 29. $g - \frac{7}{16} = 3\frac{1}{3}$ 30. $8\frac{5}{6} = e + 8\frac{5}{6}$

Apply Solve each problem.

31. After $38\frac{3}{4}$ yards of fabric was sold, there was a remnant of $2\frac{5}{8}$ yards left on the bolt. How much fabric was on the bolt originally?
$\left(\text{HINT}: f - 38\frac{3}{4} = 2\frac{5}{8}\right)$

32. Flora's Fabrics placed an order for 420 bolts of cotton. This was $3\frac{1}{2}$ times the order for wool. How many bolts of wool were ordered?
$\left(\text{HINT}: 3\frac{1}{2}k = 420\right)$

Problem Solving: Write an Equation

Read Alma bought a $3\frac{1}{2}$-yard remnant of broadcloth to make aprons for the spring bazaar. Each apron uses $\frac{3}{4}$ yard of fabric. How many aprons can she make?

Plan Write an equation that uses n for the number of aprons.

Yards of fabric for 1 apron	Number of aprons	Total number of yards of fabric

$$\frac{3}{4}n \;=\; 3\frac{1}{2}$$

Solve To find n, multiply both sides of the equation by the reciprocal of $\frac{3}{4}$.

$$\frac{3}{4}n = 3\frac{1}{2}$$

$$\left(\frac{4}{3}\right)\frac{3}{4}n = \left(\frac{4}{3}\right)\frac{7}{2}$$

$$n = 4\frac{2}{3}$$

Answer Alma can make 4 aprons.

Look Back It does not make sense to talk about $\frac{2}{3}$ of an apron, so only the whole number 4 is used in the answer.

Try Write an equation. Then find the answer.

a. A total of $4\frac{7}{8}$ yards of fabric is needed to make a suit. The jacket requires $2\frac{5}{8}$ yards of fabric. How much fabric is needed for the skirt?

Apply Write an equation. Then find the answer.

1. A size-12 blouse requires $2\frac{3}{8}$ yards of material, $\frac{5}{8}$ yard more than a size-8 blouse. How much material is needed for the size-8 blouse?

2. Dora bought a $2\frac{7}{8}$-yard remnant of quilted cotton to make placemats. Each placemat uses $\frac{3}{8}$ yard of fabric. How many placemats can she make?

3. An infant's sleeper requires $\frac{2}{3}$ the amount of fabric needed for a toddler's sleeper. The infant's sleeper uses $1\frac{1}{2}$ yards of fabric. How much fabric is needed for the toddler's sleeper?

4. Tim took in $1\frac{1}{2}$ inches on the waistband of a pair of slacks. The band now measures $28\frac{1}{2}$ inches. What did the waistband originally measure?

5. Mary used $5\frac{1}{4}$ yards of material to make a tablecloth and napkins. She used $2\frac{1}{2}$ yards of material for the napkins. How much material did she use for the tablecloth?

6. Claire is sewing a ruffle along the hemline of a skirt. She needs 96 inches of lace, $1\frac{1}{2}$ times the width of the skirt at the hem. How many inches does the skirt measure at the hem?

7. Mr. Nuyen used $3\frac{3}{4}$ yards of fabric to make vests for his triplet sons. How much fabric was used for each vest?

8. It took Shelly $4\frac{1}{2}$ times as long to sew a blouse as to cut out the fabric. She sewed the blouse in 3 hours. How long did it take her to cut out the fabric?

Solving Two-Step Equations with Fractions

A. Mr. Hutchinson bought $16\frac{1}{4}$ yards of velvet to reupholster his couch. He needs $\frac{7}{8}$ yard of fabric to cover each matching throw pillow and an additional $9\frac{1}{4}$ yards of fabric to cover the couch itself. How many throw pillows can he cover?

Yards of fabric for n pillows	Yards of fabric for couch	Total number of yards of fabric

$$\frac{7}{8}n \ + \ 9\frac{1}{4} \ = \ 16\frac{1}{4}$$ Use this equation.

$$\frac{7}{8}n + 9\frac{1}{4} - 9\frac{1}{4} = 16\frac{1}{4} - 9\frac{1}{4}$$ $9\frac{1}{4}$ has been *added to* $\frac{7}{8}n$. To get $\frac{7}{8}n$ by itself, *subtract* $9\frac{1}{4}$ from both sides of the equation.

$$\frac{7}{8}n = 7$$

$$\left(\frac{8}{7}\right)\frac{7}{8}n = \left(\frac{8}{7}\right)7$$ To find n, multiply both sides of the equation by the reciprocal of $\frac{7}{8}$.

$$n = 8$$

Mr. Hutchinson can cover 8 throw pillows.

B. Solve $3\frac{1}{5}x - 10 = 18$.

$$3\frac{1}{5}x - 10 = 18$$

$$3\frac{1}{5}x - 10 + 10 = 18 + 10$$

$$3\frac{1}{5}x = 28$$

$$\frac{16}{5}x = 28$$

$$\left(\frac{5}{16}\right)\frac{16}{5}x = \left(\frac{5}{16}\right)28$$

$$x = \frac{35}{4} = 8\frac{3}{4}$$

Try Solve each equation.

a. $\frac{2}{5}c + 32 = 54$

b. $4\frac{1}{2}d - 12 = 6$

c. $6k + 2\frac{1}{2} = 4\frac{3}{4}$

Practice Solve each equation.

1. $\frac{7}{10}m + 5 = 33$

2. $\frac{5}{8}x + 10 = 45$

3. $12 + \frac{7}{16}x = 33$

4. $\frac{2}{3}y + 6 = 18$

5. $6 = \frac{4}{5}y - 18$

6. $74 = \frac{1}{2}d - 28$

7. $\frac{b}{8} - 3 = 15$

8. $\frac{3}{4}x - 7 = 8$

9. $3\frac{1}{4}x + 7 = 33$

10. $18 + 1\frac{7}{8}n = 78$

11. $7r + \frac{4}{5} = 4\frac{3}{10}$

12. $10w - \frac{1}{3} = 3\frac{2}{3}$

13. $\frac{4}{9}b + \frac{9}{10} = \frac{9}{10}$

14. $\frac{n}{7} - \frac{1}{10} = \frac{1}{30}$

15. $2m + \frac{7}{8} = 7\frac{3}{8}$

16. $1\frac{11}{12} = 1\frac{2}{3}a + \frac{1}{4}$

17. $5s + \frac{1}{4} = 6\frac{1}{12}$

18. $21\frac{1}{20} = 8\frac{4}{5} + 3\frac{1}{2}c$

Apply Solve each problem.

19. Mr. Tabishu paid $194 to have his recliner reupholstered. He paid $12 per yard for the fabric plus $125 for labor. How many yards of fabric were used?

20. Ms. Day used $33\frac{1}{2}$ yards of fabric to redecorate her dining room. She covered each chair seat with $\frac{1}{2}$ yard of fabric and used $29\frac{1}{2}$ yards of fabric for the draperies. How many chair seats did Ms. Day cover?

Chapter 4 Test

Give each missing number.

1. $\frac{4}{5} = \frac{\blacksquare}{30}$ 2. $\frac{18}{63} = \frac{2}{\blacksquare}$

Compare these fractions.
Use >, <, or =.

3. $\frac{3}{4} \bullet \frac{9}{16}$ 4. $\frac{3}{5} \bullet \frac{2}{3}$

5. Write $\frac{7}{20}$ as a decimal.

6. Write 0.875 as a fraction in lowest terms.

Write each number as an improper fraction.

7. $9\frac{1}{2}$ 8. $3\frac{5}{6}$

Multiply.

9. $\frac{3}{8} \times \frac{2}{3}$ 10. $12\left(\frac{3}{4}\right)$

11. $3\frac{4}{7} \times 1\frac{1}{5}$ 12. $3\frac{1}{3} \times \frac{3}{10}$

Divide.

13. $\frac{1}{2} \div \frac{7}{8}$ 14. $5\frac{2}{5} \div \frac{9}{10}$

Add.

15. $\begin{array}{r} \frac{5}{9} \\ + \frac{2}{3} \\ \hline \end{array}$ 16. $\begin{array}{r} \frac{3}{4} \\ + \frac{5}{6} \\ \hline \end{array}$

17. $\begin{array}{r} 7\frac{5}{8} \\ + \ \frac{3}{8} \\ \hline \end{array}$ 18. $\begin{array}{r} 6\frac{1}{3} \\ + 3\frac{4}{5} \\ \hline \end{array}$

Subtract.

19. $\begin{array}{r} \frac{3}{4} \\ - \frac{2}{3} \\ \hline \end{array}$ 20. $\begin{array}{r} 3\frac{1}{2} \\ - 2\frac{5}{16} \\ \hline \end{array}$

21. $\begin{array}{r} 9 \\ - 2\frac{3}{5} \\ \hline \end{array}$ 22. $\begin{array}{r} 15\frac{5}{8} \\ - \ 5\frac{5}{6} \\ \hline \end{array}$

Solve each equation.

23. $m + 2\frac{1}{2} = 7$ 24. $\frac{b}{5} = \frac{7}{10}$

25. $4k - 3\frac{1}{3} = 1\frac{1}{9}$ 26. $\frac{n}{2} + \frac{1}{4} = 1$

Solve the problem.

27. A small reel holds 900 feet of film. How many of these reels are needed for 2,800 feet of film?

Write an equation. Then find the answer.

28. A size-9 skirt requires $3\frac{1}{8}$ yards of material, $\frac{3}{8}$ yard more than a size-7 skirt. How much material is needed for the size-7 skirt?

CHALLENGE
Writing Repeating Decimals as Fractions

When changed to decimals, some fractions are repeating decimals.
For example, $\frac{8}{11} = 0.\overline{72}$.

Here is a method for changing a repeating decimal to a fraction.

1. Write an equation with n representing the repeating decimal.

2. Multiply both sides of the equation by a power of 10 (1, 10, 100, . . .) so that the number of zeros in the power of 10 is equal to the number of digits in the repetend.

3. Subtract the original equation from the equation found in step 2.

4. Solve the resulting equation.

A. Write $0.\overline{6}$ as a fraction.

Let $n = 0.\overline{6} = 0.6666 \ldots$	Step 1
$10n = 6.6666 \ldots$	Step 2
$-\quad n = 0.6666 \ldots$	
$9n = 6$	Step 3
$9n = 6$	Step 4
$n = \frac{2}{3}$	
$0.\overline{6} = \frac{2}{3}$	

B. Write $0.8\overline{23}$ as a fraction.

Let $n = 0.8\overline{23} = 0.8232323 \ldots$

$$100n = 82.3232323 \ldots$$
$$-\quad n = \;\;0.8232323 \ldots$$
$$99n = 81.5$$

$99n = 81.5$

$n = \frac{81.5}{99}$ Multiply numerator and denominator by any nonzero whole number that will eliminate the decimal. 10 will work.

$n = \frac{815}{990}$

$0.8\overline{23} = \frac{815}{990}$

Write each repeating decimal as a fraction.

1. $0.\overline{3}$ **2.** $0.\overline{27}$ **3.** $0.\overline{8}$ **4.** $0.\overline{54}$ **5.** $0.9\overline{4}$

6. $0.7\overline{3}$ **7.** $0.\overline{148}$ **8.** $0.9\overline{54}$ **9.** $0.\overline{9}$ **10.** $0.91\overline{3}$

MAINTENANCE

Simplify.

1. $8(6) - 4$
2. $14 + 8(3)$
3. $5 + 4(2) + 5$
4. $4(3) + 2(8)$

5. $6 \times 3 - 5$
6. $12 + 4 \times 8$
7. $5(4 + 3)$
8. $2(8 + 2) - 2$

9. $\dfrac{48}{2(5 - 2)}$
10. $\dfrac{5 \times 6}{2 \times 2 + 2}$
11. $\dfrac{5(8 - 4)}{2(9 - 7)}$
12. $\dfrac{8 + 6 \times 3}{5 \times 3 - 2}$

Evaluate each expression for $a = 6$ and $b = 2$.

13. $a + b$
14. $2a - b$
15. $3a + 2b$
16. $7(a + b)$

17. ab
18. $ab - (a + b)$
19. $ab - b$
20. $a(b + b)$

21. $\dfrac{a + b}{b}$
22. $\dfrac{a}{b}$
23. $\dfrac{(a + b)}{2(a - b)}$
24. $\dfrac{3a - 2(b + 1)}{ab}$

Solve each problem.

25. The boa constrictor, a large snake, is 3.6 meters long. The anaconda is 2.5 times as long as the boa constrictor. Find the length of the anaconda.

26. A whole egg contains 6.5 grams of fat. There are 3.6 grams of fat in the white of the egg. How much fat is there in the yolk?

27. The star Rigel is 25 times as far from Earth as Arcturus is. Arcturus is 36 light-years away. How far from Earth is Rigel?

28. *Estimation* Estimate the total cost to the nearest dollar of: circular saw, $39.98; extension cord, $4.79; sandpaper, $1.29.

29. The Sernas were charged $89.78 for using 918 kilowatt-hours of electricity. To the nearest tenth of a cent, what was the cost per kilowatt-hour?

30. The weights of the three puppies in Goldie's litter were 580 grams, 612 grams, and 662 grams. Find the average weight of the puppies.

31. There are 42 seats on Marty's school bus. If 35 students rode the bus on Monday, what fraction of the seats were filled?

32. A scanning machine at the post office sorts 400 letters per minute. How many letters does it sort per hour (60 minutes)?

Ratio, Proportion, and Percent

List price:
$109.95

20%
OFF

anFM

OPR/BATT
FM STEREO

Ratio and Proportion

A *ratio* is a pair of numbers that describes a rate or comparison.

A. The telephone *modem* for Ms. Hamilton's home computer costs $1.25 for each 3 minutes she uses the service.

Dollars ⟶ $\dfrac{1.25}{3}$ Minutes ⟶

1.25 to 3 is one ratio that compares the cost to minutes.

You can multiply to find *equal ratios* for the same cost.

$$\text{Dollars} \longrightarrow \dfrac{1.25}{3} = \overset{2 \times 1.25}{\underset{2 \times 3}{\dfrac{2.50}{6}}} = \overset{3 \times 1.25}{\underset{3 \times 3}{\dfrac{3.75}{9}}} \cdots \overset{20 \times 1.25}{\underset{20 \times 3}{\dfrac{25.00}{60}}} \cdots$$

Discuss How can you divide to find equal ratios?

B. If two ratios are equal, they form a *proportion*, and the *cross-products* are equal.

$\dfrac{2.50}{6} = \dfrac{3.75}{9}$

2.50 × 9 and 6 × 3.75 are the cross-products.

2.50 × 9 = 22.5

6 × 3.75 = 22.5

The cross-products are equal.

c. Do these ratios form a proportion?

$\dfrac{8}{11} \overset{?}{=} \dfrac{5}{7}$

Write the cross-products.

$8 \times 7 \overset{?}{=} 11 \times 5$

The cross-products are not equal.

$56 \neq 55$

The ratios do not form a proportion.

If two ratios form a proportion, then the cross-products are equal.
If the cross-products of two ratios are equal, the ratios form a proportion.

Try

a. Write four equal ratios to describe "8 students for every 3 computers."

b. Do $\frac{8}{9}$ and $\frac{12}{135}$ form a proportion?

Practice Write four equal ratios to describe each situation.

1. 22 lines to 55 lines

2. $1.75 for 5 minutes

3. $45 for 10 disks

Do the ratios form a proportion? Write *yes* or *no*.

4. $\frac{16}{12}$ $\frac{12}{9}$ **5.** $\frac{7}{6}$ $\frac{6}{7}$

6. $\frac{75}{100}$ $\frac{4}{3}$ **7.** $\frac{18}{14}$ $\frac{54}{42}$

8. $\frac{36}{68}$ $\frac{9}{17}$ **9.** $\frac{3}{11}$ $\frac{55}{200}$

10. $\frac{0.3}{0.5}$ $\frac{4}{6.4}$ **11.** $\frac{0.2}{0.9}$ $\frac{0.6}{2.7}$

12. $\frac{0.2}{1.6}$ $\frac{0.7}{5.6}$ **13.** $\frac{0.15}{3}$ $\frac{0.45}{10}$

Apply Solve each problem.

14. If it costs $1.50 to use a telephone modem for 4 minutes, how much does it cost for 20 minutes?

15. If a printer prints 50 lines per page, how many pages would it take to print 250 lines?

Solving Proportions

Liam found that the printer for his home computer prints 4 lines every 5 seconds. How long would it take the printer to print a page 56 lines long?

Write a ratio. Then write a proportion. Use *n* for the number of seconds for 56 lines.

Lines $\longrightarrow$
Seconds $\longrightarrow$ $\dfrac{4}{5} = \dfrac{56}{n}$

$4 \times n = 5 \times 56$ Write the cross-products.

$4n = 280$

$\dfrac{4n}{4} = \dfrac{280}{4}$ Find *n*.

$n = 70$

It would take the printer 70 seconds.

Check

$\dfrac{4}{5} \overset{?}{=} \dfrac{56}{70}$ Substitute 70 for *n* in the proportion.

$4 \times 70 \overset{?}{=} 5 \times 56$

$280 = 280$ The cross-products are equal, so the answer checks.

Try   Solve each proportion.

a. $\dfrac{5}{8} = \dfrac{t}{24}$

b. $\dfrac{a}{15} = \dfrac{8}{3}$

c. $\dfrac{0.15}{n} = \dfrac{0.4}{0.16}$

Practice Solve each proportion.

1. $\frac{3}{5} = \frac{m}{25}$

2. $\frac{7}{2} = \frac{42}{x}$

3. $\frac{n}{4} = \frac{21}{6}$

4. $\frac{15}{25} = \frac{6}{a}$

5. $\frac{4}{24} = \frac{3}{r}$

6. $\frac{8}{n} = \frac{6}{15}$

7. $\frac{18}{63} = \frac{4}{g}$

8. $\frac{64}{n} = \frac{24}{9}$

9. $\frac{36}{54} = \frac{r}{15}$

10. $\frac{21}{49} = \frac{s}{14}$

11. $\frac{9}{b} = \frac{1}{12}$

12. $\frac{65}{h} = \frac{1}{5}$

13. $\frac{32}{64} = \frac{9}{x}$

14. $\frac{a}{8} = \frac{49}{14}$

15. $\frac{d}{8} = \frac{70}{80}$

16. $\frac{36}{63} = \frac{12}{n}$

17. $\frac{16}{21} = \frac{q}{42}$

18. $\frac{7}{3.5} = \frac{6}{a}$

19. $\frac{2.5}{5} = \frac{m}{4}$

20. $\frac{c}{56} = \frac{0.4}{1.4}$

21. $\frac{0.9}{3.3} = \frac{0.6}{x}$

22. $\frac{1.1}{t} = \frac{44}{12}$

23. $\frac{3}{d} = \frac{14}{2.8}$

24. $\frac{n}{0.9} = \frac{35}{21}$

25. $\frac{21}{12} = \frac{4.9}{v}$

Apply Solve each problem.

26. If Alan's printer prints 3.5 lines in 5 seconds, how many lines does it print per minute?

$\left(\text{HINT: } \frac{3.5}{5} = \frac{n}{60}\right)$

27. Some *ink-jet* printers print 3 pages in 0.5 second. How long does it take to print 200 pages?

$\left(\text{HINT: } \frac{3}{0.5} = \frac{200}{x}\right)$

28. An *electrostatic* printer prints 6,000 lines in 10 seconds. At this rate, how many lines would it print in 15 seconds?

$\left(\text{HINT: } \frac{6,000}{10} = \frac{m}{15}\right)$

★29. Which is faster, a *matrix* printer that prints 400 lines a minute, or a *thermal* printer that prints 140 characters a second? There are 133 characters in a line.

CHALLENGE

Copy the diagram. Arrange the numbers from 1 through 8 in the squares in such a way that no two consecutive numbers are next to each other horizontally, vertically, or diagonally.

Problem Solving: Use Ratios

Read   A certain computer has 8,000 connections, and for quality control, each connection must be checked. If a robot can check 320 connections in 0.15 hour (9 minutes), how many hours will it take the robot to check all the connections?

Plan   Write a proportion using ratio of hours to the number of checks.

$$\frac{0.15}{320} = \frac{n}{8{,}000} \begin{array}{l} \leftarrow \text{Hours} \\ \leftarrow \text{Checks} \end{array}$$

Solve

$$\frac{0.15}{320} = \frac{n}{8{,}000}$$

$$0.15 \times 8{,}000 = 320 \times n$$

$$1{,}200 = 320n$$

$$3.75 = n$$

Answer   It will take the robot 3.75 hours.

Look Back   Be sure that you used a correct proportion and that the answer checks.

Try   Use a proportion to solve the problem.

a. How many connections can the robot in the example check in 2 hours? Round your answer to the nearest whole number.

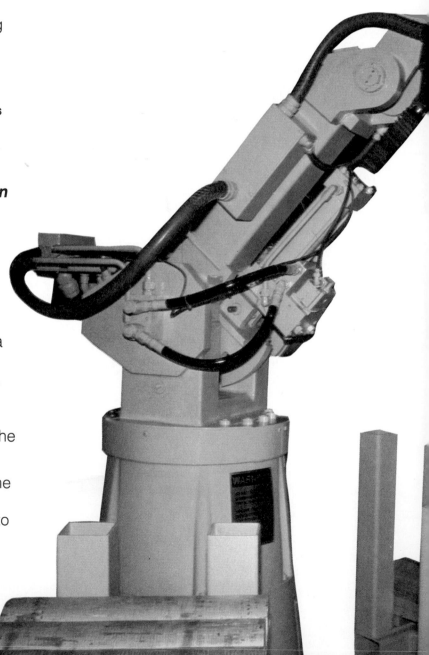

Apply Use a proportion to solve each problem.

1. A certain robot can weld 200 connections in 0.3 hour. How long would it take this robot to weld 1,500 connections?

2. One type of robot can move 83 feet in 5 seconds. How far can this robot move in 60 seconds?

3. If the number of robots in the United States increases at an average rate of 1,600 every 3 months, how many more robots will there be in 2 years than there are now?

★4. How many connections per hour can the robot in Problem 1 weld? Round to the nearest whole number.

Each problem gives the speed of a computer printer. Find the number of seconds it would take the printer to print 1,000 lines.

5. Chain: 100 lines in 3 seconds

6. Matrix: 20 lines in 3 seconds

7. Laser-light: 300 lines in 1 second

8. Thermal: 11 lines in 10 seconds

Each 8K of memory in a microcomputer can store 8,192 bytes of information. Find the number of bytes that can be stored in computers with the given memory.

9. 32K   **10.** 4K   **11.** 64K

Percents and Decimals

The town of Oakdale is raising money to help send boys and girls to the Special Olympics. The goal is $100.

A. $23 was raised the first week.

$23 out of $100 is 23 hundredths, or 23 percent, of the goal. *Percent* means hundredths.

23 hundredths = 0.23 = 23%

B. After two weeks, 50% of the goal had been reached. Write 50% as a decimal.

50% = 50 hundredths = 0.50 = 0.5

C. $100 is 100% of the goal. More than $100 is more than 100% of the goal.

Percents greater than 100% are shown in green on the scale at the right.

D. $1 is 1% of the goal. Less than $1 is less than 1% of the goal.

Percents less than 1% are shown in the enlarged section of the scale. 0.5% is read "five tenths of one percent."

Discuss If the goal is $275, give an amount that is more than 100% of this goal. What is 0% of this goal?

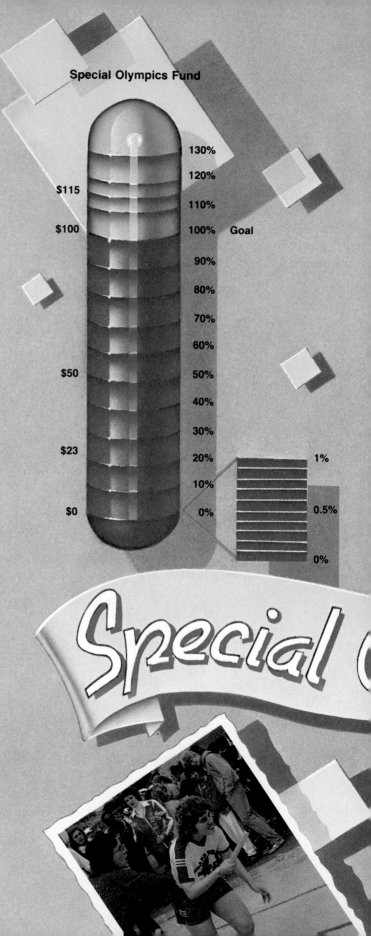

Special Olympics Fund

144

To write a percent for a decimal, move the decimal point 2 places to the right and write a percent sign.

$0.9 = 90\%$ $\qquad$ $2.75 = 275\%$

$0.33\frac{1}{3} = 33\frac{1}{3}\%$ $\qquad$ $0.0065 = 0.65\%$

To write a decimal for a percent, move the decimal point 2 places to the left and omit the percent sign.

$5\% = 0.05$ $\qquad$ $16\frac{2}{3}\% = 0.16\frac{2}{3}$

$200\% = 2.00 = 2$ $\qquad$ $72.3\% = 0.723$

Try

a. Write a percent for 0.008.

b. Write a decimal for 4.3%.

Practice Write each decimal as a percent.

1. 0.17 $\qquad$ **2.** 0.23 $\qquad$ **3.** 0.485 $\qquad$ **4.** 0.216 $\qquad$ **5.** 0.077 $\qquad$ **6.** 0.061

7. 0.08 $\qquad$ **8.** 0.06 $\qquad$ **9.** 0.005 $\qquad$ **10.** 0.004 $\qquad$ **11.** 0.4 $\qquad$ **12.** 0.2

13. 2.3 $\qquad$ **14.** 3.5 $\qquad$ **15.** 1.07 $\qquad$ **16.** 2.01 $\qquad$ **17.** 5.0 $\qquad$ **18.** 4

19. $0.66\frac{2}{3}$ $\qquad$ **20.** $0.83\frac{1}{3}$ $\qquad$ **21.** $0.12\frac{1}{2}$ $\qquad$ **22.** $0.37\frac{1}{2}$ $\qquad$ ★**23.** $0.03\frac{3}{4}$ $\qquad$ ★**24.** $0.06\frac{1}{3}$

Write each percent as a decimal.

25. 65% $\qquad$ **26.** 90% $\qquad$ **27.** 70%

28. 4% $\qquad$ **29.** 37.5% $\qquad$ **30.** 18.6%

31. 349% $\qquad$ **32.** 300% $\qquad$ **33.** 200%

34. 0.6% $\qquad$ **35.** 0% $\qquad$ **36.** 100%

37. 56.75% $\qquad$ **38.** 0.025% $\qquad$ **39.** 0.016%

40. $66\frac{2}{3}\%$ $\qquad$ ★**41.** $9\frac{3}{4}\%$ $\qquad$ ★**42.** $8\frac{1}{2}\%$

Apply If the goal is $500, name an amount that could be described as:

43. More than 100% $\qquad$ ★**44.** Less than 1%

Percents and Fractions

A. About 11 out of 20 adult Americans exercise regularly. Write a percent for 11 out of 20.

11 out of 20 is the fraction $\frac{11}{20}$.

$$\frac{11}{20} = \frac{55}{100} = 55\%$$

Percent means hundredths, so write a fraction with a denominator of 100. Then write as a percent.

B. Write a percent for $\frac{7}{8}$.

$\frac{7}{8}$ means $7 \div 8$.

$$0.87\tfrac{4}{8} = 0.87\tfrac{1}{2} = 87\tfrac{1}{2}\%$$

$$8\overline{)7.00}$$
$$\underline{64}$$
$$60$$
$$\underline{56}$$
$$4$$

Divide until the answer is in hundredths. Give the remainder as a fraction.

$$\frac{7}{8} = 87\tfrac{1}{2}\%, \text{ or } 87.5\%$$

C. Write a percent for $1\tfrac{1}{3}$.

$$1\tfrac{1}{3} = \tfrac{4}{3}$$

$$1.33\tfrac{1}{3} = 133\tfrac{1}{3}\%$$

$$3\overline{)4.00}$$

$$1\tfrac{1}{3} = 133\tfrac{1}{3}\%$$

If the number is greater than 1, the percent is greater than 100%.

Try Write each number as a percent.

a. $\frac{1}{6}$ **b.** $\frac{9}{20}$ **c.** $2\frac{1}{4}$

Practice Write each number as a percent.

1. $\frac{99}{100}$ **2.** $\frac{17}{100}$ **3.** $\frac{42}{100}$ **4.** $\frac{14}{100}$ **5.** $\frac{21}{50}$ **6.** $\frac{3}{50}$ **7.** $\frac{8}{10}$

8. $\frac{5}{10}$ **9.** $\frac{2}{25}$ **10.** $\frac{16}{25}$ **11.** $\frac{17}{20}$ **12.** $\frac{3}{20}$ **13.** $\frac{1}{2}$ **14.** $\frac{3}{4}$

15. $\frac{3}{5}$ **16.** $\frac{2}{5}$ **17.** $\frac{5}{8}$ **18.** $\frac{3}{8}$ **19.** $\frac{5}{16}$ **20.** $\frac{11}{16}$ **21.** $\frac{31}{40}$

22. $\frac{29}{40}$ **23.** $\frac{2}{3}$ **24.** $\frac{1}{3}$ **25.** $\frac{1}{9}$ **26.** $\frac{5}{6}$ **27.** $1\frac{1}{2}$ **28.** $2\frac{1}{3}$

29. $4\frac{2}{3}$ **30.** $3\frac{9}{10}$ **31.** $\frac{7}{7}$ **32.** $\frac{0}{9}$ **★33.** $\frac{1}{200}$ **★34.** $\frac{3}{500}$ **★35.** $\frac{9}{1,000}$

Apply Trish Stephens teaches a one-hour exercise class. The graph shows what fraction of the hour she spends on each kind of exercise. Tell what percent of the hour she spends on each type of exercise.

36. Warm-up exercises

37. Stomach exercises

38. Leg exercises

39. Hip exercises

40. Aerobic exercises

★41. Warm-up and cool-down exercises

★42. Stomach, hip, arm, and leg exercises

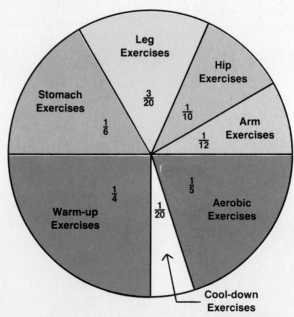

Percents, Decimals, and Fractions

A. Manuel jogs 30 minutes a day. He estimates that this exercise uses about 8% of his daily Calorie intake. Write 8% as a decimal and as a fraction.

8% = 8 hundredths = 0.08

8% = $\frac{8}{100}$ = $\frac{2}{25}$

B. Write $83\frac{1}{3}\%$ as a fraction.

$$83\frac{1}{3}\% = \frac{83\frac{1}{3}}{100}$$ Write a fraction in hundredths.

$$83\frac{1}{3} \div 100$$ $\frac{83\frac{1}{3}}{100}$ means $83\frac{1}{3} \div 100$.

$$\frac{250}{3} \div \frac{100}{1}$$

$$\frac{250}{3} \times \frac{1}{100} = \frac{\overset{5}{\cancel{250}} \times 1}{3 \times \underset{2}{\cancel{100}}} = \frac{5}{6}$$

$$83\frac{1}{3}\% = \frac{5}{6}$$

C. Write 12.5% as a fraction.

12.5% = $\frac{12.5}{100}$ = $\frac{125}{1,000}$ = $\frac{1}{8}$

12.5% = $\frac{1}{8}$

Try Write each percent as a fraction in lowest terms or as a mixed number.

a. 24%   **b.** $41\frac{2}{3}\%$ **c.** 165%

Practice For each percent, write a fraction in lowest terms, a mixed number, or a whole number.

1. 2%   **2.** 35%   **3.** 140%   **4.** 225%   **5.** 1,000%

6. $53\frac{1}{3}\%$ **7.** 57.5%   **8.** 0.4%   **★9.** 0.25%   **★10.** $88\frac{8}{9}\%$

Do as many of these exercises as you can mentally. Write the fractions in lowest terms.

Fraction	Decimal	Percent
11.	**12.**	50%
13.	$0.33\frac{1}{3}$	**14.**
$\frac{1}{4}$	**15.**	**16.**
17.	0.1	**18.**
19.	**20.**	20%
$\frac{1}{6}$	**21.**	**22.**
23.	0.125	**24.**
$\frac{7}{8}$	**25.**	**26.**

Apply   A 120-pound person uses the following percents of 2,500 Calories for each activity. Write each percent as a decimal and as a fraction in lowest terms.

27. Walking for 1 hour: 10%

28. Jumping rope for 15 minutes: 6%

29. Cross-country skiing for 1 hour: 24%

30. Bicycling at normal speed for 30 minutes: 3.5%

Solve each equation.

1. $3.4 + x = 6.9$

2. $y + 19.4 = 28.3$

3. $s - 7.6 = 18.5$

4. $37.5 = t - 12.8$

5. $5.6t = 33.6$

6. $74.72 = 8m$

7. $\frac{a}{3.2} = 30$

8. $\frac{d}{4.8} = 6$

9. $2.7 = \frac{x}{9.3}$

10. $\frac{d}{16.7} = 0.8$

11. $\frac{3}{4}t = 9$

12. $\frac{5}{8}x = 15$

13. $2x + 17 = 33$

Finding a Percent of a Number

A. The content of grocery products must meet certain minimum standards. A product sold as a chicken dinner must contain at least 18% chicken. How many ounces of chicken must be in a 16-ounce dinner?

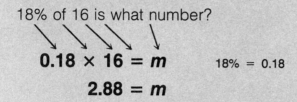

18% of 16 is what number?

$$0.18 \times 16 = m \qquad 18\% = 0.18$$

$$2.88 = m$$

The dinner must contain at least 2.88 ounces of chicken.

B. Find $66\frac{2}{3}\%$ of 250.

$$h = \frac{2}{3} \times 250 \qquad 66\frac{2}{3}\% = \frac{2}{3}$$

$$h = 166\frac{2}{3}$$

C. Estimate 73% of 12.

73% is close to 75%.

$$75\% \text{ of } 12 = \frac{3}{4} \times 12 = 9$$

73% of 12 is about 9.

Discuss Is 125% of a number greater than or less than the number? Is 68% of a number greater than or less than the number?

Try Find each answer.

a. 75% of 24

b. 75% of 0.9

c. What is 180% of 20?

d. 0.8% of 100 is what number?

Practice Find each answer.

1. 25% of 40
2. 75% of 20
3. 60% of 80
4. 40% of 90

5. 12% of 100
6. 100% of 95
7. 38% of 40
8. 52% of 20

9. $33\frac{1}{3}$% of 72
10. $66\frac{2}{3}$% of 39
11. 500% of 81
12. 120% of 60

13. 345% of 10
14. 245% of 20
15. $16\frac{2}{3}$% of 4.8
16. 37.5% of 5.6

17. 87.5% of 6.4
18. $83\frac{1}{3}$% of 3.6
19. 0.8% of 16
20. 0.7% of 83

21. 0.09% of 600 is what number?
22. What is 0.07% of 400?

23. What is $4\frac{1}{2}$% of 60?
24. $9\frac{1}{2}$% of 28 is what number?

★25. What is $\frac{1}{5}$% of 50?
★26. What is $\frac{1}{2}$% of 32?

★27. $433\frac{1}{3}$% of 18 is what number?
★28. $0.6\frac{2}{3}$% of 1,000 is what number?

Estimation Estimate each answer.

29. 51% of 38
30. 99% of 73
31. 11% of 80
32. 26% of 16

33. 19% of 25
34. 74% of 36
35. 12% of 32
36. 33% of 27

Apply Solve each problem.

37. Condensed chicken soup must contain at least 4% chicken. How many ounces of chicken must be in a 10.5-ounce can of soup?

38. A chicken pie must contain at least 14% chicken. How many ounces of chicken must be in an 8-ounce chicken pie?

Problem Solving: Multiple-Step Problems

Read   *Career* Teri Lawler is a butcher. A customer often buys a steer and has her cut and package the meat. The "dressed weight" of a 1,000-pound steer is about 615 pounds, and about 27% of this is a cut of beef called chuck. About 81% of the chuck is usable, while the rest is fat and bone. Find the number of pounds of the chuck that is usable meat.

Plan   Find the number of pounds of dressed beef that is chuck. Then find the number of pounds of chuck that is usable.

Solve   First find 27% of 615.

$n = 0.27 \times 615$

$n = 166.05$

About 166 pounds is chuck.

Now find 81% of 166.

$x = 0.81 \times 166$

$x = 134.46$

Answer   About 134 pounds of the chuck is usable.

Look Back   The weight of the chuck should be less than the dressed weight. The weight of the usable chuck should be less than the weight of all the chuck.

CHOICE

152

Try Solve the problem. Round each answer to the nearest cent.

a. A person buying a steer from Teri Lawler pays $1.60 a pound for each pound of dressed weight, plus 5% for freezing and wrapping. How much would a person pay for 615 pounds of dressed weight?

Apply Solve each problem. Round each answer to the nearest pound.

1. About 17% of the 615 pounds of dressed weight is beef loin, and 74% of the beef loin is usable. How many pounds of loin is usable?

2. About 5% of the 615 pounds of dressed weight is beef brisket, and 40% of the brisket is usable. How many pounds of the brisket is usable?

3. About 22% of the 615 pounds of dressed weight is from the round of the steer, but 38% of the round is fat and bone. How many pounds of the round is fat and bone?

4. About 27% of the 615 pounds of dressed weight is chuck, and 36% of the chuck can be used for blade pot roasts. How many pounds of the chuck can be used for blade pot roasts?

5. The dressed weight of a 1,200-pound steer is about 62% of its total weight. $66\frac{2}{3}$% of the dressed weight is usable beef. How many pounds of a 1,200-pound steer is usable beef?

★6. Suppose 15% of the total weight of a steer is chuck and 35% of the chuck can be used for pot roast. Can 15% + 35%, or 50%, of the total weight be used for pot roast? Explain your answer.

Solve each problem. Round each answer to the nearest cent.

7. Ms. Lawler got 50 pounds of beef from the ribs of a steer. She made 48% of this into standing rib roasts that sold for $3.59 a pound. How much did she receive from the sale of these roasts?

8. Ms. Lawler got 84 pounds of beef from the round. She made 12.5% of this into ground beef and sold it for $1.89 a pound. How much did she receive from the sale of the ground beef?

9. In large quantities, round steak costs $1.75 per pound plus 5% for freezing and wrapping. What is the total cost of 84 pounds of round steak?

★10. In large quantities, sirloin steak costs $2.35 per pound, which includes 5% for freezing and wrapping. What is the cost per pound of the meat only?

Finding What Percent One Number Is of Another

A. Seventy-eight sailboats started a race, but only 56 of them finished the race. What percent of the boats finished?

What percent of 78 is 56?

$$n \times 78 = 56$$

$$\frac{78n}{78} = \frac{56}{78}$$

$$n \approx 0.72$$

$$n \approx 72\%$$

About 72% of the boats finished.

B. 20 is what percent of 30?

$$20 = h \times 30$$

$$\frac{20}{30} = \frac{30h}{30}$$

$$\frac{2}{3} = h$$

$$66\frac{2}{3}\% = h$$

Try Find each percent.

a. 42 is what percent of 48?

b. What percent of 0.5 is 0.7?

Practice Find each percent.

1. 15 is what percent of 30?

2. 12 is what percent of 48?

3. 2.1 is what percent of 3?

4. 1 is what percent of 2.5?

5. What percent of 160 is 60?

6. What percent of 120 is 70?

7. What percent of 6.6 is 1.1?

8. What percent of 4.8 is 3.2?

9. 249 is what percent of 83?

10. 90 is what percent of 75?

11. What percent of 20 is 12.5?

12. 3.3 is what percent of 8.8?

13. 5 is what percent of 625?

14. 9 is what percent of 1,800?

★15. What percent of 1.25 is 0.002?

★16. 0.013 is what percent of 6.5?

Apply Solve each problem. Round each answer to the nearest percent.

17. Ray entered a 250-mile sailboat race and sailed 72 miles the first day. What percent of the total distance did he sail?

18. Joan's 22-foot boat cost $8,950. She made a $2,500 down payment. What percent of the price was the down payment?

★19. Of 132 boats that started a race, 15 dropped out the first day, 8 dropped out the second day, and 21 dropped out the third day. What percent of the boats were still in the race after three days?

Problem Solving: Write an Equation

A. Read Sue Chinn made a $100 deposit on a canoe that cost $398. What percent of the cost is the deposit?

Plan Use an equation to find the percent.

What percent of 398 is 100?

$$n \times 398 = 100$$

Solve $398n = 100$

$n \approx 0.251$

Answer The deposit is about 25% of the cost.

Look Back $398 is about $400 and 25% of $400 is $100, so the answer is reasonable.

B. Read How much is the 5% sales tax on the canoe?

Plan Use an equation to find a percent of a number.

What number is 5% of 398?

$$t = 0.05 \times 398$$

Solve $t = 0.05 \times 398$

$t = 19.9$

Answer The sales tax is $19.90.

Look Back 5% of $400 is $20, so the answer is reasonable.

Try Write an equation. Then find the answer.

a. How much is a $33\frac{1}{3}$% discount on a $24.99 life vest?

b. The sales tax on a $37.50 pair of oars is $1.50. What is the percent of the sales tax?

Apply Write an equation. Then find the answer.

1. The Witmans have completed 9 feet of a 24-foot boat dock. What percent of the dock have they completed?

2. An inflatable boat is on sale for $68. The original price was $85. What percent of the original price is the sale price?

3. A boat motor that originally sold for $588 is on sale for $33\frac{1}{3}\%$ off the original price. What is the amount of discount?

4. A boat trailer costs $449.50, plus sales tax. If the tax is 7%, what is the amount of the tax to the nearest cent?

5. Gasoline at a boat marina costs $1.60 a gallon. Of this, $0.20 is for taxes on the gasoline. What percent of the price of a gallon of gasoline is for taxes?

6. A 15-horsepower motor uses about 1.7 gallons of gasoline an hour at full power and about 60% of this amount at half power. How many gallons per hour does the motor use at half power?

7. Jerry made a $200 down payment on a boat that cost $675. The down payment is what percent of the cost of the boat? Round to the nearest percent.

8. A store is offering a $189 discount on a sailboat that costs $1,050. The discount is what percent of the cost? Round to the nearest percent.

*9. A boat that cost $1,500 ten years ago costs $2,500 now. What percent of the cost ten years ago is the cost now?

Finding a Number When a Percent of It Is Known

A. Angela Dougal has saved $18,500 toward buying a home. If a 30% down payment is required, what price home can she afford to buy?

30% of what number is $18,500?

$$0.3 \times m = 18,500$$

$$\frac{0.3m}{0.3} = \frac{18,500}{0.3}$$

$$m \approx 61,666.67$$

She can afford a $62,000 home.

B. 36 is $37\frac{1}{2}$% of what number?

$$36 = \tfrac{3}{8}k \qquad \text{Use } \tfrac{3}{8} \text{ for } 37\tfrac{1}{2}\%.$$

$$\left(\tfrac{8}{3}\right)36 = \left(\tfrac{8}{3}\right)\tfrac{3}{8}k$$

$$96 = k$$

Try Find each answer.

a. 16% of what number is 36?

b. 1.2 is $66\frac{2}{3}$% of what number?

c. 250% of what number is 8?

Practice Find each answer.

1. 70% of what number is 35?

2. 30% of what number is 18?

3. 25% of what number is 2.6?

4. 15% of what number is 2.4?

5. 13 is 10% of what number?

6. 140 is 50% of what number?

7. 66 is 55% of what number?

8. 34 is 85% of what number?

9. 1.9 is 2% of what number?

10. 2.6 is 4% of what number?

11. $33\frac{1}{3}$% of what number is 16?

12. $16\frac{2}{3}$% of what number is 45?

13. 108 is 12.5% of what number?

14. 37.5% of what number is 120?

15. 63 is 140% of what number?

16. 150% of what number is 9.6?

17. 300% of what number is 0.6?

18. 15 is 500% of what number?

★19. 9 is $166\frac{2}{3}$% of what number?

★20. 0.25% of what number is 0.65?

Apply Solve the problem.

21. The Perrones have saved $22,500. If a 25% down payment is required, what price house can they buy?

BASIC: GO TO and IF. . .THEN Statements

This program finds the total price of items including a 5% sales tax. Line 40 is an IF. . .THEN statement. When 0 is entered for P, the first part of the statement is true, so the computer will go to line 70. When a number other than 0 is entered, the first part is false, so the computer will go to the next line of the program (line 50). In line 50, the number in memory location T changes each time a number is entered. Line 60 is a GO TO statement that sends the computer back to line 20 so that another number can be entered.

```
10 LET T=0
20 PRINT "PRICE"
30 INPUT P
40 IF P=0 THEN 70
50 LET T=T+P
60 GO TO 20
70 PRINT "$";T+T*.05
80 END
```

When 3.19, 5.65, and 0 are entered, this is the output.

```
PRICE
? 3.19
PRICE
? 5.65
PRICE
? 0
$9.282
```

Give the output for the program above for the following prices.

1. $3.78, $10.32, $25.21, 0

2. $0.56, $1.77, $7.66, $4.59, 0

3. $0.47, $1.19, $0.98, $1.33, 0

4. $12.98, $22.49, $16.25, $9.99, 0

Problem Solving: Use a Formula

A. Read   Interest is the amount paid for the use of money. Jack borrowed $2,500 to make a down payment on a mobile home. He agreed to repay the money in 9 months (0.75 year) at a simple-interest rate of 15% (0.15) a year. How much interest will he have to pay?

Plan   Use the simple-interest formula.

Interest (per year)
Principal (amount borrowed)
Interest rate (per year)
Time (years)

Solve $I = P \times R \times T$

$I = (2,500)(0.15)(0.75)$

$I = 281.25$

Answer   Jack will pay $281.25 in interest.

Look Back   Be sure you substituted correctly in the formula.

B. Read   Alta invested money for 2 years at a simple-interest rate of 8.5% a year. Alta's interest was $68. How much did she invest?

Plan   Substitute in the simple-interest formula.

Solve $I = P \times R \times T$

$68 = P(0.085)(2)$

$68 = 0.17P$

$400 = P$

Answer $400 was invested.

Look Back   The interest on $400 invested at 10% for 2 years is $80. So the answer is reasonable.

Try   The total amount of a loan is the principal plus the interest.

Total   Principal   Interest
$$A = P + (P \times R \times T)$$

a. Maria borrowed $500 for 6 months at 12.5% simple interest. Find the total amount of her loan.

Apply   Find the interest

1. if $500 is borrowed at 6% simple interest for 6 months (0.5 year).

2. if $750 is borrowed for 2 years at 10% simple interest.

3. if $200 is invested at 8% simple interest for 3 years.

4. if $1,000 is invested for 3 months (0.25 year) at 6.5% simple interest.

Find the total amount that must be repaid

5. if $250 is borrowed at 7% simple interest for 2 years.

6. if $600 is borrowed at 18% simple interest for 6 months.

Find the total amount in the account

7. if $2,500 is invested at 9.5% simple interest for 5 years.

8. if $50 is invested at 17.5% simple interest for 2 years.

Find each answer. Use the simple-interest formula.

9. Some money was invested at 6% interest for 2 years. If the interest was $18, how much was invested?

10. Jay invested $100 at a simple-interest rate for 4 years. If $48 interest was earned, what was the rate of interest?

11. Judy invested $500 at 7.5% interest. For how many years was the money invested if the interest earned was $150?

12. Yuko borrowed $1,200 at a simple-interest rate for 6 months. If the interest was $51, what was the rate of interest?

13. Some money was borrowed at 12% interest for 3 months. If the interest was $21, how much was borrowed?

14. Ben borrowed $800 at 9% interest. For how many years was the money borrowed if the interest was $36?

★15. Sam borrowed $500 for 2 years at simple interest. If a total of $585 was repaid (principal plus interest), what was the interest rate?

★16. Some money was invested for 9 months at 10% interest. If the interest paid was $60, what was the total amount in the account after the 9 months?

Practice: Ratio, Proportion, and Percent

Solve each proportion.

1. $\frac{x}{18} = \frac{28}{14}$
2. $\frac{40}{m} = \frac{16}{7}$
3. $\frac{7}{55} = \frac{t}{22}$
4. $\frac{5.6}{4.8} = \frac{n}{18}$
5. $\frac{0.9}{0.5} = \frac{a}{1.5}$

Write each number as a percent.

6. 0.78
7. 0.06
8. 0.003
9. 0.5
10. 0.152
11. 2.5

12. $\frac{51}{100}$
13. $\frac{7}{10}$
14. $\frac{3}{8}$
15. $\frac{2}{3}$
16. $1\frac{1}{4}$
17. $2\frac{1}{2}$

Write each percent as a fraction in lowest terms or as a mixed number.

18. 97%
19. 75%
20. 4%
21. $33\frac{1}{3}$%
22. 87.5%
23. 150%

Write each percent as a decimal or as a whole number.

24. 43%
25. 30%
26. 8%
27. $12\frac{1}{2}$%
28. 175%
29. 200%

Find each answer.

30. 11 is what percent of 20?
31. 25% of 16 is what number?

32. What is 82% of 50?
33. 30% of what number is 18?

34. What percent of 28 is 21?
35. 2 is 8% of what number?

36. 8 is what percent of 24?
37. 35% of 14 is what number?

38. What is 40% of 6?
39. 32 is what percent of 80?

40. $66\frac{2}{3}$% of 150 is what number?
41. 16 is 12.5% of what number?

42. 98 is what percent of 200?
43. 125% of 45 is what number?

44. 1.4 is 28% of what number?
45. 2.7 is what percent of 1.8?

46. What percent of 90 is 5.4?
47. 1.2 is 48% of what number?

48. $87\frac{1}{2}$% of 6.4 is what number?
49. 130% of what number is 2.6?

Apply Solve each problem.

50. Helena borrowed $600 to buy a stereo set. She repaid the money in 3 months (0.25 year). If the interest was $24, what was the interest rate?

51. Valley City Bank makes an average of 300 loans every 4 weeks. At this rate, how many loans does the bank make in 52 weeks?

52. The North Bay volleyball team won 62.5% of their games. If they won 20 games, how many games did they play?

53. About 13% of the letters in written English are *E*s. How many *E*s would you expect in a paragraph of 1,500 letters?

54. At a rate of 25 sit-ups per minute (60 seconds), how many seconds are required for 20 sit-ups?

55. If a person weighs 120 pounds, about 78 pounds of this weight is water. What percent of a person's body weight is water?

CALCULATOR

If $250 is invested at 12% interest *compounded semiannually*, the interest is computed twice a year on the principal *plus previously earned interest*. Use the compound-interest formula below to find the total amount after 1.5 years.

Total — Principal — Rate per interest period

$$A = P(1 + R)^n \quad\text{— Number of interest periods}$$

$$A = 250(1 + 0.06)^3$$
— The number of interest periods is 1.5 × 2.
— The rate per period is 0.12 ÷ 2.

Press: 1 $+$ 0.06 $=$ **Display:** *1.06*

Press: $\times$ 1.06 $\times$ 1.06 $=$ **Display:** *1.191016*

Press: $\times$ 250 $=$ **Display:** *297.754*

The total amount after 1.5 years is $297.75.

Find the total amount at 10% interest compounded twice a year.

1. $500 for 3 years

2. $850 for 2.5 years

3. $8,500 for 2.5 years

Find the total amount at 12% interest compounded four times a year.

4. $500 for 3 years

5. $75 for 6 months

6. $200 for 1 year

7. $200 for 10 years

Problem Solving: Multiple-Step Problems

A. Read   There is a 25% discount on a radio that lists for $78.88. Find the sale price.

Plan   First find the amount of the discount. Then subtract to find the sale price.

Solve   Find the discount.
$0.25 \times \$78.88 = \$19.72$

Find the sale price.
$\$78.88 - \$19.72 = \$59.16$

Answer   The sale price is $59.16.

Look Back   The sale price should be less than the list price.

Discuss If the discount is 25%, then the sale price is 100% − 25%, or 75%, of the list price. Show that this is true for the data in Example A.

B. Read   The list price of a headset is $49.50, and the sale price is $33.00. What is the percent of discount?

Plan   Subtract to find the discount. Then find what percent of the list price the discount is.

Solve   Find the discount.
$\$49.50 - \$33.00 = \$16.50$

Find the percent of discount.

$n \times 49.5 = 16.5$
$$n = 0.33\tfrac{1}{3} = 33\tfrac{1}{3}\%$$

Answer   The discount is $33\tfrac{1}{3}\%$.

Look Back $33\tfrac{1}{3}\%$ of $49.50 is $16.50.

Try Solve each problem.

a. Mae is paid $100 a week plus a 10% commission on all of her sales. If her sales one week totaled $2,285, what was her pay for that week?

b. Paul is paid a commission on all sales over $1,000. If his sales were $8,420 and his commission was $1,855, what is the percent of his commission?

Apply Solve each problem.

1. A television set that lists for $488 is on sale for 15% off the list price. Find the sale price.

2. A $7.89 record album is on sale for $5.26. Find the percent of the discount on the album.

3. A radio costs $62.50 plus 8% sales tax. What is the total cost of the radio?

4. Vera is paid a 20% commission on all sales over $500. What is her commission on sales of $1,950?

5. Penny is paid $500 a month plus a 4% commission on all sales. What was her pay for a month in which her sales totaled $2,516?

6. Each week Frank is paid a base amount plus an 18% commission on his sales. One week his sales totaled $1,200 and his total pay was $466. What is his base pay?

7. A video player that lists for $398 is on sale for 30% off the list price. What would Ron have to pay for the video player, including 5% sales tax?

8. A $150 record player is on sale for 25% off. If you pay in cash, 10% is taken off the sale price. Find the cash-sale price of the record player.

9. José is paid $300 a week plus a commission on his sales. If his sales one week totaled $1,500, and his total pay for that week was $480, what is the percent of his commission?

★10. A stereo set is on sale for 20% off the regular price. The sale price is $220. What was the regular price of the stereo?

Chapter 5 Test

Do these ratios form a proportion? Write *yes* or *no*.

1. $\frac{4}{5}$ $\frac{5}{8}$

2. $\frac{18}{12}$ $\frac{9}{6}$

Solve each proportion.

3. $\frac{n}{3} = \frac{25}{15}$

4. $\frac{56}{64} = \frac{m}{24}$

5. What is 150% written as a decimal?

6. What is 0.065 written as a percent?

Write each number as a percent.

7. $\frac{1}{4}$

8. $\frac{7}{8}$

For each percent, write a fraction in lowest terms.

9. 60%

10. 0.1%

Find each answer.

11. 10% of 90

12. $33\frac{1}{3}$% of 51

13. 225% of 20

14. 12 is what percent of 60?

15. What percent of 7.2 is 5.4?

16. 50% of what number is 70?

17. 1.3 is 2% of what number?

Solve each problem.

18. A matrix computer printer prints 20 lines in 3 seconds. How many seconds would it take the printer to print 400 lines?

19. A giant tortoise can travel 100 meters in 22 minutes. How many minutes would it take the tortoise to travel 250 meters?

20. 40% of the 300 cars at Dave's Car Sales are used cars. 20% of the used cars are more than 5 years old. How many cars at Dave's are more than 5 years old?

21. A lumber yard charges $1.80 for a 10-foot board, plus 5% for preparation cost. What would the total cost be for 50 boards?

22. Write and solve an equation to find a 20% discount on a $560 video recorder.

23. A TV antenna costs $37.50 plus 8% sales tax. What is the total cost of the antenna?

Use the simple-interest formula ($I = P \times R \times T$) to solve each problem.

24. Find the interest if $500 is borrowed for 2 years at 10% simple interest.

25. Find the total amount that must be repaid if $300 is borrowed at 18% simple interest for 6 months (0.5 year).

CHALLENGE
Percent of Increase and Decrease

A. In ten years, the cost of gas heat in Chicago increased from $0.114 per therm to $0.485 per therm. Find the *percent of increase*.

Find the increase.
0.485 − 0.114 = 0.371

Find what percent the increase is of the original number.

What percent of 0.114 is 0.371?

$n \times 0.114 = 0.371$

$n \approx 3.25$

The increase is about 325%.

B. In thirty years, the population of New York City decreased from 7.9 million to 7.1 million. Find the *percent of decrease*.

Find the decrease.
7.9 − 7.1 = 0.8

Find what percent the decrease is of the original number.

What percent of 7.9 is 0.8?

$n \times 7.9 = 0.8$

$n \approx 0.10$

The decrease is about 10%.

Solve each problem. In Problems 1–4, round to the nearest percent.

1. The number of cars registered in the United States increased from 19.9 million in 1925 to 121.7 million in 1980. Find the percent of increase in the number of registered cars.

2. The farm population in the United States decreased from 15.7 million in 1960 to 6.1 million in 1980. Find the percent of decrease in the farm population.

3. In 1860, it cost $5.00 to send a letter across the country by Pony Express. In 1980, it cost $0.20 to mail a letter. Find the percent of decrease in cost.

4. In ten years, the gasoline tax in one state rose from $0.085 a gallon to $0.136 a gallon. Find the percent of increase in the tax.

5. In 1960, United States railroads carried 327 million passengers. By 1980, there had been a 14% decrease in the number of passengers carried. How many million passengers did the railroads carry in 1980?

6. The population of Denver was about 134,000 in 1900. The 1980 population represented an increase of 266%. What was the population of Denver in 1980?

MAINTENANCE

Write an expression for each exercise.

1. 83 subtracted from *k*

2. The sum of 34 and *c*

3. *w* divided by 13

4. *h* multiplied by 32

5. *n* increased by 33

6. 66 less than *m*

7. 46 divided by *x*

8. *k* subtracted from 4

9. 21 times *q*

10. 37 decreased by *m*

11. *b* divided by 25

12. The sum of *h* and 37

13. 65 less than *r*

14. 8 divided by *x*

15. *m* times 49

16. The result of adding *q* to 87

17. The product of 92 and *b*

18. The quotient *r* divided by 6

19. The result of multiplying *a* and 8

Solve each problem.

20. The population of California rose from 15,717,204 in 1960 to 23,668,562 in 1980. How many more people lived in California in 1980 than in 1960?

21. A model train is built to a scale of 3 inches to 8 feet. If the actual length of a train car is 44 feet, what is the length of the model?

22. Teenagers need 15 milligrams of iron a day. A hamburger provides 2.7 milligrams. What percent of the daily requirement is provided by the hamburger?

23. A toaster uses 39.5 kilowatt-hours of electricity a year. If electricity costs $0.08 per kilowatt-hour, what is the cost of using the toaster for a year?

24. A computer prints 56 lines per page. How many pages are needed to print a program 1,596 lines long?

25. A $26.95 tennis racket is on sale for 20% off the original price. What is the sale price of the racket?

26. Mexico City has $13\frac{1}{5}$ hours of daylight on June 21 and $10\frac{3}{4}$ hours on December 21. How many more hours of daylight are there on June 21?

27. A recipe for chicken pie calls for $2\frac{3}{4}$ cups of chicken. How many cups of chicken would be needed for $2\frac{1}{2}$ times the recipe?

Measurement

chapter 6

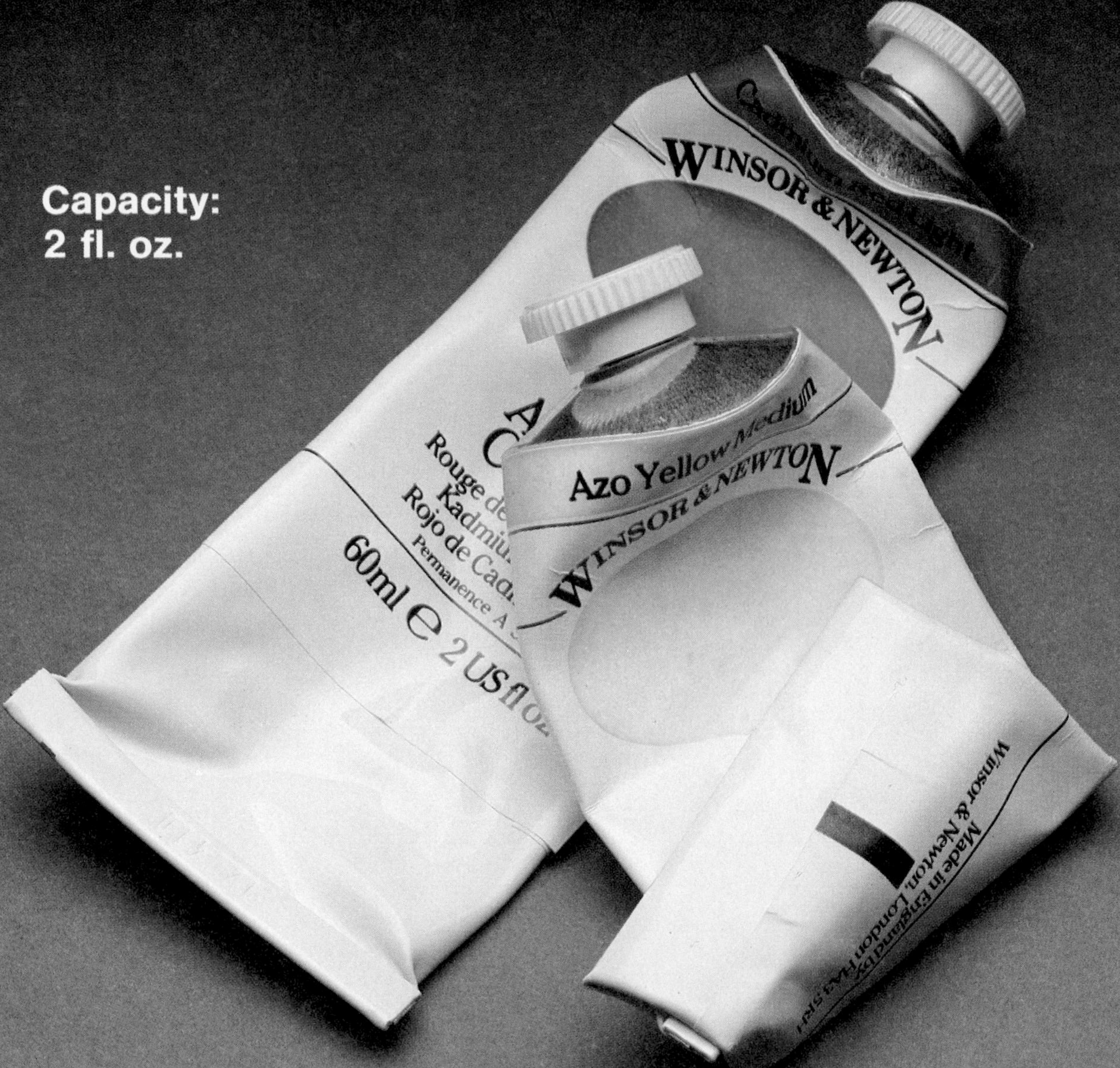

WINSOR & NEWTON
Azo Yellow Medium
WINSOR & NEWTON
Rouge de
Kadmium
Rojo de Cad
Permanence A
60ml e 2 US fl oz
Made in England by
Winsor & Newton, London HA3 5RH

Capacity:
2 fl. oz.

Overview of the Metric System

A. The metric system of measurement is used in many countries.

For length, use *meter*. The produce stand is about 1 meter (1 m) deep.

For capacity, use *liter*. Each jar contains about 1 liter (1 L) of juice.

For mass (weight), use *gram*. The mass of a small grape is about 1 gram (1 g).

B. Prefixes are used with *meter*, *liter*, and *gram*.
For example, 1 *kilo*meter is the same length as 1,000 meters.
1 *centi*gram is the same mass as 0.01 gram.

Prefix	Meaning	Length	Capacity	Mass
kilo-	1,000	kilometer (km)	kiloliter (kL)	kilogram (kg)
hecto-	100	hectometer (hm)	hectoliter (hL)	hectogram (hg)
deka-	10	dekameter (dam)	dekaliter (daL)	dekagram (dag)
	1	meter (m)	liter (L)	gram (g)
deci-	0.1	decimeter (dm)	deciliter (dL)	decigram (dg)
centi-	0.01	centimeter (cm)	centiliter (cL)	centigram (cg)
milli-	0.001	millimeter (mm)	milliliter (mL)	milligram (mg)

Try

a. Complete with *meter*, *liter*, or *gram*.

Mass of a man: kilo▧

b. Which unit has the symbol cm?

c. Give the missing number.

1 mg = ▧ g

Practice   Give or complete each unit of measure.
Use *meter*, *liter*, or *gram*.

1. Mass of an orange seed
milli▧

2. Distance around an orange
centi▧

3. Height of an apple tree
▧

4. Mass of an apple
▧

5. Length of a worm
milli▧

6. Capacity of a pail
▧

7. Capacity of a glass
milli▧

8. Mass of a pumpkin
kilo▧

9. Capacity of a crate
deka▧

Give the metric unit for each symbol.

10. mm   **11.** g   **12.** hg   **13.** hL   **14.** km   **15.** kg   **16.** cm

Use the table on page 170. Give each missing number.

17. 1 hm = ▧ m   **18.** 1 kg = ▧ g   **19.** 1 cm = ▧ m   **20.** 1 mL = ▧ L

21. 1 mm = ▧ m   **22.** 1 km = ▧ m   **23.** 1 mg = ▧ g   **24.** 1 kL = ▧ L

25. 1 hL = ▧ L   **26.** 1 dag = ▧ g   **27.** 1 dm = ▧ m   **28.** 1 cg = ▧ g

29. 1 hg = ▧ g   **30.** 1 cL = ▧ L   **31.** 1 daL = ▧ L   **32.** 1 dam = ▧ m

★33. 1 kg = ▧ mg   **★34.** 1 hL = ▧ dL   **★35.** 1 mm = ▧ cm   **★36.** 1 mL = ▧ cL

Metric Units of Length

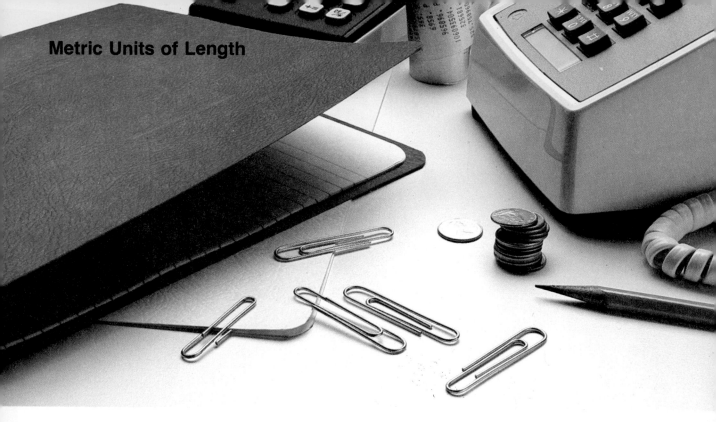

A. The paper in the red folder on Paul's desk is 1 *millimeter* (1 mm) thick. Each large paper clip is about 1 *centimeter* (1 cm) wide. The doorway of Paul's office is about 1 *meter* (1 m) wide. Paul walks 5 blocks, a distance of about 1 *kilometer* (1 km), to work at a Toronto bank.

1,000 mm = 1 m   100 cm = 1 m   1,000 m = 1 km

B. To change to a smaller unit, multiply by 10, 100, and so on.

To change to a larger unit, multiply by 0.1, 0.01, and so on.

thousands	hundreds	tens	ones	tenths	hundredths	thousandths
kilometer	hectometer	dekameter	meter	decimeter	centimeter	millimeter
km	hm	dam	m	dm	cm	mm

1 km = 10 hm	1 hm = 10 dam	1 dam = 10 m	1 m = 10 dm	1 dm = 10 cm	1 cm = 10 mm
0.1 km = 1 hm	0.1 hm = 1 dam	0.1 dam = 1 m	0.1 m = 1 dm	0.1 dm = 1 cm	0.1 cm = 1 mm

c. **1,600 cm = ▒ dam**

1,600 cm = (1,600 × 0.001) dam

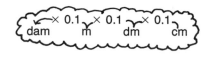

1,600 cm = 1.6 dam

Try

a. _Estimation_ Choose the best measure of the width of a wallet.

0.9 cm   9 cm   90 cm

b. Find the missing number.

45 cm = ▦ hm

Practice _Estimation_ Choose the best measure. Canadian coins and bills are about the same size as U.S. money.

1. Thickness of a dime

1 mm   10 mm   100 mm

2. Diameter of a penny

1.9 m   1.9 cm   1.9 mm

3. Length of a dollar bill

150 hm   150 m   150 mm

4. Width of a desk telephone

13 cm   1.3 cm   130 cm

5. Height of a bank guard

1.8 m   1.8 cm   1.8 mm

6. Distance from Toronto to Rome

8,000 dm   8,000 km   8,000 cm

Find the missing number. Use the table on page 172.

7. 924 cm = ▦ m

8. 48 km = ▦ m

9. 3 m = ▦ mm

10. 0.32 cm = ▦ mm

11. 8,643 dm = ▦ m

12. 52 dam = ▦ km

13. 421 cm = ▦ km

14. 678 hm = ▦ mm

15. 0.9 dam = ▦ dm

16. 5,000 mm = ▦ km

17. 0.32 hm = ▦ m

18. 8.41 dm = ▦ km

Apply Solve each problem.

19. A safe-deposit box is 125 mm wide and 500 mm long. What are its dimensions in centimeters?

★20. In Canadian money, 10 dimes have the same value as one dollar. What is the value of a stack of these dimes 140 cm tall?

Metric Units of Area and Volume

A. The top of Paul's desk had to be repaired. To measure the surface, the carpenter found its *area* in *square centimeters* (cm²).

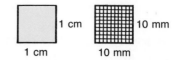

$$1 \text{ cm}^2 = 100 \text{ mm}^2$$

To change to a smaller unit of area, multiply by 100, 10,000, and so on.

To change to a larger unit, multiply by 0.01, 0.0001, and so on.

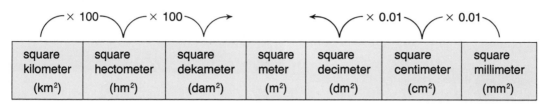

square kilometer (km²)	square hectometer (hm²)	square dekameter (dam²)	square meter (m²)	square decimeter (dm²)	square centimeter (cm²)	square millimeter (mm²)

B. The air-conditioning system at the bank was checked. To measure the space in Paul's office, the technician found the *volume* of the office in *cubic centimeters* (cm³).

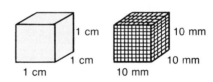

$$1 \text{ cm}^3 = 1,000 \text{ mm}^3$$

To change to a smaller unit of volume, multiply by 1,000, 1,000,000, and so on.

To change to a larger unit, multiply by 0.001, 0.000001, and so on.

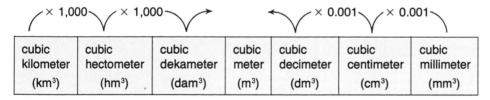

cubic kilometer (km³)	cubic hectometer (hm³)	cubic dekameter (dam³)	cubic meter (m³)	cubic decimeter (dm³)	cubic centimeter (cm³)	cubic millimeter (mm³)

c. $3 \text{ m}^2 = $ ▨ cm^2

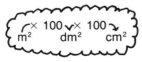

$3 \text{ m}^2 = (3 \times 10,000) \text{ cm}^2$

$3 \text{ m}^2 = 30,000 \text{ cm}^2$

D. $4,500 \text{ dm}^3 = $ ▨ m^3

$4,500 \text{ dm}^3 = (4,500 \times 0.001) \text{ m}^3$

$4,500 \text{ dm}^3 = 4.5 \text{ m}^3$

Try

a. _Estimation_ Choose the best measure for the area of a note pad.

150 cm³   150 cm²   15 cm²

b. Find the missing number.

7,700 m² = ▧ km²

Practice   _Estimation_ Choose the best measure.

1. Area of a ceiling

10 m³   2 m²   12 m²

2. Area of the city of Toronto

70 km²   70 m²   70 cm²

3. Area of a book cover

4.75 cm²   47.5 cm²   475 cm²

4. Volume of Paul's office

36 km³   36 m³   36 cm³

5. Volume of a closet

60 m²   6 m³   6 m²

6. Volume of a bank vault

210 m³   210 km³   210 mm³

Find the missing number.

7. 4 dm² = ▧ cm²

8. 4 dm² = ▧ m²

9. 4 dm² = ▧ km²

10. 0.15 hm² = ▧ m²

11. 3,000 cm² = ▧ km²

12. 892 m² = ▧ mm²

13. 7 m³ = ▧ mm³

14. 7 m³ = ▧ hm³

15. 7 m³ = ▧ dam³

16. 23 km³ = ▧ hm³

17. 5 cm³ = ▧ m³

18. 6,000,000 m³ = ▧ km³

Apply   Solve each problem.

19. The area of each teller's booth in the lobby is 60,000 cm². Express this area in square meters.

20. Would the amount of paneling on an office wall be given as square meters or cubic meters?

21. What is wrong with saying that a desktop that measures 1.5 m by 0.8 m has an area of 1.2 m³?

22. One _hectare_ (ha) = 10,000 m². The area of the province of Ontario is about 1,000,000 km². How many hectares is this?

Metric Units of Capacity and Mass

A. The container holds 1 *liter* (L) of water. The eyedropper holds about 1 *milliliter* (mL) of water.

The mass, or weight, of 1 L of water is 1 *kilogram* (kg).
The mass of 1 mL of water is 1 *gram* (g).
One grain of sand has a mass of about 1 *milligram* (mg).

1 L = 1,000 mL   1 kg = 1,000 g   1 g = 1,000 mg

kiloliter (kL)	hectoliter (hL)	dekaliter (daL)	liter (L)	deciliter (dL)	centiliter (cL)	milliliter (mL)

kilogram (kg)	hectogram (hg)	dekagram (dag)	gram (g)	decigram (dg)	centigram (cg)	milligram (mg)

B. 475 mL = ▓ L

c. 83 kg = ▓ dag

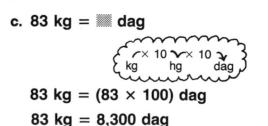

475 mL = (475 × 0.001) L

475 mL = 0.475 L

83 kg = (83 × 100) dag

83 kg = 8,300 dag

176

Try

a. *Estimation* Choose the best measure for the mass of a microscope.

5 g   5 mg   5 kg

b. Find the missing number.

40 mL = ▨ cL

Practice   *Estimation* Choose the best measure.

1. Mass of a science book

1.8 mg   1.8 g   1.8 kg

2. Mass of the scientist

7 kg   70 kg   700 kg

3. Capacity of a spoon

5 mL   5 L   15 L

4. Capacity of a sink

0.4 L   40 L   400 L

Find the missing number.

5. 768 mL = ▨ L

6. 32 L = ▨ mL

7. 65.3 L = ▨ mL

8. 4,781 mL = ▨ dL

9. 14 g = ▨ mg

10. 518 kg = ▨ g

11. 309 mg = ▨ g

12. 15.5 hg = ▨ g

13. 13,892 mg = ▨ kg

Apply   Solve each problem.

14. A can holds 3 liters of formaldehyde. How many kiloliters is this?

★15. One liter of water has a volume of 1,000 cm^3. How many liters of water can a one-cubic-meter tank hold?

MAINTENANCE

Find each answer.

1. $4\frac{1}{6} + 3\frac{1}{2}$

2. $8\frac{1}{2} - \frac{4}{5}$

3. $\frac{3}{8} + 2\frac{3}{4}$

4. $10\frac{3}{5} \times 6$

5. $\frac{2}{3} - \frac{1}{4}$

6. $13 \div 8\frac{2}{3}$

7. $5\frac{2}{5} \div \frac{3}{5}$

8. $1\frac{1}{4} \times 4\frac{1}{2}$

9. $\frac{9}{5} + \frac{9}{5}$

10. $48\frac{1}{2} - 48\frac{1}{6}$

11. $7 - 4\frac{1}{3}$

12. $1\frac{3}{4} \times 1\frac{3}{4}$

13. $2\frac{5}{8} + 3\frac{2}{3}$

14. $8\frac{1}{8} - 4\frac{5}{8}$

15. $9\frac{5}{6} \div 3$

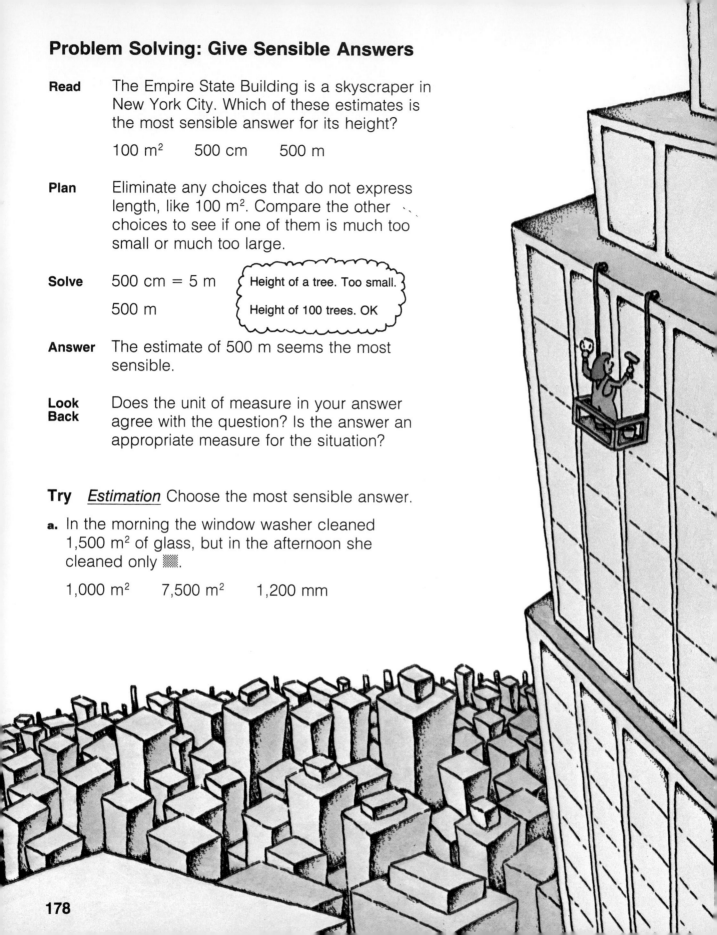

Problem Solving: Give Sensible Answers

Read   The Empire State Building is a skyscraper in New York City. Which of these estimates is the most sensible answer for its height?

       100 m^2 500 cm   500 m

Plan   Eliminate any choices that do not express length, like 100 m^2. Compare the other choices to see if one of them is much too small or much too large.

Solve   500 cm = 5 m   ⁀Height of a tree. Too small.⁀

           500 m   Height of 100 trees. OK

Answer   The estimate of 500 m seems the most sensible.

Look Back   Does the unit of measure in your answer agree with the question? Is the answer an appropriate measure for the situation?

Try   _Estimation_ Choose the most sensible answer.

a. In the morning the window washer cleaned $1,500 \text{ m}^2$ of glass, but in the afternoon she cleaned only ▒.

    $1,000 \text{ m}^2$ $7,500 \text{ m}^2$ 1,200 mm

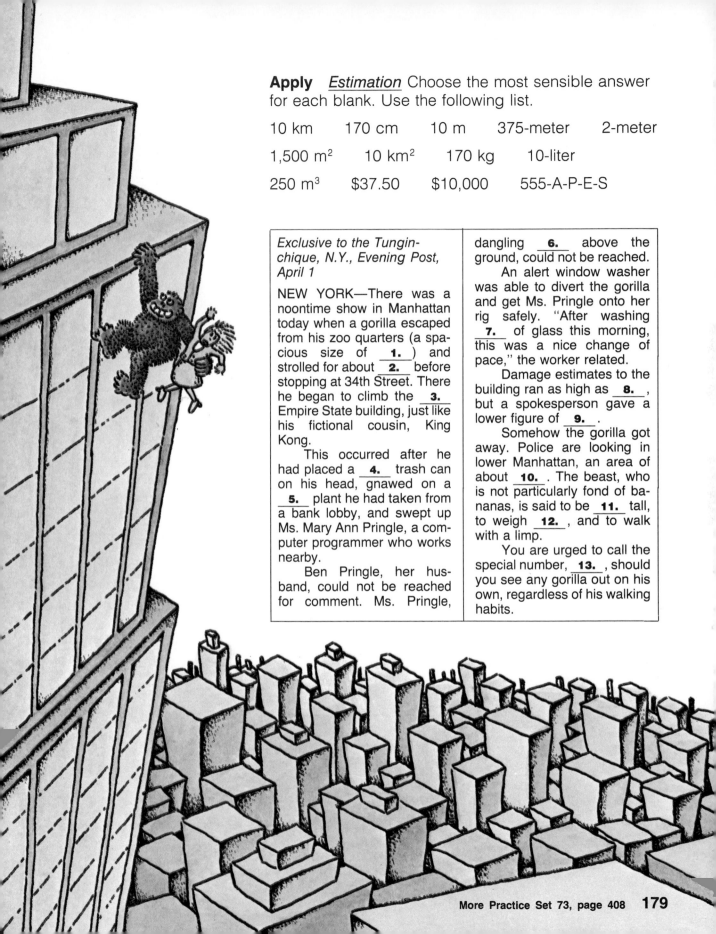

Apply *Estimation* Choose the most sensible answer for each blank. Use the following list.

10 km   170 cm   10 m   375-meter   2-meter

1,500 m²   10 km²   170 kg   10-liter

250 m³ $37.50 $10,000   555-A-P-E-S

Exclusive to the Tunginchique, N.Y., Evening Post, April 1

NEW YORK—There was a noontime show in Manhattan today when a gorilla escaped from his zoo quarters (a spacious size of __1.__) and strolled for about __2.__ before stopping at 34th Street. There he began to climb the __3.__ Empire State building, just like his fictional cousin, King Kong.

This occurred after he had placed a __4.__ trash can on his head, gnawed on a __5.__ plant he had taken from a bank lobby, and swept up Ms. Mary Ann Pringle, a computer programmer who works nearby.

Ben Pringle, her husband, could not be reached for comment. Ms. Pringle, dangling __6.__ above the ground, could not be reached.

An alert window washer was able to divert the gorilla and get Ms. Pringle onto her rig safely. "After washing __7.__ of glass this morning, this was a nice change of pace," the worker related.

Damage estimates to the building ran as high as __8.__ , but a spokesperson gave a lower figure of __9.__ .

Somehow the gorilla got away. Police are looking in lower Manhattan, an area of about __10.__ . The beast, who is not particularly fond of bananas, is said to be __11.__ tall, to weigh __12.__ , and to walk with a limp.

You are urged to call the special number, __13.__ , should you see any gorilla out on his own, regardless of his walking habits.

Practice: Metric Units

Estimation Choose the best measure.

1. Mass of a bicycle

   12 kg   120 kg   1,200 kg

2. Length of a swimming pool

   20 km   20 m   20 mm

3. Mass of a football player

   110 g   110 mg   110 kg

4. Volume of a closet

   3.5 m^3 3.5 m^2 3.5 m

5. Distance from Miami to Houston

   1,950 km   1,950 m   1,950 cm

6. Area of a record cover

   9.2 cm^2 92 cm^2 920 cm^2

7. Capacity of a paint can

   4 mL   40 mL   4 L

8. Capacity of a swimming pool

   20,000 L   20,000 mL   20,000 g

9. Area of a kitchen floor

   15 mm 15 m^2 15 cm^2

10. Width of a fingernail

   1 cm   10 cm   100 cm

11. Height of a closet

   2.7 m^2 2.7 m^3 2.7 m

12. Mass of a guitar pick

   14 mg   14 g   14 kg

13. Volume of a lunch box

   3 m^3 300 cm^3 $3,000 \text{ cm}^3$

14. Capacity of a car's gas tank

   6 L   60 L   600 L

Find each missing number.

15. $6 \text{ km} = \blacksquare \text{ m}$

16. $4 \text{ cm}^2 = \blacksquare \text{ mm}^2$

17. $23.4 \text{ kg} = \blacksquare \text{ g}$

18. $12 \text{ cm}^3 = \blacksquare \text{ mm}^3$

19. $5.6 \text{ L} = \blacksquare \text{ mL}$

20. $781 \text{ mm} = \blacksquare \text{ m}$

21. $45.6 \text{ g} = \blacksquare \text{ mg}$

22. $7,000 \text{ g} = \blacksquare \text{ kg}$

23. $1,000 \text{ m}^2 = \blacksquare \text{ dam}^2$

24. $1,600 \text{ dm}^3 = \blacksquare \text{ m}^3$

25. $90 \text{ cm} = \blacksquare \text{ dm}$

26. $5.2 \text{ L} = \blacksquare \text{ kL}$

27. $4,836 \text{ mL} = \blacksquare \text{ L}$

28. $49 \text{ mg} = \blacksquare \text{ g}$

29. $5,000 \text{ hm}^3 = \blacksquare \text{ km}^3$

30. $1,000 \text{ m}^2 = \blacksquare \text{ km}^2$

31. $707 \text{ mL} = \blacksquare \text{ L}$

32. $3 \text{ km}^2 = \blacksquare \text{ m}^2$

33. $89 \text{ mm} = \blacksquare \text{ cm}$

34. $3,000 \text{ m} = \blacksquare \text{ hm}$

35. $4,200 \text{ cm}^3 = \blacksquare \text{ dm}^3$

36. $0.005 \text{ kL} = \blacksquare \text{ mL}$

37. $0.03 \text{ kg} = \blacksquare \text{ mg}$

38. $0.1 \text{ km} = \blacksquare \text{ m}$

Apply Solve each problem.

39. A mechanical movie monster has a mass of 35 kilograms. How many grams is this?

40. Toronto is about 60,000 m from Niagara Falls. Express this distance in kilometers.

41. Should the area of a gorilla habitat at the zoo be expressed in square kilometers or in cubic kilometers?

42. Labels for single-serving cans of tomato juice were printed *Capacity: 0.2 L.* Are the labels probably correct?

★43. The mechanical monster is 2.1 m tall. Will it fit into a shipping box that is 225 cm long?

★44. Does it seem sensible to try to store 1,300 mL of sulfuric acid in a 1-liter container? Why?

BASIC: FOR . . . NEXT Loops

This program changes feet to yards. It uses a FOR . . . NEXT loop. The lines between the FOR and NEXT statements are done each time the loop is executed. Line 10 tells the computer to use 3 as the first value for F. Line 30 sends the computer back to line 10, and STEP 3 tells the computer to increase the value of F by 3. If there is no STEP in the FOR statement, the value of F will increase by 1 each time. The loop is completed after 6 is used for F.

```
10 FOR F=3 TO 6 STEP 3
20 PRINT F;" FEET = ";F/3;" YARDS"
30 NEXT F
40 END
```

Output

```
3 FEET = 1 YARDS
6 FEET = 2 YARDS
```

Give the output for each program.

1.
```
10 FOR F=1 TO 6
20 PRINT F;" FT, = ";F*12;" IN,"
30 NEXT F
40 END
```

2.
```
10 FOR P=2 TO 10 STEP 2
20 PRINT P;" LB, = ";P*16;" OZ,"
30 NEXT P
40 END
```

3.
```
10 FOR W=0 TO 24 STEP 4
20 PRINT W;" WEEKS = ";W*7;" DAYS"
30 NEXT W
40 END
```

Customary Units of Length, Area, and Volume

A. *Career* Kim Chan, a sculptor, designed the marble cube shown below. She often uses customary measures like these.

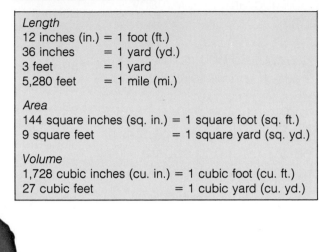

Length
12 inches (in.) = 1 foot (ft.)
36 inches   = 1 yard (yd.)
3 feet   = 1 yard
5,280 feet   = 1 mile (mi.)

Area
144 square inches (sq. in.) = 1 square foot (sq. ft.)
9 square feet   = 1 square yard (sq. yd.)

Volume
1,728 cubic inches (cu. in.) = 1 cubic foot (cu. ft.)
27 cubic feet   = 1 cubic yard (cu. yd.)

B. 140 in. = ▨ ft. ● in.

140 in. = 11 ft. 8 in.

12 in. = 1 ft.
It takes *fewer* feet than inches to measure a distance, so *divide* by 12. 140 ÷ 12 = 11 R8

C. $\frac{2}{3}$ sq. yd. = ▨ sq. ft.

$\frac{2}{3}$ sq. yd. = 6 sq. ft.

1 sq. yd. = 9 sq. ft.
It takes *more* square feet than square yards to cover a surface, so *multiply* by 9. $9\left(\frac{2}{3}\right) = 6$

Length of each edge:
2 feet

Area of top face:
4 square feet

Volume of cube:
8 cubic feet

Try

a. *Estimation* Choose the best measure of Kim's height.

5 in.   5 ft.   5 yd.

Find each missing number.

b. 72 in. = ▓ ft.   **c.** 90 in. = ▓ yd.

d. 3 mi. = ▓ ft.   **e.** 4 yd. 2 ft. = ▓ ft.

Practice   *Estimation* Choose the best measure.

1. Width of a room

1 ft.   15 ft.   150 ft.

2. Area of the same room

1 sq. ft.   15 sq. ft.   150 sq. ft.

3. Volume of the same room

45 cu. yd.   45 cu. ft.   45 cu. in.

4. Length of a paint brush

9 in.   9 sq. in.   9 cu. in.

Find each missing number.

5. 2 ft. = ▓ in.

6. 1 ft. 1 in. = ▓ in.

7. 3 sq. ft. = ▓ sq. in.

8. 15 yd. = ▓ ft.

9. 65 in. = ▓ ft. ▓ in.

10. 288 sq. in. = ▓ sq. ft.

11. 46 in. = ▓ ft.

12. 41 ft. = ▓ yd. ▓ ft.

13. $\frac{1}{3}$ cu. yd. = ▓ cu. ft.

14. $1\frac{1}{2}$ ft. = ▓ yd.

15. 110 in. = ▓ yd. ▓ in.

16. 4 cu. yd. = ▓ cu. ft.

17. $\frac{3}{4}$ mi. = ▓ ft.

18. 1 mi. 60 ft. = ▓ ft.

19. $\frac{2}{3}$ sq. ft. = ▓ sq. in.

20. 66 ft. = ▓ mi.

21. 8 yd. 8 ft. = ▓ ft.

★22. $\frac{1}{2}$ cu. yd. = ▓ cu. in.

★23. 1 mi. = ▓ yd.

★24. 100 in. = ▓ yd. ▓ ft. ▓ in.

Apply   Solve each problem.

25. The cube measures 2 ft. by 2 ft. by 2 ft. Express these dimensions in inches.

26. Kim needs 7.5 ft. of copper tubing for a sculpture. Should she buy 90 in. or 90 cu. in.?

★27. Three art studios have areas of 675 sq. ft., 75 sq. yd., and 600 sq. ft. Which studio is the smallest?

★28. Kim made a wooden cube the same size as the marble one. She painted all six faces. How many square feet did she paint?

Customary Units of Capacity and Weight

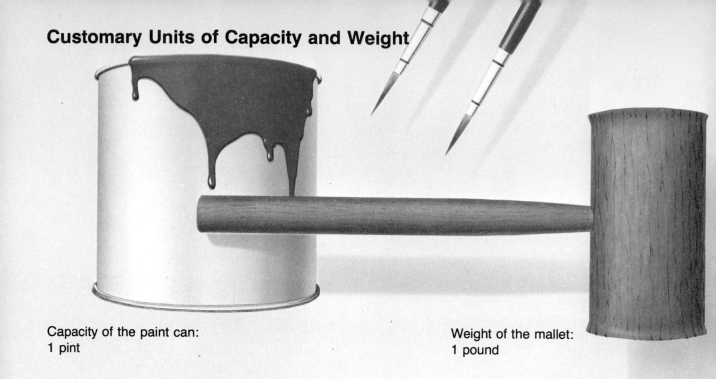

Capacity of the paint can:
1 pint

Weight of the mallet:
1 pound

Capacity		Weight	
8 fluid ounces (fl. oz.)	= 1 cup (c.)	16 ounces (oz.) = 1 pound (lb.)	
2 cups	= 1 pint (pt.)	2,000 pounds = 1 ton	
2 pints	= 1 quart (qt.)		
4 quarts	= 1 gallon (gal.)		

A. 13 qt. = ▨ gal. ● qt.

4 qt. = 1 gal.
It takes *fewer* gallons
than quarts to fill a
container, so *divide* by 4.
13 ÷ 4 = 3 R1

13 qt. = 3 gal. 1 qt.

B. $6\frac{1}{4}$ lb. = ▨ oz.

1 lb. = 16 oz.
It takes *more* ounces than
pounds to express the weight
of an object, so *multiply* by 16.
$16\left(6\frac{1}{4}\right) = 100$

$6\frac{1}{4}$ lb. = 100 oz.

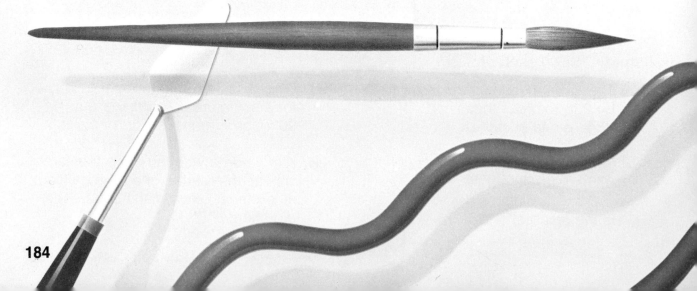

Try

a. *Estimation* Choose the best measure for the weight of the paint can on page 184 when it is empty.

3 oz.   3 lb.   3 tons

Find each missing number.

b. 9,000 lb. = ▨ tons

c. 4 lb. 11 oz. = ▨ oz.

Practice   *Estimation* Choose the best measure.

1. Weight of a paint brush

1 oz.   100 oz.   1 lb.

2. Weight of the sculptor

100 oz.   100 tons   100 lb.

3. Capacity of waste basket

6 oz.   6 qt.   60 gal.

4. Capacity of a drinking glass

8 fl. oz.   8 pt.   8 qt.

Find each missing number.

5. 10 c. = ▨ pt.

6. 20 oz. = ▨ lb. ▨ oz.

7. 5 gal. 5 qt. = ▨ qt.

8. 7 gal. = ▨ qt.

9. 33 pt. = ▨ qt. ▨ pt.

10. 9 lb. 1 oz. = ▨ oz.

11. 18 qt. = ▨ gal.

12. 18 qt. = ▨ gal. ▨ qt.

13. 2 tons 20 lb. = ▨ lb.

14. $5\frac{1}{4}$ tons = ▨ lb.

15. 54 oz. = ▨ lb. ▨ oz.

16. 7 pt. 5 c. = ▨ c.

Apply   Solve the problem.

17. Kim Chan ordered some art supplies. The total shipping weight was 74 oz. How many pounds and ounces is this?

CHALLENGE

How long does it take a train one mile long to pass through a tunnel one mile long if the train is traveling 30 miles per hour?

Computing with Customary Units

A museum prepared a special exhibit of items from the tomb of King Tutankhamun, who died about 3,300 years ago.

A. A museum worker measured the coffin as 5 ft. 11 in. If the coffin is placed on a 2-foot 6-inch pedestal, how tall would the coffin and pedestal be together?

Find 5 ft. 11 in. + 2 ft. 6 in.

$$\begin{array}{r} 5 \text{ ft. } 11 \text{ in.} \\ + 2 \text{ ft. } 6 \text{ in.} \\ \hline 7 \text{ ft. } 17 \text{ in.} \end{array}$$

7 ft. + 1 ft. 5 in. = 8 ft. 5 in.

The coffin and pedestal together would be 8 ft. 5 in. tall.

B. Find 4 lb. 7 oz. − 1 lb. 10 oz.

You cannot subtract 10 oz. from 7 oz., so rename 4 lb. 7 oz.
Remember, 1 lb. is 16 oz.

$$\begin{array}{rcl} 4 \text{ lb. } 7 \text{ oz.} & = & 3 \text{ lb. } 23 \text{ oz.} \\ - 1 \text{ lb. } 10 \text{ oz.} & = & 1 \text{ lb. } 10 \text{ oz.} \\ \hline & & 2 \text{ lb. } 13 \text{ oz.} \end{array}$$

Try   Add or subtract.

a. 7 ft. 2 in. + 8 ft. 10 in.

b. 45 lb. 9 oz. + 13 lb. 12 oz.

c. 14 gal. 3 qt. − 2 gal. 1 qt.

d. 23 ft. − 12 ft. 9 in.

Practice Add or subtract.

1. 4 ft. 7 in. + 6 ft. 3 in.

2. 37 lb. 4 oz. + 22 lb. 11 oz.

3. 17 gal. 2 qt. − 4 gal. 1 qt.

4. 4 yd. 1 ft. − 3 yd. 1 ft.

5. 11 lb. 7 oz. + 11 lb. 9 oz.

6. 10 gal. 3 qt. + 6 gal. 1 qt.

7. 3 ft. − 10 in.

8. 7 lb. − 8 oz.

9. 4 qt. 3 pt. + 2 qt. 2 pt.

10. 5 ft. 8 in. + 5 ft. 8 in.

11. 7 lb. 5 oz. − 3 lb. 8 oz.

12. 9 gal. 1 qt. − 4 gal. 3 qt.

13. 6 yd. 25 in. + 13 in.

14. 20 lb. 12 oz. + 14 oz.

15. 19 lb. − 8 lb. 5 oz.

16. 10 ft. − 2 ft. 9 in.

17. 4 yd. 2 ft. − 1 yd. 9 in.

18. 6 gal. 1 qt. − 2 gal. 1 pt.

Multiply or divide. Simplify each product if necessary. Give each quotient with a fraction and also without a fraction.

★19. 3 × 6 ft. 4 in.

★20. 6 × 5 lb. 1 oz.

★21. 2 × 4 gal. 3 qt.

★22. 5 gal. ÷ 4

★23. 8 ft. ÷ 3

★24. 10 lb. ÷ 20

Apply Solve each problem.

25. How much taller is the coffin than its pedestal?

26. Dolores Chavez bought this poster that shows an ointment jar. The poster is 2 ft. 9 in. tall and 1 ft. 10 in. wide. How much taller is it than it is wide?

27. What is the total distance around the poster?

Time		
60 seconds (sec.)	=	1 minute (min.)
60 minutes	=	1 hour (hr.)
24 hours	=	1 day

Every April an official marathon is run in Lake County, Illinois, to benefit medical research.

A. Last year, one race official left her home at 5:30 the morning of the race and returned at 2:07 that afternoon. How long was she gone?

Think of each reading as an amount of time past midnight.

Midnight   A.M.   Noon   P.M.   Midnight
12   3   6   9   12   3   6   9   12
        ↑   ↑
     5:30 A.M.   2:07 P.M.

$$2 \text{ hr. } 7 \text{ min. (P.M.)} \longrightarrow 14 \text{ hr. } 7 \text{ min.} = 13 \text{ hr. } 67 \text{ min.}$$
$$-5 \text{ hr. } 30 \text{ min. (A.M.)} \longrightarrow -5 \text{ hr. } 30 \text{ min.} = 5 \text{ hr. } 30 \text{ min.}$$
$$8 \text{ hr. } 37 \text{ min.}$$

The official was gone 8 hr. 37 min.

B. What time is it 6 hr. 25 min. after 10:35 A.M.?

10:35 A.M. is 10 hr. 35 min. past midnight.

10 hr. 35 min.
+ 6 hr. 25 min.
16 hr. 60 min. =
17 hr. past midnight, or 5 P.M.

Try

a. Find 4 days 8 hr. − 2 days 14 hr.

Practice   In the same day, what is the amount of time between

1. 8:32 P.M. and 11:59 P.M.?

2. 1:13 A.M. and 2:05 A.M.?

3. 7:18 A.M. and 9:08 A.M.?

4. 11:15 A.M. and 4:00 P.M.?

What time is it

5. 6 hr. 29 min. after 1:07 P.M.?

6. 10 hr. 30 min. after 1:46 P.M.?

7. 3 hr. after 11:50 A.M.?

8. 8 hr. 25 min. after 5:00 A.M.?

Add or subtract.

9. 4 min. 6 sec. − 2 min. 38 sec.

10. 1 min. 54 sec. + 6 min. 6 sec.

11. 3 days 10 hr. + 1 day 14 hr.

12. 7 days 11 hr. − 3 days 16 hr.

Apply   Solve the problem.

*13. In 1983, the first woman finished the race in 3 hr. 51 sec.
How much slower was this time than the winning time
of 2 hr. 16 min. 55 sec.?

Problem Solving: Use a Formula

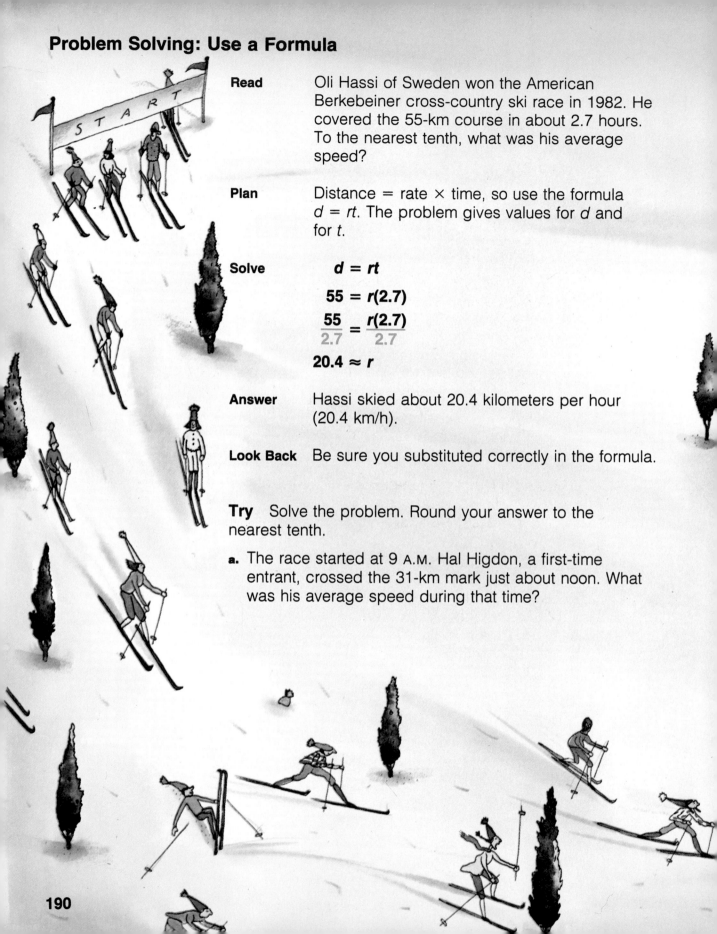

Read

Oli Hassi of Sweden won the American Berkebeiner cross-country ski race in 1982. He covered the 55-km course in about 2.7 hours. To the nearest tenth, what was his average speed?

Plan

Distance = rate × time, so use the formula $d = rt$. The problem gives values for d and for t.

Solve

$$d = rt$$
$$55 = r(2.7)$$
$$\frac{55}{2.7} = \frac{r(2.7)}{2.7}$$
$$20.4 \approx r$$

Answer

Hassi skied about 20.4 kilometers per hour (20.4 km/h).

Look Back Be sure you substituted correctly in the formula.

Try Solve the problem. Round your answer to the nearest tenth.

a. The race started at 9 A.M. Hal Higdon, a first-time entrant, crossed the 31-km mark just about noon. What was his average speed during that time?

Apply Solve each problem. When necessary, round your answer to the nearest tenth.

1. In 1932, Amelia Earhart became the first woman to fly solo across the Atlantic Ocean. She flew at about 135 mph for about 15 hr. About how far did she fly?

2. In the 1983 Boston Marathon, winner Greg Meyer ran the 26.21875 miles in 2.15 hr. What was his average speed?

3. Tom Bulger finished the 55-km Berkebeiner with an overall rate of about 8.15 km/h, but he had to borrow someone else's boots to finish at all. How long was he on the course?

4. How long would it take to ski from the 10-km marker to the 31-km marker if you skied at a rate of 12 km/h? Use $(d_f - d_s) = rt$, where d_f is the reading on the final marker and d_s is the reading on the beginning marker.

5. In the 1983 Boston Marathon, Joan Benoit's average rate was about 11.75 mph for the first 10 miles. To find how many minutes it took her to run this far, use the formula $t = 60\frac{d}{r}$.

★6. Howie Bean of New Hampshire was the first American to complete the Berkebeiner race. He finished at 2:42 P.M. What was his average speed? Try to use the formula $d = r(t_f - t_s)$.

More Practice Set 78, page 409

CALCULATOR

1 mi. ≈ 1.6094 km

1 qt. ≈ 0.946 L

1 lb. ≈ 0.4536 kg

Use your calculator to find each missing number. Round your answers to the nearest hundredth.

6 mi. ≈ ▦ km

$6 \times 1.609 = 9.654$

6 mi. ≈ 9.65 km

10 km ≈ ▦ mi.

$10 \div 1.609 \approx 6.2150403$

10 km ≈ 6.22 mi.

1. 3 mi. ≈ ▦ km

2. 4 qt. ≈ ▦ L

3. 10 lb. ≈ ▦ kg

4. 1 L ≈ ▦ qt.

5. 1 km ≈ ▦ mi.

6. 1 kg ≈ ▦ lb.

7. 5 L ≈ ▦ qt.

8. 5 qt. ≈ ▦ L

9. 100 mi. ≈ ▦ km

10. 100 km ≈ ▦ mi.

11. 2.2 lb. ≈ ▦ kg

Precision

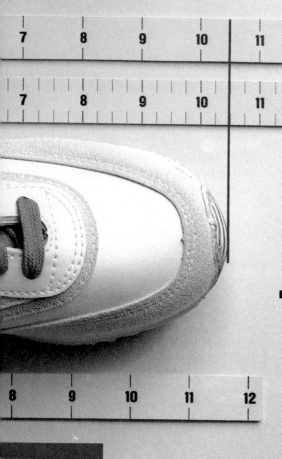

A. No measurement is truly exact, but you can get closer to the real length of this shoe if you measure with smaller and smaller units.

Measured to the
nearest inch: 10 in.

nearest fourth inch: $10\frac{2}{4}$ in.

The smaller the unit, the more **precise** the measurement. $10\frac{2}{4}$ in. is more precise than 10 in.

B. Any object that is $9\frac{1}{2}$ to $10\frac{1}{2}$ inches long is "10 inches to the nearest inch." The **greatest possible error** (GPE) of a measurement is one half the unit.

Measurement	Unit of measure	GPE
10 in.	inch	$\frac{1}{2}$ in.
$10\frac{2}{4}$ in.	quarter inch	$\frac{1}{8}$ in.
2.8 m	tenth of a meter	0.05 m

C. Find 6 in. $+ 3\frac{1}{2}$ in. $+ 4\frac{1}{4}$ in.

$$
\begin{array}{r}
6 \text{ in.} \\
3\frac{1}{2} \text{ in.} \\
+\, 4\frac{1}{4} \text{ in.} \\
\hline
13\frac{3}{4} \text{ in.} \approx 14 \text{ in.}
\end{array}
$$

The least precise measurement is given to the nearest inch, so give the answer to the nearest inch.

When you add or subtract measurements, your answer should be as precise as the least precise measurement you work with.

Try Give the unit of measure and the GPE.

a. $5\frac{3}{4}$ ft.   **b.** 14.3 cm

c. Which measurement is more precise, 40 cm or 4 m?

d. Find 5.0 m − 3.77 m. Round your answer.

Practice Give the unit of measure and the GPE.

1. 6 in.   **2.** 41 ft.   **3.** $4\frac{1}{2}$ yd.   **4.** $5\frac{3}{8}$ oz.   **5.** 77 qt.   **6.** $3\frac{9}{10}$ gal.

7. 4.0 m   **8.** 99 cm   **9.** 6.05 km   **10.** 2 L   **11.** 1.07 g   **12.** 107 cg

Which measurement is more precise?

13. $3\frac{1}{2}$ ft. or 3 ft.   **14.** 11 yd. or 3 ft.   **15.** 12.3 sec. or 14.15 sec.

16. 5.1 cm or 6 cm   **17.** 8 mm or 37.1 mm   **18.** 9 cm or 2 mm

Compute. Round your answer.

19. $3\frac{1}{8}$ in. + 9 in. + $2\frac{3}{32}$ in.   **20.** 42.17 sec. − 18.3 sec.

21. 12.4 kg − 8.0 kg   **22.** 4.3 cm + 5.466 cm

23. 3.2 min. + 2.7 min. + 0.25 min. + 0.9873 min.

Apply Solve each problem. In Problem 25, round your answer.

24. Which winning time for the Olympic 100-meter race is more precise?

1960: 10.2 sec.
1980: 10.25 sec.

25. The 100-meter freestyle swimming race was won in 57.3 sec. in the 1948 Olympics. In 1972, the winning time was 51.22 sec. How much faster was the 1972 time?

Chapter 6 Test

Complete each unit of measure.

1. Mass of a melon: kilo▨

2. Capacity of a mug: milli▨

Choose the best measure for the

3. length of an envelope.

   2.4 cm   24 cm   240 cm

4. volume of a room.

   45 m³   45 m²   45 cm²

5. area of a rug.

   12 km²   12 mm³   12 m²

6. mass of a camera.

   1.3 kg   1.3 g   1.3 mg

7. height of a bicycle.

   26 cu. in.   26 in.   26 sq. in.

8. weight of a moose.

   900 lb.   9 lb.   90 lb.

Find the missing number.

9. 21 km = ▨ m   **10.** 57 dm = ▨ m

11. 450 mL = ▨ L   **12.** 18 kg = ▨ g

13. $\frac{1}{2}$ mi. = ▨ ft.   **14.** 20 c. = ▨ pt.

15. 3 lb. = ▨ oz.

16. 27 sq. ft. = ▨ sq. yd.

Choose the most sensible answer.

17. The Mackinac Straits bridge in Michigan is one of the longest bridges in the United States. How long is it?

   1,158 cm   1,158 km   1,158 m

Add or subtract.

18. 3 ft. 6 in. + 2 ft. 8 in.

19. 6 lb. 7 oz. − 4 lb. 9 oz.

20. 8 gal. 1 qt. + 2 gal. 3 qt.

21. In the same day, what is the amount of time between 10:30 A.M. and 4:25 P.M.?

22. What time is it 5 hours after 9:05 P.M.?

Solve each problem. Use the formula $d = rt$.

23. A runner ran 20 miles in 3.2 hr. What was her rate of speed?

24. A car is traveling at a rate of 90 km/h. How long will it take to travel 684 km?

25. Give the unit of measure and the GPE for 1.3 L.

26. Which measurement is more precise, $2\frac{1}{2}$ yd. or 2 yd.?

CHALLENGE
Significant Digits and Accuracy

Suppose a ski pole is 12.6 decimeters long. Then the unit of measure is one tenth of a decimeter, and the length can be expressed as 126 tenths of a decimeter.
1, 2, and 6 are *significant digits* in this measurement.

Significant digits are those digits that are needed to tell the number of units in a measurement.

If one measurement has a greater number of significant digits than another, the first measurement is more *accurate*.

When you find area, the answer should have the same number of significant digits as the least accurate of the given measurements.

3.05 m by 7.4 m: 23 m²

Complete this table.

Measurement	Unit	Number of units	Significant digits	Number of significant digits
12.6 dm	0.1 dm	126	1, 2, 6	3
490 m	1 m	**1.**	**2.**	**3.**
490 m	10 m	**4.**	**5.**	**6.**
0.075 cm	**7.**	**8.**	**9.**	**10.**
6.034 km	**11.**	**12.**	**13.**	**14.**
52 km	**15.**	**16.**	**17.**	**18.**

Which measurement is more accurate? Which is more precise?
In some cases, you may have to write *equally accurate* or *equally precise*.

19. 0.0022 cm or 5 cm   **20.** 8.3 dm or 12 km   **21.** 792 cm or 7.92 m

Find the area of a rectangle with the given dimensions.
Round your answer according to the rule given above.

22. 6.13 m by 5.04 m   **23.** 5 cm by 0.85 cm   **24.** 2.04 dm by 442.04 dm

MAINTENANCE

Write each fraction as a decimal.

1. $\frac{1}{8}$ **2.** $\frac{3}{4}$ **3.** $\frac{1}{2}$ **4.** $\frac{7}{8}$ **5.** $\frac{3}{5}$ **6.** $\frac{4}{9}$

7. $3\frac{1}{10}$ **8.** $14\frac{1}{4}$ **9.** $3\frac{1}{40}$ **10.** $\frac{1}{100}$ **11.** $\frac{7}{10}$ **12.** $\frac{5}{11}$

Write each decimal as a fraction in lowest terms.

13. 0.2   **14.** 0.75   **15.** 0.89   **16.** 0.14   **17.** 0.04

18. 0.12   **19.** 0.24   **20.** 0.76   **21.** 0.001   **22.** 0.125

Write each decimal as a mixed number. Reduce fractions to lowest terms.

23. 3.1   **24.** 4.75   **25.** 8.04   **26.** 7.125   **27.** 8.32

Write each mixed number as an improper fraction.

28. $4\frac{1}{2}$ **29.** $6\frac{1}{3}$ **30.** $8\frac{2}{5}$ **31.** $7\frac{4}{9}$ **32.** $4\frac{5}{7}$

Write each improper fraction as a whole or a mixed number.

33. $\frac{15}{2}$ **34.** $\frac{14}{3}$ **35.** $\frac{11}{5}$ **36.** $\frac{20}{4}$ **37.** $\frac{35}{8}$

Solve each problem.

38. A taco stand last weekend sold 300, 452, and 389 tacos. How many tacos were sold in all?

39. A baseball team played 21, or 75%, of its June games at night. How many games did it play in June?

40. In ten days the taco stand has sold 1,625 tacos. At this rate, how many tacos should be sold in 28 days?

41. How many times at bat should it take a baseball player to get 10 hits if he has had 4 hits in the last 10 times at bat?

42. Eight tenths of the 30 students in Mr. Ortega's class play basketball. How many students is this?

43. Mr. Ortega's basset hound weighs 33 lb. His poodle weighs 6 lb. The basset's weight is what percent of the poodle's weight?

196

Cumulative Test, Chapters 1–6

Give the letter for the correct answer.

1. Multiply.

$$\begin{array}{r} 548 \\ \times\ 37 \\ \hline \end{array}$$

- **A** 5,480
- **B** 18,726
- **C** 20,276
- **D** 22,076

2. Choose the operation that should be used to solve this problem. Then solve the problem.

The current in Lava Falls is 15 times as fast as the current in the Black River. The speed of the Lava Falls current is 30 mph. What is the speed of the current in the Black?

- **A** Multiplication: 450 mph
- **B** Subtraction: 15 mph
- **C** Division: 2 mph
- **D** Addition: 45 mph

3. Solve the equation.

$h + 20 = 60$

- **A** 80
- **B** 40
- **C** 3
- **D** 1,200

4. Solve the equation.

$4d = 16$

- **A** 12
- **B** 20
- **C** 64
- **D** 4

5. Choose the equation that should be used to solve this problem. Then solve the problem.

Rosie worked 10 more hours this week than she did last week. Last week she worked 32 hours. How many hours did she work this week?

- **A** $\frac{x}{10} = 32;\ x = 320$
- **B** $x - 10 = 32;\ x = 42$
- **C** $x + 10 = 32;\ x = 22$
- **D** $10x = 32;\ x = 3.2$

6. Multiply.

$(0.14)(0.4)$

- **A** 0.056
- **B** 0.56
- **C** 5.6
- **D** 56

7. Divide.

$25\overline{)1.5}$

- **A** 0.6
- **B** 6
- **C** 0.06
- **D** 0.006

8. Divide.

$0.83\overline{)22.41}$

- **A** 2.7
- **B** 0.27
- **C** 0.027
- **D** 27

9. Multiply.

$\frac{4}{5} \times \frac{5}{7}$

- **A** $\frac{3}{4}$
- **B** $\frac{4}{7}$
- **C** $\frac{25}{28}$
- **D** $1\frac{3}{4}$

10. What is $\frac{12}{30}$ written in lowest terms?

- **A** $\frac{2}{5}$
- **B** $\frac{1}{3}$
- **C** $\frac{6}{15}$
- **D** $\frac{4}{10}$

11. Multiply.

$2\frac{5}{8} \times 1\frac{1}{3}$

A $3\frac{5}{24}$

B $1\frac{31}{32}$

C 7

D $3\frac{1}{2}$

12. Add.

$5\frac{7}{10}$
$+\ 2\frac{1}{2}$

A $7\frac{3}{4}$

B $7\frac{9}{10}$

C $8\frac{1}{5}$

D $8\frac{4}{5}$

13. Subtract.

$7\frac{1}{6}$
$-\ 2\frac{1}{3}$

A $5\frac{1}{3}$

B $4\frac{5}{6}$

C $4\frac{2}{3}$

D $5\frac{5}{6}$

14. Find the value of x.

$\frac{7}{3} = \frac{x}{21}$

A 49   **B** 9   **C** 7   **D** 63

15. What is $\frac{3}{5}$ written as a percent?

A 35%   **C** 75%
B 53%   **D** 60%

16. What is 75% of 72?

A 96   **B** 18   **C** 54   **D** 48

17. 9 is what percent of 60?

A 15%   **C** 12%
B 18%   **D** 25%

18. A radio costs $63 plus 7% sales tax. What is the total cost of the radio?

A $72.00   **C** $4.41
B $44.10   **D** $67.41

19. Which is the best estimate for the width of a bridge?

A 3 km   **C** 3 m
B 30 m   **D** 30 km

20. Which is the best estimate for the weight of a hamster?

A 5 lb.   **C** 50 lb.
B 5 oz.   **D** 5 T.

Triangle

Rectangle

YIELD

SPEED
LIMIT
35

CITY C

STOP

CITY OF CHICAGO

CITY OF CHICAGO

Pentagon

Octagon

Basic Geometric Concepts

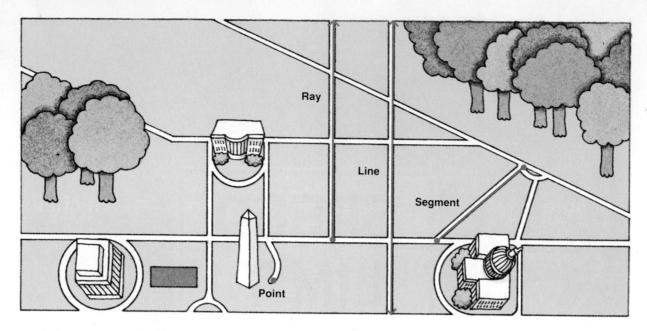

A. A flat surface, such as the map, suggests a geometric *plane*. A straight street on the map suggests a *line*, and a dot showing a location suggests a *point*.

B. Two points in a line can be used to name the line. $\overleftrightarrow{XY}$ is read "line *XY*."

A *segment* is part of a line. The two *endpoints* of the segment are used to name the segment. $\overline{YX}$ is read "segment *YX*."

A *ray* is part of a line with only one endpoint. That endpoint is given first when naming the ray. $\overrightarrow{YX}$ is read "ray *YX*."

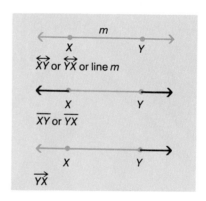

C. *Parallel lines* in plane $\mathcal{K}$ never intersect. $a \parallel b$ is read "line *a* is parallel to line *b*."

Intersecting lines in plane $\mathcal{K}$ intersect at a point. Line *c* intersects line *b* at point *T*.

D. Intersecting segments in a plane meet at a point. $\overline{RS}$ and $\overline{UV}$ intersect at point *T*. $\overline{RS}$ and $\overline{AB}$ are parallel segments because they are in parallel lines.

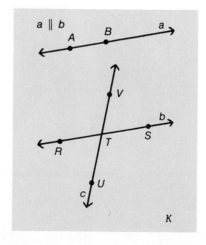

200

Try

a. Name the geometric concept suggested by the picture.

b. Name the segments shown.

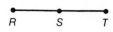

c. Give another name for $\overleftrightarrow{GH}$.

d. Sketch $\overleftrightarrow{ST}$ intersecting $\overline{XY}$ at Z.

Practice Name the geometric concept suggested by each picture.

1.

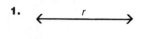

2.

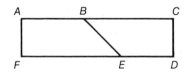

3.

4.

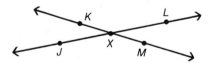

For each of Exercises 5–13, make a sketch.

5. $\overrightarrow{JK}$ **6.** $\overleftrightarrow{YZ}$ **7.** $\overline{VW}$ **8.** line s ∥ line t **9.** $\overline{AB}$ ∥ $\overline{XY}$

10. $\overleftrightarrow{MN}$ intersecting $\overleftrightarrow{PQ}$ at T **11.** $\overrightarrow{CD}$ and $\overrightarrow{CF}$ with common endpoint C

12. Line r intersecting parallel lines a and b **13.** $\overline{GH}$ intersecting $\overline{KM}$ at M

14. Name the segments shown.

15. Name the rays with endpoint X.

Apply Draw one map for which all of the following are true.

16. Maple, Elm, and Oak streets suggest parallel lines.

17. Lincoln Street suggests a segment. It starts at Maple and ends at Oak.

18. Washington Street suggests a ray. It starts at Elm and intersects Maple but does not intersect Oak.

19. The library suggests a point. It is located near the intersection of Washington and Elm.

Angles and Angle Measurement

A. An *angle* is formed by two rays that have a common endpoint. The picture of these intersecting paths suggests angles.

$\overrightarrow{AP}$ and $\overrightarrow{AQ}$ are the *sides* of the angle shown in red. Point *A* is the *vertex* of this angle.

The angle can be named ∠*PAQ*, ∠*QAP*, or ∠*A*.

B. A *protractor* can be used to measure or draw an angle. The measure of ∠*PAQ* is 70 degrees.

m∠*PAQ* = 70°

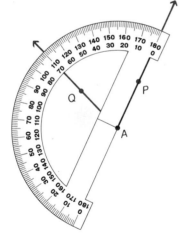

C. To draw a 30° angle, put the center of the protractor at point *A* of $\overrightarrow{AR}$. Mark point *C* at 30 and draw $\overrightarrow{AC}$.

m∠*RAC* = 30°

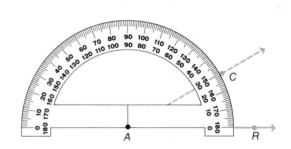

D. Angles can be classified according to their measures.

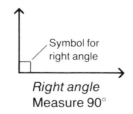

Acute angle
Measure less than 90°

Symbol for right angle

Right angle
Measure 90°

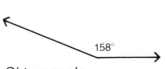

Obtuse angle
Measure greater than 90° and less than 180°

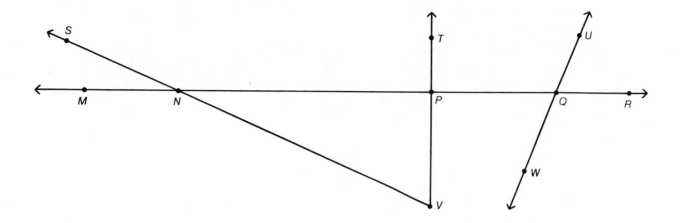

Try Use a protractor.

a. Measure ∠*NVP*, shown above. Is the angle acute, right, or obtuse?

b. Draw a 110° angle. Is the angle acute, right, or obtuse?

Practice Use a protractor to find the measure of each angle. Then tell whether the angle is acute, right, or obtuse.

1. ∠*UQR*   **2.** ∠*PQW*   **3.** ∠*TPN*   **4.** ∠*PNS*   **5.** ∠*MNS*   **6.** ∠*WQR*

Use a protractor to draw an angle with the given measure. Then tell whether the angle is acute, right, or obtuse.

7. 42°   **8.** 90°   **9.** 78°   **10.** 135°   **11.** 171°   **12.** 10°

13. Name the vertex of ∠*PQW*.

14. Name the sides of ∠*MNS*.

15. Give another name for ∠*NVP*.

16. What is *m*∠*RQU* + *m*∠*RQW*?

Apply Draw one map for which all of the following are true.

17. Iowa and York streets suggest intersecting lines. They meet to form a 90° angle.

18. Main Street suggests a ray. It starts at York Street and forms a 45° angle with York Street.

19. Give the measure of each of the four angles at the intersection of Iowa and York streets.

20. Give the measure of both of the angles at the intersection of Main and York streets.

Complementary and Supplementary Angles

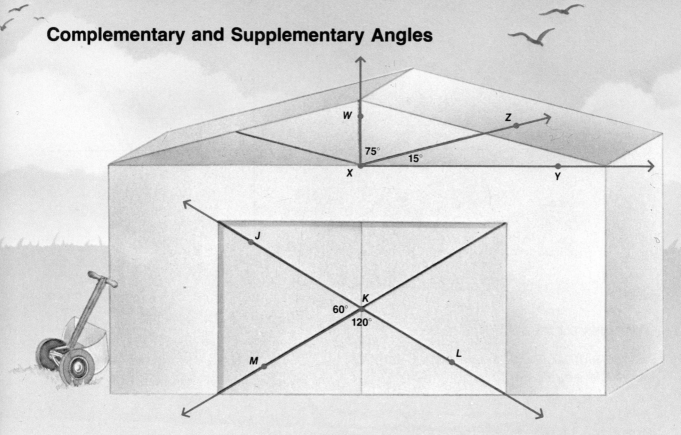

Luisa built this storage shed. Some parts of the shed suggest lines and angles.

A. Two angles are *supplementary* if the sum of their measures is 180°.

∠JKM and ∠MKL are supplementary angles since 60° + 120° = 180°. $\overrightarrow{KJ}$ and $\overrightarrow{KL}$ form a straight line.

B. Two angles are *complementary* if the sum of their measures is 90°.

∠WXZ and ∠ZXY are complementary angles since 75° + 15° = 90°.

C. Angles need not have a side in common to be complementary or supplementary.

12° + 78° = 90°, so ∠X and ∠Y are complements of each other.

78° + 102° = 180°, so ∠Y and ∠Z are supplements of each other.

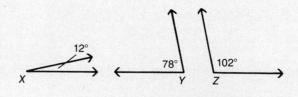

D. If lines, segments, or rays intersect to form right angles, they are *perpendicular*. ⊥ is read "is perpendicular to."

$\overleftrightarrow{AD} \perp \overleftrightarrow{BC}$ $\qquad$ $\overline{AD} \perp \overline{BC}$ $\qquad$ $\overrightarrow{ED} \perp \overrightarrow{EB}$

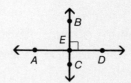

Try   Give the measure of each angle.

a. Supplement of a 76° angle

b. Complement of a 19° angle

Practice   Use this diagram for Exercises 1–4.

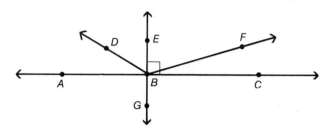

1. Name two pairs of complementary angles.

2. Name two pairs of supplementary angles.

3. Name a pair of perpendicular lines.

4. Name a pair of perpendicular rays.

Give the measure of a supplement of an angle with measure:

5. 58°   **6.** 14°   **7.** 36°   **8.** 90°

Give the measure of a complement of an angle with measure:

9. 45°   **10.** 84°   **11.** 73°   **12.** 5°

Apply   Sketch the angles suggested.

13. Two support boards on a gate form complementary angles. The angles have the same measure.

14. Two other boards meet to form supplementary angles with unequal measures.

Pairs of Lines and Related Angles

Betty is assembling this storage unit. You can see that parts of the unit suggest lines and angles.

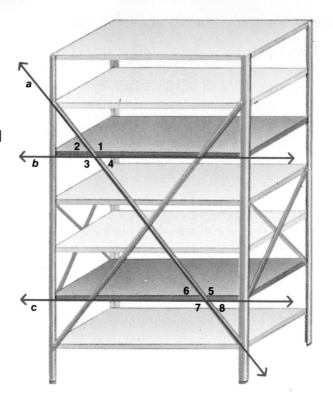

A. Lines *a* and *b* intersect. The measures of the four angles formed are given in the table.

Angle	1	2	3	4
Measure	130°	50°	130°	50°

$\angle 1$ and $\angle 3$ are **vertical angles**. $\angle 2$ and $\angle 4$ are also vertical angles.

Vertical angles have the same measure.

$m\angle 1 = m\angle 3$

$m\angle 2 = m\angle 4$

B. Lines *b* and *c* are parallel. Line *a* is a **transversal** of lines *b* and *c*. The measures of the angles formed are given in the table.

Angle	1	2	3	4	5	6	7	8
Measure	130°	50°	130°	50°	130°	50°	130°	50°

$\angle 3$ and $\angle 5$ are **alternate interior angles**. $\angle 4$ and $\angle 6$ are also alternate interior angles.

When a transversal cuts parallel lines, the alternate interior angles have the same measure.

$m\angle 3 = m\angle 5$

$m\angle 4 = m\angle 6$

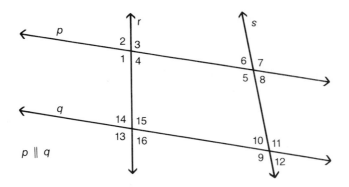

p ∥ q

Try Use the diagram. Tell whether the angles are vertical angles, alternate interior angles, or neither.

a. $\angle 1$ and $\angle 3$ b. $\angle 1$ and $\angle 14$ c. $\angle 1$ and $\angle 15$

Practice Use the diagram. Tell whether the angles are vertical angles, alternate interior angles, or neither.

1. $\angle 8$ and $\angle 10$ 2. $\angle 1$ and $\angle 13$ 3. $\angle 12$ and $\angle 10$

4. $\angle 4$ and $\angle 14$ 5. $\angle 6$ and $\angle 8$ 6. $\angle 9$ and $\angle 4$

7. $\angle 14$ and $\angle 16$ 8. $\angle 1$ and $\angle 5$ 9. $\angle 2$ and $\angle 4$

In the diagram, $m\angle 5 = 110°$. Give each of these measures.

10. $m\angle 7$ 11. $m\angle 11$ ★12. $m\angle 12$

Apply Sketch each figure and give the measure of each angle formed.

13. Two boards cross to form a 45° angle.

14. The shelves of a storage unit suggest parallel lines and the braces on the back suggest transversals. The braces meet the shelves at a 35° angle.

Basic Constructions

In geometry, to **construct** a figure means to draw the figure using only a **compass** and a straightedge.

A. *Congruent segments* have the same measure. Construct a segment congruent to $\overline{EF}$.

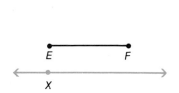

Step 1 Draw a line. Label point X.

Step 2 Open the compass to the length of $\overline{EF}$.

Step 3 With X as center, draw an arc that intersects the line at Y. $\overline{XY} \cong \overline{EF}$. $\cong$ is read "is congruent to."

B. *Congruent angles* have the same measure. Construct an angle congruent to $\angle G$.

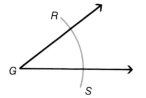

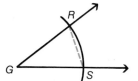

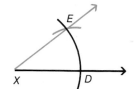

Step 1 With G as center, draw an arc that intersects both sides of $\angle G$.

Step 2 Draw a ray. Label its endpoint X. With X as center and the same compass opening, draw an arc to intersect the ray.

Step 3 Set the compass opening to the length of $\overline{RS}$.

Step 4 With D as center, draw an arc that intersects the first arc at E. Draw $\overrightarrow{XE}$. $\angle X \cong \angle G$

C. To **bisect** a segment or an angle means to divide it into two congruent parts. Construct the perpendicular bisector of $\overline{ST}$.

Step 1 Open the compass to more than one half the length of $\overline{ST}$. With S as center, draw an arc that intersects $\overline{ST}$.

Step 2 Keep the same compass opening. With T as center, draw an arc to intersect the first arc.

Step 3 Draw $\overrightarrow{QR}$, the perpendicular bisector of $\overline{ST}$. Point N is the **midpoint** of $\overline{ST}$. $\overline{SN} \cong \overline{NT}$

208

Try Construct the bisector of ∠M.

a. Trace ∠M. With M as center, draw an arc that intersects both sides of ∠M. Label points J and K.

b. Draw an arc with K as center. With the same compass opening and J as center, draw an intersecting arc. Label point L.

c. Draw $\overrightarrow{ML}$. $\overrightarrow{ML}$ bisects ∠M. ∠JML ≅ ∠KML

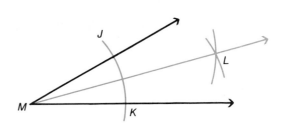

Practice Trace $\overline{AB}$, $\overline{CD}$, ∠E, and ∠F. Construct a segment or an angle congruent to each of the following.

1. $\overline{AB}$ **2.** $\overline{CD}$ **3.** ∠E   **4.** ∠F

Construct the bisector of:

5. $\overline{AB}$ **6.** $\overline{CD}$ **7.** ∠E   **8.** ∠F

9. Construct a 90° angle. HINT: A segment and its perpendicular bisector form a right angle.

10. Construct a 45° angle. HINT: What is the measure of each angle when you bisect a 90° angle?

11. Trace triangle HNV. Construct the perpendicular bisector of each side.

★12. What do you notice about the perpendicular bisectors of the sides of triangle HNV?

13. Trace triangle HNV again. Bisect each angle.

★14. What do you notice about the angle bisectors of triangle HNV?

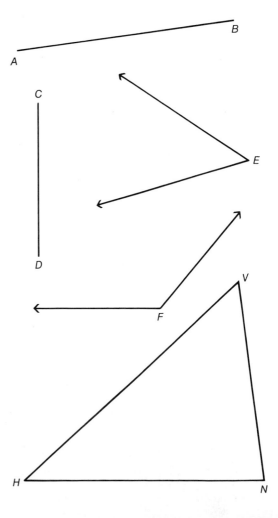

Constructing Triangles

A triangle is determined by three points (*vertices*) that are not in the same line. It has three *sides*, which are segments, and three angles. The vertices can be used for naming the triangle. △*FGH* means "triangle *FGH*."

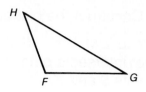

△ *FGH*
Sides: $\overline{FG}$, $\overline{GH}$, $\overline{HF}$
Angles: ∠*F*, ∠*G*, ∠*H*

A. Congruent triangles have the same size and shape. You can construct a triangle that is congruent to △*FGH* by using two angles of △*FGH* and the side between them. Use ∠*F*, ∠*G*, and $\overline{FG}$.

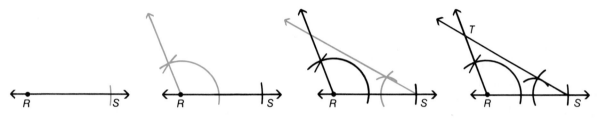

Step 1 Draw a line. Label point *R*. Construct $\overline{RS} \cong \overline{FG}$.

Step 2 At *R*, construct ∠*R* ≅ ∠*F*.

Step 3 At *S*, construct ∠*S* ≅ ∠*G*.

Step 4 Label the intersection point *T*. Draw $\overline{ST}$. △*RST* ≅ △*FGH*

B. You can construct a triangle congruent to a given triangle by using three sides of the triangle. Construct a triangle congruent to △*FGH* by using $\overline{FG}$, $\overline{GH}$, and $\overline{HF}$.

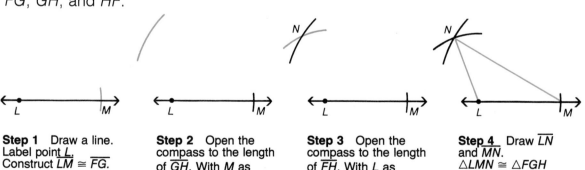

Step 1 Draw a line. Label point *L*. Construct $\overline{LM} \cong \overline{FG}$.

Step 2 Open the compass to the length of $\overline{GH}$. With *M* as center, draw an arc.

Step 3 Open the compass to the length of $\overline{FH}$. With *L* as center, draw an arc to intersect the first arc. Label point *N*.

Step 4 Draw $\overline{LN}$ and $\overline{MN}$. △*LMN* ≅ △*FGH*

Try Trace △FGH on page 210. Construct a congruent triangle by using ∠F, $\overline{FG}$, and $\overline{FH}$.

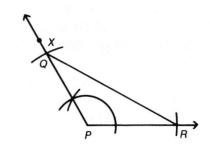

a. Draw a line and label point P. Construct $\overline{PR} \cong \overline{FG}$.

b. At P, construct ∠P ≅ ∠F. Label point X.

c. On $\overrightarrow{PX}$, construct $\overline{PQ} \cong \overline{FH}$. △PRQ ≅ △FGH

Practice Trace △DEF. Construct a congruent triangle by using only the parts given.

1. $\overline{DE}$, $\overline{EF}$, and $\overline{DF}$

2. $\overline{DE}$, ∠E, and $\overline{EF}$

3. $\overline{DE}$, ∠E, and ∠D

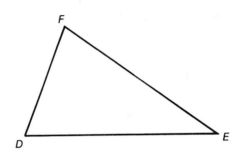

Trace △QST. Construct a congruent triangle by using only the parts given.

4. $\overline{QS}$, $\overline{ST}$, and $\overline{TQ}$

5. $\overline{QS}$, ∠S, and $\overline{ST}$

6. $\overline{QT}$, ∠Q, and ∠T

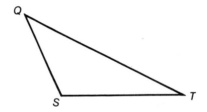

Trace the segments and angles shown at the right. Construct a triangle by using only the parts given.

7. Sides a, b, and c

8. ∠Y between sides a and b

9. Side a between ∠X and ∠Y

10. ∠X between sides b and c

11. Side c between ∠X and ∠Y

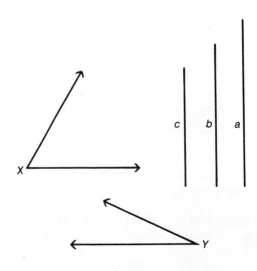

Problem Solving: Try and Check

The student council is conducting a contest to select a school flag. The flags must be triangular, and the length of each side must be a *whole number*.

Read   The lengths of two sides of Rosie's flag are 8 cm and 12 cm. What is the least possible length for the third side?

Plan   Choose a number. Then check your choice by trying to draw the triangle. Continue trying and checking until you find the answer.

Solve   Try 2 cm. Draw a segment 12 cm long and label it $\overline{KL}$. Open your compass to 8 cm and draw an arc from point K. Open your compass to 2 cm and draw another arc from point L. Since the arcs do not intersect, it is impossible to draw a triangle.

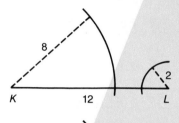

Try 4 cm. This is also impossible because the two arcs intersect on the 12-cm segment.

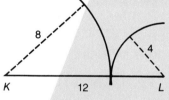

Try 5 cm. It is possible to draw a triangle whose sides measure 5 cm, 8 cm, and 12 cm.

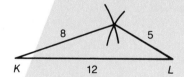

Answer   5 cm is the least possible length for the third side.

Look Back   The next whole number less than 5 is 4. Since 4 cm is too short, 5 cm is the least possible length.

Try   Choose an answer and check it. Continue trying and checking until you find the answer to the problem.

a. What is the greatest possible length for the third side of Rosie's flag? Use whole numbers only.

Apply Solve each problem. All the flags must be triangular, and the lengths of the sides must be whole numbers.

The lengths of two sides of Raul's flag are 7 cm and 9 cm.

1. What is the least possible length for the third side?

2. What is the greatest possible length for the third side?

The lengths of two sides of Theo's flag are 5 cm and 6 cm.

3. What is the least possible length for the third side?

4. What is the greatest possible length for the third side?

5. The longest side of Kim's flag is 10 cm. What might be the lengths of the other two sides? Give three possible pairs of numbers.

★6. The distance around Aiko's flag is 36 cm. What might be the lengths of the three sides? Give three possible sets of numbers.

Suppose Rosie's flag has side measures *a* and *b*, where *b* > *a*. Write an expression for

★7. the greatest possible measure of the third side.

★8. the least possible measure of the third side.

Logo: FORWARD and RIGHT Commands

In Logo, the Turtle is a small triangle on the computer monitor. This Turtle can follow commands that make it do special things.

FD 30 RT 120 FD 30 tells the Turtle to move forward 30, turn right 120° and move forward 30.

These commands will draw this angle on the computer monitor.

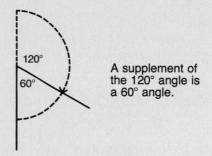

120°

60°

A supplement of the 120° angle is a 60° angle.

Give the measure of the supplement of each angle made by the following commands.

1. FD 30 RT 60 FD 30

2. FD 40 RT 90 FD 40

3. FD 10 RT 160 FD 10

4. FD 50 RT 45 FD 50

5. FD 25 RT 20 FD 25

6. FD 30 RT 100 FD 30

7. FD 60 RT 10 FD 60

8. FD 10 RT 30 FD 10

Classifying Triangles

A. Triangles can be classified according to their side measures and their angle measures. Congruent sides are marked with a slash.

Scalene Triangle
No congruent sides

Isosceles Triangle
At least 2 congruent sides

Equilateral Triangle
3 congruent sides

Acute Triangle
3 acute angles

Right Triangle
1 right angle

Obtuse Triangle
1 obtuse angle

B. The sum of the measures of the angles of △*ABC* is 180°.

$$m\angle A + m\angle B + m\angle C = 50° + 50° + 80° = 180°$$

The sum of the measures of the angles of △*DEF* is 180°.

$$m\angle D + m\angle E + m\angle F = 20° + 30° + 130° = 180°$$

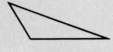

The sum of the angle measures of any triangle is 180°.

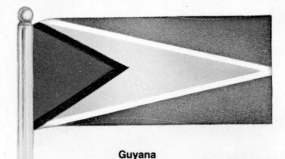

Guyana

Ohio

Try

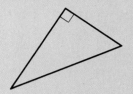

a. Which of the following describes the triangle shown?

    Right-equilateral   Scalene-right

b. The measures of two angles of a triangle are 23° and 108°. Find the measure of the third angle.

Practice   Select all the phrases that describe each triangle.

(a) Obtuse-scalene   (b) Right-isosceles
(c) Equilateral-acute   (d) Isosceles-acute

1.   **2.** 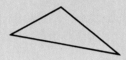   **3.**   **4.**

In Exercises 5–8, the measures of two angles of a triangle are given. Give the measure of the third angle.

5. 72° and 38°   **6.** 60° and 90°   **7.** 45° and 45°   **8.** 35° and 120°

★9. Give the measure of each angle in a right-isosceles triangle.   **★10.** Give the measure of each angle in an equilateral triangle.

Apply   Use the flags on pages 214 and 215. Tell whether the triangle appears to be scalene, isosceles, or equilateral. Then tell whether it appears to be acute, right, or obtuse.

11. Guyana: green triangles   **12.** Ohio: blue triangle

13. Samoa: white triangle   **14.** Jamaica: green triangles

American Samoa

Jamaica

Classifying Polygons

A. The outlines of these traffic signs suggest geometric figures called *polygons*. The sides of polygons are segments. A *regular polygon* has congruent sides and congruent angles. The outline of a stop sign suggests a regular polygon.

B. Polygons are named according to the number of sides and angles. For example, *tri* means *three*, and a triangle has 3 sides and 3 angles. Here are some polygons with special names.

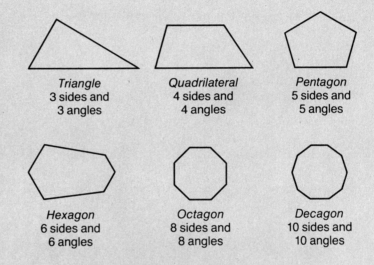

Triangle	Quadrilateral	Pentagon
3 sides and 3 angles	4 sides and 4 angles	5 sides and 5 angles

Hexagon	Octagon	Decagon
6 sides and 6 angles	8 sides and 8 angles	10 sides and 10 angles

C. Some quadrilaterals have special names. Congruent sides are marked with the same number of slashes.

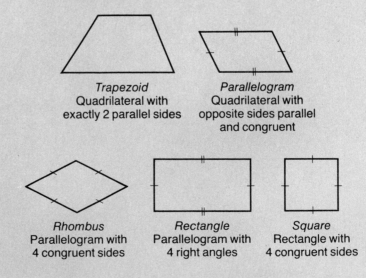

Trapezoid	Parallelogram
Quadrilateral with exactly 2 parallel sides	Quadrilateral with opposite sides parallel and congruent

Rhombus	Rectangle	Square
Parallelogram with 4 congruent sides	Parallelogram with 4 right angles	Rectangle with 4 congruent sides

D. The *diagonals* drawn from one vertex of a polygon separate it into triangles.

The two diagonals separate the pentagon into three triangles. So the sum of the measures of the angles of a pentagon is 3 × 180°, or 540°.

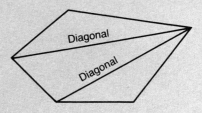

Try

a. Which of the following describes the figure shown?
Quadrilateral with opposite sides parallel
Quadrilateral with four congruent angles

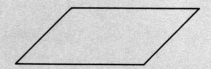

b. What is the sum of the angle measures of a rectangle?

Practice Give all the names from Example C that apply to each figure.

1.
2.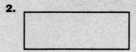
3.
4.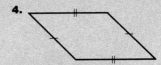

Sketch each polygon.

5. Rectangle with 4 congruent sides

6. Pentagon

7. Quadrilateral with exactly 2 right angles

8. Parallelogram with at least 1 right angle

9. Give the sum of the angle measures in an octagon.

10. Give the sum of the angle measures in a hexagon.

★11. Give the measure of each angle in a regular pentagon.

★12. Give the measure of each angle in a regular hexagon.

Apply Tell what polygon is suggested by the outline of each traffic sign. Also tell whether the polygon is regular or not regular.

13. Stop

14. Yield

15. Children Crossing

Congruent Polygons

A. Congruent polygons have the same size and shape. The outlines of the company logo are congruent polygons. The outlines of the stamps are not congruent polygons.

B. If you place one congruent polygon over another, the *corresponding parts* fit exactly. Corresponding parts of congruent polygons are congruent.

Polygon $ABCD \cong$ polygon $JKLM$. The corresponding parts are labeled in the diagram and given in this table.

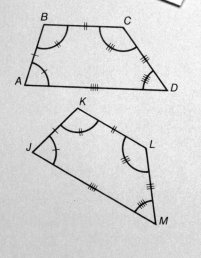

Corresponding vertices	Corresponding sides	Corresponding angles
A and J	$\overline{AB} \cong \overline{JK}$	$\angle A \cong \angle J$
B and K	$\overline{BC} \cong \overline{KL}$	$\angle B \cong \angle K$
C and L	$\overline{CD} \cong \overline{LM}$	$\angle C \cong \angle L$
D and M	$\overline{AD} \cong \overline{JM}$	$\angle D \cong \angle M$

C. $\triangle FGH \cong \triangle PQR$. Give $m\angle F$ and the length of $\overline{QR}$.

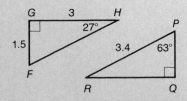

$\angle F$ corresponds to $\angle P$, so $m\angle F = m\angle P = 63°$. Side $\overline{QR}$ corresponds to side $\overline{GH}$, so the length of $\overline{QR}$ is 3.

218

Try $\triangle XYZ \cong \triangle XWZ$

a. Trace the figure. Mark the corresponding sides and angles on the figure.

b. Give the length of $\overline{ZY}$.

c. Give the measure of $\angle Y$.

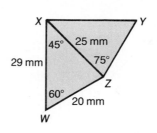

Practice Do the polygons appear to be congruent? Write *yes* or *no*.

1.

2.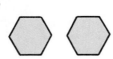

3.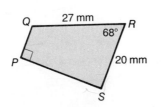

4.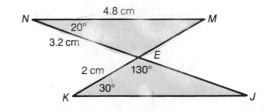

In Exercises 5–18, polygon *FCDE* $\cong$ polygon *PQRS* and $\triangle EMN \cong \triangle EKJ$.

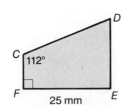

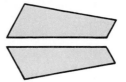

5. List all the corresponding sides and angles of *FCDE* and *PQRS* as shown in the table for Example B.

6. Trace this figure. Mark the corresponding sides and angles on the polygons as shown in Example B.

Give the measure of each segment or angle from the figures above.

7. $\overline{CD}$ 8. $\overline{DE}$ 9. $\overline{PS}$ 10. $\angle Q$ 11. $\angle D$ 12. $\angle S$

13. $\overline{KJ}$ 14. $\overline{EJ}$ 15. $\overline{EM}$ 16. $\angle J$ 17. $\angle M$ 18. $\angle NEM$

Apply Solve each problem.

19. The corresponding sides of two triangular logos are congruent. Can you be sure that the triangles are congruent?

★20. The corresponding angles of two triangular logos are congruent. Can you be sure that the triangles are congruent?

Similar Polygons

Career Andy Carson is a graphics designer. He designed this logo for Pam's Jeans. When the logo is used, it may differ in size, but it is always the same shape. The pentagons suggested by the logos are examples of **similar polygons**. Similar polygons have the same shape.

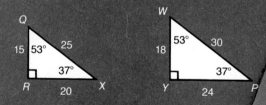

A. $\triangle RQX$ is similar to $\triangle YWP$. You can write $\triangle RQX \sim \triangle YWP$.

The corresponding angles of similar polygons are congruent.

$$\angle R \cong \angle Y \qquad \angle Q \cong \angle W \qquad \angle X \cong \angle P$$

The ratios of the lengths of corresponding sides of similar polygons form proportions.

$$\frac{RQ}{YW} = \frac{QX}{WP} = \frac{XR}{PY} \quad \begin{array}{l} \leftarrow \text{Lengths of } \triangle RQX \\ \leftarrow \text{Lengths of } \triangle YWP \end{array}$$

$$\frac{15}{18} = \frac{25}{30} = \frac{20}{24}$$

B. You can use proportions to find missing lengths of sides in similar polygons.

Polygon $ABCD \sim$ Polygon $EFGH$

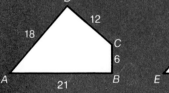

$$\frac{AD}{EH} = \frac{AB}{EF}$$

$\overline{EF}$ corresponds to $\overline{AB}$. Write a proportion using this pair. Write the cross-products and solve.

$$\frac{18}{12} = \frac{21}{n}$$

$$18 \times n = 12 \times 21$$

$$18n = 252$$

$$n = 14$$

The length of $\overline{EF}$ is 14.

Try

a. Are the polygons similar? Write *yes* or *no*.

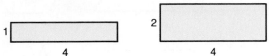

b. These polygons are similar. Find the missing length.

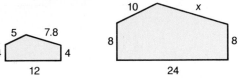

Practice Are the polygons similar? Write *yes* or *no*.

1.

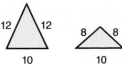

2.

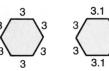

3.

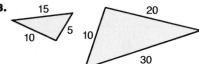

In each exercise the polygons are similar. Find the missing length.

4.

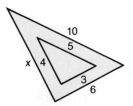

5.

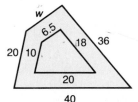

6.

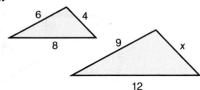

7.

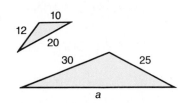

8.

★9.

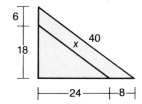

Apply Solve each problem.

10. Andy reduced this logo so that the ratio of the lengths of corresponding sides was 10 to 3. Find the length of each side in the reduced design.

11. Andy enlarged the logo so that the ratio of the lengths of corresponding sides was 2 to 5. Find the length of each side in the enlarged design.

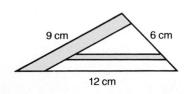

Practice: Lines, Angles, and Polygons

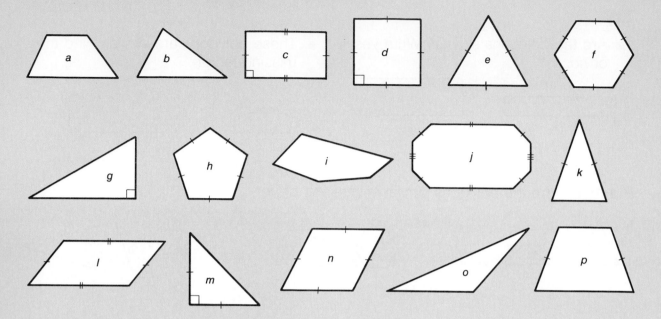

Use the pictures above. List every polygon that represents each of the following.

1. Quadrilateral

2. Scalene triangle

3. Rectangle

4. Obtuse triangle

5. Equilateral triangle

6. Pentagon

7. Acute triangle

8. Right triangle

9. Parallelogram

10. Rhombus

11. Hexagon

12. Isosceles triangle

13. Square

14. Octagon

15. Regular polygon

Draw and label each of the following.

16. $\overleftrightarrow{XY}$ intersecting $\overleftrightarrow{PQ}$ at point H

17. $\overleftrightarrow{AB}$ parallel to $\overleftrightarrow{CD}$

18. $\overrightarrow{LM}$ with its endpoint in $\overleftrightarrow{TU}$

19. $\overline{MN}$ in line x

In Exercises 20–23, use a compass and a straightedge.

20. Draw two segments and an acute angle. Construct a triangle with the two segments and the acute angle between them.

21. Draw three segments that could be the sides of a triangle. Then construct the triangle by using the three segments.

22. Draw $\overline{EF}$. Then construct the perpendicular bisector of $\overline{EF}$.

23. Draw $\angle M$. Then construct the bisector of $\angle M$.

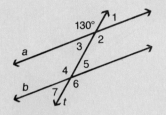 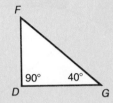

Lines a and b above are parallel. Give the measure of each angle.

24. $\angle 2$ **25.** $\angle 4$ **26.** $\angle 3$

27. In $\triangle DFG$, what is the measure of $\angle DFG$?

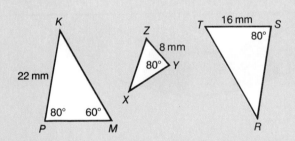

$\triangle KPM \cong \triangle RST$ and $\triangle KPM \sim \triangle XYZ$

28. Which side of $\triangle RST$ corresponds to $\overline{KM}$?

29. Give the measure of $\angle T$.

30. Give the measure of $\overline{PM}$.

31. Give the measure of $\angle Z$.

32. Give the measure of $\overline{XY}$.

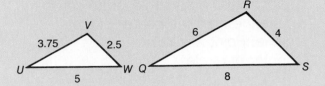

$\triangle UVW \sim \triangle QRS$. The ratio of corresponding sides of $\triangle UVW$ to $\triangle QRS$ is 5 to 8.

You can think of the ratio 5 to 8 as $5 \div 8$, or 0.625. The measure of each side of $\triangle UVW$ is 0.625 times the measure of the corresponding side of $\triangle QRS$.

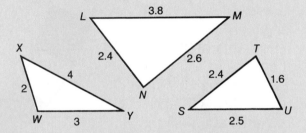

Use your calculator to find the length of each side in the resulting similar triangle.

1. $\triangle WXY$ is reduced so that the ratio of corresponding sides is 5 to 2.

2. $\triangle LMN$ is reduced so that the ratio of corresponding sides is 5 to 2.

3. $\triangle STU$ is reduced so that the ratio of corresponding sides is 20 to 9.

4. $\triangle WXY$ is enlarged so that the ratio of corresponding sides is 5 to 8.

5. $\triangle WXY$ is enlarged so that the ratio of corresponding sides is 16 to 25.

223

Circles

A. A circus ring suggests a *circle*. Every point on a circle is the same distance from the *center* of the circle. Point *X* is the center of circle *X*.

A *chord* is a segment with both endpoints on the circle. $\overline{AB}$ and $\overline{BD}$ are chords.

A *diameter* is a chord that contains the center of the circle. $\overline{BD}$ is a diameter.

A *radius* is a segment whose endpoints are the center and a point on the circle. $\overline{XB}$, $\overline{XD}$, and $\overline{XC}$ are radii.

An *arc* is part of a circle. Arc *CD* (or arc *DC*) is the shortest arc that joins points *C* and *D* on the circle. Arc *CD* can be written $\overarc{CD}$.

B. Some angles in circles have special names.

$\angle DXC$ is a *central angle* because its vertex is the center of the circle. It cuts off $\overarc{DC}$.

$\angle ABD$ is an *inscribed angle* because its vertex is on the circle. It cuts off $\overarc{AD}$.

C. Two perpendicular diameters are shown in circle *H*. Each of the four central angles is a right angle.

The number of degrees around the center of a circle is $4 \times 90°$, or $360°$.

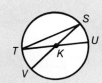

Try Use circle L above.

a. Name all the diameters shown.

b. Name the inscribed angles that cut off $\overset{\frown}{KN}$.

Practice Use the circles above. Name as many examples of each of the following as you can.

1. Radii in circle K

2. Diameters in circle K

3. Chords in circle H

4. Central angles in circle K

5. Inscribed angles in circle H

6. Name the central angle that cuts off $\overset{\frown}{SU}$ in circle K.

7. Name the inscribed angle that cuts off $\overset{\frown}{SU}$ in circle K.

8. In circle L, what is the sum of the measures of the four angles with vertex L?

9. In circle L, $m\angle MLN = 85°$. What is the measure of each of the other angles with vertex L?

Apply Solve each problem by drawing circles and measuring the segments or angles.

10. Draw 3 circles with different radii. Measure a diameter and a radius in each. What do you notice?

*11. Draw a circle with 3 inscribed angles that cut off the same arc, as shown in circle X. Measure each inscribed angle. What do you notice?

*12. Draw 3 circles with different radii. In each, draw an inscribed angle and a central angle that cut off the same arc, as shown in circle Y. In each circle, measure both angles. What do you notice?

Three-Dimensional Figures

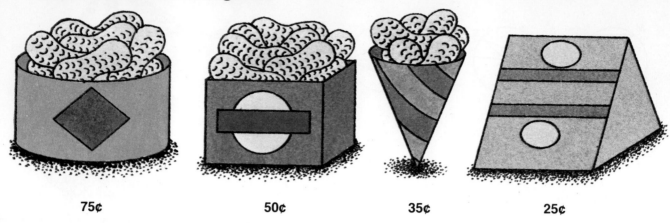

| 75¢ | 50¢ | 35¢ | 25¢ |

Vendors sell peanuts at the circus. Each container they use suggests a three-dimensional figure.

A. A *polyhedron* is a three-dimensional figure in which all the surfaces, or *faces*, are shaped like polygons.

A *prism* has two parallel and congruent bases. A prism can be described by the shape of its bases.

A *pyramid* has one base. A pyramid can also be described by the shape of its base.

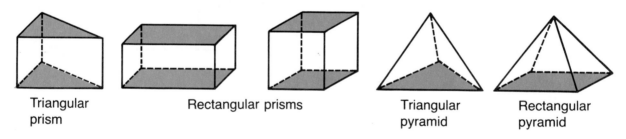

Triangular prism

Rectangular prisms

Triangular pyramid

Rectangular pyramid

B. Three-dimensional figures with curved surfaces are not polyhedrons.

A *cylinder* has two circular bases that are congruent.

A *cone* has one circular base.

A *sphere* has no base. Every point on a sphere is the same distance from its center.

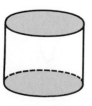

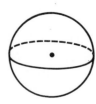

226

Try Name each figure. If the figure is a polyhedron, include the shape of the base in the name.

a.

b.

c.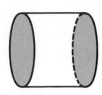

d.

Practice Name each figure. If the figure is a polyhedron, include the shape of the base in the name.

1.

2.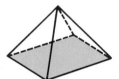

3.

4.

5.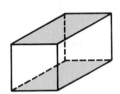

6.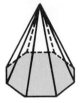

7.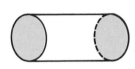

8.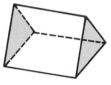

9. The bases of a prism can be shaped like any polygon. What is the shape of the other faces?

10. The base of a pyramid can be shaped like any polygon. What is the shape of the other faces?

11. If the base of a pyramid is octagonal, how many faces does the pyramid have?

12. If the bases of a prism are hexagonal, how many faces does the prism have?

★13. Imagine opening up a rectangular prism and putting it on a flat surface. Sketch the resulting figure.

★14. Imagine opening up a cylinder and putting it on a flat surface. Sketch the resulting figure.

Apply Name the three-dimensional figure suggested by each of the containers on page 226.

15. 75¢ size
16. 50¢ size
17. 35¢ size
18. 25¢ size

Problem Solving: Solve a Simpler Problem

Two faces of a polyhedron intersect to form an *edge of the polyhedron*. Three or more faces intersect to form a *vertex of the polyhedron*.

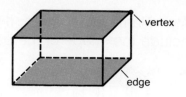

Read   Each base of a prism has 100 sides. How many edges does this prism have?

Plan   Solve simpler cases for which you can draw pictures and count. Then try to find a pattern that you can use to solve the original problem.

Solve   A triangle has 3 sides and a triangular prism has 9 edges.

Triangular prism

A rectangle has 4 sides and a rectangular prism has 12 edges.

Rectangular prism

A pentagon has 5 sides and a pentagonal prism has 15 edges.

Pentagonal prism

Observe that for each prism, the number of edges is 3 times the number of sides in a base. This pattern checks for an octagonal prism, which has 24, or 3 × 8, edges.

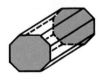

Octagonal prism

Using this pattern, you find that a prism with 100-sided bases has 3 × 100, or 300, edges.

Answer   The prism has 300 edges.

Look Back   In a prism with 100-sided bases, each of the two bases has 100 edges, and there are 100 segments connecting the corresponding vertices of the bases. Thus, there are 100 + 100 + 100, or 300, edges.

228

Try How many edges does each pyramid have?

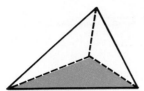 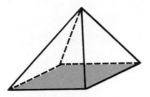 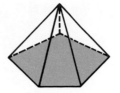 

a. Triangular pyramid

b. Rectangular pyramid

c. Pentagonal pyramid

d. Octagonal pyramid

e. For Problems a–d, compare the number of sides in the base and the number of edges. How many edges are in a pyramid with a 100-sided base?

Apply Complete the table.

	Number of edges E	Number of vertices V	Number of faces F	$V + F$	$(V + F) - E$
Triangular prism	9	**1.**	**2.**	**3.**	**4.**
Rectangular prism	12	**5.**	**6.**	**7.**	**8.**
Pentagonal prism	15	**9.**	**10.**	**11.**	**12.**
Octagonal prism	24	**13.**	**14.**	**15.**	**16.**
Prism (100-sided bases)	300	**17.**	**18.**	**19.**	**20.**
Prism (n-sided bases)	★**21.**	★**22.**	★**23.**	★**24.**	★**25.**
Triangular pyramid	**26.**	**27.**	**28.**	**29.**	**30.**
Rectangular pyramid	**31.**	**32.**	**33.**	**34.**	**35.**
Pentagonal pyramid	**36.**	**37.**	**38.**	**39.**	**40.**
Octagonal pyramid	**41.**	**42.**	**43.**	**44.**	**45.**
Pyramid (100-sided base)	**46.**	**47.**	**48.**	**49.**	**50.**
Pyramid (n-sided base)	★**51.**	★**52.**	★**53.**	★**54.**	★**55.**

★**56.** Leonhard Euler, who lived in the 18th century, made an interesting observation about the number of edges, vertices, and faces of a polyhedron. What do you think it was?

Chapter 7 Test

Make a sketch.

1. $\overline{LM}$

2. line d ∥ line e

3. Use a protractor to draw an angle of 35°.

4. Is the angle you drew acute, right, or obtuse?

5. Angle A has a measure of 60°. Give the measure of its complement.

6. Name two pairs of alternate interior angles.

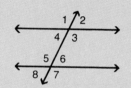

7. Construct an angle congruent to ∠G.

8. Construct the bisector of ∠G.

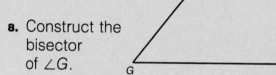

9. Construct a triangle congruent to △MNO. Use $\overline{MO}$, ∠O, and $\overline{NO}$.

Solve this problem.

10. Irma is making a triangular flag. The lengths of two sides are 9 cm and 12 cm. What is the least possible length for the third side? Use whole numbers only.

11. Which describes the triangle, right-isosceles or right-scalene?

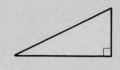

12. What is the name of a parallelogram that has exactly two parallel sides?

△ABC ≅ △DEF

13. Give the length of $\overline{DE}$.

14. Give m∠F.

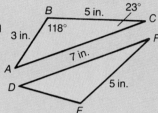

15. These polygons are similar. Find the missing length.

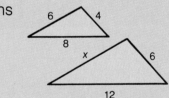

16. Name an inscribed angle of circle J.

17. Name a radius of circle J.

Name each figure.

18.

19.

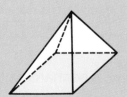

Solve this problem.

20. The base of a prism has 25 sides. How many edges does the prism have?

Numerical Prefixes

Use these prefixes and their meanings to help you match each word given below with its definition.

bi: 2	tri: 3	quad: 4	pent: 5	hex: 6
hept: 7	oct: 8	non: 9	dec: 10	dodec: 12

a. Decapod   **b.** Tripod   **c.** Trisyllable   **d.** Pentathlon

e. Quadruple   **f.** Decameter   **g.** Triweekly   **h.** Octave

i. Tricolor   **j.** Dodecahedron   **k.** Hexapod   **l.** Octopus

m. Octogenarian   **n.** Bilingual   **o.** Decagram   **p.** Bilateral

q. Triennial   **r.** Nonagenarian   **s.** Trio   **t.** Bicentennial

1. Stanza with eight lines

2. Polyhedron with twelve faces

3. A six-footed animal

4. Ten grams

5. Having three colors

6. Person in his or her eighties

7. To multiply by 4

8. Able to speak two languages

9. Animal with eight tentacles

10. Three-legged camera stand

11. Published three times a week

12. Occurring every three years

13. Having two symmetric sides

14. Animal with ten legs

15. Having three syllables

16. Two-hundredth anniversary

17. Group of three singers

18. Athletic contest with 5 events

19. Ten meters

20. Person in his or her nineties

MAINTENANCE

Find each answer.

1. What is 10% of 75?

2. 3% of 7 is what number?

3. $12\frac{1}{2}$% of 80 is what number?

4. What is 150% of 6?

5. What percent of 50 is 25?

6. 42 is what percent of 30?

7. 16.8 is what percent of 21?

8. 31 is what percent of 124?

9. 24 is 80% of what number?

10. 9 is $33\frac{1}{3}$% of what number?

11. 125% of what number is 10?

12. 1.5% of what number is 60?

13. 200% of 0.6 is what number?

14. 55 is what percent of 55?

15. 1% of 300 is what number?

16. 0.25% of what number is 2?

Solve each problem.

17. On a map of Wisconsin, 1.5 cm represents an actual distance of 50 km. Green Bay and Madison are 6.3 cm apart on the map. How many kilometers is Green Bay from Madison?

18. A car-company logo is 18 mm high. If the logo is reduced so that this figure and the corresponding parts of the reduced figure are in the ratio 3 to 2, what is the height of the reduced figure?

19. A recipe calls for $2\frac{1}{4}$ cups of diced chicken. How much chicken is needed for $2\frac{1}{2}$ times the recipe?

20. A computer prints 55 lines on a page. Marcia's program is 1,832 lines long. How many pages will be needed to print it?

21. A slice of cheese is about 0.4 cm thick. How thick is a package of 48 slices of cheese?

22. A word contains 3 vowels. If vowels represent 30% of the word, how many letters are in the word?

23. East Avenue and Third Street intersect to form four angles. If the measure of one of the angles is 35°, give the measure of each of the other angles.

24. *Estimation* The population of St. Paul is about 263,000 and the population of Minneapolis is about 346,000. Estimate the total population of these cities.

Perimeter, Area, and Volume

$V = \pi r^2 h$

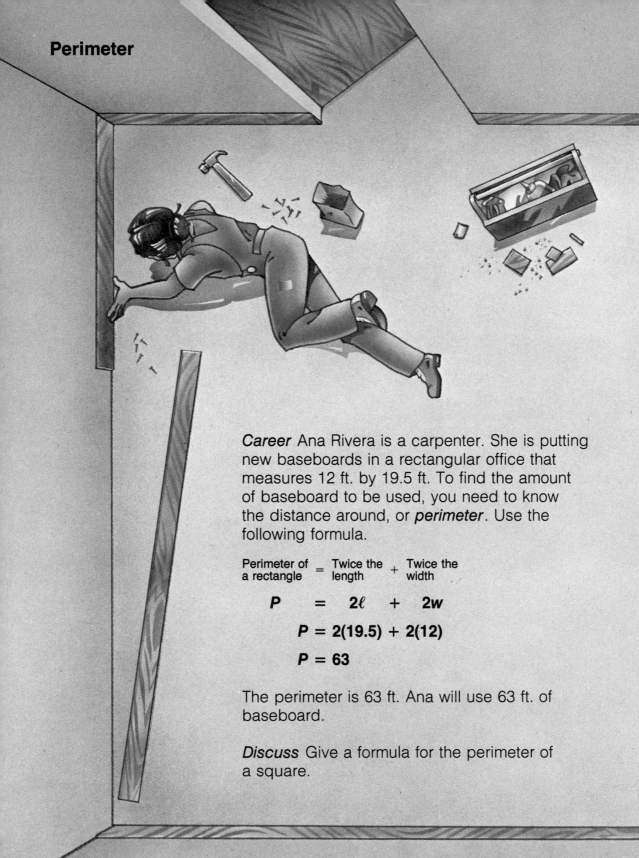

Career Ana Rivera is a carpenter. She is putting new baseboards in a rectangular office that measures 12 ft. by 19.5 ft. To find the amount of baseboard to be used, you need to know the distance around, or *perimeter*. Use the following formula.

Perimeter of a rectangle	=	Twice the length	+	Twice the width
P	=	**2ℓ**	+	**2w**

$$P = 2(19.5) + 2(12)$$

$$P = 63$$

The perimeter is 63 ft. Ana will use 63 ft. of baseboard.

Discuss Give a formula for the perimeter of a square.

Try Find the perimeter of each polygon.

a.

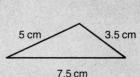

5 cm   3.5 cm

7.5 cm

b.

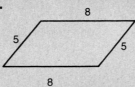

8

5   5

8

c. Square with sides 9 inches long

Practice Find the perimeter of each polygon.

1.

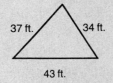

37 ft.   34 ft.

43 ft.

2.

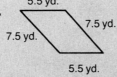

5.5 yd.

7.5 yd.   7.5 yd.

5.5 yd.

3.

12 in.

12 in.

4.

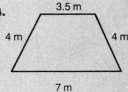

3.5 m

4 m   4 m

7 m

5.

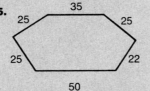

35

25   25

25   22

50

*6.

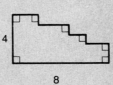

4

8

7. A rectangle 0.2 m by 4.1 m

8. A rhombus with sides 3 ft. long

9. A parallelogram whose sides are 3.8 cm and 9.2 cm

10. A regular hexagon with sides 4.5 ft. long

Apply Solve each problem.

11. How much baseboard is needed for a rectangular office 8 ft. by 10 ft.?

12. How much ceiling molding is needed for a room that is 14 ft. by 12 ft.?

Area

A. *Career* Thomas Redhawk, a building manager, has a vacant office that measures 10 ft. by 15 ft. One of his clients needs 200 sq. ft. of office space. Is the office large enough for the client?

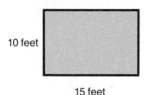

10 feet

15 feet

The number of square units that a figure encloses is its area. Find the area of the office.

Formula for the area of a rectangle

$A = \ell w$ *The area of a rectangle is equal to the length times the width.*

$$A = \ell w$$
$$A = (15)(10)$$
$$A = 150$$

The area of the available office is 150 sq. ft. This office is not large enough for the client.

Note that area is always measured in square units.

Discuss If each side of a square is s units, how might you express the area of the square?

B. To find the area of this parallelogram, you can "rearrange" the parts to form a rectangle with the same dimensions.

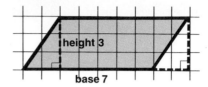

height 3

base 7

$$A = 7(3)$$
$$A = 21$$

The area of the parallelogram is 21 square units.

Formula for the area of a parallelogram

$A = bh$ *The area of a parallelogram is equal to the base times the height.*

C. You can think of a triangle as one half of a parallelogram that has the same base and height.

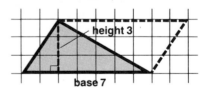

height 3

base 7

$$A = \tfrac{1}{2}(7)(3)$$
$$A = 10.5$$

The area of the triangle is 10.5 square units.

Formula for the area of a triangle

$A = \tfrac{1}{2}bh$ *The area of a triangle is equal to one half the base times the height.*

Try Find the area of each polygon.

a.

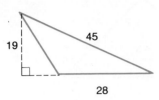

b.

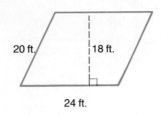

c. A rectangle 8 m by 6 m

d. A square with sides 8 cm long

Practice Find the area of each polygon.

1.

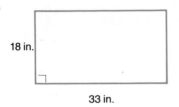

18 in.

33 in.

2.

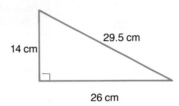

14 cm

29.5 cm

26 cm

3.

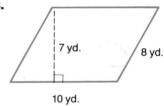

7 yd.

8 yd.

10 yd.

4.

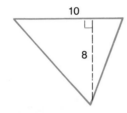

10

8

5.

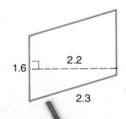

1.6

2.2

2.3

6.

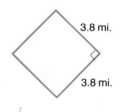

3.8 mi.

3.8 mi.

7. A parallelogram with base 6 and height 9

8. A triangle with base 20 inches and height 7 inches

9. A rectangle with length 12 feet and width 5 feet

10. A square with sides 6 m long

Apply Solve each problem.

11. Find the area of an office with length 18 feet and width 24 feet.

12. How much carpeting is needed for a hallway that is 25 yards by 3 yards?

★13. How many 1-foot-square ceiling tiles are needed for the office in Problem 11?

★14. How many 3-foot-square carpeting tiles are needed for the office in Problem 11?

Area of Trapezoids and Composite Figures

A. A conference room has some tables with tops shaped like congruent trapezoids. When two of these tables are placed together as shown, they form a parallelogram. Find the area of one of the table tops.

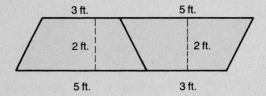

First find the area of the two table tops. Then multiply by $\frac{1}{2}$.

$A = bh$

$A = (3 + 5)2$

$A = 16$

The area of one table top is $\frac{1}{2}(16)$ sq. ft., or 8 sq. ft.

Formula for the area of a trapezoid

$$A = \tfrac{1}{2}(b_1 + b_2)h$$

The area of a trapezoid is one half times the sum of the bases times the height.

B. Find the area of the figure.

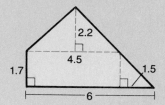

Partition the figure into two triangles and a rectangle. Find the area of each polygon and add.

Area of
top triangle $= \frac{1}{2}(4.5)(2.2)$
$= 4.95$

Area of
rectangle $= 4.5(1.7)$
$= 7.65$

Area of
small triangle $= \frac{1}{2}(1.5)(1.7)$
$= 1.275$

Area of
quadrilateral $= 4.95 + 7.65 + 1.275$
$= 13.875$

The area of the figure is 13.875, or nearly 14, square units.

Try Find the area of each polygon. Give answers to the nearest tenth.

a.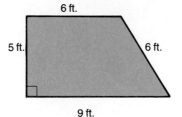

b.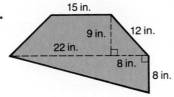

c. A trapezoid with bases 1.5 feet and 4.5 feet and a height of 2 feet

Practice Find each area. Give decimal answers to the nearest tenth.

1.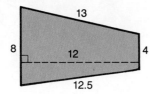

2.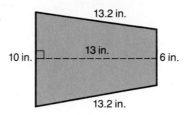

3.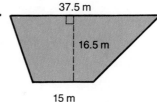

4.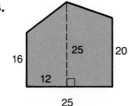

5.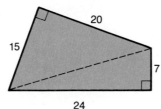

6.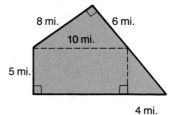

7. A trapezoid with bases 3 m and 2 m and a height of 1.5 m

8. A trapezoid with bases 5 m and 8 m and a height of 3 m

Apply Solve each problem. Give answers to the nearest tenth.

9. Six of the tables in Example A are arranged as shown below. Find the area of the work space formed.

10. An office floor-plan is shown below. Find the amount of carpeting needed for the office.

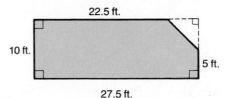

Circumference and the Number Pi

The distance around
a circle is its *circumference.*
The ratio of the circumference *C* to
the diameter *d* is the same for all circles.
This ratio is called *pi* (π).

$$\frac{C}{d} = \pi$$

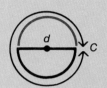

π is a decimal that never ends and
that has no repeating pattern. The
numbers 3.14 and $3\frac{1}{7}$ are often used as
approximations for π.

$\pi = 3.141592653589 \ldots$

Formula for the circumference of a circle

$C = \pi d$ *The circumference of a circle is equal to π times the diameter.*

$C = 2\pi r$ *The circumference of a circle is equal to
2 times π times the radius.*

The length of the *semicircle*, or half circle, is one half
the circumference of the circle.

Carolyn runs on a circular track that has a diameter of 420 feet. How
far does she run in one lap around the track?

Find the circumference of the track. Use 3.14 for π.

$$C = \pi d$$
$$C \approx (3.14)(420)$$
$$C \approx 1{,}318.8$$

Carolyn runs about
1,319 feet.

Try

a. Find the circumference of a circle with a radius of $5\frac{3}{4}$. Use $3\frac{1}{7}$ for π.

b. To the nearest tenth, find the length of a semicircle with a diameter of 7.2 m. Use 3.14 for π.

Practice Find the circumference of a circle with the given diameter d or radius r. Use 3.14 or $3\frac{1}{7}$ for π. Round each decimal answer to the nearest whole unit.

1. $d = 20$ in.

2. $d = 40$ yd.

3. $r = 8$

4. $r = 20$

5. $r = 1$ mi.

6. $d = 8.4$ mi.

7. $d = 2.5$ cm

8. $r = 6.1$ cm

9. $r = 13$

10. $r = 4.2$

11. $d = 6\frac{1}{2}$ yd.

12. $r = \frac{1}{3}$ yd.

13. Find the length of a semicircle with a diameter of $1\frac{2}{5}$ miles. Use $3\frac{1}{7}$ for π.

14. To the nearest tenth, find the length of a semicircle with a radius of 5.6 km. Use 3.14 for π.

Apply Solve each problem.

15. Find the distance around a circular track with a radius of 150 ft. Use $3\frac{1}{7}$ for π.

*16. Carolyn wants to run about 2 miles. How many laps would she need to make around the track in the example on page 240?

MAINTENANCE

Give the value of the 5 in each decimal.

1. 0.2534

2. 1.3452

3. 16.501

4. 0.00125

5. 2.12754

Compare the decimals. Use $<$, $>$, or $=$.

6. 0.64 ● 0.06

7. 0.5478 ● 0.54781

8. 0:01 ● 0.001

Write a number that is between the two given numbers.

9. 0.54   0.546

10. 6.3   6.37

11. 0.002   0.003

Area of Circles

The drawings show how the area of a circle can be related to the area of a parallelogram. The parallelogram that encloses the wedges from the circle has an area of bh, or about $\left(\frac{1}{2}C\right)r$.

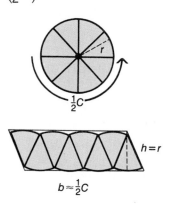

You can find the area of a circle by multiplying one half the circumference and the radius.

$$\tfrac{1}{2}Cr = \tfrac{1}{2}(2\pi r)r = \pi r^2$$

Formula for the area of a circle

$A = \pi r^2$ *The area of a circle is equal to pi times the radius squared.*

The center jump circle on a basketball court has a radius of 2 ft. Find its area.

$A = \pi r^2$

$A \approx 3.14(2)^2$

$A \approx 3.14(4)$

$A \approx 12.56$

The area of the jump circle is about 12.56 sq. ft.

Try Find the area of each circle. Use 3.14 for π. Round to the nearest tenth.

a. Radius of 7.0 ft.

b. Diameter of 8.5

c. Find the area of a semicircle with a radius of $3\frac{1}{2}$ ft. Use $3\frac{1}{7}$ for π.

Practice Find the area of a circle with the given diameter or radius. Use 3.14 or $3\frac{1}{7}$ for π. Round each decimal answer to the nearest tenth.

1. $r = 2.0$ cm

2. $d = 5.0$ m

3. $d = 3$ yd.

4. $r = 4$ ft.

5. $d = 7$ in.

6. $d = 18$ yd.

7. $r = 7$ in.

8. $d = 15$ ft.

9. $r = 3.8$ yd.

10. $r = 5.0$

11. $r = 14.0$

12. $d = 9.0$

13. $r = 13.0$

14. $d = 8.6$ mi.

15. $d = 5.2$ m

16. $r = 7.6$ cm

17. Find the area of a semicircle with a diameter of 20 in. Use 3.14 for π.

18. Find the area of a semicircle with a radius of 7 ft. Use $3\frac{1}{7}$ for π.

Apply Solve each problem. Use 3.14 for π. Round each answer to the nearest whole unit.

19. The foul circle has a diameter of 12 ft. Find its area.

20. The restraining ring has a radius of 6 ft. Find its area.

*21. The free-throw key is made up of a semicircle and a rectangle. Find its area.

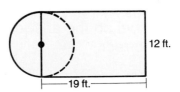

19 ft.   12 ft.

Some calculators have a $\boxed{\pi}$ key. To find the area of a circle with radius 5, use this sequence.

Press: $\boxed{\pi}\ \boxed{\times}\ 5\ \boxed{\times}\ 5\ \boxed{=}$

Display: *78.539816*

Find the area and circumference of a circle with the given radius or diameter. Round each answer to the nearest tenth.

1. $r = 10.1$ cm

2. $r = 25.25$ ft.

3. $d = 18.6$ m

4. $d = 36.5$ in.

Problem Solving: Multiple-Step Problems

Read   Mr. Grabowski wants to put plastic edging around his garden. How much edging does he need?

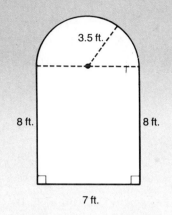

Plan   Find the length of the semicircle. Add it to the other three distances.

Solve   The length of a semicircle is one half the circumference of a circle with the same radius, so find $\frac{1}{2}C$. Use 3.14 for π.

$$\tfrac{1}{2}C = \tfrac{1}{2}(2\pi r)$$

$$\tfrac{1}{2}C = \pi r$$

$$\tfrac{1}{2}C \approx 3.14(3.5)$$

$$\tfrac{1}{2}C \approx 10.99$$

Add the four distances.

$$P \approx 8 + 7 + 8 + 10.99$$

$$P \approx 33.99$$

Answer   Mr. Grabowski needs about 34 feet of edging.

Look Back   Check that you put the correct label on the answer. "Feet" is correct.

Try   Solve the problem. Use 3.14 for π.

a. How much fertilizer does Mr. Grabowski need for his garden if 1 pound of fertilizer is needed for every 10 square feet of land?

Apply Solve each problem. Use 3.14 for π.

1. The edging in the example on page 244 is sold in packages that contain 30 feet and cost $9.99. How much will it cost Mr. Grabowski to buy enough edging to go around his garden?

2. Mr. Grabowski has 6 trees in his yard. He wants to put edging in a 3-foot-diameter circle around each tree. How much edging will he need for the trees?

3. The Grabowskis' house and lot are both rectangular. The house is 50 feet by 30 feet and the lot is 92 feet by 140 feet. How much land is available for lawn?

4. The Grabowskis' backyard is 92 feet by 80 feet. How many pounds of bluegrass seed are needed to seed the lawn if one pound seeds 650 square feet?

Suppose Mr. Grabowski's garden looked like this.

5. What is the area of this garden?

★6. How much more or less fertilizer would be needed?

★7. How much more or less edging would be needed?

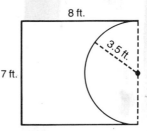

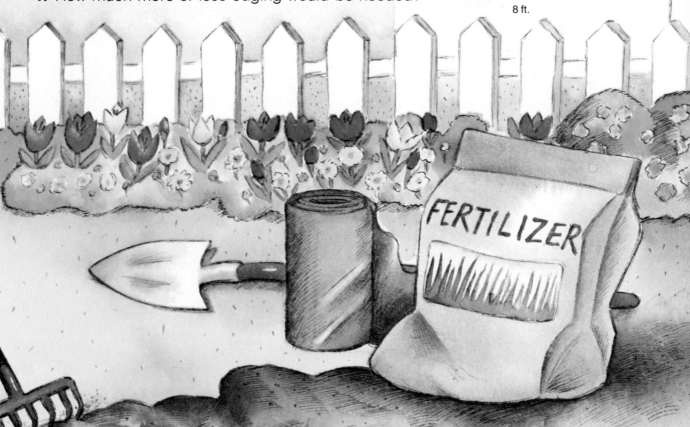

Surface Area of Polyhedrons

Ken and Corrine Wong are making a tent in the shape
of a square pyramid. The floor of the tent is a 6-foot
square. The four triangular sides have a height of
5 feet. How much canvas is used in the tent?

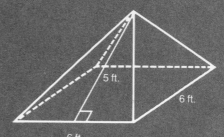

The triangular faces have the same height because the
base is shaped like a regular polygon. This height is
the **slant height** of the pyramid.

*The surface area of a polyhedron is the sum of the
areas of its bases and its other faces.*

$$A = \text{area of the base} + \text{areas of the other faces}$$

$$\text{Area of the base} = 6 \times 6$$
$$= 36$$

$$\text{Area of each of the other four faces} = \tfrac{1}{2}(6)(5)$$
$$= 15$$

$$\text{Surface area} = 36 + 15 + 15 + 15 + 15$$
$$= 96$$

96 square feet of canvas is
used in the tent.

Try Find the surface area of each polygon.

a. Triangular prism

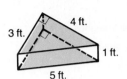

3 ft.
4 ft.
1 ft.
5 ft.

b. Rectangular prism

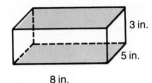

3 in.
5 in.
8 in.

c. Rectangular pyramid

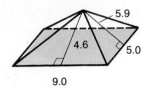

5.9
4.6
5.0
9.0

Practice Find the surface area of each polyhedron. Give each decimal answer to the nearest tenth.

1. Rectangular prism

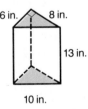

6 cm
8 cm
10 cm

2. Cube

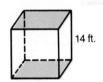

14 ft.

3. Rectangular pyramid

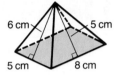

6 cm
5 cm
5 cm
8 cm

4. Triangular prism

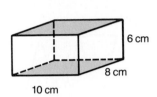

6 in.
8 in.
13 in.
10 in.

5. Square pyramid

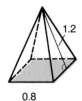

1.2
0.8

6. Rectangular prism

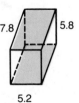

7.8
5.8
5.2

Apply Solve each problem.

7. How much canvas is needed for this tent? Be sure to include the rectangular floor.

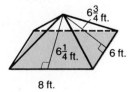

$6\frac{3}{4}$ ft.
$6\frac{1}{4}$ ft.
6 ft.
8 ft.

★8. How many 6-inch-square tiles are needed to tile the sides and bottom of this swimming pool?

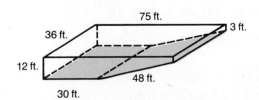

75 ft.
3 ft.
36 ft.
12 ft.
48 ft.
30 ft.

Surface Area of Cylinders and Cones

A. Corrine is making a tote bag for some of her camping gear. It has the shape of a cylinder with a diameter of 8 in. and a height of 18 in. How much canvas does she need for the tote?

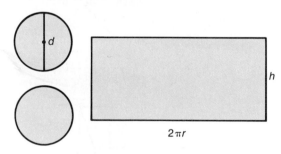

8 in.

18 in.

The two bases are circular, and the curved portion forms a rectangle when "opened up."

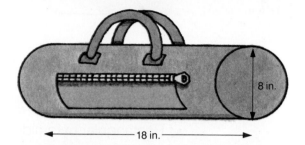

d

h

$2\pi r$

Add these areas to find the surface area.

$$A = \begin{array}{c}\text{Areas} \\ \text{of the} \\ \text{bases}\end{array} + \begin{array}{c}\text{Area of} \\ \text{the curved} \\ \text{surface}\end{array}$$

$A = 2\pi r^2 + 2\pi rh$

$A \approx 2(3.14)(4)^2 + 2(3.14)(4)(18)$

$A \approx 100.48 + 452.16$

$A \approx 552.64$

Corrine needs about 553 sq. in. of canvas for the tote.

B. Find the surface area of this cone. Use 3.14 for π.

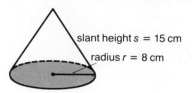

slant height s = 15 cm

radius r = 8 cm

A cone consists of two pieces. The base is circular, and the curved surface is fan shaped when "opened up." It can be cut into smaller pieces and rearranged to resemble a parallelogram.

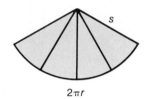

s

$2\pi r$

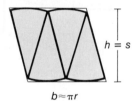

$h = s$

$b \approx \pi r$

Add these areas to find the surface area.

$$A = \begin{array}{c}\text{Area} \\ \text{of the} \\ \text{base}\end{array} + \begin{array}{c}\text{Area of} \\ \text{the curved} \\ \text{surface}\end{array}$$

$A = \pi r^2 + \pi rs$

$A \approx 3.14(8)^2 + 3.14(8)(15)$

$A \approx 200.96 + 376.8$

$A \approx 578 \text{ cm}^2$

Try Find the total surface area. Use 3.14 for π, and round each answer to the nearest whole unit.

a.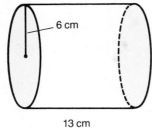

6 cm

13 cm

b.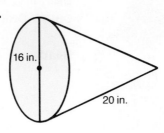

16 in.

20 in.

Practice Find the total surface area. For Exercises 1 and 2, use $3\frac{1}{7}$ for π. For Exercises 3–6, use 3.14 for π, and round each answer to the nearest tenth.

1.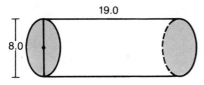

19.0

8.0

2.

3 in.

22 in.

3.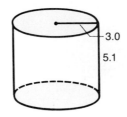

14 in.

18 in.

4.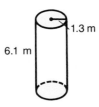

1.3 m

6.1 m

5.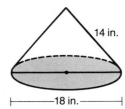

3.0

5.1

*6.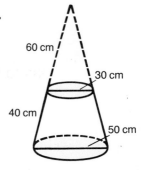

60 cm

30 cm

40 cm

50 cm

Apply Solve each problem. Use $3\frac{1}{7}$ for π.

7. How much canvas is needed for a cylindrical tent case that has a 14-inch diameter and that is 29 inches long?

8. How much canvas is needed for a cylindrical tent-frame case with an 8-inch diameter and a length of 75 inches?

Problem Solving: Use Estimation

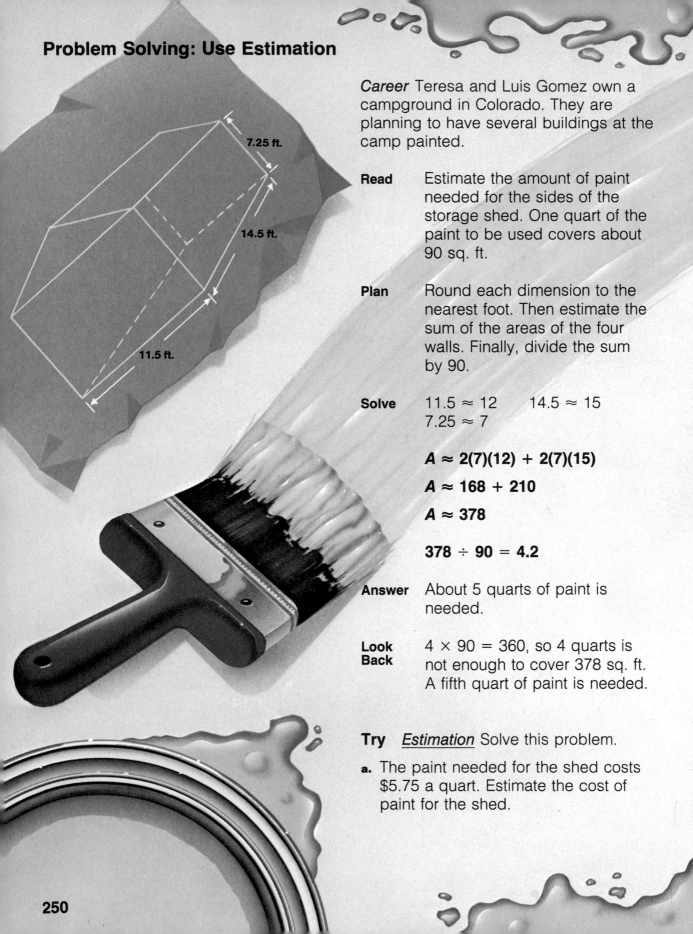

7.25 ft.

14.5 ft.

11.5 ft.

Career Teresa and Luis Gomez own a campground in Colorado. They are planning to have several buildings at the camp painted.

Read   Estimate the amount of paint needed for the sides of the storage shed. One quart of the paint to be used covers about 90 sq. ft.

Plan   Round each dimension to the nearest foot. Then estimate the sum of the areas of the four walls. Finally, divide the sum by 90.

Solve $11.5 \approx 12$ $14.5 \approx 15$
           $7.25 \approx 7$

$$A \approx 2(7)(12) + 2(7)(15)$$

$$A \approx 168 + 210$$

$$A \approx 378$$

$$378 \div 90 = 4.2$$

Answer   About 5 quarts of paint is needed.

Look Back $4 \times 90 = 360$, so 4 quarts is not enough to cover 378 sq. ft. A fifth quart of paint is needed.

Try *Estimation* Solve this problem.

a. The paint needed for the shed costs $5.75 a quart. Estimate the cost of paint for the shed.

Apply *Estimation* Solve each problem. Use 3.14 for π.

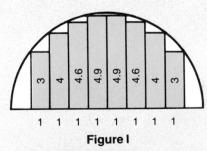

7.25 ft.

18.25 ft.

9.5 ft.

1. Estimate the amount of paint required for the walls of this garage. One quart of the paint to be used covers about 110 sq. ft.

2. Estimate the cost of paint for a garage that has 280 sq. ft. to be painted. One quart of the paint costs $6.25 and covers about 110 sq. ft.

3. Estimate the amount of paint needed to paint the outside of 6 storage drums, each with a diameter of 4.5 ft. and a height of 8.75 ft. The tops and bottoms of the drums are to be painted also. One gallon of paint covers about 425 sq. ft.

★4. Estimate the cost of the paint in Problem 3 if the paint costs $18.75 a gallon.

★5. Estimate the amount of paint needed to paint both sides of a 6-ft. solid fence around a lot that is 75 ft. by 125 ft. One gallon of paint covers about 450 sq. ft.

★6. Estimate the cost of the paint in Problem 5 if the paint costs $21.65 a gallon.

The area of a semicircle is one half the area of a circle with the same radius.

1. Find the shaded area in Figure I.

2. Find the shaded area in Figure II.

3. To approximate the area of the semicircle, find the average of your answer to Exercises 1 and 2.

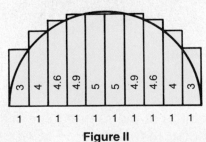

Figure I

Figure II

Volume of Prisms and Cylinders

Prism   Cylinder

These food containers are manufactured by the Boxco Container Company.

Formula for the volume of a prism or a cylinder

V = Bh   *The volume of any prism or cylinder is equal
to the area of the base times the height.*

A. Find the volume of this rectangular prism.

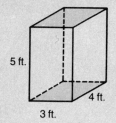

5 ft.

4 ft.

3 ft.

V = Bh   Since the base is
                  rectangular,
V = ℓwh $B = \ell(w)$.

V = 3(4)(5)

V = 60

The volume of the rectangular prism is 60 cubic feet.

B. Find the volume of this cylinder. Use 3.14 for π.

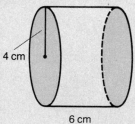

4 cm

6 cm

V = Bh   Since the base
                  is circular,
$V = \pi r^2 h$ $B = \pi r^2$.

$V \approx 3.14(4)^2(6)$

$V \approx 301.44$

The volume of the cylinder is about 301 cubic centimeters.

Try Find the volume of each prism or cylinder. In Exercise b, use $3\frac{1}{7}$ for π.
In Exercise d, use 3.14 for π and round the answer to the nearest unit.

a.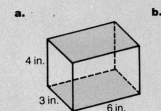
4 in.
3 in.
6 in.

b.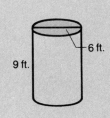
6 ft.
9 ft.

c. Hexagonal prism with base area 25 cm² and height 15 cm

d. Cylinder with radius 5 and height 11

Practice Find the volume of each prism or cylinder. Use 3.14 or $3\frac{1}{7}$ for π.
Round each decimal answer to the nearest unit.

1.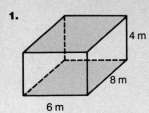
4 m
8 m
6 m

2.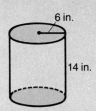
6 in.
14 in.

3.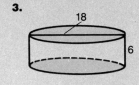
18
6

4.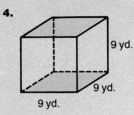
9 yd.
9 yd.
9 yd.

5.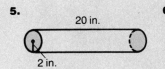
20 in.
2 in.

6.
3 ft. 4 ft.
9 ft.

7.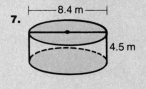
8.4 m
4.5 m

8.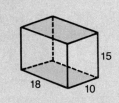
15
18 10

9. Cylinder with diameter 18 inches and height 7 inches

10. Square prism with side length 8 cm and height 20 cm

11. Pentagonal prism with base area 38 cm² and height 6 cm

12. Cube with each edge 7 inches long

Apply Solve each problem. Use 3.14 for π. Round answers to the nearest tenth.

13. Find the volume of a soup can that has a diameter of 7 cm and a height of 10 cm.

14. Find the volume of a cracker box that is a square prism. One side of the square base is 4.5 inches. The height is 9.0 inches.

★15. How many square centimeters of metal are needed to make the container in Problem 13?

★16. How much cardboard is needed for the cracker box in Problem 14?

Volume of Pyramids and Cones

Pyramid   Cone

The Boxco Company also makes these cartons.

Formula for the volume of a pyramid or a cone

$V = \frac{1}{3}Bh$ *The volume of any pyramid or cone is equal to one third times the area of the base times the height.*

A. Find the volume of the pyramid.

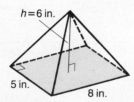

$h=6$ in.

5 in.

8 in.

$V = \frac{1}{3}Bh$ Since the base is rectangular, $B = \ell(w)$.

$V = \frac{1}{3}(\ell)(w)(h)$

$V = \frac{1}{3}(5)(8)(6)$

$V = 80$

The volume of the pyramid is 80 cu. in.

B. Find the volume of the cone. Use 3.14 for π.

$h=9$ cm

$r=4$ cm

$V = \frac{1}{3}Bh$ Since the base is circular, $B = \pi r^2$.

$V = \frac{1}{3}(\pi)(r^2)(h)$

$V \approx \frac{1}{3}(3.14)(4^2)(9)$

$V \approx 150.72$

The volume of the cone is about 151 cm³.

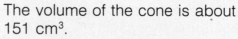

Try Find the volume of each pyramid or cone. In Exercise b, use 3.14 for π and round the answer to the nearest unit. In Exercise c, use $3\frac{1}{7}$ for π.

a.

b.

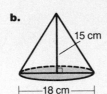

c. Cone with diameter 12 in. and height 6 in.

d. Pyramid with base area 81 sq. ft. and height 18 ft.

Practice Find the volume of each pyramid or cone. Use 3.14 or $3\frac{1}{7}$ for π. Round each decimal answer to the nearest unit.

1.

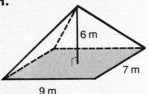

2.

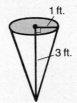

3.

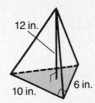

4.

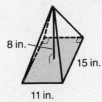

5.

6.

7.

8.

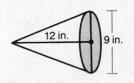

9. A triangular pyramid with base area 40 sq. in. and height 8 in.

10. Cone with radius 8 cm and height 10 cm

11. Cone with diameter 4 ft. and height 2 ft.

12. An octagonal pyramid with base area 8 sq. ft. and height 3 ft.

Apply Solve each problem. Use 3.14 for π. Round answers to the nearest tenth.

13. Find the volume of a cardboard cone with radius 4.2 in. and height 14.2 in.

14. Find the volume of a plastic square pyramid with sides of the base 8.5 in. and height 12.5 in.

★15. The slant height of the container in Problem 13 is 14.9 in. The container in Problem 14 has a slant height of 13.2 in. Which container requires more material to make?

Practice: Perimeter, Area, and Volume

A

8 in.
9 in.
6 in.
9 in.
8 in.

B

20 cm
17 cm
36 cm
41 cm

C

9 m
3.3 m
3 m
4 m
5 m

D

12 in.

E

20 cm
23 cm
20 cm

F

19 cm
4 cm

G

3 ft.   4 ft.
6.5 ft.
5 ft.

H

30 in.
16 in.
20 in.
12 in.

I

11.3 m   12 m
8 m
8 m

Find the perimeter or circumference for each figure. Use $3\frac{1}{7}$ for π.

1. Figure A
2. Figure B
3. Figure C
4. Figure D

Find the area for each figure. Use $3\frac{1}{7}$ for π.

5. Figure A
6. Figure B
7. Figure C
8. Figure D

Find the surface area for each figure. Use 3.14 for π, and round each answer to the nearest whole unit.

9. Figure E
10. Figure F
11. Figure G
12. Figure I

Find the volume for each figure. Use 3.14 for π, and round each answer to the nearest whole unit.

13. Figure E
14. Figure F
15. Figure G
16. Figure I

17. Find the perimeter of Figure H. Use $3\frac{1}{7}$ for π.

18. Find the area of Figure H. Use $3\frac{1}{7}$ for π.

Apply Solve each problem. For Problems 19–22, use 3.14 for π and round each answer to the nearest whole unit.

19. Find the volume of a cylindrical container with diameter 10 cm and height 9 cm.

20. Find the volume of a container shaped like a pyramid whose rectangular base has dimensions 8 in. by 12 in. and whose height is 7 in.

21. Find the amount of cardboard needed to make a container shaped like a cone with radius 5 cm and slant height 6 cm.

22. The height of the container in Problem 21 is 3.3 cm. Find its volume.

23. Find the area of a lot shaped like a trapezoid with bases 70 ft. and 115 ft. and height 90 ft.

24. *Estimation* A garage is 12.5 ft. long, 9.25 ft. wide, and 7.5 ft. high. Estimate the amount of paint needed for the sides of the garage. One quart of paint will cover about 90 sq. ft.

COMPUTER

BASIC: READ and DATA Statements

This program finds the area of rectangles using READ and DATA statements. Each time the computer is at line 10, it reads two new numbers from the DATA statement. After the last number is read, the computer will print a message that it is out of DATA and stop. The DATA statement can be anywhere in the program before END.

In Exercise 3, the symbol $\wedge$ means to raise to a power.

```
10 READ L,W
20 PRINT "AREA = ";L*W
30 GO TO 10
40 DATA 15,10,22,16
50 END
```

This is the output.

```
AREA = 150
AREA = 352
OUT OF DATA IN 10
```

Give the output for the program above using each DATA statement.

1. 40 DATA 3,7,5,3,10,6,14,8

2. 40 DATA 8,2,6,8,17,5,9,22,2, 37,6

3. Give the output for this program.

```
10 READ R
20 PRINT "AREA = ";3,14*R∧2
30 GO TO 10
40 DATA 5,8,2,3,6,8
50 END
```

Problem Solving: Use a Table

Read   The water tank in the town of Vado is a cylinder with radius of 30 feet and a height of 20 feet. The city council has decided to buy a tank with twice the capacity of the current tank. Which dimension or dimensions of the current tank should be doubled?

Plan   Make a table in which you double each dimension and find the effect on the volume.

Solve

	Radius r	Height h	Volume $= \pi r^2 h$
Current Tank	30 ft.	20 ft.	18,000π cu. ft.
Double Radius	60 ft.	20 ft.	72,000π cu. ft.
Double Height	30 ft.	40 ft.	36,000π cu. ft.
Double Both	60 ft.	40 ft.	144,000π cu. ft.

Answer   Doubling the height of the tank doubles its volume.

Look Back   Notice that when the radius is doubled the volume is quadrupled, or multiplied by 4.

Try   Use the table to solve this problem.

a. How does doubling both the height and the radius affect the volume?

Apply Use a table to solve each problem.

A rectangular parking lot has dimensions 2 km by 3 km. Complete the table.

	Width w	Length ℓ	Perimeter	Area
Original Dimensions	2 km	3 km	10 km	6 km^2
Double Dimensions	4 km	6 km	**1.**	**2.**
Triple Dimensions	6 km	**3.**	**4.**	**5.**
Quadruple Dimensions	8 km	**6.**	**7.**	**8.**

What is the effect on the perimeter when both dimensions of the parking lot are

9. doubled?　　**10.** tripled?　　**11.** quadrupled?　　**★12.** multiplied by 5?

What is the effect on the area when both dimensions of the parking lot are

13. doubled?　　**14.** tripled?　　**15.** quadrupled?　　**★16.** multiplied by 5?

A storage bin is shaped like a rectangular prism with dimensions 2 ft. by 3 ft. by 4 ft. Complete the table.

	Width w	Length ℓ	Height h	Surface area	Volume
Original Dimensions	2 ft.	3 ft.	4 ft.	52 sq. ft.	24 cu. ft.
Double Dimensions	**17.**	**18.**	**19.**	**20.**	**21.**
Triple Dimensions	**22.**	**23.**	**24.**	**25.**	**26.**
Quadruple Dimensions	**27.**	**28.**	**29.**	**30.**	**31.**

What is the effect on the surface area when the three dimensions of the storage bin are

32. doubled?　　**33.** tripled?　　**34.** quadrupled?　　**★35.** multiplied by 5?

What is the effect on the volume when the three dimensions of the storage bin are

36. doubled?　　**37.** tripled?　　**38.** quadrupled?　　**★39.** multiplied by 5?

Chapter 8 Test

Find the perimeter or circumference of each figure. Use 3.14 for π.

1. A circle with radius 8 cm

2. A parallelogram with sides 11 in. and 18 in.

3. A triangle with sides 12 in., 15 in., and $19\frac{1}{2}$ in.

Find the area of each figure. Use 3.14 for π. Round each answer to the nearest whole unit.

4.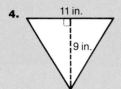

5. Parallelogram

6.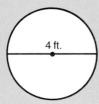

7. Trapezoid

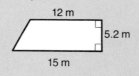

8.

9. Garden fencing costs $28.95 for a 50-foot roll. How much will it cost to buy enough fencing to enclose a rectangular garden that is 25 ft. by 12 ft.?

A

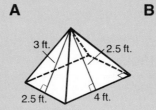

B

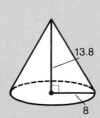

C

D

Find the surface area of

10. figure A.

11. figure B. Use 3.14 for π.

Find the volume of

12. figure C.

13. figure D. Use 3.14 for π.

14. A house has about 850 sq. ft. of siding. One gallon of paint costs $23.89 and covers about 450 sq. ft. Estimate the cost of paint for the siding.

A rectangular garden has dimensions 10 ft. by 25 ft. Complete the table.

	Width	Length	Area
Original Dimensions	10 ft.	25 ft.	**15.**
Triple Dimensions	30 ft.	**16.**	**17.**

18. What is the effect on the area of the garden when the two dimensions are tripled?

CHALLENGE

Spheres

A sphere consists of all points in space that are an equal distance from a point called the center. Circles on the sphere with the same center as the sphere are called *great circles*. Other circles on the sphere are called *small circles*.

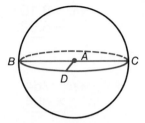

Sphere with radius $\overline{DA}$ and diameter $\overline{BC}$

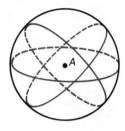

Sphere with great circles shown

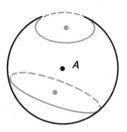

Sphere with small circles shown

The surface area of a sphere with radius r is $A = 4\pi r^2$.

The volume of a sphere with radius r is $V = \frac{4}{3}\pi r^3$.

For each sphere, find the surface area and volume. Use 3.14 for π. Round each answer to the nearest whole unit.

1. $r = 3$ cm

2. $d = 12$ ft.

3. $r = 10$ m

4. $d = 10$ in.

5. $d = 7$ cm

6. $r = 4$ ft.

7. $d = 13$ in.

8. $r = 3.5$ m

The radius of the earth is about 6,400 km.

9. Find the distance around the earth at the equator.

10. Find the surface area of the earth.

11. This silo has the shape of a cylinder with a hemisphere (half a sphere) on top. Find the total surface area, including the base, and the volume of the silo.

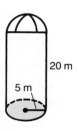

20 m

5 m

MAINTENANCE

Find each answer.

1. $\begin{array}{r} 17,583 \\ +\ 9,789 \\ \hline \end{array}$

2. $\begin{array}{r} 48.64 \\ -\ 39.452 \\ \hline \end{array}$

3. $2\frac{3}{4} \times 3\frac{1}{5}$

4. $6.05\overline{)48.4}$

5. $\begin{array}{r} 9.273 \\ +\ 6.945 \\ \hline \end{array}$

6. $\begin{array}{r} 828,828 \\ -\ 74,299 \\ \hline \end{array}$

7. $\frac{3}{4} \div \frac{5}{8}$

8. $\begin{array}{r} 0.38 \\ \times\ 8.793 \\ \hline \end{array}$

9. $12\overline{)3,496}$

10. $\begin{array}{r} 8.101 \\ -\ 6.923 \\ \hline \end{array}$

11. $\begin{array}{r} 92,841 \\ -\ 3,975 \\ \hline \end{array}$

12. $6\frac{1}{2} \div 2\frac{1}{4}$

13. $\begin{array}{r} 64,839 \\ +\ 78,584 \\ \hline \end{array}$

14. $\frac{5}{9} \times \frac{4}{15}$

15. $\begin{array}{r} 764 \\ \times\ 804 \\ \hline \end{array}$

16. $\frac{2}{3} \times \frac{4}{5}$

17. $\begin{array}{r} 16.8 \\ \times\ 0.43 \\ \hline \end{array}$

18. $\begin{array}{r} 4\frac{3}{4} \\ -\ 3\frac{2}{5} \\ \hline \end{array}$

19. $65\overline{)390,980}$

20. $\begin{array}{r} 10\frac{1}{4} \\ +\ 15\frac{5}{6} \\ \hline \end{array}$

21. $253\overline{)6,016}$

22. $\begin{array}{r} 8\frac{5}{6} \\ +\ 7\frac{7}{12} \\ \hline \end{array}$

23. $\begin{array}{r} 3,916 \\ \times\ \ \ \ 45 \\ \hline \end{array}$

24. $\begin{array}{r} 2\frac{3}{8} \\ +\ 3\frac{4}{5} \\ \hline \end{array}$

25. $5\frac{1}{2} \div 4\frac{2}{3}$

Solve each problem.

26. A dozen golf balls cost $9.99. How much does 1 golf ball cost?

27. A can of 3 tennis balls costs $2.98. How much will 4 cans of tennis balls cost?

28. *Estimation* Lorraine wants to buy a new tennis racket that costs $42.50. She can save $6.75 a week. Estimate how many weeks it will take her to save the money for the racket.

29. Ron is buying a bowling bag for $22.00. If the sales-tax rate is 6%, what is his change from $25.00?

30. On a bike trip Maura rode 29.5 km the first day, 24.6 km the second day, and 26.3 km the third day. How far did she ride in the three days?

31. Tim ran 6.3 miles one day, 5.8 miles the next day, and 4.1 miles the third day. Find the average number of miles he ran per day.

Statistics and Probability

Winning times:

54.8

54.95

55.01

Frequency Tables and Bar Graphs

A. Each student in Ms. Holm's class selected one of four books to read for a report. Ms. Holm recorded the number of students who read each book. She organized the information, or *data*, in a *frequency table*.

Book	Tally	Frequency
Time Machine	卌 II	7
Little Women	IIII	4
Sounder	卌 卌	10
The Hobbit	卌 IIII	9

The *range* is the difference between the greatest and the least number in the set. The range for the data above is 10 − 4, or 6.

B. A *bar graph* is one way to show the data in the frequency table.

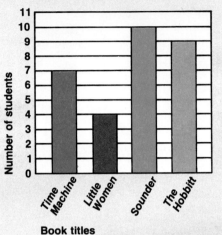

Books Read by Ms. Holm's Class

Number of students

Book titles

Try Use this double bar graph.

a. How many fiction books were checked out on Wednesday?

b. How many fewer fiction books than nonfiction books were checked out on Wednesday?

c. What is the range of the data for fiction books?

Practice Use the double bar graph. Give the number of books checked out each day.

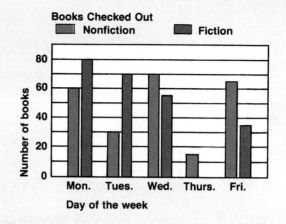

Books Checked Out
☐ Nonfiction   ■ Fiction

Number of books / Day of the week

1. Fiction on Monday

2. Fiction on Thursday

3. Nonfiction on Tuesday

4. Nonfiction on Friday

5. Fiction on Friday

6. Total on Wednesday

7. On which days were more than 50 nonfiction books checked out?

8. On which days were more fiction than nonfiction books checked out?

9. What is the range of the data for nonfiction books?

Apply Solve this problem.

10. The students in Mr. Garcia's class read the following books: *Treasure Island*, 4; *Sounder*, 9; *20,000 Leagues Under the Sea*, 8; *Time Machine*, 4. Make a bar graph for these data.

Broken-Line Graphs

Data collected over a period of time can be shown in a *broken-line graph*.

A. The graph below shows the circulation of daily newspapers in the United States each year from 1972 through 1980.

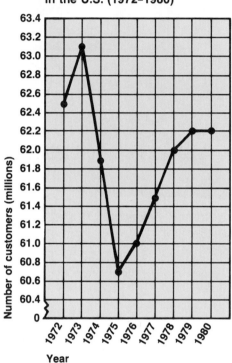

Daily Newspaper Circulation in the U.S. (1972–1980)

B. The graph below shows the circulation of two newspapers from 1973 through 1982. The red line represents *The Daily Bugle* and the blue line represents *The Evening Star*.

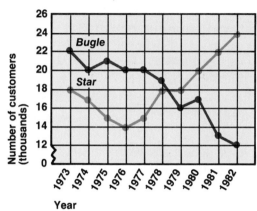

Circulation, 1973–1982

Try Use the graph in Example A.

a. In which year was the circulation about 61,900,000?

b. What was the circulation in 1977?

c. What is the range for these data?

d. Use the graph in Example B. In which years was the circulation of *The Star* greater than that of *The Bugle*?

266

Practice For Exercises 1–14, use the graph in Example A.
In which year was the circulation about

1. 62.5 million? **2.** 62.0 million? **3.** 61,000,000? **4.** 63,100,000?

What was the circulation in

5. 1972? **6.** 1973? **7.** 1974? **8.** 1975? **9.** 1976? **10.** 1978?

11. During which year or years did the circulation increase?

12. During which year or years did the circulation stay the same?

13. *Estimation* Estimate the increase in circulation from 1975 to 1980.

14. *Estimation* Estimate the decrease in circulation from 1973 to 1975.

For Exercises 15–21, use the graph in Example B.

15. In which year was the circulation of *The Star* about 20,000?

16. *Estimation* Estimate the circulation of *The Bugle* in 1981.

17. What is the range of the data for *The Bugle*?

18. What is the range of the data for *The Star*?

19. In which year was the circulation of *The Bugle* less than that of *The Star* for the first time?

20. *Estimation* Estimate the difference in the circulations of the two papers in 1982.

★21. If the trend continued, what was the circulation of *The Star* in 1983?

Apply The data below give the circulation of Sunday newspapers in the United States.

Year	1972	1973	1974	1975	1976	1977	1978	1979	1980
Circulation (millions)	49.9	51.7	51.7	51.1	51.6	52.4	54.0	54.4	54.7

22. Make a broken-line graph to show these data.

23. From 1975 to 1980, is the circulation increasing or decreasing?

24. In which year was the circulation the greatest?

Circle Graphs

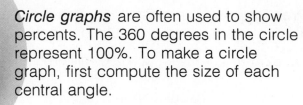

A. This table shows about how frequently each vowel occurs in ordinary written English.

A	E	I	O	U
8%	13%	7%	8%	3%

Add the numbers given. Vowels appear in 39% of written English.

The frequency of all other letters (consonants) is 100% − 39%, or 61%.

Circle graphs are often used to show percents. The 360 degrees in the circle represent 100%. To make a circle graph, first compute the size of each central angle.

A: 0.08(360°) = 28.8° ≈ 29°

E: 0.13(360°) = 46.8° ≈ 47°

I: 0.07(360°) = 25.2° ≈ 25°

O: 0.08(360°) = 28.8° ≈ 29°

U: 0.03(360°) = 10.8° ≈ 11°

Percent of Use of Vowels

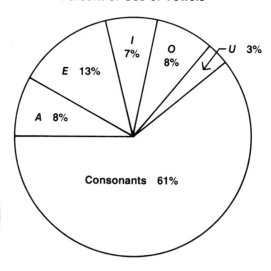

I 7%
O 8%
U 3%
E 13%
A 8%
Consonants 61%

B. About how many *E*s would you expect in a paragraph of 350 letters?

Find 13% of 350.

0.13 × 350 = 45.5 ≈ 46

You would expect about 46 *E*s.

Try   Use the graph on page 268.

a. About how many *A*s would you expect in a page of 1,500 letters?

b. How many degrees are in the central angle for 61%?

Practice   For Exercises 1–4, use the graph on page 268.

1. About how many *I*s would you expect in a paragraph of 250 letters?

2. About how many *U*s would you expect in a paragraph of 1,000 letters?

3. About how many consonants would you expect in a paragraph of 500 letters?

4. About how many vowels would you expect in a paragraph of 500 letters?

The graph shows how $1,200,000 was spent by a library. How much was spent in each category?

5. Salaries

6. Printed material

7. Films and records

8. Building and maintenance

9. How many degrees are in the central angle for 37.5%?

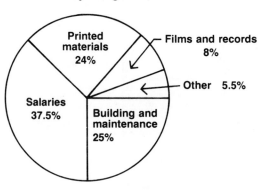

Library Budget

Apply   Solve each problem.

10. Last year the Kaplans spent $250 on these reading materials.

Newspapers	$120
Magazines	$50
Paperback books	$35
Hardcover books	$45

Make a circle graph. Round the measure of each central angle to the nearest degree.

Measures of Central Tendency

TEST SCORES

Harold	92
Marie	62
Betty	81
Linda	85
Carlos	75
Dennis	100
Jerry	92
Sandy	89
Ricardo	89
Norman	52
Kinuko	89
Beverly	74

The mean, the median, and the mode are three statistical measures commonly used to describe a set of data.

A. The *mean* is another name for average. To find the mean of the test scores, first find the sum of the scores. Then divide by the number of scores.

$$92 + 62 + 81 + 85 + 75 + 100 + 92 + 89 + 89 + 52 + 89 + 74 = 980$$

$$980 \div 12 \approx 81.7$$

The mean score is about 81.7.

B. The *median* is the number in the middle when the numbers are listed in order. If there are two middle numbers, the median is their average.

52   62   74   75   81   85   89

$$(85 + 89) \div 2 = 87$$

89   89   92   92   100

The median test score is 87.

C. The *mode* is the number that occurs most often in a set of data. To find the mode for the set of test scores, look at the list in Example B.

Since 89 occurs most frequently, the mode is 89.

If all the numbers in a set of data occur the same number of times, there is no mode. This set of data has no mode.

16, 17, 18, 19, 20, 21

Sometimes there are two or more modes. This set of data has two modes.

6, 7, 7, 9, 10, 15, 15, 18, 20

Try Use the set of numbers at the right.

a. Find the mean. Round to the nearest tenth.

b. Find the median.   **c.** Find the mode.

> 115, 100, 126,
> 104, 115, 108,
> 117, 109, 126

Practice For each set of data, find the mean, the median, and the mode. If necessary, round to the nearest tenth.

> 3, 8, 9, 14, 5, 16, 8, 7, 5, 6

1. Mean   **2.** Median   **3.** Mode

> 4.2, 5.9, 0.4, 3.9, 5.0, 7.0, 4.1

4. Mean   **5.** Median   **6.** Mode

> 23, 16, 24, 14, 24, 16, 21,
> 32, 27, 35, 36, 15, 17, 30

7. Mean   **8.** Median   **9.** Mode

> 242, 245, 251, 249, 252, 262,
> 254, 239, 238, 254, 254

10. Mean   **11.** Median   **12.** Mode

Apply Solve each problem. If necessary, round to the nearest tenth.

13. On her English tests Brenda got scores of 82, 89, 76, 80, 92, 96, and 85. Find her average score.

14. The number of students enrolled in five French classes are: 22, 16, 16, 18, and 21. What is the average number per class?

15. Mr. Jung's students earned these grades. Find the median grade.

B D C A D F A B D
C B A C B B C F C
A B C D B D A

16. Find the mode of the grades listed in Problem 15.

★17. Jenny had scores of 96, 92, 85, and 87 on her mathematics tests. After her test today, she had an average of 91. What was her score on today's test?

★18. Terry had scores of 82, 85, 87, and 92 on his mathematics tests. What is the lowest grade he can get on his next test and have an average of at least 87?

Practice: Statistics and Graphing

Use the broken-line graph.

1. How many students were enrolled at Clarke School in 1980?

2. In which years did Clarke School have under 400 students?

3. What year showed the first decrease in enrollment?

4. What was the decrease in enrollment from 1980 to 1982?

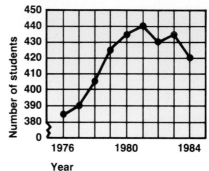

Enrollment at Clarke Junior High

Use the circle graph.

5. How many of the 420 students at Clarke are in eighth-grade mathematics?

6. How many of the 420 students at Clarke are in pre-algebra?

7. How many degrees are in the central angle for 30%?

8. About how many degrees are in the central angle for 7%?

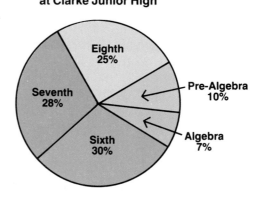

Mathematics Class Enrollment at Clarke Junior High

Use these test scores from Ms. Diaz's science class.

A C D A A C C C B C A B F D A C
C B A B B B C C C D A F D C B

9. Make a frequency table.

10. Make a bar graph.

Use these enrollment data for District 38 schools.

1978: 10,500	1979: 11,000	1980: 10,800
1981: 10,400	1982: 10,200	1983: 10,300

11. What is the range of these data?

12. Make a broken-line graph.

Use these enrollment data for Lowe Junior High School.

Sixth grade: 36%
Seventh grade: 33%
Eighth grade: 27%
Special: 4%

13. Make a circle graph. Round the measure of each central angle to the nearest degree.

For Exercises 14–17, use these test scores in Mrs. Fong's history class.

100	100	100	96	94	94
92	86	86	85	84	84
82	80	79	76	75	72
70	67	56	46		

Find each of the following.

14. Range **15.** Mean

16. Median **17.** Mode

For Exercises 18–21, use these heights of the players on the girls' basketball team.

64 in.	59 in.	66 in.	62 in.
67 in.	72 in.	69 in.	59 in.
63 in.	65 in.	66 in.	

Find each of the following. Round to the nearest tenth when necessary.

18. Range **19.** Mean

20. Median **21.** Mode

BASIC: TAB Functions

This program shows graphically the number of students in computer class by grade. The TAB function is used to print the output in a specific position. TAB(9) prints the first character at position 9.

```
10 LET A=0
20 LET B=0
30 LET C=0
40 PRINT "NUMBER OF STUDENTS BY
GRADE"
50 PRINT TAB(9);"0 1 2 3 4 5 6 7
8"
60 READ G
70 IF G=999 THEN 160
80 IF G=6 THEN 140
90 IF G=7 THEN 120
100 LET C=C+1
110 GO TO 60
120 LET B=B+1
130 GO TO 60
140 LET A=A+1
150 GO TO 60
160 PRINT "GRADE 6";TAB(9+2*A);"X"
170 PRINT "GRADE 7";TAB(9+2*B);"X"
180 PRINT "GRADE 8";TAB(9+2*C);"X"
190 DATA 6,8,6,7,8,6,7,8,6,6,999
200 END
```

This is the output.
```
NUMBER OF STUDENTS BY GRADE
         0 1 2 3 4 5 6 7 8
GRADE 6                 X
GRADE 7           X
GRADE 8             X
```

1. Give the output for this DATA list.
```
190 DATA 8,8,8,7,6,8,7,6,8,7,
999
```

Interpreting Statistics

A. The four Chicago Bears running backs earned $300,000, $70,000, $70,000, and $30,000 in 1982.

The mean of their salaries was $117,500. The mode was $70,000. The median was $70,000.

The mean is the least representative measure of these data, since it is greater than three of the four salaries. The median and the mode, which are the same in this case, give better indications of the 1982 salary of a Bears running back.

B. Both graphs show a player's salary from 1980 to 1984, but they give different impressions because the vertical scales are different.

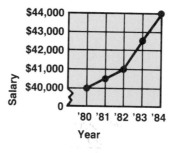

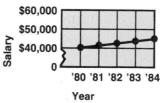

The first graph gives the impression that the salary increased sharply. The second graph gives the impression that the salary increased slowly.

Try Tell which measure, the mean, the median, or the mode, is least representative of these data.

a. Heights of 12 basketball players in centimeters: 83, 77, 78, 83, 79, 84, 80, 82, 77, 82, 78, 77

Practice For each exercise, find the mean, the median, and the mode. Tell which is *least* representative of these data.

1. Distances to road games in miles: 93, 166, 117, 1,410, 117, 263, 195, 47

2. Weights of high-school football players in pounds: 178, 143, 205, 198, 143, 191, 150, 202, 187, 154, 196, 189

Describe each graph. Use the words *increasing* or *decreasing*, and *slowly* or *rapidly*.

3. Salaries

4. Attendance

5. Ticket sales

Apply The salaries of the 16 employees of a company are:

$7,000 $8,000 $8,000 $8,000 $8,000 $9,000 $9,000 $9,000
$9,000 $9,000 $10,000 $22,000 $50,000 $65,000 $74,000 $85,000

6. Would the company use the mean, the median, or the mode to show that it pays well?

7. Would the employees use the mean, the median, or the mode to show that their salaries are low?

The circulation of *Sports Weekly* is given below.
1980: 250,000   1981: 250,100
1982: 250,200   1983: 250,500

Make a broken-line graph to suggest

8. a sharp increase in circulation.

9. a slow growth in circulation.

More Practice Set 110, page 419

Scattergrams

In making predictions, statisticians sometimes plot points for data. Then they try to draw a straight line as close to the points as possible. The graph is called a *scattergram*. The line is called the *line of best fit*.

The line of best fit below suggests that someone would have jumped about 92 inches in 1980. Actually, Gerd Wessig jumped almost 93 inches in the 1980 Olympics.

Olympic Records for Men's High Jump, 1948–1976

Year	Height (nearest inch)
1948	78
1952	80
1956	81
1960	85
1964	86
1968	88
1972	88
1976	89

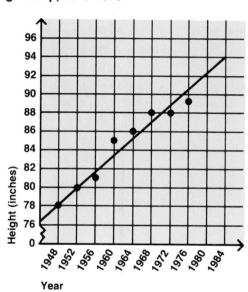

Try Give each answer. Use the graph above.

a. In which years was the record above the line of best fit?

b. What would you expect the height of the jump in 1984 to be?

Practice   Use the graph below for Exercises 1–5.

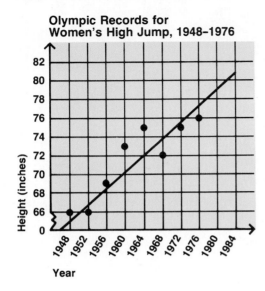

**Olympic Records for
Women's High Jump, 1948–1976**

1. In what year was the record jump 73 inches?

2. What was the record jump in 1976?

3. In which years were the records above the line of best fit?

4. In 1980, Sara Simeoni jumped 77.5 inches. Is this close to the line of best fit?

5. What would you expect the record jump in 1984 to be?

Apply   Make a scattergram. Draw a line of best fit. Then tell what you would expect the winning time in 1984 to be.

6. Olympic Records: Women's 100-Meter Freestyle Swimming (seconds)

1948: 66.3	1952: 66.3	1956: 62.0
1960: 61.2	1964: 59.5	1968: 60.0
1972: 58.6	1976: 55.7	1980: 54.8

Compare the numbers.
Use <, >, or =.

1. 3.8 ● 3.75

2. 1.09 ● 1.8

3. 0.606 ● 0.66

4. 22.02 ● 22.020

5. $\frac{1}{2}$ ● $\frac{1}{3}$

6. $\frac{1}{9}$ ● $\frac{1}{8}$

7. $2\frac{5}{6}$ ● $2\frac{4}{5}$

8. $1\frac{3}{4}$ ● $1\frac{7}{10}$

9. $8\frac{2}{3}$ ● $8\frac{7}{8}$

List the numbers in order from least to greatest.

10. 1.0, 1.01, 1.001, 1.011, 1.111

11. 0.8, 0.08, 0.008, 0.808, 0.088

12. $\frac{1}{3}, \frac{1}{8}, \frac{1}{7}, \frac{1}{12}$

13. $\frac{2}{3}, \frac{5}{6}, \frac{1}{2}, \frac{7}{12}$

14. $3\frac{1}{8}, 3\frac{1}{2}, 3\frac{3}{8}, 2\frac{3}{4}$

More Practice Set 111, page 419

Counting Choices

A. Joel plays drums and bass. Joan plays banjo, guitar, and violin. Jim plays piano and mandolin. How many combinations of instruments can they play?

Make a tree diagram to show all the possible combinations.

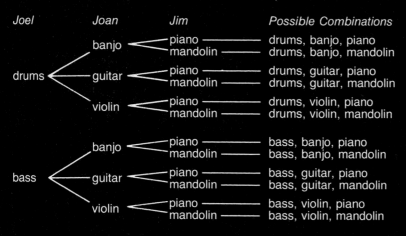

Joel	Joan	Jim	Possible Combinations
	banjo	piano	drums, banjo, piano
		mandolin	drums, banjo, mandolin
drums	guitar	piano	drums, guitar, piano
		mandolin	drums, guitar, mandolin
	violin	piano	drums, violin, piano
		mandolin	drums, violin, mandolin
	banjo	piano	bass, banjo, piano
		mandolin	bass, banjo, mandolin
bass	guitar	piano	bass, guitar, piano
		mandolin	bass, guitar, mandolin
	violin	piano	bass, violin, piano
		mandolin	bass, violin, mandolin

There are 12 possible combinations.

B. You can also multiply.

Choices for Joel		Choices for Joan		Choices for Jim		Total number
2	×	3	×	2	=	12

If successive choices are to be made, then the total number of choices can be found by multiplying the number of choices at each stage.

Practice For Exercises 1 and 2, make a tree diagram.

1. How many 2-letter codes can be made from the letters *D-R-U-M* if the letters can repeat?

2. How many 2-letter codes can be made from the letters *D-R-U-M* if the letters cannot repeat?

For Exercises 3–6, multiply to find the answer.

3. How many 5-digit codes can be written? Any digit from 0 to 9 can be used, but a digit cannot repeat.

4. How many 5-letter codes can be written with the letters *C-L-A-R-I-N-E-T* if the letters cannot repeat?

5. How many 7-digit telephone numbers can be written with the digits 0 to 9? Any digit can repeat.

6. Find the answer to Exercise 5 if the first digit cannot be 0 or 1.

Apply Solve each problem.

7. Jill plays the flute. If she joins the three musicians in Example A, how many combinations of instruments will there be?

*8. How many different ways can Joel, Joan, Jim, and Jill stand on the stage from left to right?

Probability

There are 60 students in the Lakewood Orchestra. 40 of them are in the string section, 9 are in the woodwind section, 8 are in the brass section, and 3 are in the percussion section.

A. Each year, one student is chosen at random to attend a music camp. What is the chance that he or she will be from the string section?

There are 60 *possible outcomes*, each of which is *equally likely* to occur. There are 40 students in the string section, so there are 40 *favorable outcomes*.

40 ← Number of favorable outcomes
60 ← Number of possible outcomes

The chance, or *probability*, that a student from the string section will be chosen is $\frac{40}{60}$, or $\frac{2}{3}$.

When all outcomes are equally likely, the probability of a favorable outcome is given by this formula.

$$\text{probability} = \frac{\text{number of favorable outcomes}}{\text{number of possible outcomes}}$$

B. Find the probability that a student will be chosen from either the woodwind section or the brass section.

9 + 8 ← Number of favorable outcomes
60 ← Number of possible outcomes

The probability is $\frac{17}{60}$.

If an outcome can never occur, then its probability is 0.

If an outcome is certain to occur, then its probability is 1.

Discuss Use the data about the orchestra. Give an example for which the probability is 0. Give an example for which the probability is 1.

Try Kikuye will toss a number cube labeled with the numbers 1 through 6. What is the probability of tossing

a. a 5?   **b.** a 0?   **c.** an even number?

Practice Laura will select a digit from 0 through 9 at random. What is the probability of selecting

1. a 2?   **2.** an 8 or a 9?   **3.** an odd number?   **4.** a number less than 7?

Lenny will choose a letter of the alphabet at random. What is the probability of choosing a

5. *T*?   **6.** vowel?   **7.** *B*, a *C*, or a *D*?   **8.** letter in his first name?

Monty will toss a coin once. What is the probability of tossing a

9. head?   **10.** tail?   **11.** head or a tail?   **12.** head and a tail?

Apply Use the table to solve Problems 13–18. If a student from the orchestra is chosen at random, what is the probability of choosing

13. a boy?

14. a girl?

15. a seventh-grade boy?

16. an eighth-grade girl?

17. a seventh-grade boy or an eighth-grade girl?

18. a seventh-grade girl or an eighth-grade boy?

Number of students in the orchestra			
	Seventh grade	Eighth grade	Total
Boys	16	12	28
Girls	13	19	32
Total	29	31	60

*19. For a particular eighth-grade class, the probability of selecting a girl at random is $\frac{3}{8}$. What is the probability of selecting a boy?

Independent Events

Career Bob Boyd is a disk jockey. Every day he chooses at random one of the songs from the Top Six list. The choice on any day has no effect upon the choice on any other day. The choices are *independent*.

A. What is the probability that Bob will choose the song *Wild Prairie* two days in a row?

The probability of choosing *Wild Prairie* on any one day is $\frac{1}{6}$. To find the probability that Bob will choose it twice, multiply the probabilities for each day.

Probability of choosing *Wild Prairie* one day	Probability of choosing *Wild Prairie* the next day	Probability of choosing *Wild Prairie* both days
$\frac{1}{6}$ ×	$\frac{1}{6}$ =	$\frac{1}{36}$

The probability that Bob will choose *Wild Prairie* two days in a row is $\frac{1}{36}$.

B. What is the probability that Bob will choose a song on Red Label Records the first day and a song on Blue Dot Records the second day?

Probability of choosing Red Label the first day	Probability of choosing Blue Dot the second day	Probability of choosing Red Label then Blue Dot
$\frac{4}{6}$	$\frac{1}{6}$	$\frac{4}{36}$

$$\frac{4}{6} \times \frac{1}{6} = \frac{4}{36}$$

The probability is $\frac{4}{36}$, or $\frac{1}{9}$.

Try Use the spinners.

a. What is the probability of spinning a C two times in a row?

b. What is the probability of spinning a B on the first spinner and a 3 on the second spinner?

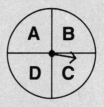 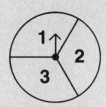

Practice Patrick will spin each spinner once. What is the probability of spinning

1. an A and a 1?

2. an A and either a 1 or a 2?

3. an A and a 1, a 2, or a 3?

4. an A or a B and a 1?

5. either a C or a D and a 1 or a 2?

6. an A, a B, or a C and a 3?

Tina chose two of the digits 0 through 9 at random. If the digits could be repeated, what is the probability that

7. both digits were 2s?

8. both digits were even?

Apply Use the information on page 282 to solve each problem.

9. What is the probability that Bob will select *Wild Prairie* three days in a row?

10. What is the probability that Bob will select *Wild Prairie* five days in a row?

Dependent Events

Bob has 12 records to give away. Five of them are folk records, five are rock, and two are jazz.

A. If Bob chooses two records at random, find the probability that both will be folk records.

The probability that the first record is folk music is $\frac{5}{12}$. If a folk record is chosen, 11 records remain, 4 of which are folk music. Thus the probability that the second record is folk music is $\frac{4}{11}$.

Notice that the outcome of the first selection influences the outcome of the second. The two selections are *dependent*.

Probability first is folk		Probability second is folk		Probability both are folk
$\frac{5}{12}$	$\times$	$\frac{4}{11}$	$=$	$\frac{20}{132} = \frac{5}{33}$

The probability that folk records will be chosen both times is $\frac{20}{132}$, or $\frac{5}{33}$.

B. If Bob chooses three records at random, find the probability that the first will be rock, the second will be jazz, and the third will be folk.

Probability first is rock
Probability second is jazz
Probability third is folk

$$\frac{5}{12} \times \frac{2}{11} \times \frac{5}{10} = \frac{5 \times 2 \times 5}{12 \times 11 \times 10} = \frac{50}{1,320} = \frac{5}{132}$$

The probability is $\frac{50}{1,320}$, or $\frac{5}{132}$.

Try There are 5 red marbles and 3 green marbles in a jar. If two marbles are drawn and not returned to the jar, what is the probability that

a. both are red?

b. the first is red and the second is green?

Practice Carlotta wrote each of the digits 0 through 9 on a card, put the cards in a hat, and mixed them up. If Carlotta draws two cards and does not replace them, what is the probability that

1. both digits are even?

2. both digits are less than 6?

3. the first digit is 2 and the second is 7?

4. the first is even and the second is odd?

If Carlotta draws three cards and does not replace them, what is the probability that

5. all three digits are odd?

6. all three digits are greater than 6?

★7. all three digits are 9s?

★8. all three digits are less than 10?

Apply Each day Bob selects two tapes at random from the top 40 songs. 24 of the tapes feature vocal groups and 16 of them feature instrumental groups. Bob never selects the same tape twice.

9. What is the probability that both tapes are vocal groups?

10. What is the probability that both tapes are instrumental groups?

11. What is the probability that the first tape is a vocal group and the second one is an instrumental group?

Experimental Probability

Joanna observed the rush-hour traffic on the expressway one evening and recorded these data.

Cars with 1 person	424
Cars with 2 people	336
Cars with 3 people	175
Cars with more than 3 people	65
	1,000

Based on these data, what is the probability that a car traveling on the expressway during rush hour is carrying exactly 3 people?

A car carrying exactly 3 people is a favorable outcome.

$\dfrac{175}{1,000}$ ← Number of favorable outcomes
← Number of possible outcomes

The probability is $\frac{175}{1,000}$, or $\frac{7}{40}$.

Experimental probability is determined by observing and counting outcomes from a sample.

Try Use the data on page 286.

a. What is the probability that a car is carrying 1, 2, or 3 people?

Practice Use the data on page 286. What is the probability that a car is carrying

1. more than 3 people?　　**2.** 1 person?

3. more than 1 person?　　**4.** 1 or 2 people?

Apply Solve each problem.

John observed 500 vehicles at a four-way stop and recorded these data.

Number turning left	170
Number turning right	132
Number going straight	198
Number of passenger cars	355
Number of buses	5

Based on these data, what is the probability that a vehicle coming to the stop will

5. turn left?　　　　　**6.** turn right?

7. turn left or right?　　**8.** be a passenger car?

9. be a bus?　　　　　**10.** be a bus or a car?

★11. be a vehicle other than a bus or a car?

An automated traffic survey of 10,000 vehicles recorded this information.

Number turning onto Highway 45	3,135
Number turning onto State Road A	2,640
Number staying on Interstate 8	4,225

Based on these data, what is the probability that a car will

12. turn onto Highway 45?　　**13.** turn onto Road A?

The product $3 \times 2 \times 1$ can be written 3!. It is read "three factorial."

$$1! = 1 \qquad\qquad = 1$$
$$2! = 2 \times 1 \qquad\quad = 2$$
$$3! = 3 \times 2 \times 1 \quad = 6$$
$$4! = 4 \times 3 \times 2 \times 1 = 24$$

Use your calculator to compute each factorial.

1. 5!　　　**2.** 6!

3. 7!　　　**4.** 8!

5. 9!　　　**6.** 10!

7. $(7 + 3)!$

8. $(15 - 4)!$

Find the value of each expression.

9. $8! + 4!$

10. $8! - 4!$

11. $8! \times 4!$

12. $8! \div 4!$

13. Is $6! + 3!$ the same as 9!?

14. Is $2! \times 4!$ the same as 8!?

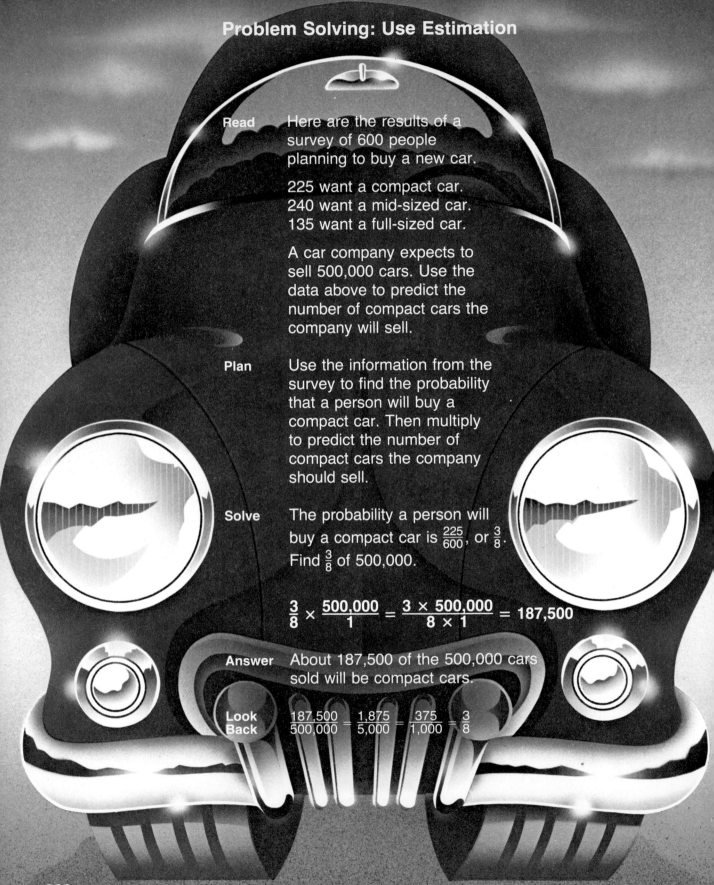

Problem Solving: Use Estimation

Read Here are the results of a survey of 600 people planning to buy a new car.

225 want a compact car.
240 want a mid-sized car.
135 want a full-sized car.

A car company expects to sell 500,000 cars. Use the data above to predict the number of compact cars the company will sell.

Plan Use the information from the survey to find the probability that a person will buy a compact car. Then multiply to predict the number of compact cars the company should sell.

Solve The probability a person will buy a compact car is $\frac{225}{600}$, or $\frac{3}{8}$. Find $\frac{3}{8}$ of 500,000.

$$\frac{3}{8} \times \frac{500,000}{1} = \frac{3 \times 500,000}{8 \times 1} = 187,500$$

Answer About 187,500 of the 500,000 cars sold will be compact cars.

Look Back $\frac{187,500}{500,000} = \frac{1,875}{5,000} = \frac{375}{1,000} = \frac{3}{8}$

Try *Estimation* Use the data on page 288.

a. A company expects to sell 100,000 cars. Predict the number of full-sized cars it will sell.

Apply *Estimation* Give the answer to each problem to the nearest whole number.

Single-speed	12
3-speed	20
5-speed	24
10-speed	18
All other	16
No bicycle	10

A bicycle dealer asked 100 randomly selected students what kind of bicycle they owned. Use the results shown at the right for Problems 1–6.

1. Estimate the number of students out of 500 that do not have a bicycle.

2. Estimate the number of students out of 500 that have a 5-speed bicycle.

3. Estimate the number of students out of 250 that have a 10-speed bicycle.

4. Estimate the number of students out of 250 that have a 3-speed bicycle.

5. How many students out of 1,000 would you expect to have either a 3-speed or a 5-speed or a 10-speed bicycle?

6. How many students out of 1,000 would you expect to have a bicycle, regardless of the kind?

7. A tire company found that 3 of 200 randomly selected tires were defective. How many defective tires would they expect in 10,000 tires?

8. Five out of 250 randomly selected vehicles had defective headlights. How many vehicles out of 1,500 would be expected to have defective headlights?

*9. Using the data on page 288, a car dealer placed an order that included 27 compact cars. How many cars were in the total order?

CHALLENGE

Using only 4s, write each of the whole numbers 0 through 10. You may use fractions or whole numbers and addition, subtraction, multiplication, or division.

Two ways to write the number 1 are shown.

$$1 = \frac{4}{4} \times \frac{4}{4}$$

$$1 = 4 - 4 + \frac{4}{4}$$

Chapter 9 Test

The number of books checked out of the school library is given below.

Mon. 180   Tues. 150   Wed. 180
Thurs. 125   Fri.   60

1. Use the data to make a bar graph.

2. Find the range of the data.

3. Find the mean for the data.

4. Tell which is least representative of the data, the mean, the median, or the mode.

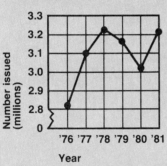

U.S. Passports Issued 1976–1981

5. In which year were about 3 million passports issued?

6. In which year were the fewest number of passports issued?

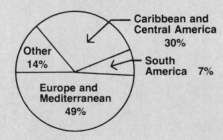

U.S. Travel to Foreign Countries 1981

7. For United States residents traveling abroad, which location was chosen most often?

8. In the graph, how many degrees are in the central angle for 30%?

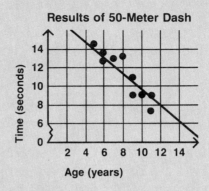

Results of 50-Meter Dash

9. Use the graph above. How long would you expect it to take a 12-year-old to run the 50-meter dash?

10. How many 4-letter codes can be made with the letters *G-R-A-P-H* if the letters cannot repeat?

11. There are 12 girls and 15 boys in a class. If a student is chosen at random, what is the probability of choosing a boy?

12. If two digits are chosen at random and the digits can repeat, what is the probability of choosing two even digits? The even digits are 0, 2, 4, 6, and 8.

13. Two socks are picked at random from 6 blue socks and 4 brown socks. What is the probability that both socks will be blue?

In a survey, 125 people out of 200 said they would vote for Mrs. Lopez.

14. What is the probability that a person will vote for Mrs. Lopez?

15. Predict the number of people out of 10,000 that will vote for Mrs. Lopez.

CHALLENGE

Simulation

Suppose ten cards were placed in a hat with a different digit on each card. If you were to repeatedly draw a card, record the digit, and replace the card, you would get a *table of random digits*. Such a table is shown at the right.

Tables of random digits can be used to imitate, or *simulate*, an event. If a ball player hits .400, or 40%, how likely is this player to get a hit three or more times in a row?

Pick any four of the ten digits to represent ''hits'' (40% of 10 is 4). Then circle the digits each time they occur in the table.

This portion of the table is a simulation of 120 times at bat. The digits 0, 1, 2, and 3 were selected to represent hits. In 120 times at bat, a player can be expected to get three or more hits in a row about 10 times. A better estimate would be obtained if more of the table were used.

```
1 9 1 0 3 8 8 3 4 4 3 7 2 1 3 9 0 2 3 5 5 3 2 2
7 9 5 1 6 7 8 8 3 5 3 1 4 3 6 5 0 2 6 1 7 1 3 3
5 2 8 4 3 3 7 3 1 0 5 2 6 9 2 0 1 0 5 4 7 0 7 1
3 1 2 3 9 1 6 3 5 8 1 6 8 3 5 5 3 4 7 9 5 5 2 8
2 0 0 4 6 3 9 0 2 2 4 0 7 6 1 3 5 8 2 3 8 8 4
4 3 0 0 1 9 9 0 7 4 3 7 1 8 0 1 9 5 7 0 2 3 0 0
2 2 7 6 3 9 6 8 5 3 6 4 2 2 2 5 6 2 9 8 8 6 3 5
9 5 6 6 7 5 0 6 4 8 8 6 7 5 4 2 0 7 0 8 3 5 2 8
4 1 2 0 2 4 5 9 1 1 0 1 1 1 3 6 6 8 6 5 8 9 9 8
7 5 4 7 5 6 8 8 7 9 6 5 5 9 6 3 9 2 6 8 8 2 6 3
1 0 1 4 5 7 0 0 8 6 9 1 2 8 2 9 8 3 3 0 2 3 6 5
3 9 2 3 3 5 8 1 9 0 9 9 5 0 5 0 7 3 5 0 3 7 7 5
3 1 5 9 5 7 6 5 8 3 3 3 7 4 1 8 8 5 2 7 1 5 4 2
6 4 7 0 4 8 7 9 9 5 6 9 7 9 3 9 7 9 5 6 8 5 1 2
9 2 3 4 7 9 7 6 9 9 0 5 3 1 1 6 5 8 2 8 4 8 0 5
```

```
①9①0③8 8③4 4③7②①3 9 0②③5 5③2②
7 9 5①6 7 8 8③5③①4③6 5 0②6①7①③③
5②8 4③③7③①0 5②6 9②0①0 5 4 7 0 7①
③①②③9①6③5 8①6 8③5 5③4 7 9 5 5②8
②0 0 4 6③9 0②②4 0 7 6①③5 8②③8 8 4
```

1. What is the longest string of hits that seems likely in 120 times at bat?

2. Did the player ever go to bat four or more times without getting a hit?

3. Use the entire table of random digits. What is the longest string of hits that seems likely?

4. Use the entire table of random digits. How many times can the player be expected to get three or more hits in a row?

5. For a player who hits .250, or 25%, ignore the 0s and 1s in the table and work with only eight digits. Since 25% of 8 is 2, use any two of the eight digits to represent hits, say, 6 and 7. What is the longest string of hits that seems likely for this player?

MAINTENANCE

Find each answer.

1. $9(7) + 4$

2. $6(26 + 4)$

3. $8(4) - 2(6)$

4. $3 + 4(12)$

5. $(3 + 4)12$

6. $85 - 5(11 - 9)$

7. $10(6 - 4) + 8$

8. $(30 - 12) - 4(3)$

9. $80 - 5(15 - 5)$

10. $\dfrac{5(4)}{10}$

11. $\dfrac{30}{10} - \dfrac{12}{6}$

12. $\dfrac{4(2 + 6)}{8}$

13. $\dfrac{12(10)}{5(8)}$

14. $9 + \dfrac{(36 - 6)}{5(6)}$

Find the value of each expression for $k = 3$.

15. $2k$

16. $23 - k$

17. $54 + k$

18. $4k - 9$

19. $6(k - 1)$

Find the value of each expression for $a = 4$.

20. $\dfrac{6a}{8}$

21. $\dfrac{36}{a} - 5$

22. $19 - \dfrac{9a}{12}$

23. $\dfrac{2(a + 4)}{a}$

24. $\dfrac{28}{a} - \dfrac{2(a + 6)}{4}$

Solve each problem.

25. The main ski lodge is 1,483.5 m above sea level. The lodge at the summit of the mountain is 1,963.4 m above sea level. How much higher is the summit lodge than the main lodge?

26. The normal body temperature is 98.6°F. When Ruth was ill, her temperature rose to 101°. How many degrees above normal is this?

27. A train from Seattle to Minneapolis uses an average of 625 L of fuel per hour. Find the amount of fuel used in the 38.5-hour trip.

28. A basketball team won 70% of the games it played in one season. The team won 14 games. How many games did it play?

29. Ramona bought a pair of shoes for $35. The sales tax was 4% of the price. What was the total price of the shoes, including sales tax?

30. Kip made a model of an airplane that has a scale of 1 to 96. The wingspan of the model is 34 cm. What is the wingspan of the actual airplane?

Cumulative Test, Chapters 1–9

Give the letter for the correct answer.

1. Add.

$$\begin{array}{r} 11,624 \\ +\ 8,377 \\ \hline \end{array}$$

- **A** 21,001
- **B** 19,991
- **C** 20,001
- **D** 19,001

2. Solve this equation.

$$\frac{b}{5} = 50$$

- **A** 250
- **C** 10
- **B** 55
- **D** 500

3. Round 57.2849 to the nearest tenth.

- **A** 57.28
- **C** 57.3
- **B** 57
- **D** 60

4. Subtract.

$$15.2 - 0.584$$

- **A** 9.36
- **B** 9.46
- **C** 14.416
- **D** 14.616

5. What is 0.45 written as a fraction in lowest terms?

- **A** $\frac{1}{15}$
- **B** $\frac{4}{5}$
- **C** $\frac{9}{20}$
- **D** $\frac{9}{25}$

6. Multiply.

$$\frac{2}{3} \times \frac{7}{8}$$

- **A** $\frac{7}{24}$
- **B** $\frac{7}{12}$
- **C** $\frac{3}{28}$
- **D** $\frac{9}{11}$

7. Subtract.

$$\begin{array}{r} 5\frac{1}{4} \\ -2\frac{4}{5} \\ \hline \end{array}$$

- **A** $3\frac{3}{4}$
- **B** $2\frac{9}{20}$
- **C** $2\frac{1}{2}$
- **D** $3\frac{19}{20}$

8. What is 30% of 60?

- **A** 20
- **B** 6
- **C** 30
- **D** 18

9. Of the 400 students at Plainfield Junior High, 50% study a foreign language. Of those students studying a foreign language, 20% study French. How many students study French?

- **A** 40
- **C** 80
- **B** 200
- **D** 280

10. Add.

$$\begin{array}{r} 3 \text{ ft. } 9 \text{ in.} \\ +2 \text{ ft. } 8 \text{ in.} \\ \hline \end{array}$$

- **A** 6 ft. 7 in.
- **C** 6 ft. 5 in.
- **B** 6 ft. 1 in.
- **D** 5 ft. 7 in.

11. The measure of ∠M is 35°. What is the measure of its supplement?

- **A** 45°
- **C** 35°
- **B** 55°
- **D** 145°

12. These polygons are similar. What is the missing length?

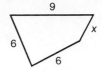

A 3   **B** 2   **C** 4   **D** 6

13. Which is an inscribed angle?

A ∠DCB   **C** ∠ACD
B ∠BAD   **D** ∠BCD

14. What is the area of this figure?

8 in.
12 in.

A 96 sq. in.   **C** 48 sq. in.
B 44 sq. in.   **D** 31 sq. in.

15. A circle has a diameter of 10 inches. What is its circumference? Use 3.14 for π.

A About 62.8 in.   **C** About 15.7 in.
B About 78.5 in.   **D** About 31.4 in.

16. How many pounds of grass seed are needed for a yard 90 ft. by 70 ft. if one pound of grass seed is needed for each 600 square feet?

A 63 pounds   **C** 1 pound
B 11 pounds   **D** 2 pounds

17. What is the volume of this prism?

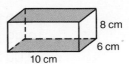

8 cm
6 cm
10 cm

A 480 cm³   **C** 240 cm³
B 160 cm³   **D** 48 cm³

18. In which year was the circulation the greatest?

Circulation, 1980-1983

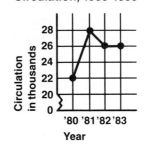

A 1980   **C** 1983
B 1982   **D** 1981

19. What is the mode of this set of test scores?

85 45 85 50 95 80 85 65
70 70

A 73   **B** 70   **C** 85   **D** 75

20. Dolores will select a digit from 0 through 9 at random. What is the probability that she will select a number greater than 4?

A $\frac{1}{2}$ **B** $\frac{4}{9}$ **C** $\frac{5}{9}$ **D** $\frac{3}{5}$

Noon   5 p.m.

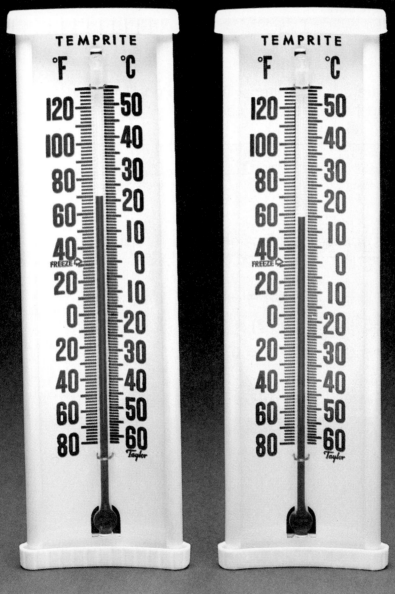

Hourly change: −2°F

Meaning of Integers

A. In December of 1982, the level of the Mississippi River at Grafton, Illinois, rose to 9 feet above flood stage. At the same time, the water level at Memphis was still 11 feet below flood stage.
Integers can be used to describe these situations.

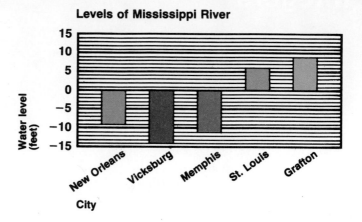

Levels of Mississippi River

$$+9 \qquad -11$$

positive nine   negative eleven

B. Positive integers are usually written without the positive sign. The integer 0 is neither positive nor negative.

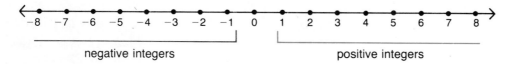

negative integers   positive integers

C. An integer and its *opposite* are located the same distance from zero on the number line. They are on opposite sides of zero.

The opposite of 8 is −8.   **−(8) = −8**

The opposite of −3 is 3.   **−(−3) = 3**

The opposite of 0 is 0.   **−(0) = 0**

Try Give an integer for each exercise.

a. 8 degrees below zero   **b.** The opposite of 19   **c.** $-(-4)$

Practice Give each answer.

1. If 22 represents a deposit of $22, what does -22 represent?

2. If 240 means 240 feet above sea level, what does -240 mean?

3. If -18 represents 18 miles south, what does 455 represent?

4. If -82 represents a loss of $82, what does 671 represent?

Give an integer for each exercise.

5. A profit of $60

6. A gain of 23 yards

7. A decrease of 456

8. A withdrawal of $17

9. A deposit of $4,058

10. 19 degrees below 0

11. 123 degrees above 0

12. The opposite of -25

13. The opposite of 14

14. $-(17)$

15. $-(100)$

16. $-(-2)$

17. $-(-74)$

18. 19 units to the right of zero

19. 45 units to the left of zero

Apply Use the graph on page 296. Give an integer for the water level at each city. Write *yes* or *no* to tell whether there was flooding.

20. New Orleans

21. Vicksburg

22. St. Louis

Comparing and Ordering Integers

A. *Tide height* refers to the number of feet above or below the average low-water level. This table shows approximate heights of the ocean tides at Boston, Massachusetts, on a certain day.

Tide	Height (feet)
Morning low tide	−1
Morning high tide	10
Evening low tide	0
Evening high tide	11

The evening high tide of 11 ft. is higher than the morning high tide of 10 ft. The morning low tide of −1 ft. is lower than the evening low tide of 0 feet.

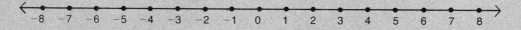

B. For any two integers on a number line, the number farther to the right is greater. Any positive integer is greater than any negative integer. Zero is greater than any negative integer.

$7 > -3$ $-10 < 6$ $-6 < 0$

$-1 > -7$ $-5 < -2$

C. List 4, −8, −13, and −1 in order from least to greatest.

Think of the numbers on a number line. The farther to the right, the greater the number.

-13 -8 -1 4

Try Compare these integers. Use < or >.

a. 7 ● −15   **b.** −8 ● −3

c. −13 ● 3   **d.** 0 ● −9

e. List 0, −4, 5, and −14 in order from least to greatest.

Practice Compare these integers. Use < or >.

1. 8 ● 4   **2.** 1 ● 7   **3.** 9 ● −2   **4.** 3 ● −7

5. −6 ● 6   **6.** −16 ● 2   **7.** 0 ● −5   **8.** −4 ● −5

9. −7 ● −4   **10.** 10 ● 0   **11.** −19 ● −11   **12.** −8 ● −20

13. −12 ● 6   **14.** −15 ● −3   **15.** −22 ● −36   **16.** −50 ● −21

List these integers in order from least to greatest.

17. 8   −8   −3   **18.** −1   −5   0   **19.** 5   −2   −9   3

20. −23   6   −18   0   **21.** 0   8   −9   −12   **22.** −18   4   −6   9

Apply This table shows the approximate tide heights at Savannah, Georgia, on a certain day.

Tide	Height (feet)
Morning low tide	0
Morning high tide	7
Evening low tide	−1
Evening high tide	8

23. Which low tide is lower?

24. Which high tide is higher?

25. List the tides in order from lowest to highest.

★26. Which has the greater change in water level, Boston or Savannah?

Adding Integers

A. A negative integer in this table shows the number of seats not booked on a flight. A positive integer shows that the flight is overbooked by that number of seats. How many seats are available on the Chicago flights?

Flight	Destination	Booking status
72	Miami	4
166	Detroit	−15
293	Chicago	−3
297	Chicago	−5
481	Los Angeles	3
493	Los Angeles	0
612	New York	−12
627	New York	9

Find $-3 + (-5)$.

Use a number line. Starting at zero, move 3 units to the left. From there, move 5 more units to the left.

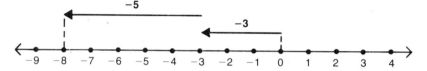

$$-3 + (-5) = -8$$

The Chicago flights are underbooked by 8 seats.
Eight seats are available.

To add integers with the same sign, add without regard to the signs. Then use the sign of the numbers in your answer.

B. Find 2 + (−6).

Starting at zero, move 2 units to the right. From there, move 6 units to the left.

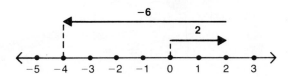

2 + (−6) = −4

To add two integers with different signs, consider the distance each integer is from zero. Subtract the shorter distance from the longer distance. Then use the sign of the number farther from zero in your answer.

Try Add.

a. −5 + (−1)   **b.** −13 + 10   **c.** −2 + 16 + (−11)

Practice Add.

1. −4 + (−6)   **2.** −8 + (−4)   **3.** 7 + 4   **4.** 9 + 5

5. 6 + (−9)   **6.** −7 + 2   **7.** 9 + (−2)   **8.** −4 + 8

9. −7 + 7   **10.** 3 + (−3)   **11.** 0 + (−8)   **12.** −6 + 0

13. −18 + (−4)   **14.** −15 + (−7)   **15.** 25 + (−14)   **16.** 19 + (−22)

17. −16 + 19 + 12   **18.** 18 + (−11) + (−10)   **19.** 4 + (−2) + (−8) + 3

20. −17 + 9 + 9 + (−1)   **21.** −4 + 22 + (−32) + 4   **22.** −8 + 27 + 8 + (−21)

Apply For each problem, refer to the flight information on page 300.

23. How many seats are available on the New York flights?

24. How many seats are available on the Los Angeles flights?

25. A family of five returned their tickets for Flight 72. How many seats are now available on that flight?

⋆26. The seating capacity on each flight to New York is 248. What is the total number of tickets sold for these flights?

Subtracting Integers

Flight _____
Week of _____

Day	Arrival Status in minutes
Monday	18
Tuesday	4
Wednesday	-9
Thursday	22
Friday	-16
Saturday	-6
Sunday	-4

A. During one week, Flight 418 left Capers Bay at the same time every day. Its early arrivals at Oakville are indicated in the table by negative integers. Positive integers show late arrivals. How many minutes later was Monday's flight than Tuesday's flight?

Find $18 - 4$.

$$18 - 4 = 14$$

Monday's flight was 14 minutes later.

B. Study these pairs of equations. In each case, adding the opposite integer gives the same result as subtracting.

$18 - 4 = 14$ $50 - 27 = 23$ $928 - 100 = 828$

$\mathbf{18 + (-4) = 14}$ $\mathbf{50 + (-27) = 23}$ $\mathbf{928 + (-100) = 828}$

To subtract an integer, add its opposite.

c. Find $-6 - 9$.

$$\mathbf{-6 - \quad 9}$$

Change to addition.   Change to the opposite.

$$\mathbf{-6 + (-9) = -15}$$

D. Find $8 - (-4)$.

$$\mathbf{8 - (-4)}$$

Change to addition.   Change to the opposite.

$$\mathbf{8 + \quad 4 = 12}$$

Try Subtract.

a. $-7 - 5$ **b.** $12 - 16$ **c.** $-3 - (-5)$ **d.** $7 - (-10)$

Practice Subtract.

1. $-6 - 2$

2. $-7 - 6$

3. $-4 - (-3)$

4. $-5 - (-2)$

5. $3 - 8$

6. $6 - 5$

7. $14 - 12$

8. $11 - 13$

9. $-7 - (-7)$

10. $24 - (-19)$

11. $28 - (-10)$

12. $-17 - (-17)$

13. $16 - (-16)$

14. $0 - 22$

15. $0 - (-34)$

16. $-29 - 29$

17. $-13 - 17$

18. $-24 - 6$

19. $-14 - (-22)$

20. $-19 - (-17)$

21. $20 - 90$

22. $-50 - (-30)$

23. $59 - 44$

24. $-35 - 28$

25. $18 - (-7) - (-6)$

26. $18 + (-7) - (-6)$

27. $24 - (-2) - 30$

28. $24 + (-2) - (-30)$

Apply Solve each problem. Use the table on page 302.

29. How much longer was Thursday's flight than Monday's?

30. How much longer was Thursday's flight than Friday's?

31. How much longer was Tuesday's flight than Wednesday's?

32. How much longer was Wednesday's flight than Friday's?

★33. Flight 418 was scheduled to take 95 minutes. For each day, find the actual length of the flight.

★34. The scheduled arrival time for Flight 418 was 1:35 P.M. For each day, find the actual arrival time.

Evaluating Addition and Subtraction Expressions

You can find the ground speed of an airplane in flight by using the expression $a + w$, where a is the airspeed of the plane and w is the speed of the wind. If the plane flies in the same direction as the wind, w is positive. If the plane flies directly into the wind, w is negative.

A. What is the ground speed of a plane flying directly into a 45-mile-per-hour (45-mph) wind if the airspeed is 680 mph?

Evaluate $a + w$ for $a = 680$ and $w = -45$.

$a + w$

$680 + (-45)$ Substitute 680 for a and -45 for w.

635

The ground speed of the plane is 635 mph.

B. Evaluate $-m - 12$ for $m = -8$.

$-m - 12$

$-(-8) - 12$ Substitute -8 for m.

$8 - 12$ $-(-8)$ is 8.

$8 + (-12)$

-4

C. Evaluate $6 - (t + 4)$ for $t = 7$.

$6 - (t + 4)$

$6 - (7 + 4)$ Substitute 7 for t.

$6 - 11$ Do computation inside the parentheses first.

$6 + (-11)$

-5

Try Evaluate each expression.
Use $n = -6$, $p = -4$, and $q = 3$.

a. $n + 3$ **b.** $-n + 5$ **c.** $8 - (2 + q)$ **d.** $2 + (p - q)$

Practice Evaluate each expression.
Use $h = -4$, $k = -7$, $x = 4$, and $y = -5$.

1. $-h - 10$ **2.** $-h + 7$ **3.** $-16 - h$ **4.** $-6 + h$ **5.** $h + 4$

6. $(k + 3) - 5$ **7.** $(-2 + k) + 4$ **8.** $-9 - (k - 2)$ **9.** $-3 - (1 + k)$

10. $x + (9 + y)$ **11.** $(y - x) + 14$ **12.** $-y - (x - 9)$ **13.** $-x - (y + 1)$

Complete each table.

	u	$7 - u$
14.	6	
15.	-4	
16.	0	

	v	$-v + 12$
17.	-5	
18.	8	
19.	0	

	z	$8 - (z - 10)$
20.	-3	
21.	-10	
22.	18	

Apply Solve each problem.

23. A plane's airspeed is 720 mph. What is its ground speed if it flies into a 75-mph wind?

24. A plane's airspeed is 540 mph. What is its ground speed if it flies with a 20-mph wind?

★25. An airplane flies with a 30-mph wind. Its ground speed is 590 mph. Find its airspeed.

★26. An airplane flies into a 55-mph wind. Its ground speed is 685 mph. Find its airspeed.

Multiplying Integers

A. Kristie's Bookstore sold 4 books at a loss of $2 each. What was the loss on the 4 books?

Find 4 × (−2).

Since one integer is positive, think of multiplication as repeated addition.

4 × (−2) = (−2) + (−2) + (−2) + (−2) = −8

The loss on the 4 books was $8.

B. Find (−3)(−7).

Look for a pattern in these examples.

(3)(−7) = −21

(2)(−7) = −14

(1)(−7) = −7   The product increases
                 by 7 each time.

(0)(−7) = 0
                 Continue to increase
(−1)(−7) = 7   by 7 each time to
                 maintain the pattern.

(−2)(−7) = 14

(−3)(−7) = 21

If two integers have the same sign, their product is positive.

If two integers have different signs, their product is negative.

Try   Multiply.

a. 8 × (−7)

b. (−10)(2)

c. (−6)(−5)

d. (−2)(−4)(−9)

Practice Multiply.

1. 8×3
2. $2 \times (-5)$
3. $(-9)(3)$

4. $12(4)$
5. $(-6)(-4)$
6. $(-7)(-1)$

7. $10 \times (-9)$
8. $(-2)(-15)$
9. $(-12)(12)$

10. $7(-7)$
11. $(-5)(0)$
12. 13×6

13. $(-8)(-8)$
14. $(8)(8)$
15. $(18) \times 7$

16. $9(-45)$
17. $-16(400)$
18. $-16(-400)$

19. $(-3)^2$
20. $(3)^2$
21. $(5)^3$

22. $(-5)^3$
23. $(-2)^4$
24. $(-2)^5$

25. $(-2)(-6)(8)(2)$
26. $(-6)(-1)(3)(-2)$

27. $-2(-3)(-1)(-5)$
28. $(-4)(-2)(7)(0)$

★29. $6(-3)^3(-4)^3$
★30. $2^3(-2)^5(-3)^2$

Simplify.

★31. $3 - (7)(2)$
★32. $(-3)(4 + 1)$

★33. $(-4)(6 - 8)$
★34. $6(-1) - (-2)(-3)$

Apply Use integers to solve each problem.

35. Kristie's Bookstore showed a $150 loss for each of 4 weeks. Find the total loss.

36. In December, Kristie's Bookstore made twice the profit made in November. The profit for November was $4,100. How much was the profit for December?

Dividing Integers

A. Kristie's Bookstore had a loss of $600 in a three-week period. What was the average loss per week?

Find $(-600) \div 3$.

To find the quotient of two integers, think of the related multiplication.

Since $3(-200) = -600$:

$$(-600) \div 3 = -200$$

The average loss per week was $200.

B. Find $-56 \div 8$.

Since $8(-7) = -56$:

$$-56 \div 8 = -7$$

C. Find $45 \div (-9)$.

Since $(-9)(-5) = 45$:

$$45 \div (-9) = -5$$

D. Find $-72 \div (-8)$.

Since $(-8)(9) = -72$:

$$-72 \div (-8) = 9$$

If two integers have the same sign, their quotient is positive.

If two integers have different signs, their quotient is negative.

Try Divide.

a. $-49 \div (-7)$

b. $132 \div 12$

c. $\dfrac{-160}{20}$

d. $\dfrac{1,400}{-70}$

Practice Divide.

1. $48 \div (-8)$

2. $-64 \div 8$

3. $-99 \div (-9)$

4. $-84 \div (-7)$

5. $39 \div 13$

6. $45 \div (-5)$

7. $-72 \div 36$

8. $140 \div 14$

9. $0 \div (-7)$

10. $0 \div (-4)$

11. $20 \div (-1)$

12. $-53 \div (-1)$

13. $\dfrac{-42}{6}$ **14.** $\dfrac{35}{-7}$ **15.** $\dfrac{0}{-18}$

16. $\dfrac{-51}{-17}$ **17.** $\dfrac{-60}{-15}$ **18.** $\dfrac{0}{-25}$

19. $\dfrac{-500}{100}$ **20.** $\dfrac{320}{-32}$ **21.** $\dfrac{-924}{-28}$

22. $\dfrac{-798}{19}$ **23.** $\dfrac{578}{-34}$ **24.** $\dfrac{-696}{-24}$

25. $\dfrac{-9,000}{-10}$ **26.** $\dfrac{12,500}{-25}$

Simplify.

⋆27. $\dfrac{8 - (2 - 12)}{-14 + 11}$ **⋆28.** $\dfrac{9(-2 + 7)}{-3(2 - 7)}$

Apply Use integers to solve each problem.

29. Last year Kristie's Bookstore showed a loss of $36,000. What was the average loss per month?

30. Kristie's Bookstore sold 3,500 books and earned $3 profit on each book. Find the total profit.

⋆31. Last year Kristie's Bookstore earned $2 profit on each of 800 copies of a book and lost $1,400 on sales of another book. To the nearest cent, give the average monthly profit or loss.

COMPUTER

BASIC: INT Function

This program finds the numbers from 1 to 20 that are divisible by 3. Line 20 uses the INT (integer) function. INT(N) means the greatest integer less than or equal to N. Here are some examples.

INT(6) = 6   INT(0.09) = 0
INT(3.68) = 3   INT(8/3) = 2
INT(−3.4) = −4

```
10 FOR N=1 TO 20              Output
20 IF INT(N/3)=N/3 THEN 40      3
30 GO TO 50                     6
40 PRINT N                      9
50 NEXT N                      12
60 END                         15
                               18
```

Give the output for each program.

1.
```
10 FOR N=1 TO 40
20 IF INT(N/5)=N/5 THEN 40
30 GO TO 50
40 PRINT N
50 NEXT N
60 END
```

2. Use 3, 8, 12, 17, 24, and 0 for X.
```
10 PRINT "GIVE A NUMBER"
20 PRINT "USE 0 TO STOP"
30 INPUT X
40 IF X=0 THEN 100
50 IF INT(X/2)=X/2 THEN 80
60 PRINT X;" IS AN ODD NUMBER"
70 GO TO 10
80 PRINT X;" IS AN EVEN NUMBER"
90 GO TO 10
100 END
```

Practice: Computing with Integers

Give each answer.

1. If −154 means 154 feet below sea level, what does 490 mean?

2. If 16 represents 16 miles north, what does −42 represent?

3. If 62 indicates 62 degrees above zero, what does −30 indicate?

4. If −7,070 represents a withdrawal of $7,070, what does 1,354 represent?

Give an integer for each exercise.

5. A decrease of 14

6. A growth of 5 feet

7. A profit of $3,788

8. A loss of 16 pounds

9. The opposite of 49

10. −(−31)

Give each answer.

11. $12(-7)$

12. $(-6)(-8)$

13. $15 + (-4)$

14. $13 + (-16)$

15. $-88 \div (-11)$

16. $-45 \div 15$

17. $-7 - (-12)$

18. $4 - (-3)$

19. $\dfrac{800}{-20}$

20. $\dfrac{-620}{-62}$

21. $-17 \times (-4)$

22. -26×8

23. $-94 + 94$

24. $0 - 77$

25. $0 - (-38)$

26. $63 + (-63)$

27. $(-6)^2$

28. $(-2)^3$

29. $-377 \div 29$

30. $864 \div 16$

31. $-13 + 4 + 8 + (-6)$

32. $7 + (-9) + 8 + (-5)$

33. $6(-3)(-4)(-1)$

34. $-2(8)(-2)(0)(3)$

35. $5(-5)(7)(0)(-3)$

36. $6(3)(2)(-3)$

37. $12 - (-2 + 3)$

38. $30 - (-10) - 18$

39. List − 3, 0, 9, and −10 in order from least to greatest.

40. List 6, −12, 0, and 3 in order from least to greatest.

Evaluate each expression. Use $x = -4$, $y = 6$, and $a = -10$.

41. $x + 8$

42. $x + y - 13$

43. $7 - (a + 9)$

44. $(-6 + a) - 11$

Apply Solve each problem.

45. Futura Productions produced two concerts in March. The first resulted in a $2,200 loss. The second concert earned a $5,400 profit. Find the company's profit or loss for March.

46. Flight 433 to Fort Worth is overbooked by 4 seats. If 6 people return their tickets, how many seats will be available on Flight 433?

47. On Monday the Hawk River was 8 feet below flood stage. On Tuesday the water rose 2 feet and on Wednesday it rose 1 more foot. What was the water level at the end of the day on Wednesday?

⋆48. At noon the temperature in St. Paul was 8 degrees below zero. Six hours later it was 10 degrees above zero. Find the average increase or decrease in temperature per hour.

CHALLENGE

Try this with a friend. Cut two pieces of string, each about 40 inches long. Make loops at the end of each piece. Slip the loops over your wrists so that the strings are intertwined as shown. Try to separate the two strings without slipping them off your wrists or untying the loops.

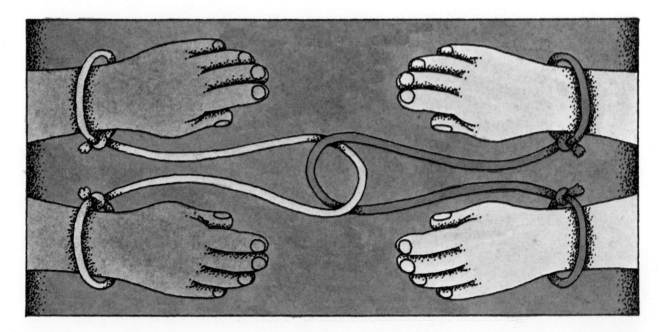

Evaluating Expressions

A. Each year the Rivercrest Schools sponsor a math competition for eighth-grade students. The following expression is used to calculate each contestant's score. Missing answers are not counted.

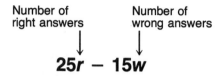

Number of right answers → 25*r*

Number of wrong answers → − 15*w*

$$25r - 15w$$

Penny had 30 right answers and 7 wrong answers. Find her score.

Evaluate 25*r* − 15*w* for *r* = 30 and *w* = 7.

25*r* − 15*w*

25(30) − 15(7)   Substitute 30 for *r* and 7 for *w*.

750 − 105   Multiply.

645   Subtract.

Penny's score was 645.

When you compute with integers, follow the standard order of operations.

B. Evaluate $\dfrac{10 - t}{s(t + 17)}$ for *t* = −20 and *s* = 5.

$\dfrac{10 - t}{s(t + 17)}$

$\dfrac{10 - (-20)}{5(-20 + 17)}$ Substitute −20 for *t* and 5 for *s*.

$\dfrac{10 - (-20)}{5(-3)}$ Do the operations inside the parentheses.

$\dfrac{30}{5(-3)}$ Do the operations above the division bar.

$\dfrac{30}{-15}$ Do the operations below the division bar.

−2   Divide.

Try

a. Evaluate −3*w* − 7*z* for *w* = 2 and *z* = −4.

b. Evaluate 9(*m* − 6) for *m* = −12.

c. Evaluate $\dfrac{-h(5 + k)}{2 + (k + 3)}$ for *h* = −1 and *k* = −3.

d. Evaluate $d^3 - e^3$ for *d* = 4 and *e* = −2.

Practice Evaluate each expression for $a = -8$.

1. $3a$

2. $-7a$

3. $\dfrac{-16}{a}$

4. $\dfrac{a}{2}$

Evaluate each expression for $b = 3$.

5. $7 + 2b$

6. $40 - 3b$

7. $\dfrac{12}{b} - 8$

8. $17 - \dfrac{9}{b}$

9. $\dfrac{b + 17}{4}$

10. $\dfrac{14}{10 - b}$

11. $7(-2 - b)$

12. $-2(b + 15)$

13. $b^2 - 6b$

14. $-12b + b^3$

15. $-7b(2 - b)$

16. $4b(-b + 9)$

17. $\dfrac{42 - 4b}{-3 + 6b}$

18. $\dfrac{3b + 6}{-2b + 1}$

19. $b - \dfrac{8 + 9b}{-7}$

Evaluate each expression for $s = 10$ and $t = -6$.

20. $\dfrac{3s}{t} + t^2$

21. $t^3 - \dfrac{10t}{-2s}$

22. $\dfrac{s + t}{2s - 18}$

23. $\dfrac{2s - 5t}{s - 12}$

24. $\dfrac{s(t - 2)}{4(s + t)}$

25. $\dfrac{3(-4t + s)}{-7t - 4s}$

Apply Solve each problem. Use the expression from Example A.

26. Amy had 22 right answers and 8 wrong answers in the math competition. Find her score.

27. Fran had 4 right answers and 8 wrong answers. Find her score.

★28. Lin answered 16 problems. His score was 0. How many problems did he answer correctly?

★29. There were 42 problems in all. Aaron's score was -5. If he got 7 right answers, how many problems did he skip?

Solve each equation.

1. $k - 19 = 101$

2. $m + 13 = 52$

3. $11.98 = c + 4.72$

4. $3.5 = x - 2.8$

5. $9 + m = 17\frac{1}{2}$

6. $y - \frac{3}{4} = 1\frac{7}{8}$

7. $8a = 168$

8. $13x = 91$

9. $\frac{a}{13} = 19$

10. $\frac{m}{23} = 15$

11. $6z + 17 = 65$

12. $3w - 52 = 17$

13. $3.8 = \frac{s}{5}$

14. $0.3 = \frac{r}{9}$

15. $\frac{c}{6} = \frac{35}{42}$

16. $\frac{1.8}{3.6} = \frac{x}{2.4}$

17. $\frac{12}{g} = \frac{0.8}{1.0}$

Problem Solving: Use a Table

Read Awards are given to students who score 80 points or more on a 10-item bicycle safety test. 15 points are given for each right answer, and 5 points are subtracted for each wrong answer. Missing answers are not counted. Melissa had 6 right answers and received an award. How many wrong answers did she have?

Plan Make a table showing the scores for all combinations of right and wrong answers.

Solve In the table, locate the column for 6 right answers. Find all scores equal to or greater than 80.

Number of right answers

	0	1	2	3	4	5	6	7	8	9	10
0	0	15	30	45	60	75	90	105	120	135	150
1	−5	10	25	40	55	70	85	100	115	130	
2	−10	5	20	35	50	65	80	95	110		
3	−15	0	15	30	45	60	75	90			
4	−20	−5	10	25	40	55	70				
5	−25	−10	5	20	35	50					
6	−30	−15	0	15	30						
7	−35	−20	−5	10							
8	−40	−25	−10								
9	−45	−30									
10	−50										

Number of wrong answers

Answer Melissa had 0 or 1 or 2 wrong answers.

Look Back 6 right answers earn 90 points for Melissa. For a score of at least 80, no more than 10 points can be subtracted. So there can be no more than 10 ÷ 5, or 2, wrong answers.

Try Use the table on page 314 to solve each problem.

a. Glenn's score was 0. How many right answers could he have?

b. Yumiko had the same number of right and wrong answers. What was her score?

Apply Use the table on page 314 to solve each problem.

1. Mel's score was 70. How many problems did he get right?

2. Francisca's score was 95. How many problems did she answer in all?

3. Bonita had 8 right answers. What might have been her score?

4. Do any students with 5 right answers earn an award?

To be hired as a lifeguard at Mages Lake, an applicant must score at least 85 points on a 12-item first-aid test. Each right answer earns 10 points. 5 points are subtracted for each wrong answer. Missing answers are not counted.

5. Make a table showing the scores for all combinations of right and wrong answers.

6. Jill had 8 right answers. Could she be hired as a lifeguard?

7. Sarah, a lifeguard, had 9 right answers on the test. How many wrong answers did she have?

8. How many wrong answers could result in a score of 0?

9. Tomas answered 10 questions. What are the highest and lowest scores he could earn?

10. Pedro's score was 80. How many wrong answers did he have?

Problem Solving: Multiple-Step Problems

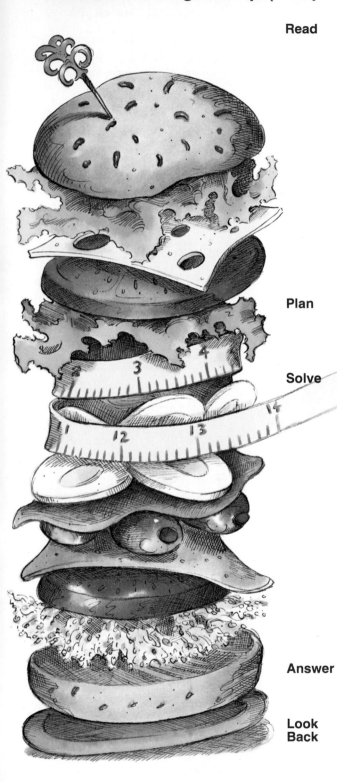

Read Ted and five of his friends are in a weight loss program. They meet regularly and record their weights. Find the average weight change for the first month.

Member	Weight in pounds		
	Starting	**1st month**	**2nd month**
Ted	143	137	134
Ken	125	127	125
Bill	140	136	144
Sam	117	114	107
Frank	115	115	112
Ramon	161	154	154

Plan Subtract to find each person's change in weight. Add these weight changes and divide the sum by the number of members.

Solve Subtract.

Ted $137 - 143 = 137 + (-143) = -6$
Ken $127 - 125 = 127 + (-125) = 2$
Bill $136 - 140 = 136 + (-140) = -4$
Sam $114 - 117 = 114 + (-117) = -3$
Frank $115 - 115 = 115 + (-115) = 0$
Ramon $154 - 161 = 154 + (-161) = -7$

Add the weight changes.

$-6 + 2 + (-4) + (-3) + 0 + (-7) = -18$

Divide by 6.

$-18 \div 6 = -3$

Answer The average weight change the first month was a loss of 3 pounds.

Look Back Four of the six boys lost weight the first month, so it is reasonable that the change is a loss rather than a gain.

Try Solve the problem.

a. Find the average weight change from the first month to the second month.

Apply Solve each problem.

1. Find the average weight of the boys at the beginning.

2. Find the average weight of the boys at the end of the first month.

3. Find the average weight of the boys at the end of the second month.

4. Find the average weight loss of the four boys who showed a weight loss the first month.

5. Begin with the starting weights. Find the average weight change after 2 months.

The weights of five preschool-age children were recorded at the beginning and at the end of the school year.

| Name | Weight in pounds | |
	September	June
Jimmy	44	47
Rosanne	38	38
Maria	34	37
Ronnie	41	40
Ginny	43	48

6. Find the average weight of the children in September.

7. Find the average weight of the children in June.

8. Find the average weight change.

CALCULATOR

Some calculators have a *change-sign* key that looks like this: $\boxed{+/-}$

This key allows you to do problems with integers. Try this key sequence for $-9 \times (-23)$.

Press: 9 $\boxed{+/-}$ $\boxed{\times}$ 23
$\boxed{+/-}$ $\boxed{=}$

Display: *207*

Use the change-sign key when you work these problems on your calculator. Enter the digits of a negative integer first. Then press the change-sign key.

1. $-15 \times (-7)$

2. $86 \times (-64)$

3. $-1,162 \div 14$

4. $3,053 \div (-71)$

5. $-679 + 805$

6. $-98 + (-866) + (-4)$

7. $68 - (-79)$

8. $-544 - (-12,988)$

9. $-16(-22)(453)(-8)$

10. $598 \div (-23) - (-62)$

Chapter 10 Test

1. What is the opposite of -7?

2. What integer represents a loss of 5 pounds?

3. Compare these integers. Use $>$ or $<$.

   $-3 \bullet -9$

4. List these integers in order from least to greatest.

   $-6 \quad 3 \quad -7 \quad 0$

Add or subtract.

5. $-9 + 5$

6. $-15 + (-5)$

7. $-4 - (-8)$

8. $12 - (-2)$

9. Evaluate $b + 2$ for $b = -3$.

10. Evaluate $-k - 1$ for $k = -5$.

11. Evaluate $(m - 6) + 3$ for $m = 2$.

Multiply or divide.

12. $10 \times (-3)$

13. $(-4)(-7)$

14. $(-5)^2$

15. $16 \div (-2)$

16. $\dfrac{-40}{-4}$

17. $-54 \div (-6)$

18. Evaluate $\dfrac{-18}{c}$ for $c = -3$.

19. Evaluate $4(-2 - s)$ for $s = 9$.

20. Evaluate $\dfrac{12}{w} - 5$ for $w = -6$.

The table shows the scoring system for a five-item test. Each right answer earns 20 points; 10 points are subtracted for each wrong answer.

		0	1	2	3	4	5
	0	0	20	40	60	80	100
	1	−10	10	30	50	70	
Number of wrong answers	2	−20	0	20	40		
	3	−30	−10	10			
	4	−40	−20				
	5	−50					

Number of right answers

21. Dorothea had 3 right answers and 2 wrong answers. What was her score?

22. Mario's score was 70. How many wrong answers did he have?

The table shows the weights of five members of a weight-reducing club.

Member	Weight in pounds		
	Starting	1st month	2nd month
Joe	134	129	127
Bob	145	142	139
Ari	127	125	122
Cal	158	150	149
Erik	121	119	118

23. Find the average starting weight.

24. Find the average weight loss for the first month.

25. Find the average weight loss between the first and second months.

CHALLENGE

Absolute Value

The *absolute value* of a number is its distance from zero on a number line, without regard to its direction from zero.

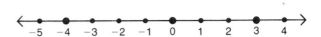

A. $|-4|$ is "the absolute value of negative four." Notice that -4 is 4 units from zero. The absolute value of -4 is 4. This fact is written $|-4| = 4$.

B. 3 is located 3 units from zero, so its absolute value is 3. $|3| = 3$.

C. Evaluate $|-9| + |4|$.

$$|-9| + |4|$$

$9 + 4$ Find each absolute value.

13 Then add.

D. Evaluate $-|6 + m|$ for $m = -8$.

$$-|6 + m|$$

$-|6 + (-8)|$ Substitute -8 for m.

$-|-2|$ Find the sum of 6 and -8.

$-(2)$ The absolute value of -2 is 2.

-2 The opposite of 2 is -2.

Express without absolute-value signs.

1. $|5|$ **2.** $|-3|$ **3.** $|0|$ **4.** $|13|$ **5.** $|-22|$ **6.** $|22|$

7. $-|12|$ **8.** $-|19|$ **9.** $-|-6|$ **10.** $-|-15|$

11. $|-7| + |4|$ **12.** $|-7 + 4|$ **13.** $|-2 - (-9)|$ **14.** $|-2| - |-9|$

Evaluate each expression for $x = 3$ and $y = -4$.

15. $|y|$ **16.** $|x|$ **17.** $|-x|$ **18.** $|-y|$ **19.** $-|y|$ **20.** $-|-y|$

21. $|x - 7|$ **22.** $|y \div 2|$ **23.** $|3x - y|$ **24.** $|3x| - |y|$

MAINTENANCE

Give or complete the unit of measure that could be used in each situation. Use *meter*, *liter*, or *gram*.

1. Mass of a person
kilo▨▨▨

2. Distance to a city
kilo▨▨▨

3. Capacity of a pail
▨▨▨

4. Mass of a grape
▨▨▨

5. Length of a baby
centi▨▨▨

6. Capacity of a spoon
milli▨▨▨

Choose the most sensible measure.

7. Mass of a bicycle
1.5 kg   15 kg   150 kg

8. Length of a child's sled
0.18 m   1.8 m   18 m

9. Height of a garage
5 m   50 m   500 m

10. Capacity of a sprinkling can
0.3 L   3 L   30 L

Complete the following.

11. 507 km = ▨▨ m

12. 238 cm = ▨▨ m

13. 5.9 g = ▨▨ mg

14. 274 mL = ▨▨ L

15. 2,874 g = ▨▨ kg

16. 8.3 L = ▨▨ mL

Choose the more precise measurement.

17. 34.7 cm   45.83 cm

18. 51 m   469 m

19. 16 g   47 kg

20. 16 L   156 mL

Solve each problem.

21. Would you measure the area of Indiana in square kilometers or cubic kilometers?

22. Would you measure the volume of a fish tank in square centimeters or cubic centimeters?

23. The mass of a can of peaches is 454 g. How many kilograms is this?

24. Dallas and Fort Worth are about 50 km apart. Express this distance in meters.

Rational Numbers and Irrational Numbers

Distance to the sun:
1.492×10^8 km

A. This board shows gains and losses of company stocks in fractions of a dollar. "$-\frac{1}{4}$" means a loss of $0.25. Express -2, $-\frac{1}{4}$, -0.25, and $1\frac{5}{8}$ as quotients of two integers in four different ways.

-2: $\frac{-2}{1}$ $\frac{2}{-1}$ $-\frac{2}{1}$ $-\frac{-2}{-1}$

> There are countless answers.
> Recall the sign rules for dividing integers.
> $-2 \div 1 = -2$ $\qquad$ $2 \div (-1) = -2$
> $-(2 \div 1) = -2$ $\qquad$ $-(-2 \div (-1)) = -2$

$-\frac{1}{4}$: $-\frac{1}{4}$ $\frac{-1}{4}$ $\frac{1}{-4}$ $\frac{-2}{8}$

-0.25: $-\frac{25}{100}$ $\frac{-25}{100}$ $\frac{25}{-100}$ $-\frac{1}{4}$ $\qquad$ $1\frac{5}{8}$: $\frac{13}{8}$ $\frac{-13}{-8}$ $-\frac{-13}{8}$ $\frac{-26}{-16}$

Any number that can be written as the quotient of two integers is a *rational number*. The divisor cannot be 0. The only rational number that is neither positive nor negative is 0.

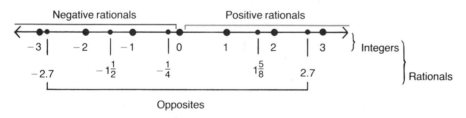

B. Compare $-\frac{1}{4}$ and $-1\frac{1}{2}$. Use $<$, $>$, or $=$.

All rational numbers are ordered on a number line the way integers are. The greater number is on the right.

$-\frac{1}{4} > -1\frac{1}{2}$

C. List 0, -2.7, $1\frac{5}{8}$, and $-\frac{3}{4}$ in order from least to greatest.

Read the numbers from left to right as they appear on a number line.

-2.7 $\quad$ $-\frac{3}{4}$ $\quad$ 0 $\quad$ $1\frac{5}{8}$

Try Write each number as the quotient of two integers in four ways.

a. 4   **b.** $-\frac{2}{3}$ **c.** $-2\frac{1}{8}$ **d.** 0.2

e. Compare -2.7 and 1. Use $>$, $<$, or $=$.

f. List $3\frac{1}{2}$, -1, and $-\frac{7}{8}$ in order from least to greatest.

Practice Write each number as the quotient of two integers in four ways.

1. -4 **2.** 0   **3.** $\frac{2}{5}$ **4.** $-\frac{3}{4}$ **5.** $5\frac{3}{8}$ **6.** $-2\frac{1}{2}$ **7.** -1.6 **8.** 2.3

Compare. Use $>$, $<$, or $=$.

9. $-\frac{1}{6}$ ⬤ $-\frac{1}{4}$ **10.** $-\frac{1}{9}$ ⬤ $\frac{1}{9}$ **11.** $-\frac{2}{3}$ ⬤ $-\frac{4}{6}$ **12.** 0 ⬤ $-\frac{1}{8}$

13. $-3\frac{2}{5}$ ⬤ -4 **14.** $\frac{3}{2}$ ⬤ -2 **15.** -0.8 ⬤ -0.7 **16.** -5.1 ⬤ -2.1

List the numbers in order from least to greatest.

17. 0 $-\frac{1}{2}$ $\frac{3}{4}$ **18.** $-\frac{1}{3}$ $-\frac{1}{10}$ $-\frac{1}{5}$ **19.** $2\frac{4}{5}$ -1 $\frac{3}{2}$ **20.** 0.6 -0.6 -1 6

Give the opposite of each rational number.

21. $-\frac{3}{4}$ **22.** $\frac{1}{2}$ **23.** $2\frac{1}{3}$ **24.** $-1\frac{4}{5}$ **25.** $-5\frac{1}{8}$ **26.** -2.7 **27.** -0.4 **28.** 3.1

Apply Solve each problem.

29. Which companies listed on the board showed losses?

★30. List the rational numbers on the board from least to greatest.

Adding and Subtracting Rational Numbers

A. One share of Abco stock gained $\frac{1}{2}$ on Monday and lost $\frac{5}{8}$ on Tuesday. What was the overall change?

Find $\frac{1}{2} + \left(-\frac{5}{8}\right)$.

Write the numbers as fractions with a common positive denominator. Then add the numerators, which are integers.

$\frac{1}{2} + \left(-\frac{5}{8}\right)$

$\frac{1}{2} + \left(\frac{-5}{8}\right)$ Write $-\frac{5}{8}$ as $\frac{-5}{8}$.

$\frac{4}{8} + \left(\frac{-5}{8}\right)$ Write the numbers with a common denominator.

$\frac{4 + (-5)}{8}$ Add the numerators.

$\frac{-1}{8}$, or $-\frac{1}{8}$

The overall change was a loss of $\frac{1}{8}$.

B. Find $-\frac{7}{10} - \frac{3}{4}$.

To subtract a rational number, add its opposite.

$-\frac{7}{10} - \frac{3}{4}$

$-\frac{7}{10} + \left(-\frac{3}{4}\right)$

$\frac{-7}{10} + \frac{-3}{4}$

$\frac{-14}{20} + \frac{-15}{20}$

$\frac{-14 + (-15)}{20}$

$\frac{-29}{20}$, or $-\frac{29}{20}$, or $-1\frac{9}{20}$

Discuss What is the opposite of $-\frac{2}{3}$? What is the sum of a number and its opposite?

c. Find $-0.3 + 0.57$.

Add these decimals the same way you add integers.

$-0.3 + 0.57$

$-0.30 + 0.57$

0.27

D. Find $1.25 - (-5.89)$.

$1.25 - (-5.89)$

$1.25 + 5.89$ Add the opposite.

7.14

Try   Add or subtract.

a. $-\frac{3}{5} + \frac{9}{10}$ **b.** $\frac{7}{8} - \left(-\frac{1}{4}\right)$ **c.** $-6 + 1.3$ **d.** $-7.25 - 0.5$

Practice   Add or subtract.

1. $\frac{2}{5} + \left(-\frac{7}{5}\right)$ **2.** $\frac{3}{5} + \left(-\frac{3}{5}\right)$ **3.** $-\frac{1}{8} + \left(-\frac{3}{4}\right)$ **4.** $\frac{2}{3} + \left(-\frac{1}{6}\right)$ **5.** $\frac{1}{2} + \left(-\frac{11}{10}\right)$

6. $-\frac{12}{5} + \left(-\frac{1}{2}\right)$ **7.** $-5 + \frac{1}{4}$ **8.** $-\frac{2}{3} + 6$ **9.** $\frac{7}{8} - \left(-\frac{3}{8}\right)$ **10.** $\frac{3}{10} - \frac{9}{10}$

11. $-\frac{1}{3} - \frac{1}{2}$ **12.** $-\frac{3}{4} + \left(+\frac{7}{8}\right)$ **13.** $\frac{1}{5} - \left(-\frac{2}{3}\right)$ **14.** $-1 - \frac{5}{16}$ **15.** $0 - \frac{3}{8}$

16. $-1.2 + 4.5$ **17.** $-9.7 + 9.7$ **18.** $-1.3 + (-0.03)$ **19.** $4 + (-7.82)$

20. $-0.7 - 0.5$ **21.** $3.2 - 3.85$ **22.** $-1 - 9.6$ **23.** $0 - 37.1$

Apply   Solve each problem.

24. On the five trading days last week, Abco gained $\frac{1}{2}$, lost $\frac{5}{8}$, lost 1, gained $\frac{1}{8}$, and gained 1. What was the overall change?

★25. What loss, followed by a gain of $\frac{1}{2}$, results in an overall change of $-\frac{1}{4}$?

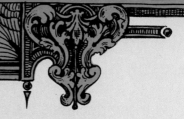

Multiplying and Dividing Rational Numbers

A. Juanita owns 500 shares of stock in CMR, Inc. Last Monday, the stock had a loss of $\frac{3}{4}$ per share. What was the change in the value of her stock?

Find $500\left(-\frac{3}{4}\right)$.

Rewrite each negative factor with a negative numerator.
Multiply the numbers as you multiplied fractions.
Use the sign rules for multiplying integers.

$$500\left(-\tfrac{3}{4}\right) = \tfrac{500}{1}\left(\tfrac{-3}{4}\right) = \tfrac{\overset{125}{\cancel{500}}(-3)}{\underset{1}{\cancel{4}}} = \tfrac{-375}{1} = -375$$

The change was a loss of $375.

B. Find $-3\frac{1}{2} \div \left(-\frac{2}{3}\right)$.

To divide by a rational number in fraction form, multiply by its reciprocal.

$$-3\tfrac{1}{2} \div \left(-\tfrac{2}{3}\right)$$

$$-\tfrac{7}{2} \times \left(-\tfrac{3}{2}\right) = \tfrac{-7}{2} \times \tfrac{-3}{2} = \tfrac{-7(-3)}{2(2)} = \tfrac{21}{4} = 5\tfrac{1}{4}$$

C. Find $-3.5(0.31)$.

$-3.5(0.31)$

-1.085 Two numbers with different signs have a negative product and quotient.

D. Find $-9.35 \div (-2.5)$.

$-9.35 \div (-2.5)$

3.74 Two numbers with the same sign have a positive product and quotient.

Try Multiply or divide.

a. $-\frac{1}{2}\left(-\frac{5}{8}\right)$ **b.** $-\frac{3}{4} \div \frac{3}{8}$ **c.** $6(0.125)$ **d.** $-1.72 \div 4$

Practice Multiply or divide.

1. $-\frac{5}{6}\left(-\frac{2}{5}\right)$ **2.** $-\frac{3}{4}\left(\frac{4}{7}\right)$ **3.** $-\frac{1}{2}\left(\frac{3}{8}\right)$ **4.** $\frac{9}{4}\left(-\frac{1}{12}\right)$

5. $-\frac{1}{8}(-12)$ **6.** $3\frac{1}{2}\left(-\frac{7}{9}\right)$ **7.** $\frac{7}{10}\left(\frac{10}{7}\right)$ **8.** $-\frac{1}{2}(-2)$

9. $\frac{3}{5} \div \frac{7}{10}$ **10.** $\frac{5}{8} \div \left(-\frac{1}{2}\right)$ **11.** $\frac{7}{8} \div -\frac{7}{8}$ **12.** $-\frac{1}{2} \div \left(-\frac{1}{2}\right)$

13. $\frac{3}{4} \div (-2)$ **14.** $-5 \div \left(-\frac{1}{6}\right)$ **15.** $4\frac{1}{2} \div \left(-\frac{1}{2}\right)$ **16.** $-\frac{3}{7} \div 5\frac{1}{7}$

17. $-4(1.5)$ **18.** $-0.7(-0.3)$ **19.** $8.5(-0.1)$

20. $-16 \div (-0.5)$ **21.** $-4.9 \div 0.49$ **22.** $-5.76 \div 1.8$

Apply Solve each problem.

23. Mrs. Smith owns 50 shares of Tri-X stock. One day the stock lost $\frac{5}{8}$ per share. What was the change in the value of her stock?

24. The value of Arturo's stock decreased by $75 Tuesday. He owns 100 shares. What was the loss per share?

★25. On Wednesday, Arturo's stock gained $1\frac{1}{8}$ per share. What was the change in the value of his stock from Monday to Wednesday?

Exponents and Powers of 10

A. A certain computer can do 1,000,000 computations per second. Each computation takes one microsecond (0.000001 sec.).

Powers of 10, such as 1,000,000 and 0.000001, can be written with exponents.

$$1,000,000 = 10 \times 10 \times 10 \times 10 \times 10 \times 10 = 10^6$$

$$0.000001 = \frac{1}{1,000,000} = \frac{1}{10^6} = 10^{-6}$$

If n is a positive integer, 10^n means that 10 is a factor n times, and 10^{-n} means $\frac{1}{10^n}$.

B. The chart below shows that when the exponent decreases by 1, the number is divided by 10. To maintain this pattern, mathematicians agree that:

$$10^1 = 10 \qquad 10^0 = 1$$

Powers of 10	
Exponential form	Standard form
10^3	1,000
10^2	100
10^1	10
10^0	1
10^{-1}	$\frac{1}{10} = 0.1$
10^{-2}	$\frac{1}{100} = 0.01$
10^{-3}	$\frac{1}{1,000} = 0.001$

Try Write with an exponent.

a. 1,000　　**b.** 0.01　　**c.** $\frac{1}{10}$　　**d.** $\frac{1}{1,000}$

Write in standard form.

e. 10^2　　**f.** 10^{-2}　　**g.** 10^0　　**h.** 10^{-5}

Practice Write with an exponent.

1. 10　　　　**2.** 1　　　　**3.** 100

4. 10,000　　**5.** 100,000　　**6.** 10,000,000

7. 0.001　　**8.** 0.00001　　**9.** 0.1

10. $\frac{1}{100}$　　**11.** $\frac{1}{10,000}$　　**12.** $\frac{1}{100,000}$

Write in standard form.

13. 10^4 **14.** 10^3 **15.** 10^5 **16.** 10^{-4}

17. 10^{-3} **18.** 10^{-7} **19.** 10^0 **20.** 10^1

21. 10^{-1} **22.** 10^{-8} **23.** 10^{10} **24.** 10^{-10}

Apply   Solve each problem.

25. A certain computer completes one step of a program in 10^{-8} seconds. Write this number in standard form.

26. Another computer can store, locate, and organize trillions of items of data. Write 1,000,000,000,000 with exponents.

27. A *googol* is written with 1 followed by one hundred zeros. Write a googol with exponents.

28. One quadrillion is 1 added to 999,999,999,999,999. Write one quadrillion with exponents.

★29. Write one hundred quadrillion with exponents.

★30. Quintillions follow quadrillions. Write one quintillion with exponents.

A *nanosecond* is 0.000000001 second. If you let a 1-inch piece of string represent a nanosecond, would a piece of string that represents a microsecond reach

★31. across your desk?

★32. across your classroom?

★33. from one end of a city block to the other?

Solve each proportion.

1. $\frac{3}{4} = \frac{t}{24}$

2. $\frac{d}{8} = \frac{70}{80}$

3. $\frac{12}{42} = \frac{5}{n}$

4. $\frac{h}{0.7} = \frac{9}{2.1}$

5. $\frac{0.5}{1.5} = \frac{3}{k}$

6. $\frac{14}{z} = \frac{8}{12}$

7. $\frac{6}{19} = \frac{v}{38}$

8. $\frac{12}{15} = \frac{8}{x}$

9. $\frac{8.1}{3.6} = \frac{2.7}{m}$

10. $\frac{45}{81} = \frac{10}{s}$

11. $\frac{6}{t} = \frac{1.2}{0.8}$

12. $\frac{x}{7.2} = \frac{0.3}{2.4}$

13. $\frac{4.5}{5.0} = \frac{9.0}{q}$

14. $\frac{3}{80} = \frac{n}{1,200}$

15. $\frac{5}{72} = \frac{4.9}{r}$

16. $\frac{1}{20} = \frac{n}{1,390}$

Multiplying Powers of 10

A. *Career* Evelyn Jackson is a statistician for an insurance company. She requested a printout of data that took 1,000 seconds to produce. How many lines did the computer print altogether if it printed 100 lines per second?

You know the answer is 1,000 × 100, or 100,000, lines.

1,000   100   100,000

$$10^3 \times 10^2 = 10^5 = 10^{3+2}$$

You can multiply powers of 10 by adding their exponents.
If m and n are integers, then $10^m \times 10^n = 10^{m+n}$.

B. Find $10^4 \times 10^{-3}$.

$10^4 \times 10^{-3}$

$10^{4+(-3)}$

10^1, or 10

Check

$10^4 \times 10^{-3} \stackrel{?}{=} 10$

$10,000 \times \frac{1}{1,000} \stackrel{?}{=} 10$

$10 = 10$

Try Use exponents to find each product. Write the answer with an exponent.

a. 10×10^3

b. $10^{-2} \times 10^2$

c. 0.001×0.01

Practice Use exponents to find each product. Write the answer with an exponent.

1. $10^4 \times 10^3$
2. $10^5 \times 10^8$
3. $10^{-3} \times 10^{-5}$
4. $10^{-2} \times 10^{-11}$
5. $10^3 \times 10^{-1}$
6. $10^8 \times 10^{-6}$
7. $10^{-4} \times 10^{-4}$
8. $10^{-5} \times 10^5$
9. $10^{-7} \times 10$
10. $10^{-6} \times 10^0$
11. $10^4 \times (10^6 \times 10^{-3})$
12. $(10^4 \times 10^6) \times 10^{-3}$
13. $1,000 \times 100$
14. $10 \times 10,000$
15. 10×0.01
16. $1,000 \times 0.001$
17. 0.001×10
18. $0.0001 \times 10,000$
19. 0.1×0.01
20. 0.01×0.001
21. $100 \times 10 \times 0.01$
★22. 10 nanoseconds

Apply Solve each problem. Give your answer with an exponent and also in standard form.

23. A certain computer can do 10^8 calculations per second. How many can it do in 10 seconds?

24. In half a day, a computer can make 100,000 transactions for a major airline. How many transactions can it make in five days?

★25. A loop in Larry's program must be done 1,000 times. How long will it take the computer to do this if one loop is completed in a microsecond?

More Practice Set 132, page 425

331

CHALLENGE

Use the circles above each puzzle to fill in the missing circles. The product must be the same along each row, column, and diagonal.

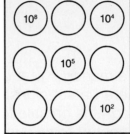

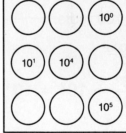

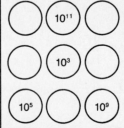

Dividing Powers of 10

A. The manager of a computer store offered a set of instructional programs on sale for $100. He expected to take in $10,000 from the sale of these sets. How many sets did he expect to sell?

You know the answer is $\frac{10,000}{100}$, or 100, sets.

$$\frac{10,000}{100} \quad 100$$

$$\frac{10^4}{10^2} = 10^2 = 10^{4-2}$$

You can divide powers of 10 by subtracting their exponents.

If m and n are integers, then $\frac{10^m}{10^n} = 10^{m-n}$.

B. Find $\frac{10}{10^4}$.

$$\frac{10}{10^4}$$

$$10^{1-4}$$

$$10^{-3}, \text{ or } 0.001$$

Try Use exponents to find each quotient. Write the answer with an exponent.

a. $\frac{10^4}{10^6}$

b. $\frac{10^5}{10^{-5}}$

c. $\frac{10^6}{10^0}$

d. $\frac{0.001}{0.1}$

e. $\frac{100,000}{1,000}$

332

Practice Use exponents to find each quotient. Write the answer with an exponent.

1. $\dfrac{10^5}{10^2}$

2. $\dfrac{10^6}{10^5}$

3. $\dfrac{10^1}{10^3}$

4. $\dfrac{10^4}{10^9}$

5. $\dfrac{10^6}{10^{-5}}$

6. $\dfrac{10^8}{10^{-6}}$

7. $\dfrac{10^{-4}}{10^{-5}}$

8. $\dfrac{10^{-5}}{10^{-6}}$

9. $\dfrac{10^4}{10^{-4}}$

10. $\dfrac{10^{-2}}{10^4}$

11. $\dfrac{10^{-3}}{10^{-3}}$

12. $\dfrac{10^2}{10^2}$

13. $\dfrac{10^0}{10^3}$

14. $\dfrac{10^3}{10^0}$

15. $\dfrac{10^{-1}}{10}$

16. $\dfrac{100}{1,000}$

17. $\dfrac{10}{100}$

18. $\dfrac{100}{10,000}$

19. $\dfrac{1,000}{1,000}$

20. $\dfrac{0.001}{0.001}$

21. $\dfrac{10}{0.1}$

22. $\dfrac{100}{0.01}$

23. $\dfrac{0.1}{0.01}$

24. $\dfrac{0.0001}{0.01}$

Apply Solve each problem. Give each answer with an exponent and also in standard form.

25. If a computer takes 100 seconds to print 10,000 lines, how many lines can it print per second?

26. If a computer takes 100 seconds to print 10,000 lines, how long does it take to print one line?

*27. How many items can a computer locate in a millisecond if it locates one item per nanosecond?

CALCULATOR

You can multiply or divide powers of 2 by adding or subtracting exponents.

$$16 \times 8 = 2^4 \times 2^3$$
$$= 2^7$$
$$= 128$$

$$\frac{256}{8} = \frac{2^8}{2^3}$$
$$= 2^5$$
$$= 32$$

Use your calculator to find the powers of 2 from 2^1 to 2^{15}. Record your results in a table. Find each product or quotient by using your table.

1. 32×32

2. $8 \times 1,024$

3. 16×256

4. 512×64

5. 256×8

6. 64×64

7. $\dfrac{512}{16}$

8. $\dfrac{2,048}{64}$

9. $\dfrac{8,192}{128}$

10. $\dfrac{16,384}{1,024}$

Scientific Notation for Large Numbers

Astronomers often use large numbers. They write these numbers compactly in **scientific notation**. To express a number in scientific notation, write it as a product so that:

1. the first factor is greater than or equal to 1 and less than 10, and
2. the second factor is a power of 10 in exponential form.

A. The earth is about 149,200,000 km from the sun. Write this number in scientific notation.

149,200,000   Imagine a decimal point after the first nonzero digit. Count the number of places from there to the actual decimal point.

8 places
to the right

1.492 × 100,000,000   Moving 8 places to the right is the same as multiplying by 100,000,000.

1.492 × 10⁸

B. Write 3,654.5 in scientific notation.

3,654.5

3 places
to the right

3.6545 × 10³

C. Write 9.87×10^5 in standard form.

9.87 × 10⁵

9.87 × 100,000

987,000

Try Write each number in scientific notation.

a. 779   **b.** 104,595   **c.** 330.26

Write each number in standard form.

d. 6.004×10^3 **e.** 6.004×10^7 **f.** 6.004×10^1

Practice Give each missing exponent.

1. $75 = 7.5 \times 10^{\blacksquare}$ **2.** $325.6 = 3.256 \times 10^{\blacksquare}$ **3.** $7,856.2 = 7.8562 \times 10^{\blacksquare}$

Write each number in scientific notation.

4. 150   **5.** 3,900   **6.** 836,000   **7.** 579,200

8. 3,200,000   **9.** 67,100,000   **10.** 875.2   **11.** 937.56

12. 6,000,000   **13.** 6   **14.** 10   **15.** 17.010

Write each number in standard form.

16. 8.12×10^5 **17.** 4.698×10^2 **18.** 1.03×10^2 **19.** 5×10^8

Apply Complete the table.

	Planet	Distance from sun	Scientific notation
20.	Mercury	57,900,000 km	
21.	Venus	108,100,000 km	
22.	Jupiter	778,100,000 km	
23.	Saturn	1,427,200,000 km	

★24. The mass of the earth is about 5.98×10^{24} kg. Write this number in standard form.

Scientific Notation for Small Numbers

When a number between 0 and 1 is expressed in scientific notation, the power of 10 has a negative exponent.

A. In 1969, the pulsar star at the core of the Crab Nebula pulsed every 0.033099324 second. Write this number in scientific notation.

0.033099324

2 places
to the left

Imagine a decimal point after the first nonzero digit. Count the number of places from there to the actual decimal point.

3.3099324 × 0.01

Moving 2 places to the left is the same as multiplying by 0.01.

3.3099324 × 10^{-2}

B. Write 0.000004 in scientific notation.

0.000004

6 places
to the left

4 × 10^{-6}

C. Write 6.57 × 10^{-3} in standard form.

6.57 × 10^{-3}

6.57 × 0.001

0.00657

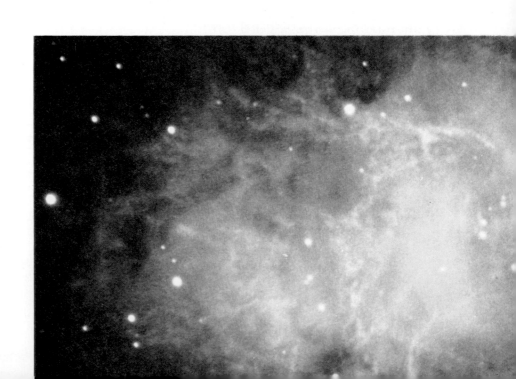

Try Give each number in scientific notation.

a. 0.00345 **b.** 0.345 **c.** 0.0345

Give each number in standard form.

d. 3.8×10^{-3} **e.** 5.217×10^{-2} **f.** 3.01×10^{-4}

Practice Give each missing exponent.

1. $0.043 = 4.3 \times 10^{\blacksquare}$ **2.** $0.005 = 5 \times 10^{\blacksquare}$

3. $0.000056 = 5.6 \times 10^{\blacksquare}$ **4.** $0.111 = 1.11 \times 10^{\blacksquare}$

Write each number in scientific notation.

5. 0.471 **6.** 0.011 **7.** 0.0000016 **8.** 0.000201

9. 0.003 **10.** 0.0034 **11.** 0.00007 **12.** 0.00503

∗13. 0.000000000555 **∗14.** 0.00000094448 **∗15.** 0.000000000000016

Write each number in standard form.

16. 3.7×10^{-1} **17.** 3.46×10^{-2} **18.** 5.7234×10^{-4} **19.** 4.26×10^{-5}

20. 7.964×10^{-3} **21.** 1.23×10^{-7} **22.** 4.7×10^{-8} **23.** 1×10^{-1}

Apply Solve each problem.

24. Scientists have calculated that the rate of the pulsar at the core of the Crab Nebula is slowing down 0.0012 second per century. Write 0.0012 in scientific notation.

25. The light from the pulsar travels one mile in 0.00000538 second. Write this number in scientific notation.

Computing with Scientific Notation

A. In its orbit around the sun, the earth travels about 2,560,000 km each day. It completes one orbit in about 365 days. Find the length of one orbit.

Find 2,560,000 × 365.

(2.56 × 10⁶) × (3.65 × 10²)	Write each number in scientific notation.
(2.56 × 3.65) × (10⁶ × 10²)	You can rearrange factors without changing their product.
9.344 × 10⁸	Multiply.
934,400,000	Write in standard form.

The length of one orbit is about 934,400,000 km.

B. Find $\dfrac{29,650,000}{0.005}$.

$\dfrac{29,650,000}{0.005}$	
$\dfrac{2.965 \times 10^7}{5 \times 10^{-3}}$	Write each number in scientific notation.
$\dfrac{2.965}{5} \times \dfrac{10^7}{10^{-3}}$	Separate into two divisions.
0.6 × 10¹⁰	Divide. Round the quotient of the decimals to the nearest tenth.
6,000,000,000	Write in standard form.

Try Compute, using scientific notation. Round the quotient of the decimals to the nearest tenth. Give each answer in standard form.

a. 250,000 × 500

b. 63,700 × 0.07

c. $\dfrac{1.56 \times 10^3}{1.2 \times 10^{-4}}$

d. $\dfrac{6,000,000}{0.017}$

Practice Multiply, using scientific notation. Give each answer in standard form.

1. (3.5 × 10⁴) × (2.7 × 10³)

2. (1.6 × 10⁻²) × (4.8 × 10⁻⁵)

3. 1,900 × 170

4. 0.000302 × 0.029

5. 50,000 × 1,200

6. 0.000518 × 0.0027

7. 0.0058 × 63

8. 65,000 × 0.00033

338

Divide, using scientific notation. Round the quotient of the decimals to the nearest tenth. Give each answer in standard form.

9. $\dfrac{5.1 \times 10^5}{1.7 \times 10^2}$

10. $\dfrac{6.4 \times 10^1}{4 \times 10^{-3}}$

11. $\dfrac{1.57 \times 10^{-3}}{5.3 \times 10^{-2}}$

12. $\dfrac{6.2 \times 10^{-2}}{2.78 \times 10^4}$

13. $\dfrac{323,000,000}{160}$

14. $\dfrac{930}{81,000}$

15. $\dfrac{0.0032}{0.00064}$

16. $\dfrac{0.792}{22,000}$

17. $\dfrac{8,000,000}{0.032}$

18. $\dfrac{0.0079}{50,000}$

19. $\dfrac{630,000}{0.75}$

20. $\dfrac{0.00068}{2,176}$

Apply Use scientific notation to compute each answer. Give each answer in standard form.

21. In its orbit around the sun, Neptune travels 467,000 km each day. It completes one orbit in 59,900 days. Find the length of Neptune's orbit.

22. The length of Pluto's orbit around the sun is 37,046,400,000 km. It completes one orbit in 90,800 days. Find the distance it travels each day.

Practice: Rational Numbers

Compare. Use >, <, or =.

1. $1\frac{1}{3}$ ⬤ -2 **2.** $-\frac{1}{2}$ ⬤ $-\frac{3}{4}$ **3.** -1.8 ⬤ 0 **4.** -2.4 ⬤ -1.6

List the numbers in order from least to greatest.

5. $-1, \frac{3}{4}, -\frac{1}{2}$ **6.** $0, -\frac{5}{8}, -\frac{1}{8}$ **7.** $2\frac{2}{3}, -2\frac{2}{3}, -2$ **8.** $-3, 0.4, -1.3$

Give each answer.

9. $\frac{5}{8} + \left(-\frac{1}{4}\right)$ **10.** $\frac{2}{3}\left(-\frac{1}{2}\right)$ **11.** $-\frac{5}{6} \div \left(-\frac{1}{3}\right)$ **12.** $-\frac{3}{5} - \frac{7}{10}$

13. $-3\frac{3}{5} \div \frac{2}{5}$ **14.** $\frac{2}{3} - 1\frac{5}{6}$ **15.** $-\frac{1}{5} + \left(-\frac{2}{3}\right)$ **16.** $-1\frac{1}{4}\left(-\frac{1}{3}\right)$

17. $0.8 - 0.16$ **18.** $-3.1 - 0.7$ **19.** $-4.6 + 2.5$ **20.** $-5.2 - (-3.7)$

21. -7.4×0.5 **22.** $25.2 \div (-0.9)$ **23.** $(-1.3)(-4.1)$ **24.** $-49.5 \div (-0.15)$

Write each number in standard form.

25. 10^5 **26.** 10^{-4} **27.** 7.8×10^4 **28.** 6.09×10^{-3}

Write each answer with an exponent.

29. $10^2 \times 10^5$ **30.** $10^6 \times 10^{-3}$ **31.** $10^{-5} \times 10^{-3}$ **32.** $10,000 \times 0.001$

33. $\frac{10^4}{10^3}$ **34.** $\frac{10^2}{10^{-2}}$ **35.** $\frac{1,000}{0.01}$ **36.** $\frac{0.0001}{100}$

Write each number in scientific notation.

37. $3,062$ **38.** 0.045 **39.** $372,000$ **40.** 0.0001

41. 11.2 **42.** 0.00025 **43.** 0.0000684 **44.** $40,500,000$

Compute, using scientific notation. Give each answer in standard form.

45. $(1.35 \times 10^5)(6 \times 10^3)$ **46.** 0.045×0.008

47. $\frac{7.13 \times 10^{-4}}{3.1 \times 10^{-1}}$ **48.** $\frac{234,000,000}{1,300}$

Apply Solve each problem. In Problems 49 and 50, use scientific notation to compute and give the answer in standard form.

49. In its orbit around the sun, Saturn travels about 830,000 km each day. It completes one orbit in about 10,800 days. Find the length of Saturn's orbit.

50. The length of Jupiter's orbit around the sun is about 4,849,600,000 km. It completes one orbit in about 4,330 days. Find the distance Jupiter travels each day.

51. One share of STA stock lost $1\frac{1}{4}$ on Monday and gained $\frac{1}{2}$ on Tuesday. Find the overall change.

52. Mr. Choy owns 75 shares of CMR stock. One day the stock lost $\frac{5}{8}$ per share. What was the change in the value of his stock?

⋆53. On Monday, one share of Tri-X stock sold for $16. The gains or losses for the week were: $-\frac{1}{8}$ on Monday, $1\frac{1}{8}$ on Tuesday, $-\frac{3}{4}$ on Wednesday, $-\frac{5}{8}$ on Thursday, and $\frac{3}{8}$ on Friday. What was one share worth at the close of the exchange on Friday?

COMPUTER

Interpreting Output

In BASIC, numbers are printed as integers, decimals, or in exponential form. Most computers print a maximum of six significant digits. When the number of significant digits is more than six, the number is printed in exponential form.

3.72546E−3 means 3.72546×10^{-3}.
5.5E7 means 5.5×10^{7}.

Data can be read in exponential form. This form can also be used in LET and PRINT statements.

Write each of the following numbers in decimal form.

1. 9.04E3   **2.** 4.3180E9

3. 1E7   **4.** 1.71662E−2

5. 2.97E2   **6.** 4.01872E−12

7. 6.94374E3   **8.** 8.2E8

9. 3.7201E−2   **10.** 7.13572E−3

Write each of the following numbers in exponential form.

11. 72,000,000   **12.** 0.00056792

13. 3,421.95   **14.** 0.00000021

15. 100,000,000   **16.** 4,300

17. 0.000002864   **18.** 0.000057381

19. 35,782,000   **20.** 61,947.4

Square Roots

A. If a quilt square has an area of 16 sq. in., how long is each side?

You know that each side is 4 in. long because $16 = 4 \times 4$.

16 is the *square* of 4. $\qquad 16 = 4^2$

4 is the *square root* of 16. $\qquad 4 = \sqrt{16}$

It is also true that $16 = (-4)^2$, but we will study positive square roots only.

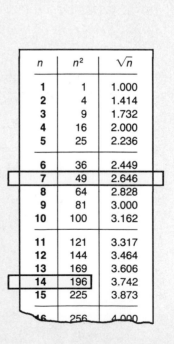

The picture shows that $\sqrt{9} = 3$, $\sqrt{4} = 2$, and $\sqrt{1} = 1$. Numbers like 1, 4, 9, and 16 are called *perfect squares* because their positive square roots are positive integers.

B. Between which two consecutive integers is $\sqrt{7}$?

7 is between the consecutive perfect squares 4 and 9. Therefore, $\sqrt{7}$ is between $\sqrt{4}$ and $\sqrt{9}$, or 2 and 3.

This table of squares and square roots is part of a larger one on page 445. Like the picture, it also shows that $\sqrt{7}$ is between 2 and 3. The table gives the value of $\sqrt{7}$ to the nearest thousandth.

c. To the nearest tenth, what is $\sqrt{7}$?

Find 7 in the *n* column.
Read across to the $\sqrt{n}$ column.

To the nearest tenth, $\sqrt{7} = 2.6$.

D. Find $\sqrt{196}$.

The table shows that $14^2 = 196$.
Therefore, $\sqrt{196} = 14$.

n	n²	√n
1	1	1.000
2	4	1.414
3	9	1.732
4	16	2.000
5	25	2.236
6	36	2.449
7	49	2.646
8	64	2.828
9	81	3.000
10	100	3.162
11	121	3.317
12	144	3.464
13	169	3.606
14	196	3.742
15	225	3.873
16	256	4.000

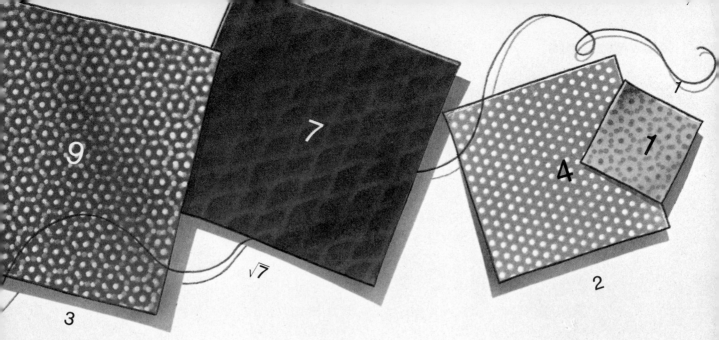

Try

a. Between which two consecutive integers is $\sqrt{45}$?

Use the table on page 445 to find each square root. If the answer is not an integer, round to the nearest tenth.

b. $\sqrt{25}$ **c.** $\sqrt{84}$ **d.** $\sqrt{2,209}$

Practice Between which two consecutive integers is

1. $\sqrt{29}$? **2.** $\sqrt{40}$? **3.** $\sqrt{72}$? **4.** $\sqrt{75}$? **5.** $\sqrt{97}$?

Use the table on page 445 to find each square root.
If the answer is not an integer, round to the nearest tenth.

6. $\sqrt{81}$ **7.** $\sqrt{36}$ **8.** $\sqrt{100}$ **9.** $\sqrt{64}$ **10.** $\sqrt{49}$

11. $\sqrt{29}$ **12.** $\sqrt{40}$ **13.** $\sqrt{15}$ **14.** $\sqrt{21}$ **15.** $\sqrt{42}$

16. $\sqrt{51}$ **17.** $\sqrt{55}$ **18.** $\sqrt{78}$ **19.** $\sqrt{80}$ **20.** $\sqrt{90}$

21. $\sqrt{400}$ **22.** $\sqrt{625}$ **23.** $\sqrt{3,249}$ **★24.** $\sqrt{12^2}$ **★25.** $(\sqrt{36})^2$

Apply Solve each problem.

26. A quilt square has an area of 2 sq. in. To the nearest tenth of an inch, how long is each side?

27. What is the area of a square whose sides each measure $\sqrt{12}$?

Real Numbers

A. Earlier in the chapter you learned that a rational number is one that can be written as the quotient of two integers, with the divisor not equal to 0. Write these rational numbers as either terminating or repeating decimals.

$$1 \quad -7 \quad \tfrac{1}{8} \quad \tfrac{3}{11} \quad -\tfrac{8}{3}$$

$$1 = \tfrac{1}{1} = 1.0 \qquad -7 = \tfrac{-7}{1} = -7.0$$

$$\tfrac{1}{8} = 0.125 \qquad \tfrac{3}{11} = 0.\overline{27} \qquad -\tfrac{8}{3} = \tfrac{-8}{3} = -2.\overline{6}$$

Every rational number can be written as either a terminating or a repeating decimal. Every terminating or repeating decimal names a rational number.

B. Nonrepeating decimals name *irrational numbers*.

3.141592653 . . .   **−2.050050005 . . .**

The value of π A number with a pattern in the digits but without a set of repeating digits.

The square roots of perfect squares are rational.

$$\sqrt{1} = 1 \qquad \sqrt{16} = 4$$

The square roots of all other positive integers are irrational.

$$\sqrt{2} = 1.4142135\ldots \qquad \sqrt{6} = 2.3393897\ldots$$

C. Decimal approximations help you locate irrational numbers on the number line.

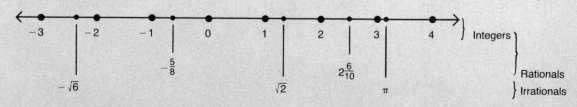

The rational numbers and irrational numbers together make up the *real numbers*.

Try Write each rational number as either a terminating or a repeating decimal.

a. $\frac{2}{5}$　　b. $-\frac{1}{3}$　　c. $\frac{10}{9}$

Decide whether the number is rational or irrational.

d. 4.7　　e. $-\frac{7}{4}$　　f. $\sqrt{23}$　　g. $\sqrt{100}$　　h. $3.\overline{14}$

Practice Write each rational number as either a terminating or a repeating decimal.

1. $\frac{1}{4}$　　2. $-\frac{2}{11}$　　3. $5\frac{2}{3}$　　4. $-1\frac{5}{8}$　　5. $\frac{65}{1,000}$

Decide whether the number is rational or irrational.

6. 0　　7. 20　　8. $-\frac{3}{5}$　　9. $\frac{8}{7}$　　10. $-\pi$

11. $\sqrt{13}$　　12. $\sqrt{24}$　　13. $\sqrt{81}$　　14. $\sqrt{4}$　　15. $-\sqrt{10}$

16. $-1.\overline{3}$　　17. -0.555　　18. 3.1416　　19. $-1.4\overline{14}$　　20. 1.0001

21. -2.683017688　　22. $6.718191\ldots$　　23. $5.\overline{142857}$

★24. 4π　　★25. $\frac{1}{2}\pi$　　★26. $\pi + 2$　　★27. $7 - \pi$　　★28. $\frac{1}{3}\sqrt{25}$

Apply A circle design in a quilt has a 35-in. diameter. Three people computed the circumference, but they used different approximations for π. Use each approximation given. Round your answer as instructed.

29. Amy used $3\frac{1}{7}$.　(ones)

30. Bill used 3.14.　(hundredths)

31. Pablo used 3.14159.　(ten-thousandths)

Pythagorean Theorem

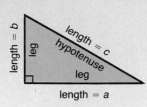

length = b
leg
length = c
hypotenuse
leg
length = a

The longest side of a right triangle is the *hypotenuse*, which is opposite the right angle. The other sides are the *legs*. The lengths of the sides are often called a, b, and c, where c is the length of the hypotenuse.

The *Pythagorean Theorem* applies to right triangles only. It relates the side lengths of any right triangle.

$$a^2 + b^2 = c^2$$

The sum of the squares of the lengths of the legs is equal to the square of the length of the hypotenuse.

A. This graduation invitation is 12 in. high and 5 in. wide. How long is the blue ribbon?

$$a^2 + b^2 = c^2$$

$$12^2 + 5^2 = c^2 \qquad \text{Lengths of the legs are given.}$$

$$144 + 25 = c^2$$

$$169 = c^2$$

$$\sqrt{169} = c$$

$$13 = c$$

The ribbon is 13 in. long.

B. Find b to the nearest tenth.

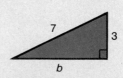

7   3
b

$$a^2 + b^2 = c^2$$

$$3^2 + b^2 = 7^2 \qquad \text{Lengths of one leg and the hypotenuse are given.}$$

$$9 + b^2 = 49$$

$$b^2 = 40$$

$$b = \sqrt{40} \qquad \text{Find } \sqrt{40} \text{ in the table on page 445.}$$

$$b \approx 6.3$$

c. Can a right triangle have side lengths of 6, 9, and 12?

$$a^2 + b^2 = c^2$$

$$6^2 + 9^2 \overset{?}{=} 12^2$$ *c should be replaced by 12, the longest length.*

$$36 + 81 \overset{?}{=} 144$$

$$117 \neq 144$$

The Pythagorean relationship is not satisfied. A right triangle cannot have sides with these lengths.

Try Two side lengths of a right triangle are given. Find the third length. If necessary, round your answer to the nearest tenth.

a. $a = 5, b = 5$

b. $a = 8, c = 17$

c. Can a right triangle have side lengths of 6, 8, and 10?

Practice Two side lengths of a right triangle are given. Find the third length. If necessary, round your answer to the nearest tenth.

1. $a = 4, b = 3$

2. $a = 24, b = 7$

3. $a = 9, b = 12$

4. $a = 10, b = 24$

5. $a = 6, b = 7$

6. $a = 2, b = 1$

7. $a = 21, c = 29$

8. $a = 24, c = 25$

9. $b = 15, c = 39$

10. $b = 12, c = 20$

11. $c = 20, a = 19$

12. $c = 40, b = 39$

Can a right triangle have these side lengths?

13. 3, 2, 4

14. 20, 21, 29

15. 15, 36, 39

16. 10, 10, 15

Apply Solve each problem. If necessary, round your answer to the nearest tenth.

17. A student designed a school pennant that is shaped like a right triangle. One side is 5 inches long, and the hypotenuse is 10 inches long. How long is the third side?

18. How long is the diagonal of a flag that is 3 ft. high and 5 ft. long?

Problem Solving: Use a Formula

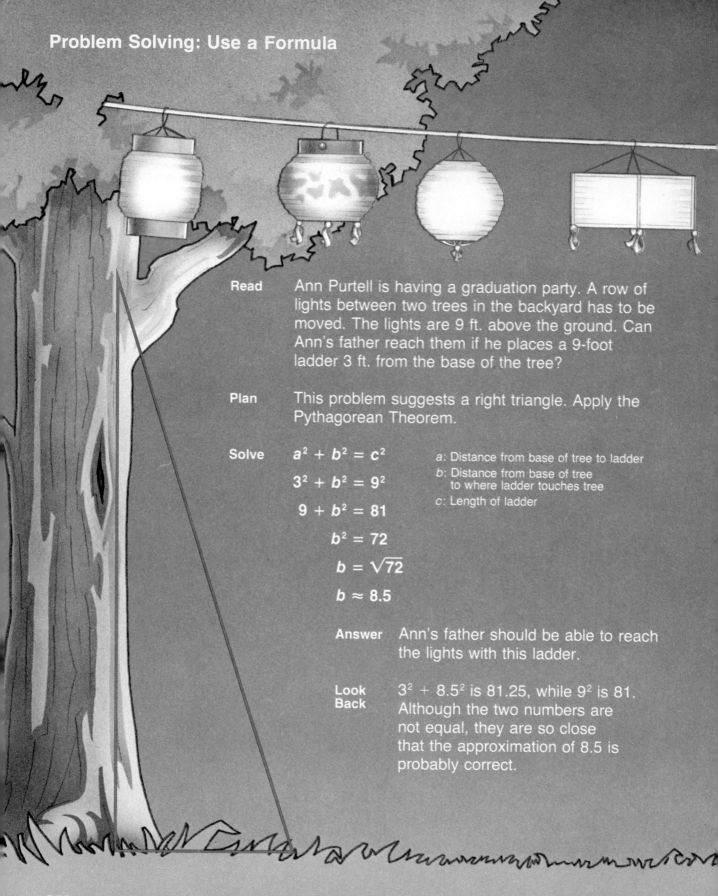

Read Ann Purtell is having a graduation party. A row of lights between two trees in the backyard has to be moved. The lights are 9 ft. above the ground. Can Ann's father reach them if he places a 9-foot ladder 3 ft. from the base of the tree?

Plan This problem suggests a right triangle. Apply the Pythagorean Theorem.

Solve

$$a^2 + b^2 = c^2$$

$$3^2 + b^2 = 9^2$$

$$9 + b^2 = 81$$

$$b^2 = 72$$

$$b = \sqrt{72}$$

$$b \approx 8.5$$

a: Distance from base of tree to ladder

b: Distance from base of tree to where ladder touches tree

c: Length of ladder

Answer Ann's father should be able to reach the lights with this ladder.

Look Back $3^2 + 8.5^2$ is 81.25, while 9^2 is 81. Although the two numbers are not equal, they are so close that the approximation of 8.5 is probably correct.

Try Solve the problem by using the Pythagorean Theorem. Round your answer to the nearest tenth, if necessary.

a. Will a round table top with an 8-foot diameter fit through a doorway that is 3 ft. by 7 ft.?

Apply Solve each problem by using the Pythagorean Theorem. Round your answer to the nearest tenth, if necessary.

1. A 12-foot ladder propped against the garage reaches the roof 11 ft. above the ground. How far from the garage is the base of the ladder?

2. The backyard is rectangular, 60 ft. wide and 80 ft. deep. What is the distance from one corner to the corner that is diagonally opposite?

3. Can a graduation gift in a 30-inch-long tube be hidden in the bottom of a dresser drawer that is 10 in. by 24 in.?

4. A tent pole is 87 in. long. Can it be stored against a closet wall that measures 35 in. by 84 in.?

5. Ann is making a gameboard with tape on the laundry room floor. Find *n*.

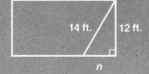

*6. How much crepe paper is needed for this design?

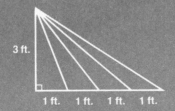

The Tangent Ratio

In any right triangle, a **trigonometric ratio** called the **tangent** can be written for each acute angle.

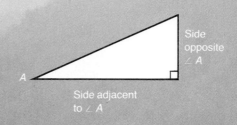

$$\tan A = \frac{\text{length of opposite side}}{\text{length of adjacent side}}$$

A. Part of U.S. Highway 40 through the Allegheny Mountains rises 55 ft. in a horizontal distance of 1,000 ft. Give the tangent of $\angle R$ as a ratio and as a decimal to the nearest thousandth.

$$\tan R = \frac{55}{1,000} = 0.055$$

The table on page 446 gives trigonometric ratios to the nearest thousandth.

$\tan 1° \approx 0.017$

$\tan 5° \approx 0.087$

$\tan 50° \approx 1.192$

Measure of angle	tan	Measure of angle	tan
1°	0.017	46°	1.036
2°	0.035	47°	1.072
3°	0.052	48°	1.111
4°	0.070	49°	1.150
5°	0.087	50°	1.192
6°	0.105	51°	1.235

B. Find n to the nearest tenth.

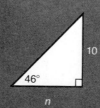

$$\tan 46° = \frac{10}{n}$$

$\dfrac{1.036}{1} \approx \dfrac{10}{n}$ Look in the table.
tan 46° ≈ 1.036

$1.036n \approx 10$ Find the cross-products.

$\dfrac{1.036n}{1.036} \approx \dfrac{10}{1.036}$

$n \approx 9.7$

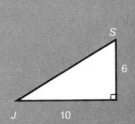

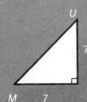

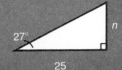
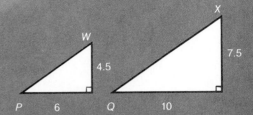

Try Use the triangles above. Give the tangent of each angle as a ratio and as a decimal to the nearest thousandth.

a. $\angle J$

b. $\angle S$

c. Find n to the nearest tenth. Use the table on page 446.

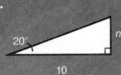

Practice Use the triangles above. Give the tangent of each angle as a ratio and as a decimal to the nearest thousandth.

1. $\angle K$ **2.** $\angle M$ **3.** $\angle N$ **4.** $\angle P$ **5.** $\angle Q$

6. $\angle T$ **7.** $\angle U$ **8.** $\angle V$ **9.** $\angle W$ **10.** $\angle X$

Find n to the nearest tenth. Use the table on page 446.

11.   **12.**   **13.**   **14.**

Apply Solve the problem.

15. On one of the steeper parts of Highway 40, $m\angle R = 4°$. In a horizontal distance of 5,000 ft., how many feet does the road rise?

If a hill rises 3 ft. for every 100 ft. of horizontal distance, the tangent of the angle at the bottom of the hill is 0.030, and the *grade* of the hill is 3%.

Read In San Francisco in 1881, cable cars traveled the Clay St. hill. A profile of the hill is shown below. What was the grade between Kearny St. and Dupont St.?

Plan Find the value of the tangent of $\angle K$ and write it as a percent.

Solve $\tan K = \dfrac{73 - 28}{412.5}$ ← Rise
← Horizontal distance

$\tan K = \dfrac{45}{412.5}$

$\tan K \approx 0.109$

Answer The grade was about 10.9%.

Look Back Be sure you chose the appropriate data from the diagram.

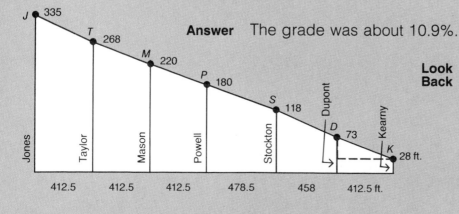

Try Solve each problem. Give percents to the nearest tenth of a percent.

a. What was the rise between Dupont and Stockton?

b. What was the grade between Dupont and Stockton?

Apply Solve each problem. Give percents to the nearest tenth of a percent.

1. What was the rise between Stockton and Powell?

2. What was the grade between Stockton and Powell?

3. What was the grade between Powell and Mason?

4. What was the grade between Mason and Taylor?

5. Between Kearny and Jones, what was the overall rise and the overall distance?

6. What was the grade between Kearny and Jones?

7. Two routes ran parallel to the Clay St. route. The rise between Kearny and Powell was 183 ft. on the California St. route and 23 ft. on the Geary St. route. List the three routes in order, starting with the steepest.

★8. Make a sketch of the following information. Label the rises and horizontal distances with numbers.

The grade of a hill between Elm St. and Pine St. is 2%. Between Pine and Main the grade is 3.5%. Consecutive streets are 660 ft. apart.

Chapter 11 Test

1. Compare. Use >, <, or =.

$-2\frac{1}{8}$ ⬤ $-1\frac{2}{3}$

2. List 0, $-\frac{1}{2}$, and $-\frac{3}{4}$ in order from least to greatest.

Give each answer.

3. $\frac{3}{4} + \left(-\frac{7}{8}\right)$

4. $1\frac{1}{2} - \left(-\frac{2}{3}\right)$

5. $-0.7 - 0.9$

6. $\left(-\frac{1}{3}\right)\left(-\frac{3}{5}\right)$

7. $4 \div \left(-\frac{2}{7}\right)$

8. $-4.96 \div 1.6$

Write each number with exponents.

9. 10,000

10. 0.001

11. $\frac{1}{100}$

Write each number in standard form.

12. 10^5

13. 10^1

14. 10^{-4}

15. 1.62×10^6

16. 4.1×10^{-2}

Write each answer with exponents.

17. $0.01 \times 10,000$

18. $\frac{10^{-3}}{10^2}$

Write in scientific notation.

19. 278,000

20. 0.0038

Compute, using scientific notation. Give each answer in standard form.

21. $87,600 \times 0.04$

22. $\frac{3.6 \times 10^{-2}}{1.5 \times 10^{-3}}$

23. Between which two consecutive integers is $\sqrt{37}$?

24. Write $-\frac{3}{4}$ as either a terminating or a repeating decimal.

25. Decide whether $\sqrt{5}$ is rational or irrational.

Use the table for Exercises 26 and 27. Round answers to the nearest tenth.

n	n^2	$\sqrt{n}$	n	n^2	$\sqrt{n}$
41	1,681	6.403	71	5,041	8.426
42	1,764	6.481	72	5,184	8.485
43	1,849	6.557	73	5,329	8.544

26. Two sides of a right triangle are $a = 5$ cm and $b = 4$ cm. Find the length of the hypotenuse.

27. How far up the side will a 9-foot ladder extend if it is placed 3 feet from the base of a house?

28. Give tan ∠D to the nearest tenth.

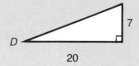

29. Find n to the nearest tenth. tan 17° ≈ 0.306.

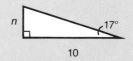

30. Find the grade from Main St. to Elm St.

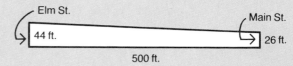

The Sine and Cosine Ratios

Besides the tangent ratio, two other common ratios are the *sine* and the *cosine*.

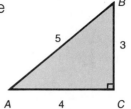

$$\sin\ A = \frac{\text{length of opposite side}}{\text{length of hypotenuse}}$$

$$\cos\ A = \frac{\text{length of adjacent side}}{\text{length of hypotenuse}}$$

$$\sin A = \tfrac{3}{5} = 0.600$$

$$\cos A = \tfrac{4}{5} = 0.800$$

Use the table on page 446 to express each of the following as a decimal.

1. cos 54°   **2.** sin 80°   **3.** sin 5°   **4.** cos 5°

Use either sine or cosine to find *n* to the nearest tenth.

5. 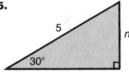   **6.** 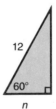   **7.** 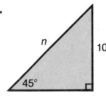   **8.**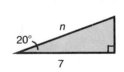

If ∠T and ∠S are the acute angles of a right triangle, describe the relationship between

9. sin *T* and cos *S*.   **10.** cos *T* and sin *S*.   **11.** tan *T* and tan *S*.

As an acute angle *R* increases, what happens to

12. sin *R*?   **13.** cos *R*?   **14.** tan *R*?

355

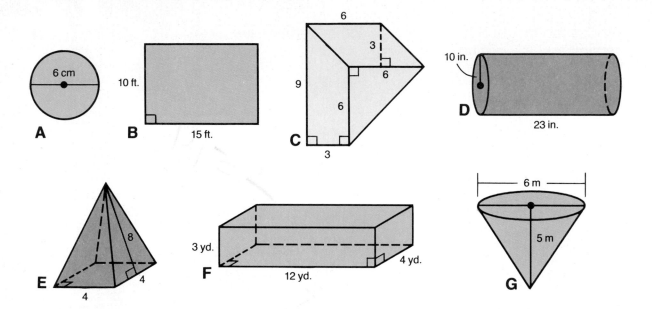

Express your answers to the nearest whole unit.
Use 3.14 for π.

Find the perimeter or circumference of each figure.

1. Figure A   **2.** Figure B

Find the area of each figure.

5. Figure A   **6.** Figure C

Find the surface area of each figure.

3. Figure D   **4.** Figure E

Find the volume of each figure.

7. Figure F   **8.** Figure G

Solve each problem.

9. What is the circumference of a $33\frac{1}{3}$-rpm record if its diameter is 30 cm?

10. A patio shaped like a right triangle has a base of 30 ft. and an altitude of 15 ft. What is the area of the patio?

11. A stereo speaker shaped like a cylinder is 15 in. high. The radius of each circular base is 4 in. What is the surface area of the speaker?

12. The Great Pyramid at Giza has a square base that measures 230 m on each side. Scientists think the original height of the pyramid was 147 m. What was its original volume?

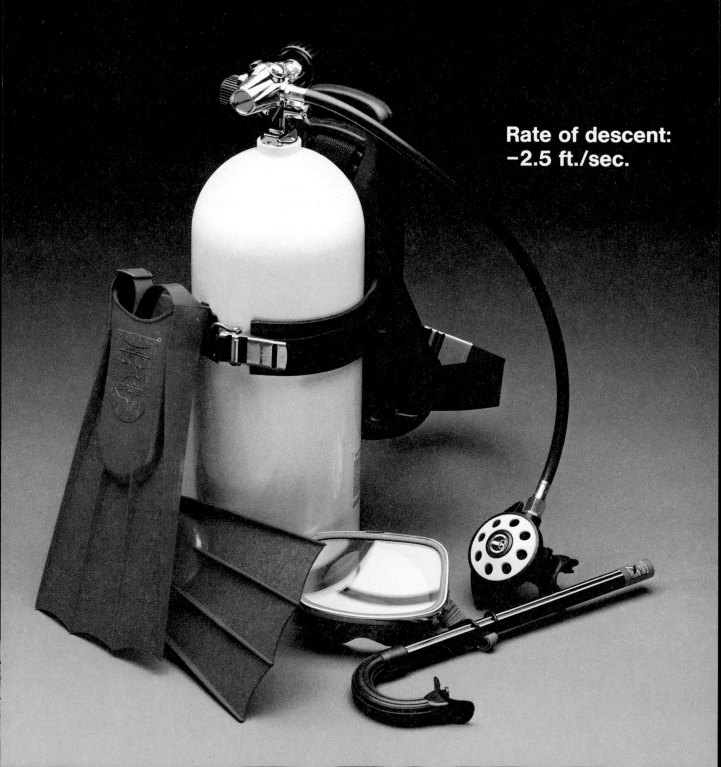

Equations, Inequalities, and Graphing

**Rate of descent:
−2.5 ft./sec.**

Expressions with Rational Numbers

A. The expression $100 - 0.003m$ can be used to find the boiling point of water in degrees Celsius at an altitude of m meters.

$$100 - 0.003m$$

$$100 - 0.003(1,600)$$ Substitute 1,600 for m.

$$100 - 4.8$$ Multiply.

$$95.2$$ Subtract.

Denver is about 1,600 meters above sea level. Find the boiling point of water in Denver.

The boiling point of water in Denver is about 95.2°C.

B. A quotient containing one variable can be written as the product of a rational number and the variable.

$$\frac{-4x}{7} = \frac{-4}{7}x = -\frac{4}{7}x$$

$$\frac{-a}{5} = \frac{-1a}{5} = \frac{-1}{5}a = -\frac{1}{5}a$$

C. Evaluate $\frac{4n}{5}$ for $n = -\frac{3}{8}$.

$$\frac{4n}{5} = \frac{4}{5}n$$ Write $\frac{4n}{5}$ as the product of a rational number and a variable.

$$= \frac{4}{5}\left(-\frac{3}{8}\right)$$ Substitute $-\frac{3}{8}$ for n.

$$= -\frac{3}{10}$$ Multiply.

D. Write an expression for -4 added to $\frac{2}{3}$ times w.

$$\frac{2}{3} \text{ times } w \text{ plus } -4$$
$$\downarrow \qquad \downarrow \quad \downarrow$$
$$\frac{2}{3}w \qquad + \quad (-4)$$

Try

a. Evaluate $x(y + 1)$ for $x = -0.4$ and $y = -0.5$.

b. Write an expression for -2 subtracted from the product of 6 and z.

Practice Write each expression as the product of a rational number and the given variable.

1. $\frac{4c}{5}$
2. $\frac{-3x}{8}$
3. $\frac{a}{4}$
4. $\frac{-m}{3}$
5. $-\frac{7s}{11}$
6. $-t$

Evaluate each expression for $a = -1.5$, $b = 0.6$, $c = 2.4$, $r = -\frac{1}{6}$, $s = \frac{2}{3}$, and $t = -\frac{1}{2}$.

7. $-4t$
8. $r + s$
9. $-r + 2s$
10. $r(s + 1)$
11. $-r(1 - t)$

12. $\frac{3r}{4}$
13. $-rst$
14. $rs + t$
15. $a + 2b$
16. $\frac{-2r}{3} - \frac{s}{2} + t$

17. $\frac{-2t}{5}$
18. $a(b + c)$
19. $ab + ac$
20. $0.5c - b$
21. $a^2 + 2a + 1$

Write an expression for each phrase.

22. -4 added to c
23. m subtracted from -2
24. -10 plus twice r

25. m divided by -4
26. 7 plus the product of -4 and x

27. $-\frac{2}{3}$ minus the product of $\frac{1}{2}$ and t

Apply Use the expression $100 - 0.003m$ to find the boiling point of water in degrees Celsius at each location. Round each answer to the nearest tenth of a degree.

28. Mt. Everest: Elevation 8,848 m
29. Mt. Whitney: Elevation 4,418 m

30. Dead Sea: Elevation -396 m
31. Death Valley: Elevation -86 m

Solving Addition and Subtraction Equations

Members of the Alpine Mountain-Climbing Club use this formula to find the outside air temperature in degrees Celsius at an elevation h meters above (+) or below (−) their base camp.

Temperature at base camp

Temperature h meters above or below camp

Meters from camp

$$T = t + 0.01h$$

A. The mountain summit is 3,000 meters above camp. If the temperature at camp is −5°C, find the temperature at the summit.

$$T = t + 0.01h$$

$$-5 = t + 0.01(3,000)$$

Substitute −5 for T and 3,000 for h.

$$-5 = t + 30$$

$$-5 + (-30) = t + 30 + (-30)$$

To get t by itself, add the opposite of 30 to both sides of the equation.
$30 + (-30) = 0$

$$-35 = t$$

The temperature at the summit is −35°C.

To solve a subtraction equation, you can first change the subtraction to addition of the opposite.

B. Solve $x - \frac{3}{4} = -\frac{1}{2}$.

$$x - \tfrac{3}{4} = -\tfrac{1}{2}$$

$$x + \left(-\tfrac{3}{4}\right) = -\tfrac{1}{2}$$

$$x + \left(-\tfrac{3}{4}\right) + \tfrac{3}{4} = -\tfrac{1}{2} + \tfrac{3}{4}$$

$$x = \tfrac{1}{4}$$

Here is another way to solve a subtraction equation.

c. Solve $-t - 2.6 = -1.2$.

$$-t - 2.6 = -1.2$$

$$-t - 2.6 + 2.6 = -1.2 + 2.6$$

$$-t = 1.4$$

$$t = -1.4$$

Multiply both sides of the equation by −1.

Try Solve each equation.

a. $t - 11 = 8$ **b.** $y + 4 = -5$ **c.** $y + \frac{1}{6} = -\frac{1}{3}$ **d.** $-1.5 - a = 2$

Practice Solve each equation.

1. $c + 7 = -3$ **2.** $-2 + a = 5$ **3.** $r + (-8) = -9$ **4.** $q + (-3) = 4$

5. $x - 9 = 7$ **6.** $v - 3 = -6$ **7.** $a - (-1) = 3$ **8.** $n - (-6) = -2$

9. $4 - x = -1$ **10.** $3 - c = 4$ **11.** $-2 - c = 8$ **12.** $-5 - h = -4$

13. $m + 6.5 = -7$ **14.** $v - 4.4 = 3$ **15.** $z - 6.1 = 2$ **16.** $x + 8.2 = -5$

17. $6.1 - x = 2.8$ **18.** $4.6 - z = 1.7$ **19.** $-6.4 = q + 3.7$ **20.** $1.3 = v - 3.2$

21. $d + \frac{3}{4} = \frac{1}{2}$ **22.** $-\frac{5}{8} + n = \frac{-3}{4}$ **23.** $\frac{2}{3} - t = -\frac{1}{6}$ **24.** $\frac{8}{9} + a = -\frac{1}{2}$

25. $m - \left(-\frac{5}{8}\right) = \frac{1}{4}$ **26.** $\frac{3}{8} + b = -3$ **★27.** $5\frac{2}{5} - x = -7\frac{5}{9}$ **★28.** $-8\frac{3}{4} + t = -7\frac{4}{5}$

Apply Suppose the temperature at the base camp is 5°C. Use the formula $5 = t + 0.01h$ to find the temperature at the given number of meters above (+) or below (−) the camp.

29. 4,000 m **30.** −1,000 m **31.** −2,000 m **32.** 6,000 m

Using Reciprocals to Solve Equations

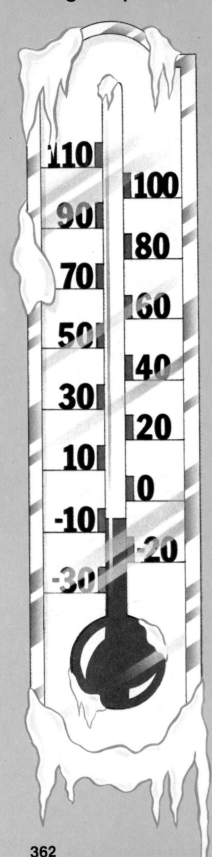

A. In 12 hours, the temperature dropped 30°F. Find the average hourly change in the temperature.

Hours   Average change   Total change

$$12n = -30$$

$$\left(\tfrac{1}{12}\right)12n = \left(\tfrac{1}{12}\right)(-30)$$

To get n by itself, multiply both sides of the equation by the reciprocal of 12. $\left(\tfrac{1}{12}\right)(12)n = 1n = n$

$$n = -2\tfrac{1}{2}$$

The average hourly change was $-2\tfrac{1}{2}$°F.

B. Solve $\frac{-2t}{5} = 4$.

$$\frac{-2t}{5} = 4$$

$$-\tfrac{2}{5}t = 4$$

$$\left(-\tfrac{5}{2}\right)\left(-\tfrac{2}{5}\right)t = \left(-\tfrac{5}{2}\right)4$$

$$t = -10$$

C. Solve $-2x - 7 = 15$.

$$-2x - 7 = 15$$

$$-2x - 7 + 7 = 15 + 7$$

$$-2x = 22$$

$$\frac{-2x}{-2} = \frac{22}{-2}$$

$$x = -11$$

Try   Solve each equation.

a. $\tfrac{2}{3}t = -\tfrac{1}{5}$ **b.** $\frac{-3x}{4} = \tfrac{1}{2}$

c. $-2m - 3 = 1$ **d.** $5x = 11.25$

Practice   Solve each equation.

1. $3x = -36$ **2.** $8n = -28$ **3.** $15y = 70$

4. $-6t = 84$ **5.** $-7a = 49$ **6.** $-4b = -40$

7. $\frac{2}{3}n = \frac{1}{2}$ **8.** $\frac{1}{2}t = \frac{5}{6}$ **9.** $-\frac{3}{4}a = -9$ **10.** $-\frac{2}{3}n = \frac{5}{12}$ **11.** $\frac{3x}{5} = \frac{9}{10}$

12. $\frac{5w}{8} = \frac{3}{4}$ **13.** $\frac{4m}{9} = -12$ **14.** $-\frac{r}{6} = -2$ **15.** $\frac{-x}{4} = -\frac{7}{12}$ **16.** $\frac{-c}{9} = \frac{5}{18}$

17. $4x - 9 = -1$ **18.** $-9 + 2y = -21$ **19.** $5t - 3 = -18$

20. $-3d + 4 = 6$ **21.** $-10x - 8 = -13$ **22.** $-8.4 = -4n + 8$

23. $2n - 1.7 = 1.3$ **24.** $5x + 0.4 = -2.6$ **★25.** $-0.24y + 0.1 = -3.2$

Apply   Solve each problem.

26. The snow melted at a rate of 6 inches a week. How many weeks did it take for 33 inches of snow to melt?

(HINT: $-6w = -33$)

27. The temperature fell an average of $\frac{3}{4}$°F an hour. In how many hours did it fall 6°F?

(HINT: $-\frac{3}{4}h = -6$)

CALCULATOR

The formula below shows how Celsius and Fahrenheit temperatures are related. To express −10°F in degrees Celsius, substitute −10 for F in the formula and solve the resulting equation.

Fahrenheit   Celsius

$$F = \frac{9}{5}C + 32$$

$$-10 = \frac{9}{5}C + 32$$

$$-10 - 32 = \frac{9}{5}C + 32 - 32$$

Press: 10 $\boxed{+/-}$ $\boxed{-}$ 32 $\boxed{=}$

$$-42 = \frac{9}{5}C$$

Display: -42

$$\left(\frac{5}{9}\right)(-42) = \left(\frac{5}{9}\right)\left(\frac{9}{5}C\right)$$

Press: $\boxed{\times}$ 5 $\boxed{\div}$ 9

$$-23\frac{3}{9} = C$$

Display: -23.333333

−10°F is about −23°C.

Express each reading in degrees Fahrenheit. Round to the nearest degree.

1. 30°C   **2.** 18°C

3. 100°C   **4.** −12°C

5. −30°C   **6.** −5°C

Express each reading in degrees Celsius. Round to the nearest degree.

7. 212°F   **8.** 25°F

9. 68°F   **10.** −20°F

11. −8°F   **12.** −40°F

Graphing Inequalities

Mathematical sentences that use the words "is less than" or "is greater than" are called *inequalities*.

The average depth of the Atlantic Ocean is −2.3 miles. The depth of any location that is lower than −2.3 miles can be expressed by the inequality $x < -2.3$.

A. Graph $x < -2.3$.

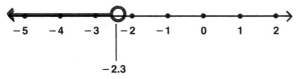

Every number to the *left* of −2.3 on the number line will make this sentence true. Use a circle to show that −2.3 is not in the graph.

B. Graph $x > -2.3$.

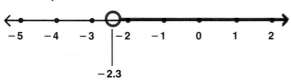

Every number to the *right* of −2.3 on the number line will make this sentence true. Use a circle to show that −2.3 is not in the graph.

Discuss How would you graph the equation $x = -2.3$?

c. Graph $x \le 2$.

This inequality is read "*x* is less than or equal to 2."

2 and every number to the left of 2 on the number line will make this sentence true. Use a filled-in circle to show that 2 is included in the graph.

Try Graph each inequality.

a. $x \geq -2$ **b.** $x < 0.5$

c. Write an inequality for this graph.

Practice Graph each inequality.

1. $x < -3$ **2.** $y > -4$ **3.** $c < 5$

4. $d \leq 5$ **5.** $z \geq 0$ **6.** $b < 0$

7. $m \geq -3$ **8.** $n < 2$ **9.** $h \geq 2.5$

Write an equation or inequality for each graph.

10.

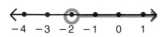

11.

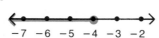

12.

13.

14.

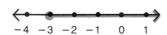

15.

Apply Solve each problem.

16. The altitude of Mt. Everest is 5.5 miles. Write an inequality to express the heights of all altitudes higher than Mt. Everest. Graph the inequality.

*17. The depth of the Mariana Trench is −6.9 miles, and the depth of the Brazil Basin is −3.8 miles. Make a graph to express all depths between these two depths.

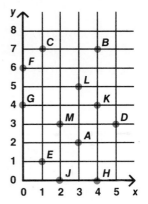

Use the figure above.

1. Which axis is the vertical axis?

2. Which axis is the horizontal axis?

3. Give the coordinates of the origin.

Name the point that each ordered pair locates.

4. (5, 3)   **5.** (3, 5)

6. (3, 2)   **7.** (1, 7)

8. (4, 0)   **9.** (0, 4)

Give the coordinates of each point.

10. J **11.** E **12.** M

13. K **14.** F **15.** B

Solving Addition and Subtraction Inequalities

A. One underwater vehicle was working at 5,000 ft. below sea level, and another vehicle was 3,000 ft. below sea level. Then both vehicles descended another 2,000 ft.

$$-5,000 < -3,000$$

This inequality compares −5,000 and −3,000. The first vehicle was lower.

$$-5,000 + (-2,000) \bullet -3,000 + (-2,000)$$

Add −2,000 to both sides of the inequality.

$$-7,000 \bullet -5,000$$

Write the new inequality. It has the same symbol as the original inequality. The first vehicle was still lower.

$$-7,000 < -5,000$$

The order of an inequality is not changed by adding the same number to both sides.

B. Solve $8.3 + t < -2.1$.

$$8.3 + t < -2.1$$
$$8.3 + t + (-8.3) < -2.1 + (-8.3)$$
$$t < -10.4$$

C. Solve $-5.1 \geq x - 2$.

$$-5.1 \geq x - 2$$
$$-5.1 + 2 \geq x - 2 + 2$$
$$-3.1 \geq x$$

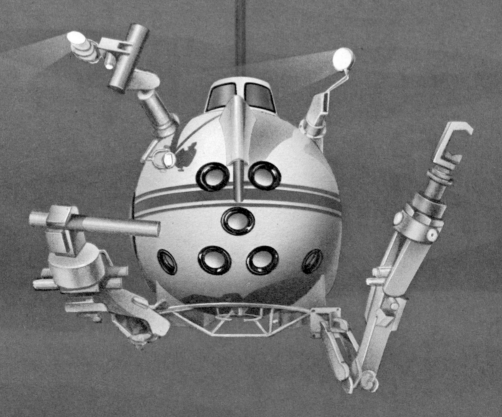

Try

a. Add −2.5 to both sides of −1 < 0. Write the new inequality.

b. Solve $g - 4 > -2$.   **c.** Solve $-1.6 \le x + 2.2$.

Practice Add the given number to both sides of the inequality. Write the new inequality.

1. 3 < 7. Add −2.

2. 3 ≥ −1. Add −4.

3. $-\frac{1}{4} \le 1$. Add $\frac{1}{4}$.

4. $-\frac{1}{2} > -1$. Add $-\frac{1}{2}$.

5. 3.2 < 4.1. Add −2.1.

6. 1.8 > −1.8. Add 0.8.

Solve each inequality.

7. $x + 6 < 8$

8. $y + 7 < 3$

9. $z - 9 > 15$

10. $a - 4 > 10$

11. $c - 6 \le -2$

12. $m + 5 \ge -7$

13. $d + (-3) > -6$

14. $x + (-9) < -8$

15. $5 < -4 + q$

16. $-8 \ge 2 + m$

17. $1 \le x - 2.1$

18. $3 < h - 4.7$

19. $-3 + r < -2.1$

20. $4 + x \ge 3.3$

21. $0 \le t - 3.7$

22. $x + 2.8 > 0$

23. $a - 4.1 > 0$

24. $k - 9.6 \ge 0$

25. $8 < n - 4.5$

26. $10 < b - 0.7$

27. $0.3 + r \le -2$

28. $0.9 + s \le -5$

29. $-7 \ge x - 1.1$

30. $-9 \ge c - 1.9$

Apply One underwater vehicle was at −8,000 ft. and another was at −6,000 ft. For each problem, write an inequality showing the new locations.

31. Both vehicles descended 1,000 ft.

32. Both vehicles ascended 1,000 ft.

33. Both vehicles descended 3,000 ft.

34. Both vehicles ascended 800 ft.

Solving Multiplication and Division Inequalities

A. While scuba diving, Rayann descended at a rate of 4 feet per second and Tammy descended at a rate of 2 feet per second. They descended for 20 seconds.

$$-4 < -2$$ This inequality compares -4 and -2. After one second, Rayann is lower.

$$20(-4) \bullet 20(-2)$$ Multiply both sides of the inequality by 20.

$$-80 \bullet -40$$ Write the new inequality. Notice that Rayann is still lower than Tammy.

$$-80 < -40$$

If both sides of an inequality are multiplied by the same positive number, the order of the inequality does not change.

B. Now observe what happens when both sides of an inequality are multiplied by a negative number.

$$-4 < -2$$

$$-3(-4) \bullet -3(-2)$$

$$12 > 6$$

$$\tfrac{1}{2} > -\tfrac{1}{2}$$

$$\left(-\tfrac{1}{3}\right)\left(\tfrac{1}{2}\right) \bullet \left(-\tfrac{1}{3}\right)\left(-\tfrac{1}{2}\right)$$

$$-\tfrac{1}{6} < \tfrac{1}{6}$$

If both sides of an inequality are multiplied by the same negative number, the order of the inequality is reversed.

c. Solve $\frac{1}{4}y < -7$.

$$\frac{1}{4}y < -7$$

$$(4)\tfrac{1}{4}y < (4)(-7)$$

$$y < -28$$

4 is positive.
The order of the inequality is not changed.

D. Solve $-2x \geq 7$.

$$-2x \geq 7$$

$$\left(-\tfrac{1}{2}\right)(-2x) \leq \left(-\tfrac{1}{2}\right)7$$

$$x \leq -3\tfrac{1}{2}$$

$-\frac{1}{2}$ is negative.
The order of the inequality is reversed.

Try Solve each inequality.

a. $-3x < 6$

b. $\frac{3}{4}y \leq -9$

c. $\frac{-3x}{2} > 6$

Practice Multiply both sides of the inequality by the given number. Write the new inequality.

1. $5 < 7$. Multiply by 2.

2. $5 < 7$. Multiply by -2.

3. $0 \geq -6$. Multiply by 4.

4. $0 > -6$. Multiply by -4.

5. $-1 \leq 3$. Multiply by -10.

6. $-6 \geq -7$. Multiply by 3.

7. $2.5 > -1$. Multiply by 4.

8. $-3.2 \leq -1.5$. Multiply by -1.

Solve each inequality.

9. $8n < 48$

10. $3m > 27$

11. $5x > -10$

12. $4t < -12$

13. $-7a \geq 35$

14. $-7b < 35$

15. $-9q \leq -36$

16. $-8h > -56$

17. $-5c \leq -30$

18. $-7f > -28$

19. $\frac{2}{3}s \geq -4$

20. $\frac{4}{5}k < -8$

21. $\frac{-3x}{4} \geq -15$

22. $\frac{-5y}{4} < 20$

★23. $\frac{2}{5}m - 2 < 14$

★24. $3 - \frac{4x}{5} \geq 11$

Apply Solve each problem.

25. From the surface, Rayann dived to more than -75 feet in 30 seconds. Describe the average number of feet she descended per second.

26. On one dive Tammy was more than twice as deep as Rayann. Rayann was at -45 feet. Describe Tammy's depth.

Practice: Equations and Inequalities

What happens when you cross a whale with a computer?

Solve each equation. Write the letters in the order of the answers given below.

1. $x - 9 = -3$ (N)

2. $x + 8 = 2$ (L)

3. $-4x = -16$ (Y)

4. $-2 - x = -7$ (N)

5. $3x = -12$ (K)

6. $-9 - x = -9$ (T)

7. $5 - x = 10$ (A)

8. $2x = -1$ (N)

9. $1.6 = x - 2.7$ (G)

10. $8.2 = x + 4.7$ (O)

11. $-2x - 1 = 13$ (E)

12. $2x + 4 = -3$ (T)

13. $\frac{5}{8} + x = -\frac{3}{8}$ (E)

14. $-3 + x = -\frac{1}{2}$ (A)

15. $-1.2x = -3.6$ (I)

16. $3x = -4.8$ (T)

17. $\frac{2}{3}x = \frac{8}{9}$ (U)

18. $-\frac{3}{5}x = \frac{2}{5}$ (T)

19. $\frac{x}{4} = \frac{-1}{3}$ (L)

20. $\frac{-4x}{5} = 2$ (O)

21. $\frac{2x}{7} = 2$ (O)

22. $\frac{-x}{4} = \frac{3}{8}$ (W)

Answer

| 4 | 3.5 | $1\frac{1}{3}$ | 4.3 | -7 | 0 |

| $2\frac{1}{2}$ | -1.6 | -1 | $-\frac{1}{2}$ | $-\frac{2}{3}$ | $-2\frac{1}{2}$ | 5 |

| -4 | 6 | 7 | $-1\frac{1}{2}$ | 3 | -3.5 | -5 | $-1\frac{1}{3}$ | -6 |

Graph each inequality.

23. $x \le -2$ **24.** $x \ge -2$

25. $y > 4$ **26.** $m < 0$

Solve each inequality.

27. $y + 3 \ge 5$ **28.** $-2m > 10$

29. $q - 6 < 9$ **30.** $j - 8 \ge 6$

31. $-8.5w \le -1.7$ **32.** $-3.5r > -10.5$

33. $\frac{2}{5}s < -\frac{1}{4}$ **34.** $-\frac{3}{8}y \le -12$

35. $-\frac{3}{4}m \ge -8$ **36.** $\frac{5}{6}q < -\frac{11}{12}$

Apply   The normal body temperature for humans is 98.6°F. This formula compares a given temperature and the normal. d is the number of degrees above or below normal.

$T = 98.6 + d$

37. After a race, a runner's temperature might be 103°F. How many degrees is this above or below the normal temperature?

38. People have been known to survive with a body temperature of 65°F. This is how many degrees above or below the normal temperature?

39. During a bout with pneumonia, an infant's temperature dropped to 87°F. How many degrees above or below the normal temperature is this?

COMPUTER

Write Programs

1. The speed of light is about 2.99776×10^8 m/s. Write a program that computes the number of meters light travels in one year.

2. Write a program that will divide any integer, N, by another integer, D, and then print the quotient and remainder.

3. Write a program that will find the mean of two numbers.

4. Write a program that will find the sum of the whole numbers from 1 to 100.

5. Write a program that will produce a table of squares and cubes from 1 to 10. Use the TAB function to print the number in one column, the square in a second column, and the cube in a third.

6. Write a program that will tell you if an integer is divisible by 2, 3, or both.

7. Write a program that can solve a linear equation $Ax + B = C$ for x when A, B, and C are input.

8. Write a program that will read a value for x and then tell you if it is a solution of the inequality $3x + 5 < 7$. Let x represent an integer.

Graphing in the Coordinate Plane

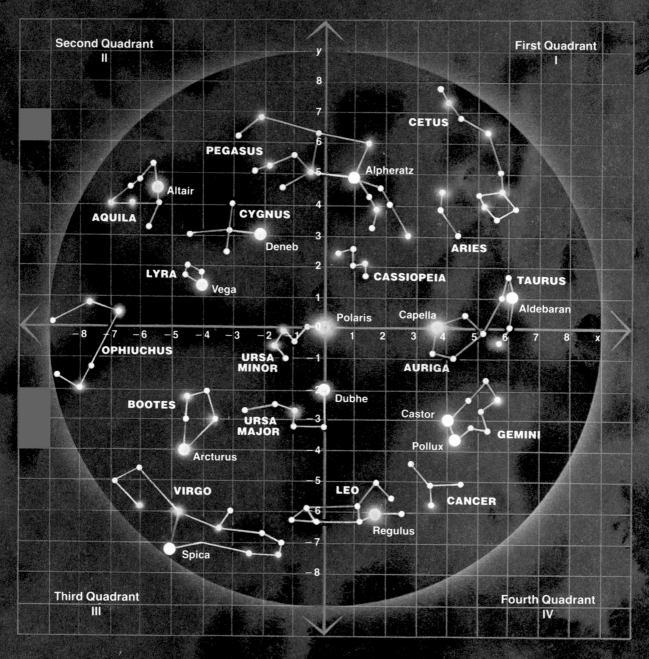

Career Luetta Hanson is an astronomer. She uses a grid to help people locate constellations and stars on a map. The *x*-axis and the *y*-axis separate the plane into four quadrants. They are labeled I through IV, as shown.

Any point can be located with an ordered pair of numbers called coordinates. The first coordinate tells how far to move to the right (+) or to the left (−) of the origin. The second coordinate tells how far to move up (+) or down (−).

A. Labels in capital letters name constellations on the map. Name the constellation near point (−4, −3).

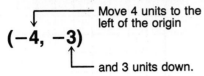

(−4, −3)

Move 4 units to the left of the origin

and 3 units down.

Bootes is near point (−4, −3).

B. The other labels, like Vega and Pollux, name stars. Give the coordinates of Vega, which is in quadrant II.

The point representing Vega is 4 units to the left of the origin (−4) and 1.5 units up (1.5).

The coordinates are (−4, 1.5).

Discuss What do the coordinates have in common for points in quadrant I? II? III? IV? On the *x*-axis? On the *y*-axis?

Try

a. Name the constellation at (−4, 2). In which quadrant is this point?

b. Give the coordinates of the star Pollux in quadrant IV.

Practice Name the constellation near each point. Tell which quadrant or which axis contains the point.

1. (−1, 6)
2. (4, 4)
3. (−7, 0)
4. (5, −3)
5. (5, 6)
6. (−6, −5)
7. (3, −5)
8. (−6, 5)
9. (0, −6)
10. (4, −1)
11. (−3, 3)
12. (1, 2)
13. (6, 1.5)
14. (−1, −0.5)
15. (−1, −2.5)

Give the coordinates of the point for each star.

16. Castor (IV)
17. Aldebaran (I)
18. Deneb (II)
19. Spica (III)
20. Capella (*x*-axis)
21. Arcturus (III)
22. Dubhe (*y*-axis)
23. Altair (II)
24. Regulus (IV)

Plot these points and connect them in order. Connect the last point with the first point.

25. (0, 7)
26. (1.5, 2)
27. (7, 1)
28. (3, −1)
29. (4, −6)
30. (0, −3)
31. (−4, −6)
32. (−3, −1)
33. (−7, 2)
34. (−2, 2)

Graphing Linear Equations

A. Gases expand when heated, and they contract when cooled. The formula below relates the volume of the gas in cubic centimeters and the temperature in degrees Celsius.

$$t = \tfrac{3}{5}V - 273$$

To graph this equation, first make a table of ordered pairs.

V (cm³)	0	200	500	800
t (°C)	−273	−153	27	207

Label a pair of axes with a convenient scale. The V-axis has to include 0 through 800, and the t-axis has to include −273 through 207. Use the ordered pairs in the table to graph points. Draw the line that the points determine.

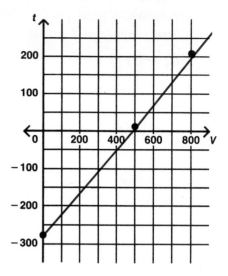

Discuss Give the volume for 100°C. Give the temperature for 50 cm³.

B. Graph both equations on the same grid.

$y = x + 2$

x	−4	−2	0	2
y	−2	0	2	4

$y = x − 2$

x	−2	0	2	4
y	−4	−2	0	2

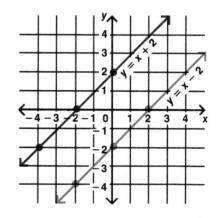

Notice that the lines are parallel and that they rise as you go from left to right.

Try Make a table and draw the graph.

a. $y = x + 4$

b. $y = -3x$

Practice In each exercise, make a table and draw the graph.
Use the same grid for Exercises 1–4.

1. $y = x$ **2.** $y = x + 3$ **3.** $y = x - 3$ **4.** $y = x - 5$

Use the same grid for Exercises 5–8.

5. $y = -x$ **6.** $y = -x + 2$ **7.** $y = -x - 4$ **8.** $y = -x - 1$

In each exercise, graph both equations on the same grid.

9. a. $y = 2x$ **10. a.** $y = 2x$ **11. a.** $y = 2x$ **12. a.** $y = 2x$

  b. $y = -2x$ **b.** $y = 4x$ **b.** $y = \frac{1}{2}x$ **b.** $y = -\frac{1}{2}x$

How are the graphs alike

13. in Exercises 1–4?

14. in Exercises 5–8?

★15. in Exercise 9?

★16. in Exercise 10?

★17. in Exercise 11?

★18. in Exercise 12?

Write an equation for a line
that goes through the origin

★19. and rises as you go
from left to right.

★20. and falls as you go
from left to right.

Apply Use the graph on page 374.

21. Give the volume for $-100°C$.

22. Give the temperature for 700 cm³.

Problem Solving: Use a Graph

ABC Car Rental
$ 20 a day
$ 0.25 a mile

Royal Car Rental
$ 50 a day
$ 0.10 a mile

Read   Carla wants to rent a car for one day. When is ABC Car Rental cheaper? When is Royal Car Rental cheaper? When is the cost the same?

Plan   Write an equation for the cost at each company. Graph the two equations on the same grid.

Solve   ABC Car Rental
$$C = 20 + 0.25m$$

m	0	100	200	300
C	20	45	70	95

Royal Car Rental
$$C = 50 + 0.10m$$

m	0	100	200	300
C	50	60	70	.80

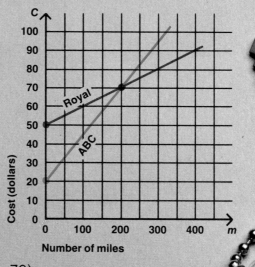

The lines intersect at (200, 70).

Answer If Carla drives 200 miles, both cars cost $70.00. ABC is cheaper for less than 200 miles, and Royal is cheaper for more than 200 miles.

Look Back   Both the graph and the tables show that the answer is correct.

Try Copy and complete the graph to solve the problem.

a. A bus left Bay City for Grafton at noon and averaged 40 mph. Two hours later, Carla left Bay City for Grafton by car and averaged 50 mph. The towns are 250 miles apart. Will Carla overtake the bus before getting to Grafton?

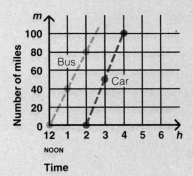

Apply Make a graph to solve the problems.

Dependable Rent-A-Bike Company charges $2 plus $0.50 an hour. Quality Bike Rental charges $1 plus $0.75 an hour.

1. When is the cost the same?

2. When is Dependable cheaper?

3. When is Quality cheaper?

Superior Car Rental charges $50 a day with no mileage charge. Reliable Car Rental charges $25 a day plus $0.10 a mile. Suppose Mr. Alvarez rents a car for 1 day.

4. When is the cost the same?

5. When is Superior cheaper?

6. When is Reliable cheaper?

Suppose Mr. Alvarez rents a car for 2 days.

7. When is the cost the same?

8. When is Superior cheaper?

9. When is Reliable cheaper?

10. A car and a train left Central City and traveled the same route. The car left at 12 noon and averaged 50 mph. The train left at 3:00 P.M. and averaged 75 mph. How far from Central City did they meet?

Graphing Inequalities in the Plane

A 40% solution of antifreeze will protect an automobile to about −12°F. The number of quarts of antifreeze needed for a radiator with a capacity of c quarts is $A = 0.4c$. Using the exact amount of antifreeze, or more, is given by the inequality $A \geq 0.4c$.

A. Graph $A \geq 0.4c$. Use only the first quadrant.

The inequality is a combination of $A = 0.4c$ and $A > 0.4c$. First graph $A = 0.4c$.

Capacity c	0	10	20
Antifreeze A	0	4	8

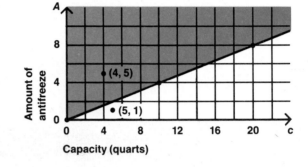

Amount of antifreeze

Capacity (quarts)

Select a point on one side of the line. If its coordinates make $A > 0.4c$ true, then that point is on the side that contains all the remaining solutions.

Try (5, 1). Is $1 \geq 0.4(5)$? No
Try (4, 5). Is $5 \geq 0.4(4)$? Yes

The line and the shaded region are the graph of $A \geq 0.4c$.

B. Graph $y < x + 2$.

Graph $y = x + 2$ with a dashed line, since this is not part of the solution.

Test a point. (0, 0) makes the inequality true, so all points on this side of the line are in the solution. The shaded region is the graph of $y < x + 2$.

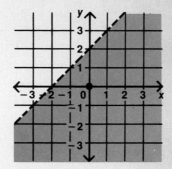

Try Graph each inequality.

a. $y > -2x$ **b.** $y \leq x - 1$

Practice Graph each inequality.

1. $y > x + 1$ **2.** $y < x + 1$ **3.** $y \leq x - 2$

4. $y \geq 2x$ **5.** $y < -x$ **6.** $y \leq -3x$

7. $y \geq x + 4$ **8.** $y < -x + 2$ **9.** $y > \frac{1}{2}x$

Apply Solve each problem.

10. A 50% solution of antifreeze will protect an automobile to about −34°F. Use $A \geq 0.5c$ and make a graph to show the number of quarts of antifreeze needed for a radiator with a capacity of c quarts.

11. A 45% solution of antifreeze will protect an automobile to about −23°F. Use $A \geq 0.45c$ and make a graph to show the number of quarts of antifreeze needed for a radiator with a capacity of c quarts.

CHALLENGE

Sam Smart said, "I have no time for school. There are 365 days in a year, and I sleep about 8 hours a day, or $\frac{1}{3}$ of a year."

$365 - 122 = 243$

"I don't go to school on Saturdays and Sundays."

$243 - 104 = 139$

"I have 90 days off for summer vacation."

$139 - 90 = 49$

"I have winter and spring vacations."

$49 - 19 = 30$

"I eat about 2 hours a day, or $\frac{1}{12}$ of a year."

$30 - 30 = 0$

"See? I have no time left."

Is Sam really so smart? Explain.

Chapter 12 Test

1. Write an expression for k subtracted from -6.

2. Evaluate $a(b - 1)$ for $a = -1.3$ and $b = 2.5$.

Solve each equation.

3. $r + (-4) = -6$

4. $5 - x = 8$

5. $4z = -28$

6. $\frac{-10y}{3} = \frac{5}{6}$

7. Use a number line to graph the inequality $d \le -1$.

8. Write an inequality for this graph.

$$\longleftarrow \overset{}{\underset{-6}{\bullet}} \overset{}{\underset{-5}{\bullet}} \overset{}{\underset{-4}{\bullet}} \overset{}{\underset{-3}{\bullet}} \overset{}{\underset{-2}{\bullet}} \overset{}{\underset{-1}{\bullet}} \overset{}{\underset{0}{\bullet}} \overset{}{\underset{1}{\bullet}} \overset{}{\underset{2}{\bullet}} \longrightarrow$$

9. Add -3.3 to both sides of $1 > 0$. Write the new inequality.

10. Solve the inequality $m + 5 < -3$.

11. Multiply both sides of the inequality $3 < 6$ by -2. Write the new inequality.

12. Solve the inequality $-4d \le -36$.

Use this graph to answer questions 13 and 14.

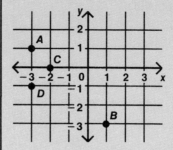

13. What are the coordinates of point C?

14. Which point is located at $(-3, 1)$?

Graph each equation and label it.

15. $y = -3x$

16. $y = \frac{1}{3}x$

Make a graph to solve the problem.

Super Car Rental charges $40 a day with no mileage charge. Ready Car Rental charges $25 a day plus $0.10 a mile. Suppose Consuela rents a car for one day.

17. When is the cost the same?

18. When is Ready cheaper?

Graph each inequality on a grid.

19. $y \le x + 2$

20. $y > -x$

CHALLENGE

Symmetry in the Coordinate Plane

If you fold the figure at the right along the *y*-axis, the two parts of the polygon will coincide. Polygon *ABCD* is *symmetric* with respect to the *y*-axis. The *y*-axis is the *line of symmetry*.

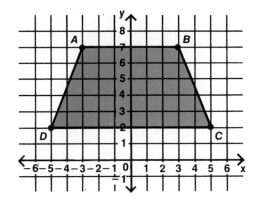

1. Compare the coordinates of *A* and *B*. Then compare the coordinates of *C* and *D*. What do you notice?

2. △*EFG* has vertices *E*(−6, −2), *F*(6, −2), and *G*(0, 5). Give a line of symmetry of △*EFG*.

3. Write the coordinates of points *H*, *L*, and *J*. Give a line of symmetry of △*HLJ*.

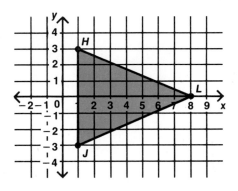

4. Plot points *M*(7, 3), *N*(−7, 3), *P*(−7, −3), and *Q*(7, −3). Give two lines of symmetry of polygon *MNPQ*.

5. Give the coordinates of the vertices of a square that has both the *x*-axis and the *y*-axis as lines of symmetry.

6. Plot points *R*(−3, 4), *S*(3, 4), *T*(5, 1), *U*(3, −2), and *V*(−3, −2). Fold the figure to find a line of symmetry of polygon *RSTUV*.

7. Plot points *R*(−3, 4), *S*(3, 4), *U*(3, −2), and *V*(−3, −2). Fold the figure to find two lines of symmetry of polygon *RSUV*.

8. Is $\overleftrightarrow{RU}$ a line of symmetry of polygon *RSUV*?

9. Is $\overleftrightarrow{SV}$ a line of symmetry of polygon *RSUV*?

10. Plot points *X*(2, 2), *Y*(12, 2), *Z*(12, 6), and *W*(2, 6). Give two lines of symmetry of polygon *XYZW*.

11. Is $\overleftrightarrow{XZ}$ a line of symmetry of polygon *XYZW*?

MAINTENANCE

Classify each triangle as scalene, isosceles, or equilateral and as acute, right, or obtuse. Congruent sides are shown with slash marks.

1.   **2.**   **3.**   **4.**    **5.**   **6.**

Classify each quadrilateral. Use as many of the following names as apply: *trapezoid, parallelogram, rhombus, rectangle, square.*

7.    **8.**   **9.**   **10.** 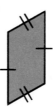   **11.** 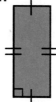   **12.**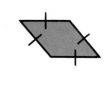

Solve each problem.

13. Fran purchased a $250 bond that paid 10.5% simple interest per year. What was the value of the bond after 2 years?

14. The circumference of the General Sherman tree at its base is 114.6 ft. Find the diameter to the nearest tenth. Use 3.14 for π.

15. One of the highest recorded temperatures was 136°F. One of the lowest was −90°F. Find the difference between these temperatures.

16. During a television special, 85 out of 250 people polled were watching the special. Predict the number of people, out of 10,000 viewers, who were watching the special.

17. A sailboat traveling with the wind traveled $5\frac{1}{2}$ nautical miles per hour for $1\frac{1}{3}$ hours. How far did the boat travel?

18. In its orbit around the sun, the earth travels about 2.56×10^6 kilometers per day. It completes one orbit in 365 days. Find the length of the earth's orbit.

Cumulative Test, Chapters 1–12

Give the letter for the correct answer.

1. Divide.

$36\overline{)3{,}046}$

A 84 R22
B 86
C 81 R30
D 80 R6

2. Solve this equation.

$4c - 12 = 24$

A 6   **B** 3   **C** 9   **D** 12

3. What does the 5 mean in 21.539?

A 5 ones
B 5 tens
C 5 hundredths
D 5 tenths

4. Which numbers are written in order from least to greatest?

A 0.09   0.094   0.2
B 0.2   0.09   0.094
C 0.094   0.09   0.2
D 0.2   0.094   0.09

5. Which fractions are written in order from least to greatest?

A $\frac{3}{8}$ $\frac{3}{4}$ $\frac{5}{16}$

B $\frac{5}{16}$ $\frac{3}{8}$ $\frac{3}{4}$

C $\frac{3}{4}$ $\frac{3}{8}$ $\frac{5}{16}$

D $\frac{5}{16}$ $\frac{3}{4}$ $\frac{3}{8}$

6. Divide.

$\frac{4}{5} \div \frac{1}{2}$

A $\frac{5}{8}$
B $\frac{2}{5}$
C $8\frac{1}{5}$
D $1\frac{3}{5}$

7. What is $\frac{13}{25}$ written as a percent?

A 65%   **C** 52%
B 38%   **D** 26%

8. 30 is $33\frac{1}{3}\%$ of what number?

A 33   **B** 90   **C** 27   **D** 120

9. Which is the best estimate of the area of a tennis court?

A 260 m²   **C** 2,600 m³
B 260 m³   **D** 26 m²

10. What is the name of this figure?

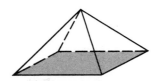

A rectangular prism
B triangular pyramid
C triangular prism
D rectangular pyramid

11. A circle has a diameter of 6 ft. What is its area? Use 3.14 for π.

  A About 113.04 sq. ft.
  B About 18.84 sq. ft.
  c About 28.26 sq. ft.
  D About 282.6 sq. ft.

12. What is the median of this group of salaries?

  $26,000 $10,000 $11,000
  $45,000 $13,000

  A $13,000   **c** $21,000
  B $11,000   **D** $20,000

13. If 11 represents a gain of eleven pounds, which integer represents a weight loss of 11 pounds?

  A 11   **c** 11%
  B 0   **D** −11

14. Which integers are written in order from least to greatest?

  A 0 −1 2 −5
  B −5 −1 0   2
  c −1 −5 0   2
  D −1   0 2 −5

15. Subtract.

  $-6 - (-2)$

  A −8
  B −4
  c 4
  D 8

16. Multiply.

  $-0.4(-0.3)$

  A −0.12
  B 1.2
  c 0.12
  D −1.2

17. What is 0.1 written with an exponent?

  A 10^0 **c** 10^1
  B 10^{-2} **D** 10^{-1}

18. The lengths of two sides of a right triangle are $a = 6$ cm and $b = 8$ cm. Find the length of the hypotenuse.

  A 14 cm   **c** 10 cm
  B 5.3 cm   **D** 3.7 cm

19. Solve the equation.

  $k + 4 = -5$

  A −9   **B** −1   **c** 9   **D** 1

20. Solve the inequality.

  $-3x \geq 5$

  A $x \geq 1\frac{2}{3}$ **c** $x \leq -1\frac{2}{3}$

  B $x \leq -\frac{3}{5}$ **D** $x \geq \frac{3}{5}$

MORE PRACTICE

Set 1 *pages 2-3* Find a pattern and list the next five numbers.

1. 4, 8, 12, 16, 20, . . .

2. 12, 20, 28, 36, 44, . . .

3. 66, 63, 60, 57, 54, . . .

4. 91, 84, 77, 70, 63, . . .

5. 0, 1, 4, 9, 16, . . .

6. 10, 11, 13, 16, 20, . . .

7. 750, 745, 735, 720, 700, . . .

8. 144, 132, 120, 108, 96, . . .

9. 11, 13, 12, 14, 13, . . .

10. 15, 25, 24, 34, 33, . . .

11. 1, 5, 13, 25, 41, . . .

12. 21, 30, 39, 48, 57, . . .

13. 73, 80, 78, 85, 83, . . .

14. 100, 90, 81, 73, 66, . . .

15. 300, 290, 295, 285, 290, . . .

16. 2, 17, 16, 31, 30, . . .

Set 2 *pages 4-5* Round to the nearest hundred.

1. 524   **2.** 217   **3.** 2,798   **4.** 1,051   **5.** 7,862   **6.** 17,213   **7.** 36,078

8. 71   **9.** 159   **10.** 3,029   **11.** 12,444   **12.** 8,150   **13.** 20,803   **14.** 93,152

Round to the nearest thousand.

15. 700   **16.** 529   **17.** 1,906   **18.** 23,014   **19.** 15,499   **20.** 80,406

21. 15,232   **22.** 77,498   **23.** 415,923   **24.** 5,032,699   **25.** 4,830,956   **26.** 57,621

Round to the nearest hundred-thousand.

27. 679,816   **28.** 956,023   **29.** 5,719,399   **30.** 123,429   **31.** 89,728   **32.** 216,611

33. 503,008   **34.** 800,527   **35.** 598,000   **36.** 716,543   **37.** 1,993,546   **38.** 590,103

Round to the nearest million.

39. 8,409,327   **40.** 19,715,619   **41.** 76,057,999   **42.** 99,605,728   **43.** 21,079,698

44. 82,359,713   **45.** 10,630,000   **46.** 49,752,522   **47.** 3,097,525   **48.** 61,902,202

Write each number in expanded form.

49. 637   **50.** 906   **51.** 1,019   **52.** 2,751   **53.** 9,072   **54.** 30,107

55. 5,974   **56.** 13,963   **57.** 20,506   **58.** 79,020   **59.** 112,568   **60.** 113,025

61. 2,304   **62.** 62,091   **63.** 170,462   **64.** 950,677   **65.** 24,315   **66.** 809,770

Set 3 *pages 6–7* Estimate each sum or difference.
First round the numbers in each problem to the same place.

1. 457 + 907

2. 852 + 575

3. 623 − 216

4. 782 − 539

5. 313 + 708

6. 426 − 172

7. 950 − 821

8. 525 − 395

9. 2,713 + 1,483

10. 8,586 − 310

11. 3,376 − 995

12. 4,258 − 1,256

13. 8,514 + 3,168

14. 3,313 − 1,121

15. 8,734 − 1,011

16. 6,798 + 3,921

17. 36,413 + 16,432

18. 48,019 + 37,817

19. 86,713 − 16,555

20. 53,957 − 29,435

21. 92,413 − 39,814

22. 27,052 + 31,813

23. 88,715 − 16,759

24. 43,013 + 22,951

25. 372,956 − 247,013

26. 961,978 − 504,321

27. 416,725 + 345,666

28. 583,802 + 966,410

29. 899,418 − 777,765

30. 208,506 + 77,544

Set 4 *pages 8–9*

1. 837 + 519

2. 932 − 514

3. 1,965 + 715

4. 2,958 + 3,582

5. 3,984 − 875

6. 9,016 + 4,889

7. 8,927 + 4,667

8. 9,988 + 3,777

9. 46,525 − 32,713

10. 57,013 + 32,109

11. 98,000 − 17,632

12. 48,785 − 39,096

13. 87,456 − 33,000

14. 39,544 + 23,005

15. 42,706 + 95,400

16. 835,000 + 82,903

17. 6,073 + 9,702 + 85 + 2,333

18. 30,015 + 13,344 + 19,278

19. 17,985 − 8,500

Set 5 *pages 10–11* Estimate each product.
Round each number so that only the first digit is not zero.

1. 506 × 313

2. 489 × 755

3. 194 × 373

4. 530 × 707

5. 3,510(8,412)

6. 8,113(1,072)

7. 2,833(4,179)

8. 3,478(8,906)

9. 92(406)

10. (817)49

11. (550)76

12. 19(562)

13. (8,425)(23)

14. (9,016)(75)

15. (82)3,110

16. 925(36)

17. 6,035(35)

18. (21)7,581

19. 89(715)

20. (93)(9,715)

21. 27,516(98)

22. 19,001(72)

23. 47(41,673)

24. 88(24,713)

25. (49)37,777

26. 82,016(91)

27. 66,715(63)

28. (77,814)(55)

MORE PRACTICE

Set 6 *pages 12–13*

1. 7(43)   **2.** 3(98)   **3.** 8(405)   **4.** 6(768)   **5.** 9(380)   **6.** 5(470)

7. 6(800)   **8.** 17(79)   **9.** 80(63)   **10.** 65(37)   **11.** 59(41)   **12.** 47(52)

13. (48)560   **14.** 15(44)   **15.** 35(505)   **16.** (309)44   **17.** (33)(604)   **18.** (24)(456)

19. 38(6,035)   **20.** 94(1,006)   **21.** (279)(500)   **22.** 715(1,325)   **23.** 624(404)

24. (677)(547)   **25.** 679(2,044)   **26.** (491)(3,026)   **27.** (209)(867)   **28.** 800(647)

29. (45)(90)(68)   **30.** 41 × 16 × 39   **31.** (58)(57)(54)   **32.** (789)(2,370)

33. (57)(32)(94)   **34.** (23)(38)(6)   **35.** 75 × 21 × 17   **36.** (3,713)(908)

37. 87 × 42 × 50   **38.** (28)(97)(84)   **39.** 68(67)(64)   **40.** 60(33)(29)

Set 7 *pages 14–15*

1. $7\overline{)746}$ **2.** $8\overline{)705}$ **3.** $4\overline{)927}$ **4.** $5\overline{)3,902}$ **5.** $6\overline{)6,233}$ **6.** $8\overline{)9,400}$

7. $27\overline{)983}$ **8.** $92\overline{)784}$ **9.** $44\overline{)607}$ **10.** $86\overline{)6,489}$ **11.** $67\overline{)7,684}$ **12.** $57\overline{)4,683}$

13. 1,007 ÷ 72   **14.** 2,082 ÷ 85   **15.** 18,978 ÷ 38   **16.** 40,500 ÷ 55   **17.** 8,621 ÷ 91

18. 5,221 ÷ 18   **19.** 6,344 ÷ 21   **20.** 15,555 ÷ 36   **21.** 37,645 ÷ 51   **22.** 16,035 ÷ 28

23. 1,756 ÷ 31   **24.** 8,718 ÷ 42   **25.** 38,709 ÷ 60   **26.** 96,000 ÷ 51   **27.** 57,400 ÷ 66

28. $\dfrac{11,315}{25}$ **29.** $\dfrac{35,000}{190}$ **30.** $\dfrac{37,631}{721}$ **31.** $\dfrac{478,320}{410}$ **32.** $\dfrac{28,509}{361}$ **33.** $\dfrac{35,648}{302}$

34. $\dfrac{17,835}{605}$ **35.** $\dfrac{9,555}{40}$ **36.** $\dfrac{52,871}{82}$ **37.** $\dfrac{333,733}{786}$ **38.** $\dfrac{254,688}{460}$ **39.** $\dfrac{77,675}{446}$

Set 8 *pages 16–17*   Tell which operation to use. Then solve each problem.

1. The attendance at the university's second basketball game was 5,376 people. That was 789 more than the attendance at the first game. How many attended the first game?

2. Charles Brown is retyping a report. If the report is 117 pages long and he types at the rate of 13 pages per hour, how long will it take him to complete the job?

3. Joan Baker is writing a book. In January, she spent 97 hours working on it; in February, 110 hours. How many hours did she spend working on the book?

4. Each month the Homestyle Bakery makes 14,250 loaves of bread. How many loaves are baked there in one year?

Set 9 *pages 20–21*   Is each number divisible by 2, 3, 4, 5, 9, or 10?
Write all the possibilities.

1. 370	**2.** 618	**3.** 603	**4.** 432	**5.** 183	**6.** 549
7. 9,123	**8.** 900	**9.** 3,150	**10.** 6,258	**11.** 8,975	**12.** 2,730
13. 7,280	**14.** 4,194	**15.** 7,264	**16.** 5,916	**17.** 33,624	**18.** 8,160
19. 48,615	**20.** 96,000	**21.** 113,226	**22.** 33,128	**23.** 70,512	**24.** 25,602
25. 325,656	**26.** 37,290	**27.** 32,112	**28.** 658,320	**29.** 810,018	**30.** 681,303

Set 10 *pages 22–23*   Tell whether each number is prime or composite.
If it is composite, list all of its factors.

1. 11	**2.** 21	**3.** 37	**4.** 51	**5.** 82	**6.** 18	**7.** 27	**8.** 31
9. 33	**10.** 65	**11.** 59	**12.** 72	**13.** 81	**14.** 93	**15.** 109	**16.** 112
17. 79	**18.** 47	**19.** 87	**20.** 200	**21.** 135	**22.** 117	**23.** 121	**24.** 120
25. 150	**26.** 167	**27.** 111	**28.** 300	**29.** 119	**30.** 141	**31.** 103	**32.** 137

Set 11 *pages 24–25*   Write the prime factorization of each number.
Use exponents when you can.

1. 16	**2.** 24	**3.** 45	**4.** 58	**5.** 69	**6.** 32	**7.** 44	**8.** 60
9. 72	**10.** 78	**11.** 84	**12.** 108	**13.** 140	**14.** 144	**15.** 110	**16.** 92
17. 128	**18.** 225	**19.** 300	**20.** 260	**21.** 420	**22.** 150	**23.** 213	**24.** 240
25. 550	**26.** 625	**27.** 900	**28.** 2,500	**29.** 5,000	**30.** 1,200	**31.** 1,440	**32.** 360

Set 12 *pages 26–27*   Find the GCF of each pair of numbers.

1. 12 and 16	**2.** 15 and 27	**3.** 14 and 42	**4.** 64 and 48	**5.** 18 and 36
6. 3 and 7	**7.** 11 and 33	**8.** 18 and 45	**9.** 31 and 47	**10.** 24 and 18
11. 60 and 15	**12.** 12 and 42	**13.** 30 and 55	**14.** 31 and 49	**15.** 16 and 48
16. 36 and 90	**17.** 25 and 75	**18.** 24 and 72	**19.** 32 and 80	**20.** 64 and 24
21. 54 and 72	**22.** 96 and 64	**23.** 81 and 45	**24.** 120 and 90	**25.** 15 and 75
26. 88 and 11	**27.** 108 and 36	**28.** 48 and 144	**29.** 108 and 27	**30.** 120 and 75

MORE PRACTICE

Set 13 *pages 28–29* For each pair of numbers, list the first three common multiples.

1. 8 and 12   **2.** 6 and 8   **3.** 4 and 10   **4.** 7 and 3   **5.** 3 and 11   **6.** 6 and 10

7. 10 and 20   **8.** 5 and 12   **9.** 4 and 15   **10.** 15 and 9   **11.** 25 and 30   **12.** 7 and 5

Use prime factorization to find the LCM of each pair of numbers.

13. 10 and 14   **14.** 12 and 18   **15.** 15 and 25   **16.** 28 and 32   **17.** 12 and 32

18. 30 and 42   **19.** 27 and 45   **20.** 16 and 40   **21.** 18 and 54   **22.** 24 and 30

23. 54 and 60   **24.** 40 and 72   **25.** 35 and 42   **26.** 24 and 40   **27.** 18 and 30

Set 14 *pages 30–31* Solve each problem. Look for a pattern.

1. Coach Smith must schedule games for his school's invitational basketball tournament. If two teams participate, he must schedule one game. If there are three teams, there will be three games; if four teams, six games. How many games must he schedule if there are eight teams participating?

2. One day Farmer Jones set out 6,561 sunflower seeds in the sun to dry. By the next day, the crows had eaten many and there were only 2,187 left. On the third day, there were only 729 left. At that rate, how many sunflower seeds would be left on the fourth day? on the ninth day?

3. Rachel Martinez is a runner who runs 3,000 meters each day. She would like to run in a marathon and wants to increase her endurance. The first week she increased her distance to 3,500 meters; the second, 4,000 meters; the third, 4,500 meters. At this rate, how many meters should she be able to run in the ninth week?

4. Bees built a hive in a garage. On the first day, Enrico counted 64 bees; on the second day, his neighbor, Darlene, counted 96 bees. On the third day, another friend, Leroy, counted 144 bees. At this rate, how many bees will the children be able to count on the fifth day?

Set 15 *pages 36–37*

1. $7 \times 9 + 2$ **2.** $3 + 25 \times 3$ **3.** $36 - 2(3)$ **4.** $40 + 6 \times 3 - 12 \div 4$ **5.** $8(9) + 6 \div 2$

6. $70 + 3(20) \div 5 \times 2$ **7.** $(15 + 3) - (14 - 2)$ **8.** $(12 - 8) + (2 + 2)$

9. $100 - 25 \times 2 + 21 \div 3$ **10.** $92 - 7 \times 4 + 9 \times 2^2$ **11.** $9 \times 8 \div 4 + 30 - 6(3)$

12. $\dfrac{25 + 3}{4}$ **13.** $\dfrac{8 + 3 \times 4}{5 - 3}$ **14.** $\dfrac{5(10 - 3)}{3 + 4}$ **15.** $\dfrac{3 + 5^2}{2^2}$ **16.** $\dfrac{5(12 + 8)}{2^2}$

17. $18 + \dfrac{30}{3}$ **18.** $49 - \dfrac{16}{2}$ **19.** $\dfrac{8^2}{2^2}$ **20.** $\dfrac{(7 + 3)^2}{(4 + 1)^2}$ **21.** $\dfrac{9(13 - 8)^2}{5 \times 3}$

Set 16 *pages 38–39* Find each missing number. Then name the property.

1. 16 + ▓ = 16

2. 12 + (6 + 3) = (12 + 6) + ▓

3. 98 + 10 = ▓ + 98

4. 29(▓) = 0

5. 10(45) = (10 × 9) + (10 × ▓)

6. 3,999 + ▓ = 3,999

Compute. Use the properties when you can.

7. 13 × 8 × 0

8. 49 × 1

9. (91 + 25) + 125

10. (15)5 + 25(5)

11. 7 × (4 × 3)

12. 31 + 15 + 0

13. (13)(5 − 5)(85)

14. 210 + 59 − 59

15. (11 − 10)27

16. (19)(17)(0)

17. (22 × 3) × 10 × 1

18. 9(10) + 9(4) + 9(16)

Set 17 *pages 40–41* Evaluate each expression when $d = 12$.

1. $d − 7$

2. $9d − 25$

3. $d + 27$

4. $15d + 2d$

5. $d + 2$

6. $7d + 13$

7. $3(d + 1)$

8. $d − 10 + 9$

9. $7 + d − 16$

10. $(d − 10) + 25$

Evaluate each expression when $k = 9$ and $n = 6$.

11. $k + n$

12. kn

13. $7kn$

14. $k(n + 4)$

15. $(k + 4) + n$

16. $n(k − 4)$

17. $(12 − n)k$

18. $(k + 5)n$

19. $3n + 4k$

20. $10k + 12n$

21. $\dfrac{9n}{k}$

22. $\dfrac{2k}{n}$

23. $n + k$

24. $(k + n)3$

25. $\dfrac{8k}{n}$

26. $4k(k + 2n)$

Evaluate $4(s + 9)$ when s is:

27. 4 **28.** 13 **29.** 57 **30.** 83 **31.** 150 **32.** 72 **33.** 55 **34.** 60 **35.** 84

36. 98 **37.** 15 **38.** 22 **39.** 35 **40.** 64 **41.** 50 **42.** 79 **43.** 58 **44.** 89

Evaluate $\dfrac{(t − 8)2}{5}$ when t is:

45. 33 **46.** 88 **47.** 103 **48.** 428 **49.** 173 **50.** 93 **51.** 358 **52.** 213 **53.** 308

Set 18 *pages 42–43* Write a mathematical expression for each problem.

1. 100 decreased by 19

2. The product of 7 and a

3. m divided by 2

4. The sum of 29 and 56

5. 15 fewer than n

6. 19 increased by n

7. b added to 4

8. The total of 73 and b

9. 203 multiplied by s

10. 73 less than x

11. 9 times b

12. 89 decreased by y

MORE PRACTICE

Set 19 *pages 44–45*   Solve each equation.

1. $m + 21 = 88$ **2.** $x - 72 = 39$ **3.** $w + 325 = 719$ **4.** $t + 83 = 707$

5. $49 = y + 13$ **6.** $44 = m - 16$ **7.** $150 = m - 29$ **8.** $136 = s - 56$

9. $115 = z + 81$ **10.** $z - 36 = 100$ **11.** $27 + q = 73$ **12.** $89 + m = 319$

13. $314 = 125 + x$ **14.** $r + 135 = 402$ **15.** $64 = 13 + s$ **16.** $172 = 78 + r$

17. $s + 5 + 16 = 95$ **18.** $m + 3 + 8 = 40$ **19.** $81 = s + 7 + 24$ **20.** $49 = z - 72$

21. $38 = x + 7 + 7$ **22.** $19 + 50 + x = 78$ **23.** $19 + s + 0 = 25$ **24.** $75 + y = 181$

25. $x - 35 = 118 + 7$ **26.** $25 + 17 + t = 55$ **27.** $m - 29 = 57$ **28.** $66 = 190 - m$

29. $x + 87 + 6 = 99$ **30.** $z - 77 = 87$ **31.** $72 + q = 119$ **32.** $184 = n - 55$

Set 20 *pages 46–47*   Solve each equation.

1. $6s = 72$ **2.** $9t = 153$ **3.** $100 = 5m$ **4.** $144 = 12y$ **5.** $35n = 280$

6. $140 = 10x$ **7.** $\frac{m}{11} = 12$ **8.** $\frac{c}{13} = 15$ **9.** $45 = \frac{x}{7}$ **10.** $\frac{x}{18} = 288$

11. $28p = 644$ **12.** $7s = 133$ **13.** $\frac{x}{6} = 606$ **14.** $\frac{132}{11} = x$ **15.** $\frac{p}{7} = 413$

16. $32 = \frac{p}{7}$ **17.** $\frac{x}{39} = 1$ **18.** $\frac{x}{7} = 42$ **19.** $87 = 3s$ **20.** $m = (7)(63)$

21. $s = 9(43)$ **22.** $9x = 99$ **23.** $7t = 91$ **24.** $92 = 4p$ **25.** $t - 53 = 105$

Set 21 *pages 48–49*   Write an equation. Then find the answer.

1. m divided by 32 is 56.   **2.** 19 less than x is 89.   **3.** p added to 113 is 149.

4. g increased by 6 is 18.   **5.** 72 decreased by 59 is r.   **6.** 765 divided by 85 is n.

7. One year a forest ranger counted 139 healthy elm trees and 67 elm trees that had died of Dutch elm disease. How many elm trees had there been originally?

8. In the eighth grade there are four homerooms which each have 27 students. How many students are in the eighth grade?

9. Genevieve divided a bag of peanuts among six people, herself and five friends, so that each received 32. How many peanuts were in the bag originally?

10. There are 29 houses on the street. 17 of the houses have trees planted in the front lawns. How many houses do not have trees in the front lawns?

Set 22 *pages 52–53*   Solve each equation.

1. $2a + 5 = 11$ **2.** $59 = 8 + 3f$ **3.** $88 = 13b + 10$ **4.** $92 = 8x + 4$

5. $17p + 4 = 123$ **6.** $4m - 72 = 144$ **7.** $19n - 38 = 95$ **8.** $15s - 72 = 78$

9. $6y - 7 = 41$ **10.** $3z + 27 = 36$ **11.** $\frac{x}{3} - 5 = 7$ **12.** $24f + 69 = 213$

13. $37 = \frac{y}{4} + 9$ **14.** $\frac{t}{5} + 29 = 44$ **15.** $\frac{3a}{4} = 45$ **16.** $\frac{4b}{8} = 44$ **17.** $\frac{12c}{4} = 15$

18. $24 = \frac{8x}{3}$ **19.** $\frac{16x}{10} = 8$ **20.** $\frac{9w}{4} = 63$ **21.** $\frac{29w}{7} = 87$ **22.** $\frac{9s}{15} = 12$

Set 23 *pages 54–55*
Use this graph and give the coordinates of:

1. A **2.** B **3.** D **4.** G **5.** Z

6. H **7.** K **8.** S **9.** T **10.** C

What point is at:

11. $(3, 1)$ **12.** $(5, 3)$ **13.** $(1, 5)$

14. $(6, 6)$ **15.** $(8, 2)$ **16.** $(2, 4)$

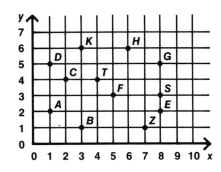

Draw the x-axis and the y-axis on grid paper.
Graph these points and label them with the ordered pairs.

17. $(6, 8)$ **18.** $(2, 2)$ **19.** $(5, 0)$ **20.** $(5, 6)$ **21.** $(0, 4)$ **22.** $(7, 3)$

Set 24 *pages 56–57*

The graph at the right shows the rate at which the printer for a microcomputer prints characters.

1. How many characters per second does the printer print?

2. How many characters does the printer print in 6 seconds?

3. How many seconds does it take to print 1,000 characters?

4. How many seconds does it take to print 400 characters?

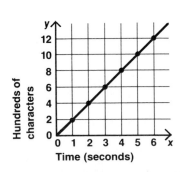

MORE PRACTICE

Set 25 *pages 58–59* Complete each table.
Then graph each equation on grid paper.

1. $x = a + 10$

a	0	1	3	5	9
x	10	11			

2. $y = 3t + 7$

t	0	2	4	6	8
y	7	13			

3. $d = 2t - 5$

t	5	10	15	20	25
d	5	15			

4. $s = 4m$

m	0	2	4	6	8
s	0	8			

Graph these equations on the same grid. Label each line
with its equation.

5. $y = 2x$ **6.** $y = x + 4$ **7.** $y = x + 1$ **8.** $y = 3x$ **9.** $y = 2x + 1$ **10.** $y = x + 5$

Set 26 *pages 60–61* Make a graph to solve each problem.

1. Frank is walking to school and is 100 meters
from the building entrance. David is walking
ahead of Frank and is only 80 meters from
the entrance. If Frank walks at the rate of four
meters per second and David walks at the
rate of three meters per second, how long
will it take Frank to catch up with David? How
far from the school will they be? (Use a graph
showing the distance from the school.)

2. Margaret and Donna were running the last
quarter of a four-person relay race. When
Donna received the baton, Margaret was
already ten meters ahead. Margaret was
running at the rate of nine meters per
second; Donna was running ten meters per
second. In how many seconds did Donna
overtake Margaret?

Set 27 *pages 62–63* Use the information in the sign.
Write your own problem about:

1. notebooks and multiplication.

2. the change received after paying for one
item.

3. division and ribbon.

4. multiplication and subtraction.

5. subtraction and notebooks.

6. puzzles and division.

7. toothpaste and addition.

VAL'S VARIETY STORE
COMBS 69¢
SHAMPOO $1.69
RIBBON 69¢ per yd.
TOOTH PASTE $1.69
NOTEBOOKS 89¢
PUZZLES $1.99
SPORT SOCKS $1.79 per pair
PENCILS 2 for 25¢
SALE!

Set 28 *pages 68–69* Write each number as a decimal.

1. $\frac{5}{10}$ 2. $\frac{609}{1,000}$ 3. $\frac{29}{100}$ 4. $\frac{38}{10,000}$ 5. $\frac{7,134}{100,000}$ 6. $\frac{52}{100}$ 7. $\frac{19}{10}$ 8. $\frac{3,709}{100,000}$

9. seventy-two hundredths

10. six and seventy-eight thousandths

11. twenty-two ten thousandths

12. sixteen and thirty-one ten thousandths

13. ten and nine tenths

14. forty-four hundred-thousandths

Write each decimal in words.

15. 0.015   16. 12.0088   17. 66.7003   18. 0.01016   19. 15.0103   20. 78.0019

21. 33.75   22. 0.0303   23. 8.311   24. 0.99099   25. 100.54   26. 0.50032

Set 29 *pages 70–71* Use <, >, or = to compare the numbers.

1. 0.6 ● 0.069   2. 0.705 ● 0.750   3. 2.78 ● 27.8   4. 0.54 ● 0.529

5. 0.382 ● 0.047   6. 29.18 ● 7.852   7. 0.666 ● 0.6667   8. 0.789 ● 0.7883

9. 0.0098 ● 0.025   10. 50.34 ● 6.888   11. 29.15 ● 29.1500   12. 0.1607 ● 0.1599

Write the numbers in order from least to greatest.

13. 7.97   7.99   0.756

14. 0.324   0.3024   0.412

15. 0.984   9.840   0.00984

16. 0.9546   16.32   1.632   9.546

17. 8.880   8.088   8.808   8.800

Set 30 *pages 72–73* Round each number to the place shown in parentheses.

1. 15.623 (ones)   2. 80.996 (ones)   3. 18.0155 (thousandths)

4. 37.735 (hundredths)   5. 13.856 (tenths)   6. 11.0188 (hundredths)

7. 99.997 (ones)   8. 0.4338 (hundredths)   9. 42.22979 (thousandths)

10. 0.801 (tenths)   11. 1.474 (hundredths)   12. 0.0084386 (millionths)

Round so that only one digit is not zero.

13. 56.3998   14. 0.05999   15. 3.1415   16. 8.0018   17. 0.08416   18. 11.387

19. 0.19199   20. 32.75   21. 99.011   22. 0.9333   23. 18.1877   24. 3916.6

25. 3.7502   26. 0.7272   27. 0.0309   28. 0.0011   29. 258.33   30. 46.725

MORE PRACTICE

Set 31 *pages 74–75*

1. 39.867 + 27.986
2. 10.6 + 8.44
3. 13.75 + 44
4. 18.78 + 47.566
5. 32 − 14.306
6. 42.135 − 28.6
7. 9.475 − 6.131
8. 57.183 − 18.25
9. 47 + 0.0569
10. 13.2 − 0.572
11. 66.408 − 32.78
12. 81 − 0.0756
13. 0.819 − 0.277
14. 54 + 27.1314
15. 2.8612 − 0.0087
16. 0.55 − 0.3417
17. 0.247 − 0.0899
18. 22 − 0.0003
19. 6.675 + 0.98003
20. 78 + 53.928
21. 0.0112 + 96 + 3.48 + 9.7
22. 4.301 + 430 + 0.431 + 30.41

Set 32 *pages 76–77*   Estimate each sum or difference.
First round each number to the nearest one.

1. 39.01 − 7.098
2. 55.36 + 8.903
3. 27.666 + 13.088
4. 14.96 − 10.078
5. 79.93 − 24.5
6. 99.19 − 13.622
7. 43.61 + 62.71
8. 67.08 + 16.2

First round each number to the nearest tenth.

9. 0.55 + 9.86 + 0.004
10. 30.39 + 18.82
11. 100.046 − 23.092
12. 21.09 + 16.57
13. 0.88 + 1.025 + 0.77
14. 56.732 − 16.444
15. 11.355 + 98.55
16. 72.37 − 28.06

First round the numbers to the same place.

17. 3.178 + 19.3
18. 19.773 − 13
19. 75.03 + 4.9821
20. 62.831 − 29
21. 0.0243 + 0.0077
22. 84 − 39.92
23. 66.398 − 15.0302
24. 41.309 − 37.55

Set 33 *pages 78–79*   If not enough information is given, write *too little information*. Otherwise, solve the problem.

1. At Ace Sport Shop how much did Mrs. Brown spend for two dozen golf balls?

2. Erik bought four baseballs. How much change did he receive?

3. Patty spent $36.75 for balls. How many did she buy?

4. What would the total bill be for one football and nine tennis balls?

5. Which is more expensive to buy, one golf ball or one tennis ball?

```
ACE SPORT SHOP
BASEBALLS     $2.99
FOOTBALLS     $10.99
BASKETBALLS   $15.95
GOLF BALLS    $21.00 per dozen
TENNIS BALLS  $5.85 per can of 3
```

Set 34 *pages 80–81*

1. 7.6×0.19 **2.** 10.8×0.5 **3.** 4.37×55.6 **4.** 93.72×10.2 **5.** $(0.12)^2$

6. $(8.7)^2$ **7.** $(0.023)^2$ **8.** $(0.37)^2$ **9.** $(28.4)^2$ **10.** $(4.4)^2$

11. $(84.57)(10)$ **12.** $(300.5)(100)$ **13.** $(9.501)(11)$ **14.** $(3.258)(17)$ **15.** $(73.5)^2$

16. $(0.0172)(0.0003)$ **17.** $(3.2)(5.4)(8.7)$ **18.** $(0.9)(0.66)(0.008)$

Set 35 *pages 82–83* Estimate each product.

1. 7.4×8.3 **2.** 2.3×5.96 **3.** 6.04×8.7 **4.** 3.15×9.01 **5.** 7.06×243

6. 44.1×7.02 **7.** 50.09×28 **8.** 17×0.3 **9.** 8.08×0.057 **10.** $0.72(0.04)$

11. 0.5×716 **12.** $8.703(0.08)$ **13.** $0.763(9.7)$ **14.** $8.44(0.012)$ **15.** 33×0.772

16. $0.784(7.08)$ **17.** $0.11(18.95)$ **18.** $0.071(3.6)$ **19.** $(0.875)(0.07)$ **20.** $(18.5)0.08$

Set 36 *pages 84–85*

1. $15\overline{)186}$ **2.** $16\overline{)60}$ **3.** $38\overline{)570}$ **4.** $45\overline{)36}$ **5.** $36\overline{)270}$

6. $63\overline{)446.67}$ **7.** $29\overline{)426.3}$ **8.** $75\overline{)617.25}$ **9.** $48\overline{)0.672}$ **10.** $62\overline{)611.94}$

11. $6.372 \div 54$ **12.** $0.7258 \div 19$ **13.** $0.0128 \div 16$ **14.** $6.12 \div 36$ **15.** $3.655 \div 43$

16. $11.5 \div 25$ **17.** $708.4 \div 10$ **18.** $0.0432 \div 27$ **19.** $63.415 \div 11$ **20.** $44.33 \div 22$

21. $\frac{3}{16}$ **22.** $\frac{23}{25}$ **23.** $\frac{114.984}{9}$ **24.** $\frac{45.099}{18}$ **25.** $\frac{21}{25}$ **26.** $\frac{79.812}{3}$ **27.** $\frac{84.474}{9}$

Set 37 *pages 86–87*

1. 748×100 **2.** $25 \times 10,000$ **3.** 10×0.049 **4.** $1.092 \times 100,000$

5. $1,000 \times 0.032$ **6.** 8.8×100 **7.** $0.007 \times 1,000$ **8.** 0.00851×10

9. $784 \div 10$ **10.** $3.6 \div 100$ **11.** $0.85 \div 1,000$ **12.** $8.8 \div 10,000$

13. $0.8659 \div 100$ **14.** $0.008 \div 100$ **15.** $100 \div 1,000$ **16.** $18 \div 10,000$

Multiply each of the following numbers by 10; 100; 1,000; and 10,000.

17. 7.6 **18.** 0.0179 **19.** 60.07 **20.** 98.6 **21.** 2.105 **22.** 3.79 **23.** 8.607

24. 10.27 **25.** 1.224 **26.** 11,865 **27.** 0.994 **28.** 1.3785 **29.** 290.3 **30.** 70.032

MORE PRACTICE

Set 38 *pages 88–89*

1. $0.08\overline{)0.6}$ **2.** $0.18\overline{)0.2268}$ **3.** $2.72\overline{)14.8512}$ **4.** $5.15\overline{)13.39}$ **5.** $2.18\overline{)14.17}$

6. $8.9\overline{)53.845}$ **7.** $0.09\overline{)810}$ **8.** $1.6\overline{)0.064}$ **9.** $0.08\overline{)0.144}$ **10.** $0.07\overline{)0.0315}$

Divide. Round the quotient to the nearest tenth.

11. $427 \div 0.8$ **12.** $8.76 \div 0.07$ **13.** $18 \div 0.362$ **14.** $10.8 \div 4.3$ **15.** $9 \div 0.46$

Divide. Round the quotient to the nearest hundredth.

16. $\dfrac{8.76}{1.8}$ **17.** $\dfrac{0.442}{7.2}$ **18.** $\dfrac{23}{0.147}$ **19.** $\dfrac{12}{1.54}$ **20.** $\dfrac{78}{0.49}$ **21.** $\dfrac{0.361}{3.9}$ **22.** $\dfrac{67.8}{8.1}$

23. $\dfrac{50}{1.7}$ **24.** $\dfrac{96}{4.5}$ **25.** $\dfrac{13.5}{1.7}$ **26.** $\dfrac{59}{6.2}$ **27.** $\dfrac{68}{4.3}$ **28.** $\dfrac{44}{7.3}$ **29.** $\dfrac{16}{0.302}$

Set 39 *pages 92–93*   Solve each equation.

1. $x + 7.2 = 11.1$ **2.** $76.8 = m + 4.9$ **3.** $c - 8.3 = 6.9$ **4.** $w - 8.3 = 17.1$

5. $6 + 10 + y = 21.3$ **6.** $t - 7 = 5.163$ **7.** $4s = 64.16$ **8.** $5.2n = 19.76$

9. $61.75 = b - 8.16$ **10.** $4.3x = 430$ **11.** $9.5 + x = 9.9$ **12.** $8s = 14.24$

13. $0.03 + m + 7.77 = 11$ **14.** $8.05y = 2.415$ **15.** $33t = 70.95$ **16.** $1.2m = 8.52$

17. $\dfrac{x}{15} = 0.675$ **18.** $100.8 = \dfrac{f}{7.2}$ **19.** $\dfrac{m}{11.5} = 0.8855$ **20.** $9.1 + 1.7 + 4.8 = c$

Set 40 *pages 94–95*   Write an equation. Then find the answer.

1. 23.5 added to a number y is 40.62.

2. The product of 75 and a number b is 30.

3. 5.478 is 14.0074 less than a number r. Find the number.

4. A number k divided by 89.7 is 431.2.

5. If four tickets to the circus cost a total of $9.00, how much does one cost?

6. If four tires for Mrs. Allen's automobile cost $291.80, how much would one tire cost?

7. Anna walked for 1.25 hours, stopped to eat for .5 hour, and then walked for 2.5 hours longer. How much time elapsed from the beginning of her walk to the end?

8. If a 15-pound bag of birdseed was to be divided evenly among four bird feeders, how many pounds should be put into each feeder?

9. 82.75 is 13.7 less than a number t. Find the number.

10. A number k increased by 3.56 is 3.597. Find the number.

Set 41 *pages 102–103* Give each missing number.

1. $\frac{3}{8} = \frac{18}{\blacksquare}$
2. $\frac{7}{\blacksquare} = \frac{1}{3}$
3. $\frac{4}{9} = \frac{36}{\blacksquare}$
4. $\frac{\blacksquare}{49} = \frac{5}{7}$
5. $\frac{7}{10} = \frac{56}{\blacksquare}$
6. $\frac{14}{63} = \frac{2}{\blacksquare}$

7. $\frac{63}{99} = \frac{7}{\blacksquare}$
8. $\frac{3}{\blacksquare} = \frac{18}{60}$
9. $\frac{45}{72} = \frac{\blacksquare}{8}$
10. $\frac{3}{11} = \frac{21}{\blacksquare}$
11. $\frac{56}{72} = \frac{\blacksquare}{9}$
12. $\frac{7}{11} = \frac{70}{\blacksquare}$

Write the answers in lowest terms.

13. $\frac{24}{30}$
14. $\frac{27}{45}$
15. $\frac{4}{9}$
16. $\frac{48}{72}$
17. $\frac{24}{64}$
18. $\frac{8}{36}$
19. $\frac{77}{84}$
20. $\frac{35}{105}$
21. $\frac{81}{108}$

Set 42 *pages 104–105* Write >, <, or = to compare the fractions.

1. $\frac{2}{3} \bullet \frac{5}{7}$
2. $\frac{7}{15} \bullet \frac{21}{45}$
3. $\frac{6}{7} \bullet \frac{7}{9}$
4. $\frac{9}{10} \bullet \frac{8}{9}$
5. $\frac{3}{5} \bullet \frac{6}{11}$
6. $\frac{7}{11} \bullet \frac{21}{33}$

7. $\frac{7}{16} \bullet \frac{3}{8}$
8. $\frac{8}{9} \bullet \frac{18}{20}$
9. $\frac{5}{8} \bullet \frac{3}{4}$
10. $\frac{9}{15} \bullet \frac{3}{5}$
11. $\frac{2}{9} \bullet \frac{4}{19}$
12. $\frac{4}{7} \bullet \frac{12}{21}$

13. $\frac{7}{12} \bullet \frac{3}{5}$
14. $\frac{9}{10} \bullet \frac{18}{25}$
15. $\frac{6}{11} \bullet \frac{14}{22}$
16. $\frac{9}{11} \bullet \frac{7}{8}$
17. $\frac{7}{15} \bullet \frac{13}{30}$
18. $\frac{5}{9} \bullet \frac{10}{19}$

Set 43 *pages 106–107* Write each decimal as a fraction in lowest terms.

1. 0.6
2. 0.28
3. 0.55
4. 0.06
5. 0.5
6. 0.032
7. 0.258

8. 0.18
9. 0.75
10. 0.9
11. 0.375
12. 0.56
13. 0.015
14. 0.745

Write each fraction as a decimal.

15. $\frac{7}{12}$
16. $\frac{5}{8}$
17. $\frac{1}{4}$
18. $\frac{9}{10}$
19. $\frac{7}{20}$
20. $\frac{7}{16}$
21. $\frac{6}{25}$
22. $\frac{11}{40}$
23. $\frac{11}{12}$

24. $\frac{4}{15}$
25. $\frac{13}{50}$
26. $\frac{4}{25}$
27. $\frac{3}{8}$
28. $\frac{3}{7}$
29. $\frac{5}{16}$
30. $\frac{17}{50}$
31. $\frac{7}{22}$
32. $\frac{11}{32}$

Set 44 *pages 108–109* Write each improper fraction as a whole number or a mixed number.

1. $\frac{13}{4}$
2. $\frac{57}{8}$
3. $\frac{36}{12}$
4. $\frac{35}{8}$
5. $\frac{57}{27}$
6. $\frac{91}{6}$
7. $\frac{72}{8}$
8. $\frac{57}{16}$
9. $\frac{12}{12}$

10. $\frac{18}{3}$
11. $\frac{88}{7}$
12. $\frac{90}{11}$
13. $\frac{38}{5}$
14. $\frac{42}{7}$
15. $\frac{83}{16}$
16. $\frac{26}{5}$
17. $\frac{19}{4}$
18. $\frac{65}{13}$

19. $\frac{33}{9}$
20. $\frac{51}{16}$
21. $\frac{28}{15}$
22. $\frac{58}{25}$
23. $\frac{15}{2}$
24. $\frac{67}{9}$
25. $\frac{31}{10}$
26. $\frac{19}{6}$
27. $\frac{58}{29}$

List the numbers in order from least to greatest.

28. $9\frac{2}{7}$ $9\frac{1}{2}$ $9\frac{3}{5}$
29. $4\frac{7}{9}$ $4\frac{3}{5}$ $4\frac{5}{8}$
30. $5\frac{1}{3}$ $5\frac{5}{6}$ $5\frac{5}{12}$
31. $10\frac{3}{4}$ $10\frac{7}{8}$ $10\frac{13}{16}$

32. $2\frac{5}{6}$ $2\frac{3}{4}$ $2\frac{7}{8}$
33. $3\frac{5}{8}$ $3\frac{3}{5}$ $3\frac{1}{2}$
34. $11\frac{3}{7}$ $11\frac{4}{5}$ $11\frac{1}{2}$
35. $4\frac{5}{6}$ $4\frac{3}{4}$ $4\frac{7}{12}$

MORE PRACTICE

Set 45 *pages 110–111*   Solve each problem.

1. Megan Brady delivers newspapers to 74 subscribers every day. She bought a box of 5,000 rubber bands for the papers. How many days will it be before she must buy another box?

2. Mr. Howard wants to purchase heavy mesh screening to install in his gutters. How many 30-foot rolls of screening must he buy to cover 439 feet of gutters?

3. Envelopes are sold in boxes of 50. How many boxes must the secretary of Elm School Parents' Club order so that she can send out announcements about the Fun Fair to the school's 708 families?

4. Jerry is entering a kite-flying contest. He wants to put 650 feet of string on his kite. How many 75-foot spools of string must he buy in order to accomplish this?

Set 46 *pages 112–113*

1. $\frac{5}{9} \times \frac{3}{4}$
2. $\frac{4}{7} \times \frac{5}{12}$
3. $\frac{7}{8} \times \frac{11}{15}$
4. $\frac{7}{10} \times \frac{3}{14}$
5. $\frac{2}{13} \times 6$

6. $18 \times \frac{5}{6}$
7. $\frac{12}{19} \times \frac{7}{20}$
8. $\frac{9}{16} \times 48$
9. $7 \times \frac{4}{21} \times \frac{5}{18}$
10. $\frac{3}{8} \times \frac{6}{25} \times \frac{11}{30}$

11. $\frac{8}{11} \times \frac{33}{40}$
12. $20 \times \frac{9}{28}$
13. $\frac{2}{5} \times \frac{5}{9}$
14. $\frac{4}{15} \times 75$
15. $\frac{1}{6} \times \frac{3}{7} \times \frac{8}{9}$

16. $27 \times \frac{11}{15}$
17. $\frac{11}{18} \times \frac{6}{7}$
18. $\frac{4}{11} \times \frac{5}{12}$
19. $\frac{17}{24} \times \frac{8}{17}$
20. $\frac{9}{14} \times \frac{1}{2} \times \frac{7}{12}$

21. $12 \times \frac{5}{9} \times \frac{3}{16}$
22. $\frac{1}{3} \times \frac{9}{13} \times \frac{26}{27}$
23. $16 \times \frac{7}{8} \times 20$
24. $\frac{5}{12} \times \frac{9}{50} \times 5$

Set 47 *pages 114–115*

1. $3\frac{3}{4} \times \frac{2}{15}$
2. $4\frac{3}{8} \times 7\frac{5}{7}$
3. $3\frac{1}{3} \times 27$
4. $8\frac{2}{5} \times 1\frac{1}{6}$
5. $5\frac{3}{4} \times 8\frac{2}{3}$
6. $9\frac{1}{2} \times 30$

7. $10\frac{2}{5} \times \frac{10}{13}$
8. $7\frac{5}{7} \times 3\frac{1}{2}$
9. $2\frac{5}{8} \times 9\frac{1}{7}$
10. $10\frac{5}{8} \times 3\frac{1}{5}$
11. $9\frac{5}{12} \times 2\frac{1}{4}$
12. $22 \times 7\frac{1}{11}$

13. $21 \times \frac{11}{24}$
14. $4\frac{1}{5} \times 5\frac{1}{4}$
15. $32 \times 6\frac{1}{2}$
16. $1\frac{1}{6} \times 1\frac{1}{6}$
17. $14 \times 7\frac{1}{2}$
18. $8\frac{1}{3} \times 7\frac{1}{5}$

19. $\frac{1}{2} \times 8\frac{3}{4} \times \frac{4}{15}$
20. $\frac{9}{10} \times 3\frac{1}{3} \times 6\frac{1}{12}$
21. $8\frac{2}{9} \times 3\frac{1}{4} \times 5\frac{1}{2}$
22. $3\frac{1}{3} \times 7\frac{1}{2} \times 9$

Give the reciprocal of each number.

23. 17
24. $\frac{4}{5}$
25. $3\frac{1}{3}$
26. $\frac{7}{8}$
27. 50
28. $6\frac{7}{8}$
29. $\frac{10}{11}$
30. $\frac{7}{9}$
31. $12\frac{3}{4}$

32. $\frac{5}{8}$
33. $12\frac{1}{2}$
34. 23
35. $\frac{9}{10}$
36. $15\frac{2}{3}$
37. $17\frac{3}{8}$
38. $9\frac{6}{11}$
39. $8\frac{7}{8}$
40. 64

Set 48 *pages 116–117*

1. $\frac{7}{8} \div \frac{1}{6}$ 2. $\frac{4}{15} \div \frac{4}{9}$ 3. $\frac{3}{4} \div \frac{8}{9}$ 4. $\frac{5}{7} \div \frac{1}{3}$ 5. $\frac{6}{13} \div \frac{9}{20}$ 6. $\frac{5}{8} \div \frac{15}{16}$

7. $\frac{7}{9} \div \frac{21}{30}$ 8. $\frac{4}{9} \div \frac{8}{15}$ 9. $5\frac{1}{5} \div 3\frac{3}{4}$ 10. $10\frac{2}{9} \div 2$ 11. $\frac{7}{12} \div 21$ 12. $\frac{8}{15} \div 24$

13. $8\frac{1}{8} \div \frac{5}{12}$ 14. $7\frac{1}{2} \div 4\frac{1}{16}$ 15. $18\frac{1}{4} \div 4\frac{1}{2}$ 16. $18 \div 12\frac{1}{2}$ 17. $\frac{8}{15} \div 6$

18. $23\frac{1}{3} \div 7\frac{5}{9}$ 19. $8\frac{4}{7} \div 3\frac{3}{7}$ 20. $7\frac{5}{8} \div 7\frac{5}{8}$ 21. $\frac{9}{10} \div \frac{8}{15}$ 22. $44\frac{3}{4} \div 16\frac{1}{4}$

Set 49 *pages 118–119*

1. $\frac{7}{8} + \frac{5}{12}$ 2. $\frac{4}{7} + \frac{3}{4}$ 3. $\frac{5}{9} + \frac{2}{3}$ 4. $\frac{9}{10} + \frac{11}{15}$ 5. $\frac{5}{8} + \frac{5}{6} + \frac{1}{4}$ 6. $\frac{5}{16} + \frac{5}{8}$

7. $\frac{8}{11} + \frac{1}{2}$ 8. $\frac{7}{8} + \frac{3}{5}$ 9. $\frac{2}{21} + \frac{6}{7}$ 10. $\frac{4}{9} + \frac{7}{12}$ 11. $\frac{5}{15} + \frac{2}{3} + \frac{1}{10}$ 12. $\frac{9}{10} + \frac{4}{5}$

13. $\frac{7}{18} + \frac{3}{4}$ 14. $\frac{11}{25} + \frac{3}{10}$ 15. $\frac{5}{6} + \frac{3}{14}$ 16. $\frac{3}{11} + \frac{4}{5}$ 17. $\frac{5}{14} + \frac{7}{10} + \frac{6}{7}$ 18. $\frac{3}{5} + \frac{3}{8} + \frac{9}{10}$

Set 50 *pages 120–121*

1. $5\frac{1}{2} + 10\frac{2}{7}$ 2. $\frac{8}{9} + 7\frac{1}{3}$ 3. $15\frac{7}{12} + 3\frac{2}{15}$ 4. $16 + 2\frac{5}{12}$ 5. $9\frac{3}{4} + 2\frac{5}{6}$

6. $11\frac{5}{8} + 9\frac{4}{5}$ 7. $\frac{7}{10} + 21\frac{1}{4}$ 8. $5\frac{7}{16} + 10\frac{1}{2}$ 9. $8\frac{3}{5} + 7\frac{4}{9}$ 10. $8\frac{9}{10} + 7\frac{3}{4}$

11. $8\frac{8}{9} + 7\frac{5}{12}$ 12. $16\frac{7}{18} + 9\frac{1}{3}$ 13. $7\frac{1}{8} + 3\frac{5}{12}$ 14. $19\frac{1}{2} + 6\frac{3}{5}$ 15. $6\frac{2}{9} + 2\frac{5}{6}$

16. $7\frac{1}{2} + \frac{8}{9} + 20\frac{1}{6}$ 17. $20\frac{3}{4} + 3\frac{7}{12} + 9\frac{5}{6}$ 18. $4\frac{7}{16} + 19\frac{7}{8} + 7\frac{1}{4}$ 19. $20\frac{3}{5} + 16\frac{3}{10} + \frac{11}{15}$

Set 51 *pages 122–123*

1. $\frac{7}{12} - \frac{1}{2}$ 2. $\frac{2}{9} - \frac{2}{15}$ 3. $\frac{7}{8} - \frac{3}{7}$ 4. $\frac{7}{12} - \frac{3}{8}$ 5. $\frac{13}{15} - \frac{3}{5}$

6. $15\frac{5}{7} - 8\frac{2}{9}$ 7. $20\frac{7}{12} - 8\frac{5}{16}$ 8. $25\frac{2}{3} - 4\frac{4}{15}$ 9. $18\frac{7}{10} - 13$ 10. $16\frac{7}{9} - 3\frac{1}{3}$

11. $53\frac{7}{9} - 18\frac{5}{12}$ 12. $31\frac{3}{5} - 19$ 13. $11\frac{7}{8} - 2\frac{2}{9}$ 14. $65\frac{9}{13} - 9\frac{2}{5}$ 15. $28\frac{5}{8} - 19$

16. $41\frac{5}{6} - \frac{7}{10}$ 17. $39\frac{5}{8} - 13\frac{3}{8}$ 18. $90\frac{5}{7} - 3\frac{1}{2}$ 19. $65\frac{5}{16} - 1\frac{3}{10}$ 20. $33\frac{7}{10} - 15\frac{2}{5}$

21. $18\frac{7}{8} - 12\frac{3}{16}$ 22. $7\frac{11}{12} - \frac{3}{8}$ 23. $3\frac{5}{12} - \frac{2}{5}$ 24. $28\frac{9}{10} - 9\frac{9}{10}$ 25. $22\frac{9}{10} - 5\frac{1}{4}$

26. $41\frac{19}{20} - \frac{3}{10}$ 27. $23\frac{1}{3} - 18$ 28. $54\frac{5}{6} - 17\frac{5}{6}$ 29. $27\frac{5}{7} - 8\frac{3}{8}$ 30. $30\frac{4}{7} - 3\frac{1}{2}$

MORE PRACTICE

Set 52 *pages 124–125*

1. $8\frac{2}{7} - 5\frac{6}{7}$ **2.** $15\frac{2}{9} - 9\frac{5}{9}$ **3.** $21\frac{1}{4} - 8\frac{3}{4}$ **4.** $30\frac{3}{11} - 14\frac{7}{11}$ **5.** $20 - 17\frac{5}{8}$

6. $24 - 7\frac{4}{5}$ **7.** $39 - 10\frac{5}{12}$ **8.** $12\frac{1}{6} - 6\frac{3}{5}$ **9.** $18\frac{3}{5} - 3\frac{5}{8}$ **10.** $17\frac{2}{5} - 10\frac{4}{5}$

11. $27\frac{3}{10} - \frac{7}{8}$ **12.** $42 - 16\frac{7}{9}$ **13.** $38 - 18\frac{7}{15}$ **14.** $22\frac{5}{12} - 10\frac{11}{12}$ **15.** $31\frac{1}{12} - 17\frac{5}{8}$

16. $17\frac{5}{12} - 14\frac{9}{10}$ **17.** $25\frac{2}{5} - 11\frac{5}{6}$ **18.** $32\frac{1}{4} - 3\frac{4}{7}$ **19.** $18\frac{1}{16} - 6\frac{1}{3}$ **20.** $81 - 18\frac{5}{16}$

Set 53 *pages 128–129* Solve each equation.

1. $m + 9\frac{2}{3} = 16$ **2.** $15\frac{1}{6} + s = 29\frac{5}{6}$ **3.** $12\frac{3}{7} + x = 22$ **4.** $y + 17\frac{5}{8} = 29\frac{1}{3}$

5. $t + 26\frac{7}{12} = 37\frac{3}{4}$ **6.** $21\frac{3}{10} = p + 19\frac{4}{5}$ **7.** $x - 17\frac{3}{5} = 56$ **8.** $d - 22\frac{3}{8} = 4\frac{2}{3}$

9. $n - 13\frac{1}{2} = 22\frac{5}{8}$ **10.** $s - 18\frac{4}{7} = 12\frac{6}{7}$ **11.** $17\frac{1}{9} = z - 8\frac{2}{3}$ **12.** $14\frac{2}{7} = t - 25\frac{7}{10}$

13. $\frac{9}{10}x = 54$ **14.** $\frac{5}{6}t = 2\frac{11}{12}$ **15.** $4\frac{5}{8}d = 7\frac{2}{5}$ **16.** $\frac{4}{5}x = \frac{4}{5}$

17. $40 = 18\frac{3}{4}y$ **18.** $r - 14\frac{7}{15} = 19\frac{3}{5}$ **19.** $14\frac{3}{7} + m = 22\frac{3}{4}$ **20.** $13 = 10\frac{1}{2}m$

21. $5\frac{5}{8}c = 40$ **22.** $7\frac{1}{2}y = 26\frac{3}{4}$ **23.** $x - 13\frac{4}{9} = 2\frac{3}{5}$ **24.** $7\frac{1}{2} = \frac{r}{20}$

25. $\frac{5}{6}d = 9\frac{3}{5}$ **26.** $18\frac{1}{2} = 9\frac{5}{6} + s$ **27.** $63 = 10\frac{1}{2}t$ **28.** $35\frac{1}{3} = n + 35\frac{1}{3}$

Set 54 *pages 130–131* Write an equation; then find the answer.

1. Mr. Washington bought a board which was 10 feet long to make a shelf which would be $6\frac{3}{4}$ feet long. How much of the board must he cut off?

2. The recipe for banana nut bread which Paul was making required $3\frac{1}{8}$ cups of flour. He wanted to double the recipe. How much flour did he need?

3. On July 10, XYZ Company's stock was trading at $36\frac{7}{8}$. At the opening of the market on July 11, the stock was trading at $40\frac{5}{8}$. How many points did the stock gain in value during the one-day period?

4. Barbara has prepared 18 ounces of potpourri with dried flowers and herbs from her garden. She would like to make sachets for gifts with the potpourri. How many $1\frac{1}{2}$-ounce sachets can she make?

5. Jay Witt has completed running $11\frac{1}{4}$ of his daily laps. How many more laps must he complete if he runs 20 laps daily?

6. How many batches of pancakes can Carol make from a 20-cup box of biscuit mix if each batch requires $1\frac{3}{4}$ cups?

Set 55 *pages 132–133*   Solve each equation.

1. $\frac{5}{9}x + 13 = 38$

2. $27 + \frac{5}{8}t = 77$

3. $\frac{5}{16}y - 11 = 19$

4. $\frac{3}{4}n + 20 = 44$

5. $\frac{7}{9}d - 15 = 69$

6. $6\frac{2}{3}n + 6 = 106$

7. $2\frac{4}{5}s - 19 = 23$

8. $66 = \frac{1}{3}d + 60$

9. $5\frac{1}{3}m + 10 = 74$

10. $4\frac{9}{10}x - 17 = 81$

11. $13\frac{1}{2}y - 25 = 56$

12. $20w - \frac{5}{8} = 7\frac{3}{8}$

13. $2\frac{3}{16}p - 37 = 33$

14. $8\frac{1}{9}d + 9 = 104$

15. $4\frac{4}{9}t + 3 = 163$

16. $6\frac{11}{15} = 2\frac{1}{2}a + 3\frac{2}{5}$

Set 56 *pages 138–139*   Name four equal ratios to describe each situation.

1. 3 tickets for $0.50

2. 6 pens for $1.98

3. 4 tables to 16 chairs

Do the ratios form a proportion? Write *yes* or *no*.

4. $\frac{5}{18}$ $\frac{10}{34}$

5. $\frac{18}{12}$ $\frac{9}{6}$

6. $\frac{27}{54}$ $\frac{12}{24}$

7. $\frac{46}{69}$ $\frac{12}{8}$

8. $\frac{5}{30}$ $\frac{7}{42}$

9. $\frac{36}{75}$ $\frac{4}{15}$

10. $\frac{1.4}{4.2}$ $\frac{6.0}{18.0}$

11. $\frac{28}{21}$ $\frac{36}{37}$

12. $\frac{45}{50}$ $\frac{54}{60}$

13. $\frac{0.9}{4.5}$ $\frac{0.7}{3.0}$

14. $\frac{25}{90}$ $\frac{5}{16}$

15. $\frac{75}{50}$ $\frac{36}{24}$

16. $\frac{8}{9}$ $\frac{9}{8}$

17. $\frac{60}{40}$ $\frac{4}{3}$

18. $\frac{45}{35}$ $\frac{27}{21}$

19. $\frac{6}{18}$ $\frac{1.5}{4.2}$

20. $\frac{35}{56}$ $\frac{10}{16}$

21. $\frac{7}{12}$ $\frac{56}{96}$

22. $\frac{0.4}{0.9}$ $\frac{2}{4.5}$

23. $\frac{28}{25}$ $\frac{35}{30}$

24. $\frac{60}{72}$ $\frac{55}{66}$

25. $\frac{1.6}{1.8}$ $\frac{3.2}{4.0}$

26. $\frac{45}{70}$ $\frac{55}{90}$

27. $\frac{4}{15}$ $\frac{20}{75}$

Set 57 *pages 140–141*   Solve each proportion.

1. $\frac{4}{9} = \frac{x}{63}$

2. $\frac{35}{14} = \frac{r}{6}$

3. $\frac{35}{s} = \frac{14}{16}$

4. $\frac{21}{49} = \frac{12}{y}$

5. $\frac{x}{9} = \frac{42}{54}$

6. $\frac{5}{d} = \frac{55}{66}$

7. $\frac{72}{m} = \frac{45}{60}$

8. $\frac{11}{12} = \frac{44}{p}$

9. $\frac{a}{26} = \frac{14}{91}$

10. $\frac{s}{9} = \frac{24}{8}$

11. $\frac{7}{m} = \frac{42}{90}$

12. $\frac{1.2}{6} = \frac{6}{n}$

13. $\frac{1.2}{t} = \frac{0.9}{3.6}$

14. $\frac{28}{16} = \frac{y}{12}$

15. $\frac{r}{35} = \frac{22}{14}$

16. $\frac{0.9}{2.4} = \frac{0.21}{t}$

17. $\frac{63}{14} = \frac{d}{8}$

18. $\frac{35}{20} = \frac{h}{2.4}$

Set 58 *pages 142–143*   Use a proportion to solve each problem.

1. Lee can sew 5 aprons in 7 hours. How long will it take her to sew 105 aprons?

2. There are 36 melons in 4 crates. How many crates will be needed for 180 melons?

3. If Tony can wash 18 cars in 6 hours, how many cars can he wash in 5 hours?

4. If 8 dinner rolls cost 79¢, how much will 24 rolls cost?

5. Three yards of ribbon cost $2.19. How much would 4 yards of the same ribbon cost?

6. There is a total of 56 needles in 4 packages. How many packages would there be for 126 needles?

MORE PRACTICE

Set 59 *pages 144–145* Write each decimal as a percent.

1. 0.12   **2.** 0.24   **3.** 0.55   **4.** 0.78   **5.** 0.925   **6.** 0.066   **7.** 0.042

8. 0.6   **9.** 0.05   **10.** 0.16   **11.** 3.2   **12.** 1.1   **13.** 0.7   **14.** 0.095

15. 3.05   **16.** 2.06   **17.** 4.9   **18.** 2.09   **19.** 3.3   **20.** 0.01   **21.** 0.014

22. $0.62\frac{1}{2}$ **23.** $0.16\frac{2}{3}$ **24.** $0.05\frac{1}{4}$ **25.** $0.80\frac{3}{4}$ **26.** $0.08\frac{1}{2}$ **27.** 9   **28.** 0.004

Set 60 *pages 146–147* Write each number as a percent.

1. $\frac{39}{100}$ **2.** $\frac{15}{100}$ **3.** $\frac{17}{50}$ **4.** $\frac{7}{10}$ **5.** $\frac{4}{25}$ **6.** $\frac{33}{50}$ **7.** $\frac{28}{100}$ **8.** $\frac{19}{25}$ **9.** $\frac{9}{10}$

10. $\frac{1}{4}$ **11.** $\frac{4}{5}$ **12.** $\frac{7}{8}$ **13.** $\frac{7}{16}$ **14.** $\frac{23}{40}$ **15.** $3\frac{1}{2}$ **16.** $4\frac{7}{10}$ **17.** $\frac{8}{8}$ **18.** $\frac{0}{10}$

19. $\frac{37}{40}$ **20.** $\frac{9}{16}$ **21.** $\frac{19}{20}$ **22.** $\frac{7}{9}$ **23.** $\frac{14}{25}$ **24.** $6\frac{3}{4}$ **25.** $5\frac{3}{10}$ **26.** $\frac{19}{19}$ **27.** $7\frac{9}{10}$

Set 61 *pages 148–149* For each percent, write a fraction in lowest terms, a mixed number, or a whole number.

1. 7%   **2.** 46%   **3.** 54%   **4.** $62\frac{1}{2}$%   **5.** 12.5%   **6.** 0.5%   **7.** 250%   **8.** 925%

9. 8%   **10.** 60%   **11.** 85%   **12.** $37\frac{1}{2}$%   **13.** 375%   **14.** 0.8%   **15.** 110%   **16.** 2,000%

Do as many of these exercises as you can mentally. Write the fractions in lowest terms.

Fraction	**17.**	**19.**	$\frac{4}{5}$	**23.**	**25.**	$\frac{5}{6}$	**29.**	$\frac{7}{12}$
Decimal	**18.**	$0.66\frac{2}{3}$	**21.**	0.15	**26.**	**27.**	0.275	**31.**
Percent	60%	**20.**	**22.**	**24.**	48%	**28.**	**30.**	**32.**

Set 62 *pages 150–151* Find each answer.

1. 40% of 30   **2.** 19% of 300   **3.** 65% of 800   **4.** 20% of 110   **5.** 70% of 80

6. 0.6% of 420   **7.** 250% of 72   **8.** $9\frac{1}{2}$% of 30   **9.** 14.5% of 98   **10.** 26% of 45

11. 350% of 44   **12.** 18% of 216   **13.** 0.75% of 120   **14.** 0.2% of 180   **15.** 125% of 60

16. 225% of 20   **17.** 145% of 50   **18.** $37\frac{1}{2}$% of 72   **19.** 12.5% of 6.4   **20.** $8\frac{1}{3}$% of 36

21. 210% of 70   **22.** 23% of 90   **23.** 175% of 44   **24.** 0.9% of 18   **25.** 0.6% of 90

Set 63 *pages 152–153* Solve.

1. In Milltown there are 1,400 children. 90% of them received measles immunizations and did not become ill. One tenth of those who did not receive the vaccine became ill with measles. How many children did not become ill?

2. Joe put $1,000 in a one-year saving certificate that will give 9% interest at the end of the year. He must pay 25% tax on that interest income. What is the total amount he will have left?

3. Two hundred twenty-five eighth graders took the U.S. Constitution test. 80% of the students passed the test. One fifth of those who did not pass the test received a score below 50. How many students received a score below 50?

4. The teen club was presenting a talent review. Two thousand tickets were printed for an admission price of $5.00. One tenth of the tickets were sold at a 20% discount. The remainder were sold at full price. What was the total income from ticket sales?

Set 64 *pages 154–155* Find each percent. Round to the nearest percent.

1. What percent of 75 is 60?

2. 24 is what percent of 160?

3. 81 is what percent of 135?

4. 7.2 is what percent of 28.8?

5. What percent of 40 is 28.5?

6. What percent of 39 is 156?

7. 175 is what percent of 350?

8. What percent of 132 is 33?

9. 38 is what percent of 200?

10. What percent of 76 is 57?

11. What percent of 50 is 22.5?

12. What percent of 400 is 120.5?

Set 65 *pages 156–157* Write an equation; then find the answer.

1. Tony has read 72 pages of a book that has 212 pages. What percent of the book has he already read? Round to the nearest percent.

2. Angela would like to buy a sweater that is being sold at 20% off the original price of $39.95. What is the amount of discount to the nearest cent?

3. The Anderson family's grocery bill was $102.32, plus sales tax. If the tax rate is 4%, what is the amount of the tax to the nearest cent?

4. A store is offering a $30 discount on a telephone that usually costs $159. The discount is what percent of the usual price? Round to the nearest percent.

5. Pierre made a $450 down payment on a used car that cost $1,250. What percent of the cost of the car has he already paid for?

6. Adam bought six computer books that cost a total of $41.70. If the sales-tax rate is 6%, what is the amount of tax to the nearest cent?

MORE PRACTICE

Set 66 *pages 158–159* Find each answer.

1. 15% of what number is 75?

2. 20% of what number is 8?

3. 75% of what number is 450?

4. 5% of what number is 3?

5. 90% of what number is 360?

6. 11% of what number is 66?

7. 2 is 0.5% of what number?

8. 304 is 95% of what number?

9. 200% of what number is 18?

10. 75 is 125% of what number?

11. 12 is 0.2% of what number?

12. $66\frac{2}{3}$% of what number is 6?

Set 67 *pages 160–161* Find the interest

1. if $850 is borrowed at 8% simple interest for 9 months (0.75 year).

2. if $400 is invested at 9% simple interest for $3\frac{1}{2}$ years.

Find the total amount that must be repaid

3. if $900 is borrowed at 12% simple interest for 3 years.

4. if $300 is borrowed at 15% simple interest for 9 months.

Find the total amount in the account

5. if $3,000 is invested at 10.5% simple interest for 10 years.

6. if $250 is invested at 5.5% simple interest for 3 years.

7. if $4,250 is invested at 8% simple interest for 8 years.

8. if $4,250 is invested at 10% simple interest for 8 years.

Set 68 *pages 164–165* Solve each problem.

1. Find the sale price of a video game if the regular price is $19.00 and there is a 30% discount now?

2. Find the total cost of four books with regular prices of $2.95, $3.95, $6.95, and $12.95 if a 10% discount is given.

3. As a special promotion $12.00 tickets for a day at the Whirl and Twirl Amusement Park were being sold at the Food Cart Supermarket at a 20% discount. How much would Mrs. Wilt save if she bought seven tickets?

4. What is the percent of discount at an appliance store if the regular price of an air conditioner is $325 and the sale price is $265? Round to the nearest percent.

5. If the regular price of a stereo set is $340 and the sale price is $255, what is the percent of discount?

6. Find the total sale price of four $6.95 t-shirts if they are being sold at a 15% discount.

Set 69 *pages 170–171* Give or complete each unit of measure.

1. Length of a house
▒▒▒

2. Capacity of a barrel
Deka▒▒▒

3. Height of a giraffe
▒▒▒

4. Mass of a grape
▒▒▒

5. Width of a wallet
Centi▒▒▒

6. Capacity of a sprinkling can
▒▒▒

Give each missing number. Use the table on page 170

7. 1 mm = ▒▒ dm

8. 1 hg = ▒▒ kg

9. 1 cL = ▒▒ dL

10. 1 km = ▒▒ hm

Set 70 *pages 172–173* Find the missing number. Use the table on page 172.

1. 82 dm = ▒▒ cm

2. 110 dam = ▒▒ hm

3. 1.7 m = ▒▒ cm

4. 7 m = ▒▒ mm

5. 79 m = ▒▒ km

6. 47 dam = ▒▒ mm

7. 1,720 cm = ▒▒ m

8. 0.44 cm = ▒▒ m

9. 5,755 hm = ▒▒ km

10. 1,242 mm = ▒▒ cm

11. 175 dm = ▒▒ hm

12. 555 hm = ▒▒ mm

13. 86 dam = ▒▒ m

14. 106 km = ▒▒ dm

15. 0.52 m = ▒▒ cm

16. 0.7 dam = ▒▒ dm

Set 71 *pages 174–175* Find the missing number.

1. $7 \text{ dm}^2 = ▒▒ \text{ m}^2$

2. $410 \text{ m}^2 = ▒▒ \text{ cm}^2$

3. $9 \text{ dm}^2 = ▒▒ \text{ km}^2$

4. $0.75 \text{ hm}^2 = ▒▒ \text{ m}^2$

5. $19 \text{ m}^3 = ▒▒ \text{ cm}^3$

6. $0.5 \text{ km}^3 = ▒▒ \text{ hm}^3$

7. $3 \text{ m}^3 = ▒▒ \text{ mm}^3$

8. $19 \text{ m}^3 = ▒▒ \text{ dam}^3$

9. $250 \text{ cm}^2 = ▒▒ \text{ km}^2$

10. $0.33 \text{ hm}^2 = ▒▒ \text{ m}^2$

11. $8,950 \text{ m}^3 = ▒▒ \text{ km}^3$

12. $12 \text{ cm}^3 = ▒▒ \text{ m}^3$

Set 72 *pages 176–177* Choose the best measure.

1. Capacity of a water cooler

   11 kL   11 cL   11 L

2. Mass of a brick

   1.5 g   1.5 kg   1.5 cg

3. Capacity of an oil tank

   3 mL   30 cL   30 L

Find the missing numbers.

4. 63 mL = ▒▒ L

5. 2,172 mg = ▒▒ g

6. 28 L = ▒▒ dL

7. 32 hL = ▒▒ L

8. 175 mg = ▒▒ dag

9. 19.7 hg = ▒▒ cg

10. 1,307 cg = ▒▒ kg

11. 382 mL = ▒▒ dL

12. 880 g = ▒▒ mg

13. 8.2 L = ▒▒ mL

14. 77 daL = ▒▒ kL

15. 8.4 hg = ▒▒ g

16. 25 cL = ▒▒ mL

17. 97 dg = ▒▒ hg

18. 0.032 kg = ▒▒ g

19. 2,781 mg = ▒▒ kg

20. 7 dg = ▒▒ g

21. 0.04 kL = ▒▒ cL

22. 37 dL = ▒▒ mL

23. 55 g = ▒▒ mg

MORE PRACTICE

Set 73 *pages 178–179* Choose the most sensible answer.

1. Mass of a bread slice

   30 mg   3 kg   30 g

2. Area of a brick patio

   1.5 m²   150 cm²   15 m²

3. Volume of a wastebasket

   7 m³   72 dm³   72 m²

4. Capacity of a frying pan

   1.5 hL   1.5 L   50 cL

5. Width of a checkbook

   7 dm   16 mm   8 cm

6. Height of an Egyptian pyramid

   50 km   50 m   50 m²

Set 74 *pages 182–183* Find each missing number.

1. $5\frac{1}{2}$ ft. = ▦ in.

2. $4\frac{3}{4}$ sq. ft. = ▦ sq. in.

3. 468 sq. in. = ▦ sq. ft.

4. 200 in. = ▦ yd. ▦ ft.

5. 37 ft. = ▦ yd.

6. 1 mi. 2 ft. = ▦ ft.

7. $1\frac{3}{8}$ sq. ft. = ▦ sq. in.

8. $\frac{5}{6}$ mi. = ▦ ft.

9. $2\frac{3}{4}$ sq. ft. = ▦ sq. in.

10. 90 cu. ft. = ▦ cu. yd.

11. 264 ft. = ▦ mi.

12. 90 in. = ▦ yd.

Set 75 *pages 184–185* Find each missing number.

1. 55 oz. = ▦ lb. ▦ oz.

2. 21 pt. = ▦ qt. ▦ pt.

3. 23 lb. 10 oz. = ▦ oz.

4. 800 lb. = ▦ ton

5. 19 c. = ▦ pt. ▦ c.

6. 5 qt. = ▦ c.

7. 37 qt. = ▦ gal. ▦ qt.

8. 3.5 tons = ▦ lb.

9. 2 gal. 3 qt. = ▦ pt.

10. $7\frac{5}{8}$ tons = ▦ lb.

11. $8\frac{1}{2}$ pt. = ▦ oz.

12. $15\frac{3}{4}$ lb. = ▦ oz.

Set 76 *pages 186–187*

1. 12 qt. 5 pt. + 6 qt. 3 pt.

2. 18 lb. 7 oz. − 13 oz.

3. 17 yd. − 2 ft. 8 in.

4. 18 gal. 3 qt. + 9 gal. 2 qt.

5. 19 lb. 12 oz. + 16 lb. 4 oz.

6. 15 lb. − 12 lb. 13 oz.

7. 14 qt. − 7 qt. 1 pt.

8. 25 yd. − 2 yd. 2 ft.

9. 4 yd. 2 ft. + 6 yd. 2 ft.

10. 27 gal. 3 qt. + 7 gal. 3 qt.

11. 27 lb. − 18 lb. 9 oz.

12. 25 yd. 30 in. + 10 in.

Set 77 *pages 188–189* What time is it

1. 7 hr. 24 min. after 12:42 A.M.?
2. 10 hr. 50 min. after 9:15 P.M.?
3. 4 hr. 10 min. after 11:30 P.M.?
4. 9 hr. 47 min. after 3:37 A.M.?

Add or subtract.

5. 11 hr. 17 min. + 5 hr. 56 min.
6. 8 hr. − 2 hr. 15 min.
7. 22 min. 40 sec. − 5 min. 49 sec.
8. 18 min. 38 sec. + 24 min. 32 sec.
9. 15 days 7 hr. + 9 days 19 hr.
10. 12 days 6 hr. − 5 days 7 hr.

Set 78 *pages 190–191* Solve each problem. When it is necessary, round your answer to the nearest tenth.

1. In the marathon race Anita was at the 8-mile mark at 1:00 P.M. and at the 15-mile mark at 6:00 P.M. What was her speed?
2. An auto increases its speed by 10 miles per hour each second. How fast is it traveling after 6 seconds if it was initially stopped?
3. If a batter hits a ball 90 miles per hour to the center fielder who is standing 265 feet away, how long is the ball in the air? (90 mph = 132 ft./second)
4. A runner in a one-mile race had a total elapsed time of 60 seconds after the first quarter mile. What was the runner's speed in miles per hour during the first quarter mile?

Set 79 *pages 192–193* Give the unit of measure and the GPE.

1. 2.7 cm
2. 3.11 dL
3. 100 ft.
4. 44.0 km
5. 55 cg
6. 75 lb.
7. 58 min.
8. 18.09 kg
9. 96 mm
10. 8.30 sec.
11. 4.65 m
12. 1.079 kL

Compute. Round your answer.

13. 15.2 m − 3.57 m
14. 18 kg + 0.27 kg + 0.781 kg
15. 18.6 kg − 9.06 kg
16. 60 sec. − 7.92 sec.
17. 14 L − 7.35 L
18. 50 sec. − 17.1 sec.
19. 36 kg + 46.5 kg
20. 88 yd. + 20.1 yd.
21. 27 in. + 19.5 in.
22. 16 cm + 258.6 cm
23. 14 min. + 70.4 min. + 89 min.
24. 8.9 cm + 6.327 cm
25. 72 g − 8.7 g
26. 66 dm + 25.63 dm
27. 200 g + 89.6 g + 4.278 g

MORE PRACTICE

Set 80 *pages 200–201*   Make a sketch.

1. $\overleftrightarrow{MA}$ intersecting $\overline{TH}$ at T.

2. $\overrightarrow{XC}$, $\overrightarrow{XO}$, $\overrightarrow{XF}$ with a common endpoint X.

3. $\overleftrightarrow{WX} \parallel \overleftrightarrow{KL}$

4. Line f intersecting parallel lines c and r.

5. Name all of the segments shown.

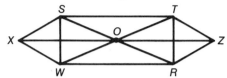

6. Name all rays with endpoint O.

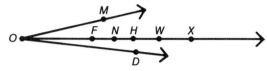

Set 81 *pages 202–203*   Use a protractor to draw an angle with the given measure. Tell if the angle is acute, right, or obtuse.

1. 96°   **2.** 85°   **3.** 115°   **4.** 6°   **5.** 179°   **6.** 18°   **7.** 100°   **8.** 60°   **9.** 45°

10. Name the rays of $\angle HER$.

11. Give two other names for $\angle XYZ$.

12. Name the vertex of $\angle HER$.

13. Name the sides of $\angle XYZ$.

Set 82 *pages 204–205*
Use the diagram at the right for the exercises.

1. Name the complement of $\angle XOT$.

2. Name two pairs of perpendicular lines.

3. Name five pairs of supplementary angles.

4. Name two pairs of complementary angles.

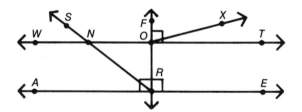

5. Name the supplement of $\angle ROX$.

Set 83 *pages 206–207*   In the diagram $m\angle 4 = 100°$. Give the measure of each of these angles.

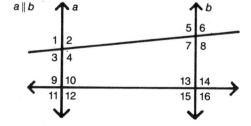

1. $m\angle 5$ **2.** $m\angle 3$ **3.** $m\angle 2$

4. $m\angle 1$ **5.** $m\angle 7$ **6.** $m\angle 8$

Use the diagram. Tell whether the angles are vertical angles, alternate interior angles, or neither.

7. $\angle 2$ and $\angle 6$ **8.** $\angle 12$ and $\angle 13$ **9.** $\angle 10$ and $\angle 11$ **10.** $\angle 4$ and $\angle 15$

11. $\angle 5$ and $\angle 8$ **12.** $\angle 9$ and $\angle 12$ **13.** $\angle 6$ and $\angle 3$ **14.** $\angle 7$ and $\angle 2$

Set 84 *pages 208–209* Copy and enlarge the figure on a separate piece of paper. With a compass construct a segment or an angle congruent to each of the following:

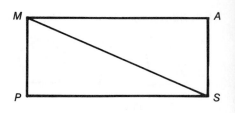

1. $\overline{AS}$ **2.** $\overline{MS}$ **3.** $\angle MPS$ **4.** $\angle ASM$

Construct the bisector of each of the following:

5. $\overline{PS}$ **6.** $\angle MAS$ **7.** $\angle ASM$ **8.** $\overline{MS}$

Set 85 *pages 210–211* Trace the segments and angles shown at the right. Using only the parts given, construct a triangle.

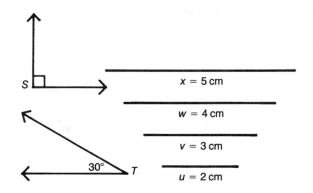

1. Sides v, w, and x.

2. $\angle T$ between sides w and x.

3. Side x between $\angle S$ and $\angle T$.

4. $\angle S$ between sides x and u.

Set 86 *pages 212–213* Solve each problem by trying and checking until you find the answer. The lengths of the sides of the triangles must be whole numbers.

1. The longest side of a triangle is 8 cm. What might be the lengths of the other two sides? Give three possible pairs of numbers.

2. The distance around a triangle is 20 cm. What might be the length of the three sides?

3. The lengths of two sides of a triangle are 15 cm and 19 cm. What is the least possible length for the third side?

4. What is the greatest possible length for the third side of a triangle which has sides of 13 cm and 7 cm?

Set 87 *pages 214–215* In the exercises, the measures of two angles of a triangle are given. Give the measure of the third angle and name the type of triangle it is.

1. 25° and 130°   **2.** 61° and 56°   **3.** 91° and 17°   **4.** 60° and 60°

5. 19°and 100°   **6.** 90° and 5°   **7.** 72° and 18°   **8.** 30° and 30°

9. 61° and 62°   **10.** 15° and 150°   **11.** 90° and 22°   **12.** 48° and 84°

13. 64° and 72°   **14.** 45° and 45°   **15.** 27° and 126°   **16.** 54° and 26°

MORE PRACTICE

Set 88 *pages 216–217* Name the polygons illustrated.

1.  **2.** **3.** **4.** **5.**

Does the exercise describe a polygon? If it does, sketch it.

6. A rhombus with 3 obtuse angles

7. A square with 1 acute angle

8. A quadrilateral with 2 congruent sides

9. A parallelogram with 3 acute angles

10. An octagon with 6 angles

11. A trapezoid with 1 pair of opposite sides parallel

12. A triangle with 2 right angles

13. A pentagon with 3 right angles

Set 89 *pages 218–219* Use the figure at the right for the exercises. $\triangle JAC \cong \triangle KAD$ and polygon *JADH* $\cong$ polygon *KACG*.

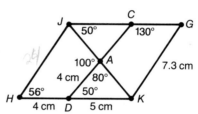

1. List all the corresponding sides and angles for the two triangles.

Give the measure of each segment or angle from the figure above.

2. $\angle AKG$ **3.** $\overline{JH}$ **4.** $\overline{JC}$ **5.** $\angle HJA$ **6.** $\angle ADK$

7. $\angle HDA$ **8.** $\angle JAC$ **9.** $\angle CGK$ **10.** $\overline{CG}$ **11.** $\angle CAK$

Set 90 *pages 220–221* Are the polygons similar? Write *yes* or *no*.

1. 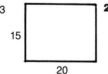 **2.** 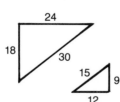 **3.** 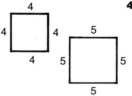 **4.**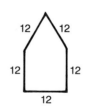

In each exercise the polygons are similar. Find the missing length.

5. 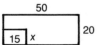 **6.** **7.**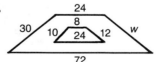

8.  **9.** **10.**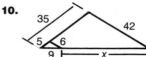

Set 91 *pages 224–225* Use the circles at the
right. Name as many examples of each of the
following as you can.

1. Radii in circle *C*

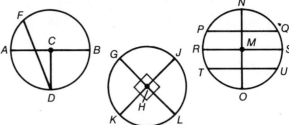

2. Central angles in circle *H*

3. Chords in circle *H*

4. Inscribed angles in circle *M*

5. Diameters in circle *M*

6. Central angles in circle *C*

7. Arcs in circle *C*

8. In circle *H*, what is the measure of central
   angle *KHG*?

Set 92 *pages 226–227*

1. How many bases does a cone have?

2. How many bases does a sphere have?

3. If the bases of a prism are square, how many
   faces does the prism have?

4. If there are five faces on a prism, what kind
   of prism is it?

5. Name the type of pyramid that has five faces.

6. Name the prism that has six faces.

7. Name two 3-dimensional figures that each
   have five faces.

8. Name two 3-dimensional figures that each
   have seven faces.

Set 93 *pages 228–229*

1. Name all the faces, edges, and vertices in
   Figure 1 and in Figure 2.

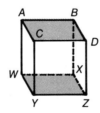

Figure I

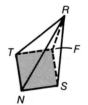

Figure II

Complete the table:

	Number of edges *E*	Number of vertices *V*	Number of faces *F*	*V* + *F*	(*V* + *F*) − *E*
Decagonal Prism (10-sided)	30	**2.**	**3.**	**4.**	**5.**
Dodecagonal Prism (12-sided)	**6.**	**7.**	**8.**	**9.**	**10.**
Decagonal Pyramid	20	**11.**	**12.**	**13.**	**14.**
Pyramid (15-sided base)	**15.**	**16.**	**17.**	**18.**	**19.**

413

MORE PRACTICE

Set 94 *pages 234–235*   Find the perimeter of each polygon.

1. 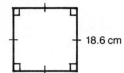 18.6 cm

2.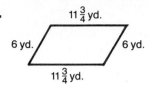
$11\frac{3}{4}$ yd.
6 yd.   6 yd.
$11\frac{3}{4}$ yd.

3.
17 in.   17 in.
17 in.

4.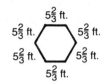
$5\frac{2}{3}$ ft.
$5\frac{2}{3}$ ft. $5\frac{2}{3}$ ft.
$5\frac{2}{3}$ ft. $5\frac{2}{3}$ ft.
$5\frac{2}{3}$ ft.

5.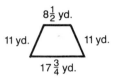
$8\frac{1}{2}$ yd.
11 yd.   11 yd.
$17\frac{3}{4}$ yd.

6. 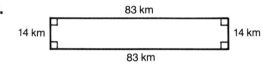

6. 5.4 m
5.4 m   5.4 m
5.4 m

7. 83 km
14 km   14 km
83 km

Set 95 *pages 236–237*   Find the area of each polygon.

1.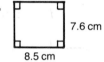
7.6 cm
8.5 cm

2.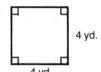
4 yd.
4 yd.

3.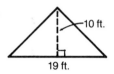
10 ft.
19 ft.

4.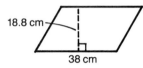
18.8 cm
38 cm

5.
16.5 m
23.1 m

6.
54 in.
41 in.

7.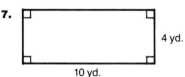
4 yd.
10 yd.

8.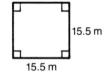
15.5 m
15.5 m

Set 96 *pages 238–239*   Find the area of each polygon.
Give answers to the nearest tenth.

1.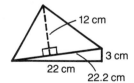
12 cm
3 cm
22 cm   22.2 cm

2.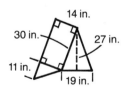
14 in.
30 in.   27 in.
11 in.   19 in.

3.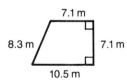
7.1 m
8.3 m   7.1 m
10.5 m

4.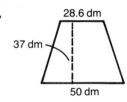
28.6 dm
37 dm
50 dm

5.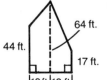
64 ft.
44 ft.
17 ft.
18 ft. 19 ft.

6.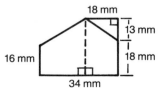
18 mm
13 mm
16 mm   18 mm
34 mm

7.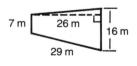
7 m   26 m   16 m
29 m

8.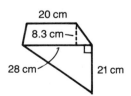
20 cm
8.3 cm
28 cm   21 cm

9. A trapezoid with bases of 72 m and 58 m and a height of 5.5 m

10. A trapezoid with bases of 15 cm and 19 cm and a height of 10 cm

414

Set 97 *pages 240–241*   Find the circumference of a circle with the given diameter or radius. Use 3.14 or $3\frac{1}{7}$ for π. Round each decimal answer to the nearest whole unit.

1. $d = 10$ in.
2. $d = 33$ yd.
3. $d = \frac{1}{2}$ ft.
4. $d = 9\frac{1}{4}$ yd.
5. $r = 30$ cm

6. $r = 2$ m
7. $d = 4.9$ m
8. $r = 2.8$ cm
9. $d = 6.3$ dm
10. $r = 42$ ft.

11. $d = 21$ ft.
12. $r = 17\frac{1}{2}$ in.
13. $d = \frac{7}{12}$ yd.
14. $d = 42$ mm
15. $r = 50$ in.

16. $r = 25$ m
17. $r = 3$ ft.
18. $d = 1.4$ m
19. $d = 80$ in.
20. $r = 70$ m

Set 98 *pages 242–243*   Find the area of a circle with the given diameter d or radius r. Use $3\frac{1}{7}$ or 3.14 for π. Round each decimal answer to the nearest tenth.

1. $r = 12$ yd.
2. $d = 7$ ft.
3. $d = 11$ ft.
4. $r = 14$ in.
5. $d = 28$ in.

6. $r = 0.5$ cm
7. $r = 20$ ft.
8. $d = 1.5$ m
9. $r = 0.14$ m
10. $d = 19$ ft.

11. $d = 35$ yd.
12. $r = 2.1$ yd.
13. $d = 24$ ft.
14. $d = 4.9$ cm
15. $r = 11$ ft.

16. $r = 10$ yd.
17. $r = 25$ in.
18. $d = 16$ ft.
19. $d = 8.4$ m
20. $d = 32$ yd.

Set 99 *pages 244–245*   Solve each problem by referring to the diagram of the City Park.

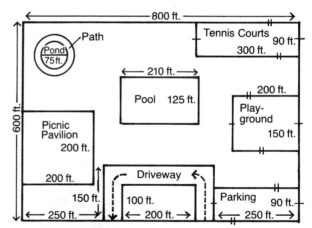

1. How many feet of chain-link fencing must the park department buy in order to replace the old fence around the playground? Two five-foot gates do not need to be replaced.

2. How wide is the driveway?

3. How many cans of asphalt sealer must be bought to resurface the parking lot if each container will cover 200 sq. ft.?

4. How many square feet of path around the pond must be covered with gravel if the path is ten feet wide?

5. How many cans of paint will be needed to paint the bottom of the pool if one can of paint covers 300 square feet?

6. How many fifty-pound bags of fertilizer must the gardener use to fertilize the playground area grass in the park if each bag covers 10,000 square feet?

7. How many metal posts must the park department buy in order to put a fence around the tennis courts if the posts must be placed six feet apart?

415

MORE PRACTICE

Set 100 *pages 246–247*   Find the surface area of each polyhedron.

1. Rectangular prism

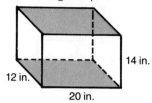

14 in.
12 in.
20 in.

2. Cube

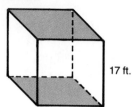

17 ft.

3. Rectangular pyramid

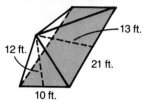

13 ft.
12 ft.
21 ft.
10 ft.

4. Square pyramid

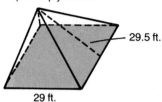

29.5 ft.
29 ft.

5. Triangular prism

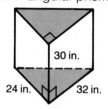

30 in.
24 in.   32 in.

6. Rectangular prism

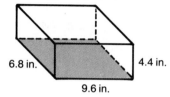

6.8 in.   4.4 in.
9.6 in.

Set 101 *pages 248–249*   Find the surface area.
Use 3.14 for π. Round answers to the nearest tenth.

1.

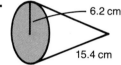

6.2 cm
15.4 cm

2.

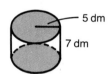

5 dm
7 dm

3.

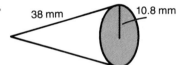

38 mm   10.8 mm

4.

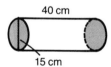

40 cm
15 cm

5.

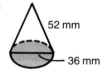

52 mm
36 mm

6.

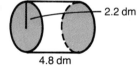

2.2 dm
4.8 dm

Set 102 *pages 250–251*   Make a sketch and solve each problem.

1. Estimate the number of square inches of chintz fabric needed to re-cover an old wicker chair cushion. The cushion is 24 in. wide, 22 in. long, and 4 in. high.

2. Estimate the amount of screening needed to make a large gerbil cage. The cage floor, which is a piece of heavy plastic, is 3.5 ft. by 4.25 ft. The height of the cage will be 2 ft.

3. How many 3-ft. by 6-ft. sections of sheet metal will Mr. Greene need in order to replace the old sheet metal on the sides of his silo? It has a diameter of 12 ft. and a height of 25 ft.

4. Mr. Johnson painted the walls and ceiling of the school cafeteria, which is 100 ft. long, 90 ft. wide, and 12 ft. high. (He did not paint the doors and windows, which had a total area of approximately 1,000 sq. ft.) If each gallon of paint covers 400 sq. ft., how many gallons did he use?

Set 103 *pages 252-253*   Find the volume of each prism or cylinder.
Use 3.14 or $3\frac{1}{7}$ for π. Round each decimal answer to the nearest whole unit.

1.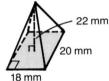
8 ft.
8 ft.
8 ft.

2.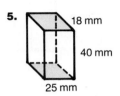
7 in.
4 in.
6 in.

3.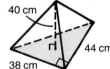
9 yd.
6 yd.
11 yd.

4.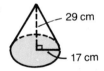
10 in.
16 in.

5.
18 mm
40 mm
25 mm

6.
15 ft.
14 ft.

Set 104 *pages 254-255*   Find the volume of each pyramid or cone.
Use 3.14 or $3\frac{1}{7}$ for π. Round each decimal answer to the nearest whole unit.

1.
22 mm
20 mm
18 mm

2.
11 dm
4 dm

3.
40 cm
44 cm
38 cm

4.
29 cm
17 cm

5.
14 mm
50 mm

6.
24 in.
20 in.
12 in.

Set 105 *pages 258-259*   Use the table to solve each problem.

A rectangular prism has the dimensions of 10 ft. by 12 ft. by 8 ft.
Complete the table to see the changes in surface area and volume
corresponding to changes in dimensions.

Rectangular prism	Length	Width	Height	Surface area	Volume
Original dimensions	10	12	8	592 sq. ft.	960 cu. ft.
Double dimensions	20	24	16	**1.**	**2.**
Triple dimensions	30	36	24	**3.**	**4.**
Quadruple dimensions	40	48	32	**5.**	**6.**

MORE PRACTICE

Set 106 *pages 264–265*   Use the graph for Exercises 1–4.
The double bar graph shows the amounts for the Stewart family's
electricity and gas bills for six months of a year.

1. What is the range for the gas bills?

2. In which months was the electricity bill higher
   than the gas bill?

3. In which months was the gas bill greater than
   $60?

4. In which months was the difference between
   the amounts of the two bills less than $30?

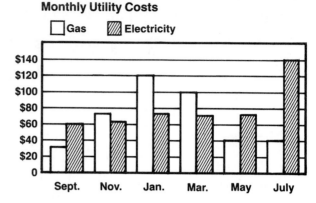

Set 107 *pages 266–267*
The graph shows the approximate average daily
high temperature readings in Tokyo, Japan, for a
one-year period.

1. What is the difference in degrees between
   the lowest and highest average
   temperatures?

2. Name the months which have the same
   average temperatures.

3. What is the increase in average temperature
   from March to June?

4. During how many months of the year is the
   average daily temperature higher than 66°?

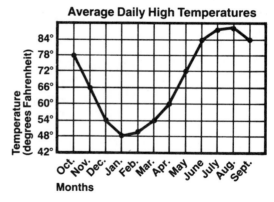

Set 108 *pages 268–269*   Use the graph. The
graph shows how $80,000 was spent on the
construction of a new home. How much was
spent on each item?

1. Electrical

2. Land

3. Plumbing

4. Roofing

5. Kitchen
   cabinets

6. Air conditioning
   and heating

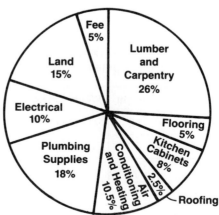

Set 109 *pages 270–271* For each set of data find the mean, the median, and the mode. If it is necessary, round to the nearest tenth.

21, 32, 16, 25, 30, 32, 27, 28, 29, 31, 32, 27, 31, 25

1. Mean   **2.** Median   **3.** Mode

7.5, 6.3, 6.0, 7.2, 7.5, 6.3, 6.9, 6.2, 6.8, 6.3, 6.4, 6.5, 7.4, 6.1

4. Mean   **5.** Median   **6.** Mode

56, 59, 61, 57, 62, 61, 65, 57, 58, 63, 64, 61, 67, 65, 64, 57, 58, 62, 66, 65, 58

7. Mean   **8.** Median   **9.** Mode

98, 96, 86, 63, 72, 95, 93, 90, 93, 90, 86, 88, 86, 92, 86, 87, 90, 91, 97, 90, 87

10. Mean   **11.** Median   **12.** Mode

Set 110 *pages 274–275* For each exercise, find the mean, the median, and the mode. Tell which is *least* representative of the data.

1. Weekly swimming pool attendance:

1,560	1,825	1,613
1,487	1,709	1,585
1,518	1,492	1,503

2. Video store sales:

$812	$1,125	$1,490
$943	$1,197	$1,056
$1,075	$1,120	$1,550

3. Annual rainfall amounts:

32 in.	39 in.	45 in.	33 in.
35 in.	35 in.	36 in.	38 in.
37 in.	33 in.	35 in.	34 in.

4. Ages of students in a computer class:

14 yr.	38 yr.	49 yr.	18 yr.
21 yr.	24 yr.	33 yr.	22 yr.
23 yr.	60 yr.	30 yr.	28 yr.

Set 111 *pages 276–277* Use the graph for Exercises 1–5.

1. In which year was the record approximately $17\frac{1}{2}$ feet?

2. What was the record in 1956?

3. In which years were the records above the line of best fit?

4. In 1960, Don Bragg of the U.S. jumped 15 ft. $5\frac{1}{8}$ in. Is this height above or below the line of best fit for 1960?

5. Make a prediction for 1984.

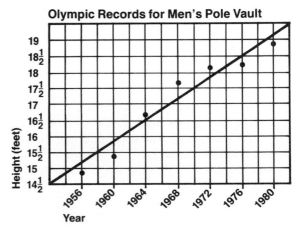

Olympic Records for Men's Pole Vault

MORE PRACTICE

Set 112 *pages 278–279*   For Exercises 1–4, make a tree diagram.

1. How many 3-letter codes can be made from the letters *H-I-D-E* if the letters can be repeated?

2. How many 3-letter codes can be made from the letters *E-N-G-L-I-S-H* if the letters cannot be repeated?

3. How many 6-character license plates can be written if the first two characters must be alphabetic and the last four characters are numerical? The letters cannot be repeated.

4. How many 4-character lock combinations can be formed if the first character must be alphabetic, A through H, and the last 3 characters are numerical? The numbers cannot be repeated.

Set 113 *pages 280–281*   There are twelve children in a music class. Each has a birthday in a different month of the year. Marty has a birthday in July. What is the probability that

1. someone has a birthday earlier in the year?

2. someone has a birthday in the same month?

3. someone has a birthday later in the year?

4. someone has a birthday in the same season of the year?

Noelle is on a baseball team. What is the probability that she is

5. an outfielder?

6. an infielder?

7. a pitcher or a catcher?

Set 114 *pages 282–283*   Blake selected a 3-character computer access code which was alphabetic. What is the probability that he chose

1. three vowels?

2. three consonants?

3. letters from only the first half of the alphabet?

Jenny chose 2 books from a shelf containing 25 biographies, 28 mysteries, and 17 romances. She replaced the first book before choosing the second. What is the probability that she chose

4. the same book twice?

5. two biographies?

6. a mystery then a romance?

Set 115 *pages 284–285*   Stephanie and Heather each wanted to buy flowers for their mother's birthday. The florist had only one of each of the following cut-flower bouquets: daisies, mums, roses, or tulips, and one of each of the following three potted plants: ivy, fern, and jade plants. What is the probability that their mother received

1. two potted plants?

2. two cut-flower bouquets?

3. a cut-flower bouquet from Stephanie and a potted plant from Heather?

4. a daisy bouquet from Stephanie and a tulip bouquet from Heather?

Set 116 *pages 286–287* Use the data in the chart. What is the probability that

1. a patron would check out books?

2. a book borrower would check out three or more books?

3. a book borrower would be a child?

4. a patron would check out two books?

CITY LIBRARY STATISTICS for October
15,000 Adults   5,000 Children
8,000 patrons checked out 1 book
4,800 patrons checked out 2 books
2,000 patrons checked out 3 books
1,200 patrons checked out 4 or more
12,800 adults checked out books
3,200 children checked out books

Set 117 *pages 288–289* A survey of 100 randomly selected students at State University were asked where they were from. Use the results shown in the table for Exercises 1–2.

1. If there are 6,000 students in all at the school, how many would be expected to be from Iowa? From the U.S.?

2. If there are 2,000 freshmen, how many would be expected to be from Indiana?

STUDENTS' HOMES	
Illinois	38
Iowa	26
Indiana	22
Other State	10
Foreign Country	4

3. Forty-five out of 100 students said that they planned to buy lunch at school. If there are 760 students, how many lunches might be purchased at school?

4. In a high school, 4 out of 19 students planned to try out for the soccer team. If there are 380 students in the school, how many students should the coach expect for tryouts?

Set 118 *pages 296–297* Name an integer for each example.

1. A gain of 4 pounds

2. A profit of $200

3. An $80 salary increase

4. A loss of 12 yards

5. 6 degrees below 0

6. A withdrawal of $20

7. $-(34)$

8. $-(-19)$

9. The opposite of -43

10. The opposite of 13

11. A descent of 150 ft.

12. An increase of 215

13. An altitude of 2,500 ft.

14. A bonus of $100

15. 200 feet above sea level

16. A $50 discount

17. An elevation of 50 ft.

18. A debt of $20

19. A depth of 6 ft.

20. A loss of $2,000

21. A $200 tax deduction

MORE PRACTICE

Set 119 *pages 298–299*   Compare the integers. Use > or <.

1. 13 ● 6   **2.** 3 ● 5   **3.** 10 ● −12   **4.** 6 ● −5   **5.** −8 ● −9   **6.** 25 ● 0

7. −5 ● −15   **8.** 4 ● −21   **9.** 0 ● −2   **10.** −9 ● −11   **11.** −57 ● −38   **12.** −19 ● −16

List these integers in order from least to greatest.

13. 12   −5   0   −9   **14.** −7   −30   −15   3   **15.** 11   −14   −30   0

16. −4   −17   −1   −25   **17.** −19   6   −12   4   **18.** 0   14   −10   −3

Set 120 *pages 300–301*

1. −11 + (−16)   **2.** −10 + (−2)   **3.** 9 + 16   **4.** 7 + 28   **5.** −15 + 17

6. 25 + (−6)   **7.** −13 + 4   **8.** 38 + (−3)   **9.** −20 + 15   **10.** 12 + 19

11. −40 + (−5)   **12.** −29 + (−19)   **13.** 56 + (−17)   **14.** 33 + (−11)   **15.** −68 + (−59)

16. −22 + 8 + 6 + (−5)   **17.** −2 + 40 + (−28) + 1   **18.** −21 + 55 + 7 + (−30)

Set 121 *pages 302–303*

1. −11 − 8   **2.** −9 − 9   **3.** −17 − (−5)   **4.** −21 − (−3)   **5.** 47 − (−28)

6. 2 − 13   **7.** 17 − 14   **8.** 35 − 2   **9.** −14 − (−14)   **10.** −65 − 26

11. −75 − 18   **12.** 70 − 56   **13.** −47 − 17   **14.** 0 − (−51)   **15.** −72 − (−19)

16. 28 − (−9) − (−8)   **17.** 39 − (−16) − (−25)   **18.** 25 − (−6) − (−7)   **19.** −16 + (−17) + 41

20. 90 − (−11) − 72   **21.** 64 − (−5) − 41   **22.** −34 − (−5) − 51   **23.** 27 + (−29) − 44

Set 122 *pages 304–305*   Evaluate each expression for $x = 9$.

1. $x − 9$ **2.** $27 − x$ **3.** $−15 − x$ **4.** $−21 + x$ **5.** $x + 39$ **6.** $−82 − x$

Evaluate each expression for $k = −12$.

7. $(k + 19) − 7$ **8.** $(−8 + k) + 10$ **9.** $−23 − (7 + k)$ **10.** $−36 − (4 + k)$

Evaluate each expression for $s = 7$ and $y = −10$.

11. $s + (10 + y)$ **12.** $(s − y) + 11$ **13.** $−y − (s − 15)$ **14.** $−s + (56 + y)$

15. $−s − (y + 1)$ **16.** $s + y + 18$ **17.** $y + (−s + 30)$ **18.** $−y − (s − 9)$

19. $−s − (42 + y)$ **20.** $17 − (s − y)$ **21.** $−s − y − 25$ **22.** $−s − (−y + 7)$

Set 123 *pages 306–307*

1. 7×9 **2.** $4 \times (-9)$ **3.** $(-11)(5)$ **4.** $8(7)$ **5.** $(-25)(-200)$

6. $(-6)(-7)$ **7.** $(-11)(-1)$ **8.** $(0)(-16)$ **9.** $(-9)(-7)$ **10.** $(-55)(12)$

11. $5(-65)$ **12.** $(-12)(700)$ **13.** $(-11)(-300)$ **14.** $(14) \times 6$ **15.** $(-37)(15)$

16. $(-5)^2$ **17.** $(7)^2$ **18.** $(-2)^2$ **19.** $(-3)^3$ **20.** $(-95)(-1)(0)$

21. $(-4)(-5)(6)(1)$ **22.** $(-7)(8)(0)(3)$ **23.** $(-1)(-6)(-5)(-3)$ **24.** $(1)(-7)(14)(0)$

Set 124 *pages 308–309*

1. $72 \div 9$ **2.** $(-81) \div (-9)$ **3.** $(-120) \div 40$ **4.** $56 \div (-4)$ **5.** $(-108) \div 12$

6. $(-36) \div 9$ **7.** $132 \div 11$ **8.** $(-63) \div (-7)$ **9.** $-48 \div 16$ **10.** $121 \div (-11)$

11. $\dfrac{-45}{9}$ **12.** $\dfrac{0}{-13}$ **13.** $\dfrac{70}{-10}$ **14.** $\dfrac{-100}{-4}$ **15.** $\dfrac{304}{-19}$ **16.** $\dfrac{-288}{-16}$ **17.** $\dfrac{-702}{27}$

18. $\dfrac{540}{-27}$ **19.** $\dfrac{-720}{90}$ **20.** $\dfrac{750}{-30}$ **21.** $\dfrac{-10,000}{-500}$ **22.** $\dfrac{-16,900}{-1,300}$ **23.** $\dfrac{-25,600}{-160}$ **24.** $\dfrac{28,900}{-17}$

Set 125 *pages 312–313*   Evaluate each expression for $t = 7$.

1. $11 + 2t$ **2.** $24 - 6t$ **3.** $\dfrac{35}{t} - 15$ **4.** $69 - \dfrac{21}{t}$ **5.** $\dfrac{t + 38}{5}$

6. $t^2 - 3t$ **7.** $-3(t + 3)$ **8.** $-15t + t^2$ **9.** $9(-6 - t)$ **10.** $-4t(8 - t)$

11. $7t - (-t + 11)$ **12.** $8(-4 - t)$ **13.** $t^2 - (-14 - 5)$ **14.** $8t(-t + 5)$ **15.** $-8t(3 - t)$

Evaluate each expression for $x = -10$.

16. $3x$ **17.** $-15x$ **18.** $8 + 5x$ **19.** $-4(x + 12)$ **20.** $x^2 + x^3$

21. $x^2 - 8x$ **22.** $-18x + x^2$ **23.** $\dfrac{3x + 15}{5}$ **24.** $\dfrac{100}{2x}$ **25.** $\dfrac{7x + 10}{-2x + 10}$

Evaluate each expression for $s = 5$ and $c = -2$.

26. $\dfrac{6s}{c} + c^2$ **27.** $c^3 - \dfrac{5c}{-2s}$ **28.** $\dfrac{4s - 10}{(c)(s)}$ **29.** $\dfrac{4s + 5c}{5c + 3s}$ **30.** $\dfrac{2(c + 8)}{-3c}$

31. $\dfrac{4s - 6c}{c - 2}$ **32.** $\dfrac{9s(s - 6)}{3(s + c)}$ **33.** $\dfrac{6(-2s + c)}{c^3}$ **34.** $s^3 - \dfrac{8s}{4c}$ **35.** $\dfrac{5(4s - c)}{cs}$

36. $\dfrac{8s}{2c} + s^2$ **37.** $\dfrac{s^2 - c^2}{s + c}$ **38.** $\dfrac{3s - 5c}{s}$ **39.** $\dfrac{6(s - 15)}{2(s + c)}$ **40.** $\dfrac{6 - 4s + c}{-c}$

423

MORE PRACTICE

Set 126 *pages 314–315* Theater tickets cost $5.00 each for an adult admission and $2.50 for a child.

1. Make a table showing the cost of admission of all combinations for groups of up to eight persons.

2. Corrine spent $20 for theater tickets. How many different combinations of adults' and children's tickets could she buy?

Mr. Samuelson builds and sells wood birdhouses as a hobby. The cost of the materials is $6.00 per birdhouse which he sells for $10.00 each.

3. Make a table showing the excess of income over expenses for six birdhouses.

4. Mr. Samuelson sold five birdhouses. For how many more birdhouses can he now buy materials?

Set 127 *pages 316–317* The savings account balances for the four children in the Banks family were recorded at the end of each of the first three months of the year.

1. Find the average account balance of the four children at the end of January.

2. Find the average balance at the end of March.

3. Find the average change in the account balances between February and March.

Savings Account Balance			
	January	February	March
Anne	$125	$153	$ 75
Brad	$ 16	$ 30	$ 42
Carol	$201	$262	$334
Steve	$118	$135	$193

Set 128 *pages 322–323* Write each number as the quotient of two integers in four ways.

1. -3 2. 10 3. 0.6 4. -3.4 5. $-7\frac{1}{2}$ 6. $9\frac{3}{4}$ 7. 1.5 8. 9 9. 0.38

Compare. Use $>$, $<$, or $=$.

10. $-\frac{2}{3} \bullet \frac{1}{9}$ 11. $\frac{8}{5} \bullet -8$ 12. $-\frac{3}{5} \bullet 1$ 13. $-6\frac{1}{2} \bullet -9\frac{1}{7}$ 14. $6.4 \bullet 4.6$

List the numbers in order from least to greatest.

15. $6 \quad \frac{3}{8} \quad -\frac{1}{3}$ 16. $-\frac{6}{11} \quad -3 \quad -\frac{9}{10}$ 17. $-\frac{1}{4} \quad -\frac{5}{12} \quad \frac{6}{7}$ 18. $-\frac{3}{7} \quad -\frac{3}{8} \quad -\frac{7}{10}$

19. $-\frac{9}{20} \quad -\frac{3}{10} \quad \frac{4}{5}$ 20. $-\frac{1}{2} \quad 0 \quad \frac{6}{7}$ 21. $-\frac{7}{8} \quad -\frac{15}{16} \quad \frac{3}{4}$ 22. $0.7 \quad -8 \quad -0.83$

Give the opposite of each rational number.

23. $-\frac{5}{6}$ 24. $\frac{7}{9}$ 25. $4\frac{3}{7}$ 26. $-3\frac{1}{3}$ 27. -7.1 28. -2.5 29. 5.9 30. $-\frac{5}{8}$ 31. $\frac{11}{14}$

32. $-\frac{4}{5}$ 33. $\frac{3}{7}$ 34. $6\frac{7}{9}$ 35. $-2\frac{5}{7}$ 36. -6.3 37. -0.1 38. 8.2 39. $-\frac{2}{9}$ 40. $\frac{10}{13}$

Set 129 *pages 324–325*

1. $-\frac{7}{12} + \frac{2}{3}$
2. $-\frac{2}{3} + \frac{4}{9}$
3. $\frac{6}{7} - \left(-\frac{5}{8}\right)$
4. $\frac{4}{13} - 3$
5. $\frac{-7}{10} - \left(-\frac{4}{15}\right)$
6. $\frac{5}{6} - \left(-\frac{3}{8}\right)$

7. $-\frac{7}{8} + \left(-\frac{7}{24}\right)$
8. $-9 - \frac{7}{12}$
9. $-4\frac{1}{3} - \frac{5}{12}$
10. $0 - \frac{11}{12}$
11. $-6\frac{5}{6} - 7\frac{3}{8}$
12. $\frac{-11}{12} - \left(\frac{5}{16}\right)$

13. $0.7 - 0.93$
14. $-7.4 + 2.9$
15. $-8.5 - (0.8)$
16. $-10.06 - 0.7$

17. $-4.8 + 12.9$
18. $-13.7 - (-1.1)$
19. $0.4 - 0.97$
20. $-7.07 - 0.4$

Set 130 *pages 326–327*

1. $5\left(-\frac{2}{5}\right)$
2. $72\left(-\frac{7}{9}\right)$
3. $-39(3.2)$
4. $9.1(-4.65)$
5. $-\frac{5}{8} \div \left(-2\frac{4}{15}\right)$

6. $-\frac{6}{11} \div (-18)$
7. $-\frac{8}{9} \div \frac{2}{3}$
8. $-6\frac{1}{4} \div \left(-\frac{5}{8}\right)$
9. $-5\frac{1}{3} \div \left(-\frac{1}{8}\right)$
10. $-0.8 \div 0.16$

11. $\frac{5}{9}\left(2\frac{3}{10}\right)$
12. $-\frac{2}{7}\left(-\frac{21}{40}\right)$
13. $\left(-\frac{1}{21}\right)\left(-4\frac{1}{5}\right)$
14. $-\frac{13}{18} \div \left(-\frac{2}{9}\right)$
15. $-1.69 \div 0.13$

Set 131 *pages 328–329* Write with an exponent.

1. 100
2. 1,000
3. 0.0001
4. $\frac{1}{10}$
5. 1,000,000
6. 0.000001
7. $\frac{1}{100}$

Write each number in standard form.

8. 10^{-1}
9. 10^1
10. 10^{-4}
11. 10^7
12. 10^{-11}
13. 10^2
14. 10^{-6}
15. 10^5

16. 10^6
17. 10^{-8}
18. 10^{-10}
19. 10^4
20. 10^{-3}
21. 10^{-5}
22. 10^3
23. 10^{-9}

Set 132 *pages 330–331* Use exponents to find each product.
Write the answer with an exponent.

1. $10^6 \times 10^0$
2. $10^3 \times 10$
3. $10^6 \times 10^2$
4. $10^{-1} \times 10^{-7}$
5. $10^2 \times 10^{-2}$

6. $10^{-3} \times 10^{-9}$
7. $10^4 \times 10^0$
8. $10^{-3} \times 10^{-3}$
9. $10^{-6} \times 10^6$
10. $10^8 \times 10^{-7}$

11. $10^5 \times 10$
12. $10^{-3} \times 10^{-7}$
13. $10^9 \times 10^{-10}$
14. 10×10^{-10}
15. $10^{-5} \times 10^7$

16. $10^3 \times (10^{-2} \times 10^4)$
17. $(10^7 \times 10^3) \times 10^{-6}$
18. $1,000 \times 10$
19. 100×0.0001

20. 100×0.001
21. $1,000 \times 0.1$
22. 0.0001×0.1
23. $1,000 \times 1,000$

24. $100 \times 100 \times 0.1$
25. $0.1 \times 0.1 \times 0.01$
26. $0.01 \times 100 \times 100$

27. $10 \times 10 \times 0.0001$
28. $10 \times 10 \times 0.1$
29. $1,000 \times 0.001 \times 10$

30. $100 \times 0.01 \times 0.01$
31. $0.01 \times 0.1 \times 10$
32. $100 \times 1000 \times 0.0001$

MORE PRACTICE

Set 133 *pages 332–333*   Use exponents to find each quotient.
Write the answer with an exponent.

1. $\frac{10^7}{10^4}$ 2. $\frac{10^7}{10^5}$ 3. $\frac{10^2}{10^3}$ 4. $\frac{10^9}{10^{10}}$ 5. $\frac{10^8}{10^{-1}}$ 6. $\frac{10^3}{10^8}$ 7. $\frac{10^4}{10^{-2}}$

8. $\frac{10^{-2}}{10^{-5}}$ 9. $\frac{10}{10^{-4}}$ 10. $\frac{10^2}{10^{-2}}$ 11. $\frac{10^{-3}}{10^2}$ 12. $\frac{10}{10^0}$ 13. $\frac{10^{-5}}{10^{-3}}$ 14. $\frac{10^7}{10^{-7}}$

15. $\frac{1,000}{10}$ 16. $\frac{0.1}{0.001}$ 17. $\frac{10^3}{100}$ 18. $\frac{1,000}{0.1}$ 19. $\frac{0.001}{10}$ 20. $\frac{100}{100}$ 21. $\frac{0.01}{100}$

Set 134 *pages 334–335*   Give each missing exponent.

1. $96 = 9.6 \times 10^{\blacksquare}$ 2. $401.8 = 4.018 \times 10^{\blacksquare}$ 3. $6,539.7 = 6.5397 \times 10^{\blacksquare}$

Write each number in scientific notation.

4. 840   5. 1,100   6. 789.3   7. 13   8. 33,000   9. 5,040.2   10. 609.75

Write each answer in standard form.

11. 9.73×10^2 12. 0.476×10^5 13. 8.04×10^4 14. 1.7×10^6 15. 7.006×10^7

Set 135 *pages 336–337*   Give each missing exponent.

1. $0.077 = 7.7 \times 10^{\blacksquare}$ 2. $0.00087 = 8.7 \times 10^{\blacksquare}$ 3. $0.0048 = 4.8 \times 10^{\blacksquare}$

Write each number in scientific notation.

4. 0.338   5. 0.098   6. 0.000076   7. 0.000372   8. 0.774   9. 0.004051

Write each number in standard form.

10. 8.5×10^{-2} 11. 6.43×10^{-3} 12. 7.892×10^{-6} 13. 2.11×10^{-1} 14. 6.8842×10^{-3}

15. 2.4×10^{-5} 16. 7×10^{-4} 17. 4.851×10^{-7} 18. 3.827×10^{-8} 19. 8.765×10^{-5}

Set 136 *pages 338–339*   Multiply, using scientific notation.
Give each answer in standard form.

1. $(2.4 \times 10^3) \times (8.8 \times 10^6)$ 2. $(4.7 \times 10^{-4}) \times (7.7 \times 10^{-3})$ 3. $3,300 \times 290$

4. $100,000 \times 3,600$ 5. 0.046×0.000999 6. 0.0052×0.0019 7. $48,000 \times 0.000036$

Divide, using scientific notation. Round the quotient of the
decimals to the nearest tenth. Give each answer in standard form.

8. $\frac{8.1 \times 10^6}{2.7 \times 10^3}$ 9. $\frac{2.88 \times 10^5}{1.44 \times 10^{-1}}$ 10. $\frac{0.0075}{0.00015}$ 11. $\frac{1,620}{27,000}$ 12. $\frac{900,000}{0.15}$ 13. $\frac{0.0064}{16,000}$

14. $\frac{342{,}000}{190}$ **15.** $\frac{1{,}080}{27{,}000}$ **16.** $\frac{7{,}200{,}000}{0.045}$ **17.** $\frac{9.6 \times 10^6}{2.4 \times 10^5}$ **18.** $\frac{2{,}560}{160{,}000}$

19. $\frac{540{,}000}{0.018}$ **20.** $\frac{8.4 \times 10^4}{2.1 \times 10^{-3}}$ **21.** $\frac{3.25 \times 10^3}{2.5 \times 10^{-1}}$ **22.** $\frac{810{,}000}{0.0009}$ **23.** $\frac{1.21 \times 10^3}{1.1 \times 10^{-1}}$

Set 137 *pages 342–343*   Between which two consecutive integers is

1. $\sqrt{34}$?   **2.** $\sqrt{48}$?   **3.** $\sqrt{60}$?   **4.** $\sqrt{77}$?   **5.** $\sqrt{86}$?   **6.** $\sqrt{91}$?   **7.** $\sqrt{99}$?

8. $\sqrt{120}$?   **9.** $\sqrt{140}$?   **10.** $\sqrt{155}$?   **11.** $\sqrt{200}$?   **12.** $\sqrt{250}$?   **13.** $\sqrt{284}$?   **14.** $\sqrt{292}$?

Use the table on page 445 to find each square root. If the answer
is not an integer, round to the nearest tenth.

15. $\sqrt{5}$ **16.** $\sqrt{38}$ **17.** $\sqrt{81}$ **18.** $\sqrt{130}$ **19.** $\sqrt{146}$ **20.** $\sqrt{172}$ **21.** $\sqrt{198}$

22. $\sqrt{196}$ **23.** $\sqrt{625}$ **24.** $\sqrt{880}$ **25.** $\sqrt{961}$ **26.** $\sqrt{700}$ **27.** $\sqrt{812}$ **28.** $\sqrt{7{,}200}$

Set 138 *pages 344–345*   Write each rational number as either a
terminating or a repeating decimal.

1. $\frac{7}{8}$ **2.** $-\frac{11}{12}$ **3.** $8\frac{4}{7}$ **4.** $-7\frac{5}{9}$ **5.** $-\frac{14}{15}$ **6.** $-3\frac{5}{6}$ **7.** $\frac{17}{100}$ **8.** $\frac{47}{1{,}000}$

Decide whether the number is rational or irrational.

9. $\sqrt{25}$ **10.** $3.\overline{12}$ **11.** 8.5 **12.** $-10.\overline{67}$ **13.** 6 **14.** $\sqrt{625}$

15. -0.22 **16.** $8.8\overline{9}$ **17.** $\sqrt{11}$ **18.** $-\frac{3}{14}$ **19.** 0.3535 **20.** 6.3742189

Set 139 *pages 346–347*   Find the length of the third side for each right
triangle. Round your answer to the nearest tenth if necessary. The variables
a and b stand for legs; c is for the hypotenuse.

1. $a = 6, b = 8$ **2.** $a = 10, b = 5$ **3.** $a = 6, b = 9$ **4.** $a = 4, b = 4$

5. $a = 11, b = 8$ **6.** $a = 15, b = 36$ **7.** $a = 20, b = 21$ **8.** $a = 7, b = 9$

9. $a = 8, b = 1$ **10.** $a = 24, b = 10$ **11.** $a = 20, b = 15$ **12.** $a = 16, b = 12$

13. $a = 30, c = 50$ **14.** $a = 16, c = 18$ **15.** $c = 11, b = 10$ **16.** $a = 12, c = 13$

17. $a = 14, c = 50$ **18.** $a = 9, c = 11$ **19.** $a = 14, c = 16$ **20.** $c = 34, b = 16$

Can a right triangle have these side lengths? Write *yes* or *no*.

21. $a = 5, b = 12, c = 13$ **22.** $a = 6, b = 6, c = 8$ **23.** $a = 7, b = 24, c = 25$

24. $a = 19, b = 17, c = 28$ **25.** $a = 12, b = 9, c = 15$ **26.** $a = 15, b = 20, c = 25$

MORE PRACTICE

Set 140 *pages 348–349* Solve each problem by using the Pythagorean theorem. Round your answer to nearest tenth if necessary.

1. A 16-foot ladder is leaning against a garage which is 10 feet high. The bottom of the ladder is 2 feet away from the garage. How far from the bottom of the ladder is the point of contact with the garage?

2. A 5-foot fishing pole is leaning against a 9-foot-high wall of a shed. The end of the pole is 3 feet from the shed. How far above the ground does the pole touch the shed?

3. A radio transmission tower has a 30-foot supporting and stabilizing cable, which is attached to the tower 20 feet above the ground. How far from the tower should the cable be anchored in the ground?

4. The two sides of the roof of a house meet at a right angle, and each side of the roof is 25 feet long from the lower edge to the peak. How wide is the house?

Set 141 *pages 350–351* Give the tangent for each angle as a ratio and as a decimal to the nearest hundredth. Find each side measure to the nearest tenth. Use the table on page 446.

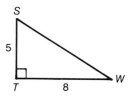
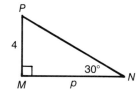

1. ∠W   **2.** ∠B   **3.** ∠S   **4.** ∠A   **5.** x   **6.** p

Set 142 *pages 352–353* Use the diagram to solve each problem. Give percents to the nearest tenth of a percent.

1. What is the grade of the cable-car wire between Tower 1 and Tower 2?

2. What is the grade between Tower 3 and Tower 4?

3. Between the start and the end of the cable-car ride, what is the overall rise and the overall distance?

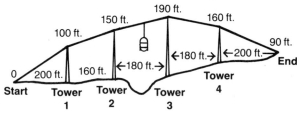

4. What is the rise between the start and Tower 3?

Set 143 *pages 358–359* Write each expression as the product of a rational number and a variable.

1. $\frac{6x}{7}$ **2.** $\frac{-7m}{9}$ **3.** $\frac{t}{4}$ **4.** $\frac{-k}{5}$ **5.** $\frac{-8s}{13}$ **6.** $-z$ **7.** $\frac{2d}{3}$ **8.** $\frac{-y}{2}$ **9.** $\frac{-9r}{10}$ **10.** $\frac{4x}{5}$

Evaluate each expression for $a = -2.2$, $b = 0.8$, $c = 4.2$, $r = -\frac{1}{3}$, $s = \frac{5}{6}$, and $t = -\frac{5}{12}$.

11. $-5t$ **12.** $s + t$ **13.** $-s + 2r$ **14.** $r(s + 2)$ **15.** $-r(1 - t)$ **16.** $s(r + 3)$

17. $\frac{4r}{5}$ **18.** $-rt$ **19.** $st + r$ **20.** $2a + b$ **21.** $\frac{-2s}{6} + t$ **22.** $4c - 3a$

23. $\frac{-2s}{15}$ **24.** $b(a + c)$ **25.** $bc + ab$ **26.** $0.4b - a$ **27.** $b^2 + 2c + 10$ **28.** $c^2 - 2a$

29. $\frac{-2r}{5}$ **30.** $c(a + b)$ **31.** $2(b + c)$ **32.** $0.5b - c$ **33.** $b^2 + a^2 + 4$ **34.** $2a + b^2$

Set 144 *pages 360–361* Solve each equation.

1. $z - 24 = -13$ **2.** $-10 + r = 9$ **3.** $s - 111 = -56$ **4.** $c + (-11.3) = -13$

5. $d + 10 = -28$ **6.** $m - 6.5 = 7$ **7.** $12.6 + a = -1.1$ **8.** $14.3 - n = 7.8$

9. $\frac{7}{8} - x = \frac{1}{8}$ **10.** $\frac{-4}{5} + y = \frac{-5}{6}$ **11.** $-9\frac{1}{2} + z = -7$ **12.** $\frac{8}{9} - b = -15$

13. $m - \frac{2}{3} = 5\frac{1}{2}$ **14.** $\frac{7}{12} + c = -17$ **15.** $-4\frac{7}{10} + s = -9$ **16.** $n - \frac{3}{4} = 6$

17. $\frac{9}{10} - d = 0$ **18.** $-\frac{1}{2} + a = \frac{-7}{12}$ **19.** $\frac{5}{11} - x = -22$ **20.** $\frac{-5}{7} + w = -19$

21. $8.3 - x = 7$ **22.** $9.9 - m = 3.1$ **23.** $-6.6 = q + 4$ **24.** $15.7 = v - 19$

Set 145 *pages 362–363* Solve each equation.

1. $5x = -60$ **2.** $6n = -32$ **3.** $16y = 75$ **4.** $-8t = 88$ **5.** $-8a = 56$

6. $-7b = -70$ **7.** $\frac{3}{8}z = \frac{9}{16}$ **8.** $\frac{9}{10}w = \frac{3}{5}$ **9.** $\frac{-4}{7}a = -16$ **10.** $\frac{-5}{6}n = \frac{11}{12}$

11. $\frac{4x}{6} = \frac{8}{21}$ **12.** $\frac{2w}{15} = \frac{2}{5}$ **13.** $\frac{7}{9}w = -18$ **14.** $-\frac{s}{15} = -10$ **15.** $\frac{-m}{9} = \frac{-5}{12}$

16. $5x - 19 = -4$ **17.** $-11 + 4y = -43$ **18.** $6t - 7 = -55$ **19.** $-8d + 10 = 12$

20. $-15x - 9 = -12$ **21.** $-8d - 6 = -10$ **22.** $-6.4 = -2n + 14$ **23.** $2y - 4.9 = 7.1$

24. $8x + 0.6 = -5.4$ **25.** $9t - 6 = -33$ **26.** $-16 + 6y = -70$ **27.** $9x - 40 = -4$

MORE PRACTICE

Set 146 *pages 364–365*   Graph each inequality.

1. $x > 6$ 2. $a < -3$ 3. $c \geq -10$ 4. $d \leq -1$ 5. $m > -11$ 6. $t \geq 3.5$

7. $y \geq 9$ 8. $b < 0$ 9. $w \leq -7$ 10. $c < 11$ 11. $d \geq -9$ 12. $a > -4.9$

13. $t \geq 14$ 14. $z \leq -5$ 15. $m \leq 1$ 16. $t \geq 7$ 17. $a \leq 12$ 18. $d < 7.1$

Set 147 *pages 366–367*   Solve each inequality.

1. $w + 7 < 19$ 2. $t + 8 < 2$ 3. $a - 11 > 26$ 4. $x - 15 < 6$

5. $t + (-7) \geq 20$ 6. $c + (-15) \leq -11$ 7. $19 < x - 7.8$ 8. $2 < m - 1.5$

9. $-5.7 > -8 + s$ 10. $-9.1 > -16 + b$ 11. $0 > y - 2.9$ 12. $0 \leq h - 6.4$

13. $z + 93 \leq 100$ 14. $y - 19 \leq 48$ 15. $-3.6 + n > -2.4$ 16. $a + 0.3 > 0.47$

17. $88 < x - 7.1$ 18. $30 < t - 5$ 19. $-7.5 > -8 + b$ 20. $c + (-29) \leq 58$

21. $a + (-1) \geq -40$ 22. $c + 0.66 > 0.77$ 23. $b + 12 \leq 61$ 24. $z - 4 \leq 100$

Set 148 *pages 368–369*   Solve each inequality.

1. $15w < 105$ 2. $17x \geq 51$ 3. $-12c > 132$ 4. $25n < 225$ 5. $13t \geq -52$

6. $-11d < -121$ 7. $7a \leq -84$ 8. $-4m > 64$ 9. $-9w > 108$ 10. $-11q < 143$

11. $-16y < 192$ 12. $11c < -5$ 13. $7n > -13$ 14. $11a < -55$ 15. $-9c \leq 153$

16. $\frac{3}{4}s \geq -36$ 17. $\frac{5}{6}t > -60$ 18. $\frac{-2}{3}k < -30$ 19. $\frac{-7}{10}m \leq 140$ 20. $\frac{4}{9}k < -16$

21. $\frac{-15}{7}d < 85$ 22. $\frac{7}{16}a > -21$ 23. $\frac{-6}{5}n < 66$ 24. $\frac{4}{9}w > -144$ 25. $\frac{-6}{7}x \geq -30$

26. $\frac{-9}{8}s > -72$ 27. $\frac{1}{2}m < 34$ 28. $\frac{6}{11}b \leq -42$ 29. $\frac{-7}{12}n < -49$ 30. $\frac{5}{8}s < -15$

31. $\frac{-8}{15}t < 75$ 32. $\frac{9}{20}a > 45$ 33. $\frac{-2}{9}t \geq -100$ 34. $\frac{1}{6}k < -9$ 35. $\frac{-12}{13}t \geq -72$

Set 149 *pages 372–373*   Plot each of these points on a coordinate graph. Tell which quadrant or axis contains the point.

1. $(0, 4)$ 2. $(1, 9)$ 3. $(4, 6)$ 4. $(6, 4)$ 5. $(-2, -3)$ 6. $(-5, 5)$

7. $(-5, -1)$ 8. $(7, -4)$ 9. $(-6, 3)$ 10. $(-8, 7)$ 11. $(-4, 0)$ 12. $(0, -7)$

13. $(4, -9)$ 14. $(-8, -1)$ 15. $(6, -3)$ 16. $(2, 7)$ 17. $(-7, -1)$ 18. $(4, -4)$

19. On a separate graph, plot (6, 9); (−6, 9); (−6, −9); (6, −9).

20. On a separate graph, plot (7, 1); (7, 3); (7, 5); (7, 7).

21. Plot: (4.5, 6); (8.5, 1); (7, −1.5); (−8, −7); (−3.5, 4).

Set 150 *pages 374–375*   Complete each table and draw the graph.

1. $y = x + 7$

x	−7	−5	−3	−1	0	1	3
y	0	2					

2. $y = 4 - x$

x	−2	−1	0	1	2	3	4
y							

3. $y = -3x$

x	−3	−2	−1	0	1	2	3
y	9						

4. $y = 2x + 2$

x	4	5	6	7	8	9	10
y							

Set 151 *pages 376–377*   Draw a graph to solve each problem.

1. Two points on a line are (−6, 6) and (2, −6). For what value of x is y = 0?

2. Two points on a line are (0, 7) and (−1, 11). For what value of x is y = 0?

3. A burning candle was 8 inches long at 5:00 P.M.; at 7:30 P.M. it was 5 inches long. How many more inches would have burned by 9:00 P.M.?

4. If a cyclist can travel a distance of 12 miles in one hour, how far could he travel in 3 hours and 15 minutes?

5. If a town planning council uses a general guide of having 3 parks for every 10,000 people, approximately how large must the population be to sustain 12 parks?

6. A pitcher throws a baseball. After 0.1 seconds the ball is 6 feet from the pitcher; after 0.15 seconds it is 10 feet from the pitcher. How long will it take for the ball to be 60.5 feet from the pitcher?

Set 152 *pages 378–379*   Graph each inequality.

1. $y \geq x + 3$ **2.** $y > 3 - x$ **3.** $y \geq 5x$ **4.** $y \leq 3x$ **5.** $y > x + 5$

6. $y \leq -2x$ **7.** $y \leq 6x$ **8.** $y > 4 - x$ **9.** $y \geq 2x + 4$ **10.** $y < -x + 3$

11. $y \leq -x + 5$ **12.** $y \leq -4x$ **13.** $y > -\frac{1}{3}x$ **14.** $y \geq -x + 6$ **15.** $y \leq -8x$

16. $y < \frac{-3}{4}x$ **17.** $y > 3x$ **18.** $y < -x + 3$ **19.** $y > \frac{1}{4}x$ **20.** $y < x - 4$

Answers to Odd-Numbered Exercises

Chapter 1

Pages 2–3
1. 30, 35, 40, 45, 50 **3.** 36, 33, 30, 27, 24 **5.** 30, 42, 56, 72, 90 **7.** 984, 978, 971, 963, 954 **9.** 9, 14, 9, 14, 9 **11.** 5, 4, 6, 5, 7 **13.** 106, 148, 197, 253, 316 **15.** 13, 21, 34, 55, 89

17.

Shirts	Dollars
7	85
8	97
9	109
10	121

19.

Shirts	Dollars
1	5
2	10
3	15
4	20
5	25
6	30
7	35
8	40

Pages 4–5
1. 400 **3.** 1,200 **5.** 8,900 **7.** 7,000 **9.** 5,700,000 **11.** 800,000 **13.** 3,000,000 **15.** 8,000,000 **17.** 10,000,000 **19.** 200 + 10 + 3 **21.** 40,000 + 4,000 + 400 + 40 + 4 **23.** 30,000 **25.** 30,200 **27.** 59,000 **29.** 70,000 **31.** 70,900 **33.** 76,000 **35.** 100,000 **37.** 104,000

Pages 6–7
1. 1,000 **3.** 500 **5.** 2,100 **7.** 4,500 **9.** 10,000 **11.** 5,000 **13.** 90,000 **15.** 20,000 **17.** 700,000 **19.** 640,000 **21.** 150,000 **23.** Any two numbers between 7,500 and 7,999 inclusive whose sum is less than 15,500; for example, 7,642 and 7,598. **25.** Any two numbers between 8,001 and 8,499 inclusive whose sum is greater than 16,499 and less than 17,499; for example, 8,496 and 8,131. **27.** About 21,000

Pages 8–9
1. 898 **3.** 8,854 **5.** 1,300 **7.** 6,043 **9.** 10,322 **11.** 222,003 **13.** 17,121 **15.** 22,378 **17.** 16,517 **19.** 405 **21.** 4,330 **23.** 4,753 **25.** 31,589 **27.** 1,359 **29.** 3,132 **31.** 1,993,033 **33.** 3,115 **35.** 6,010 **37.** 235,284 **39.** Find the sum of the differences or the difference of the two totals.

Pages 10–11
1. 160,000 **3.** 240,000 **5.** 15,000,000 **7.** 18,000,000 **9.** 63,000 **11.** 400,000 **13.** 2,000,000 **15.** 1,600,000 **17.** 162,000 **19.** 5,400,000 **21.** 600 miles

Pages 12–13
1. 234 **3.** 1,020 **5.** 4,500 **7.** 6,232 **9.** 50,112 **11.** 540,981 **13.** 232 **15.** 6,300 **17.** 3,920 **19.** 1,935 **21.** 18,270 **23.** 14,985 **25.** 137,264 **27.** 278,100 **29.** 610,589 **31.** 1,887,410 **33.** 63,112 **35.** 286,875 **37.** 216 **39.** 2,025 **41.** 1,209 **43.** Write the product of the ones digits using the two right-hand places. To the left of this, write the product of the tens digit times the number that is one greater than the tens digit. **45.** 73,500 passenger miles **47.** 1,034-mile flight

Pages 14–15
1. 54 R1 **3.** 132 **5.** 905 R3 **7.** 29 R6 **9.** 72 **11.** 165 **13.** 600 R1 **15.** 45 R10 **17.** 470 R16 **19.** 253 R20 **21.** 3 R124 **23.** 10 R120 **25.** 22 R57 **27.** 7,689 **29.** 550 miles per hour **31.** Driving $48 less

Pages 16–17
1. Multiplication **3.** Division, 5 times as long **5.** Multiplication, 780 miles **7.** Addition, 533 passengers **9.** Multiplication, 144,540 passengers

Pages 18–19
1. 1,308 **3.** 37,487 **5.** 8,426 **7.** 59,089 **9.** 892 **11.** 16,342 **13.** 129 **15.** 14,810 **17.** 11,826 **19.** 88,896 **21.** 3,645 **23.** 45 R1 **25.** 902 R3 **27.** 2,910 **29.** 1,092 **31.** 75 R634 **33.** 90 R2 **35.** 24,986 **37.** 365,681 **39.** 5,541 **41.** 508 R6 **43.** 1,602 **45.** 134 **47.** 9,021 **49.** 244,375 **51.** 321 **53.** 28,640 **55.** 7,768,358 **57.** 480 miles **59.** 187 passengers **61.** 4,086 tickets

Pages 20–21
1. Divisible by 2, 3, 5, 9, 10 **3.** Divisible by 2, 4, 5, 10 **5.** Not divisible **7.** Divisible by 2, 3, 4, 5, 9, 10 **9.** Divisible by 2, 3, 4 **11.** No **13.** 6, 18, 30, and 42 **15.** A whole number is divisible by eight if the number formed by its last three digits is divisible by 8.

Pages 22–23
1. Composite 1, 2, 5, 10 **3.** Prime **5.** Composite 1, 7, 49 **7.** Prime **9.** Composite 1, 2, 4, 5, 10, 20, 25, 50, 100 **11.** Composite 1, 3, 41, 123 **13.** Composite 1, 11, 13, 143 **15.** Composite 1, 2, 4, 8, 16, 37, 74, 148, 296, 592 **17.** Composite 1, 3, 149, 447 **19.** Composite 1, 3, 5, 7, 15, 19, 21, 35, 57, 95, 105, 133, 285, 399, 665, 1,995 **21.** 3 and 5, 5 and 7, 11 and 13, 17 and 19, 29 and 31, 41 and 43 **23.** Answers will vary. A sample is given. 24, 25, 26, 27, 28

Pages 24–25
1. Answers will vary. 2 samples are given.

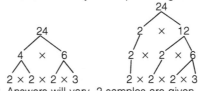

3. Answers will vary. 2 samples are given.

5. 2×7 **7.** $2^2 \times 7$ **9.** $2 \times 5 \times 7$ **11.** $5^2 \times 13$ **13.** 2×3^4 **15.** 3×97 **17.** $2^4 \times 3^4 \times 5^2$ **19.** $2^5 \times 7^2 \times 11^2$ **21.** $2^2 \times 3$ 1, 2, 3, 4, 6, 12 **23.** 5^3 1, 5, 25, 125 **25.** $2^5 \times 3$ 1, 2, 3, 4, 6, 8, 12, 16, 24, 32, 48, 96 **27.** $3 \times 5^2 \times 17$ 1, 3, 5, 15, 17, 25, 51, 75, 85, 255, 425, 1,275 **29.** 30,030, 510,510, 9,699,690

Pages 26–27
1. 1, 2 **3.** 1, 2, 4, 8 **5.** 1 **7.** 1, 3, 9 **9.** 3 **11.** 6 **13.** 1 **15.** 12 **17.** 5 **19.** 65 **21.** 1, 2, 4, 8, 16   16 **23.** 1, 2   2 **25.** 1-in. or 2-in. squares.

27. Border will be too wide in relation to whole.

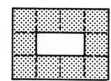

Pages 28–29
1. 5, 10, 15, 20, 25 **3.** 11, 22, 33, 44, 55 **5.** 20, 40, 60, 80, 100 **7.** 36, 72, 108, 144, 180 **9.** 12, 24, 36 ·
11. 30, 60, 90 **13.** 6, 12, 18 **15.** 16, 32, 48
17. 147, 294, 441 **19.** 78 **21.** 108 **23.** 561 **25.** 312
27. 490 **29.** 12 inches **31.** The two numbers are equal

Pages 30–31
1. 2^{10} or 1,024 paths **3.** 3^8, or $6,561 **5.** 11 **7.** 14 paths

Chapter 2

Pages 36–37
1. 14 **3.** 3 **5.** 11 **7.** 6 **9.** 5 **11.** 85 **13.** 51 **15.** 0
17. 6 **19.** 64 **21.** 10 **23.** 22 **25.** 1 **27.** 10 **29.** 10
31. 5 **33.** 7 **35.** 9

Pages 38–39
1. 80, assoc. prop. of + **3.** 8, comm. prop. of +
5. 25, comm. and assoc. prop. of × **7.** 58 **9.** 135
11. 1,300 **13.** 0 **15.** 110 **17.** 0 **19.** 279 **21.** 140
23. 44 **25.** 8 **27.** $7.90

Pages 40–41
1. 11 **3.** 54 **5.** 54 **7.** 23 **9.** 9 **11.** 9 **13.** 3 **15.** 153
17. 603 **19.** 2 **21.** 10 **23.** 7 **25.** 10 **27.** 65 **29.** 0
31. 1 **33.** 8 **35.** 975,000 bits **37.** 78,000,000 bits

Pages 42–43
1. $m + 31$ **3.** $p - 4$ **5.** $6f^3$ **7.** $\frac{t}{6}$ **9.** $k + 6$ **11.** ab
13. $c^2 + b$ **15.** $\frac{4}{n}$ **17.** $3 - x$ **19.** $60c$ **21.** $n - 1$
23. $4d + f$

Pages 44–45
1. $k = 27$ **3.** $x = 134$ **5.** $h = 65$ **7.** $t = 274$ **9.** $q = 85$
11. $r = 153$ **13.** $y = 28$ **15.** $a = 59$ **17.** $q = 0$
19. $x = 5$ **21.** $j = 3$ **23.** 42 more years **25.** 8 cellists

Pages 46–47
1. $t = 12$ **3.** $x = 13$ **5.** $w = 187$ **7.** $a = 190$ **9.** $p = 14$
11. $x = 396$ **13.** $q = 1$ **15.** $n = 448$ **17.** $u = 7$
19. $m = 38$ **21.** $r = 30$ **23.** $y = 80$ **25.** 288 min. or
4 hr. 48 min. **27.** $75

Pages 48–49
1. $\frac{t}{408} = 17$ $t = 6,936$ **3.** $408 - 17 = t$ $t = 391$
5. $b + 48 = 120$ 72 butterfly fish **7.** $\frac{224}{14} = t$ 16
readings **9.** $15(92) = f$ 1,380 fish

Pages 50–51
1. 12 **3.** 32 **5.** 47 **7.** 17 **9.** 80 **11.** 16 **13.** 17 **15.** 72
17. 2 **19.** 40 **21.** 3 **23.** 30 **25.** 165 **27.** $\frac{c}{8}$ **29.** xy

31. $h - 81$ **33.** $3y$ **35.** $e + 5$ **37.** $g - 1$ **39.** $\frac{x}{64}$
41. $100 - y$ **43.** $b = 143$ **45.** $d = 1,690$ **47.** $n = 225$
49. $m = 0$ **51.** $i = 9$ **53.** $x = 87$ **55.** $r = 1$
57. 2,380 fish **59.** $395

Pages 52–53
1. $x = 88$ **3.** $c = 160$ **5.** $r = 8$ **7.** $a = 50$ **9.** $w = 2$
11. $r = 13$ **13.** $x = 27$ **15.** $c = 3$ **17.** $d = 55$
19. 132 feet **21.** About 6 atmospheres of pressure

Pages 54–55
1. R **3.** G **5.** (5, 5) **7.** (2, 1) **9.** (0, 5)

11,13,15.

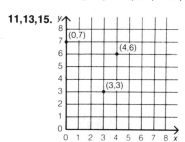

17. RUN **19.** PROGRAM **21.** PASCAL **23.** GRAPHICS
25. END

Pages 56–57
1. 1 minute **3.** 4 minutes **5.** 2,400 **7.** 3,600 **9.** 2
11. 36 **13.** 14 million calculations **15.** 35 million
calculations

Pages 58–59
1. 10, 15, 20 **3.** 9, 12, 17

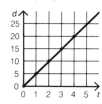

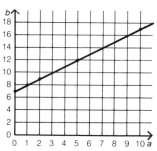

5. 58, 62, 66 **7.** 20, 30, 70, 120

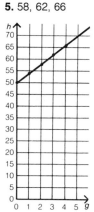

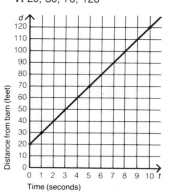

1. 90 meters

3.

Seconds	0	1	2	3
Meters (Fox)	0	10	20	30

5.

Seconds	0	1	2	3
Meters (Rabbit)	25	30	35	40
Meters (Fox)	0	10	20	30

5 seconds

7.

Seconds	0	1	2	3	10
Cm (Tortoise)	0	8	16	24	80
Cm (Snail)	100	101	102	103	110

About 14 seconds

Pages 62–63
Answers will vary. Samples are given. **1.** Chang wants to buy six goldfish. How much money does she need? **3.** Peter wants a dog without fleas. His sister also wants a dog without fleas. How much would the two dogs cost? **5.** How much would one framed poster and a tarantula cost? **7.** Together Jo, Jose, Mary, and Martin bought a dog without fleas. How much did each one pay? **9.** Sonia wants to buy three dogs with fleas and a white rat. She has $23. How much more money does she need?

Chapter 3

Pages 68–69
1. 0.8 **3.** 0.06 **5.** 0.02965 **7.** 9.017 **9.** 35.3 **11.** 8.0007 **13.** 61.000061 **15.** 4 ones **17.** 4 millionths **19.** 4 tens **21.** Two and eighty-five hundredths **23.** Forty-one and eight thousandths **25.** Nine hundred-thousandths **27.** 0.04

Pages 70–71
1. 0.70 **3.** 4.76 **5.** 0.03 **7.** 6.930 **9.** 4.200 **11.** 0.900 **13.** > **15.** < **17.** > **19.** = **21.** > **23.** = **25.** 4.26 4.62 6.42 **27.** 0.3186 0.3286 0.33 **29.** 3.03 3.033 3.303 3.330 **31.** Answers may vary. Possible answers are given. 1.1, 1.2, 1.333 **33.** Answers may vary. Possible answers are: 0.673, 0.675, 0.67683 **35.** Less **37.** Less

Pages 72–73
1. 9 **3.** 4.6 **5.** 6.05 **7.** 0.237 **9.** 1 **11.** 424.4 **13.** 0.60 **15.** 200 **17.** 4.0 **19.** 0.44444 **21.** 16.1344 **23.** 20 **25.** 7 **27.** 3,000 **29.** 0.0003 **31.** 1 **33.** 0.025 mm **35.** 0.3 mm

Pages 74–75
1. 8.42 **3.** 28.286 **5.** 28.086 **7.** 33.008 **9.** 40.97 **11.** 20.76 **13.** 70.41 **15.** 13.433 **17.** 28.18 **19.** 0.2117 **21.** 74.9678 **23.** 23.385 **25.** 0.621 g

Pages 76–77
1. 7 **3.** 25 **5.** 1.7 **7.** 0.7 **9.** 6.76 **11.** 14.2 **13.** 5.77 **15.** 5.77 **17.** 0.02 **19.** $4.20 **21.** $2.40

Pages 78–79
1. $20.21 **3.** 4.89 **5.** Too little information **7.** Too little information **9.** $0.24 **11.** Too little information

Pages 80–81
1. 5 **3.** 0.00126 **5.** 0.030025 **7.** 5.76 **9.** 62.1 **11.** 0.0064 **13.** 262.44 **15.** 2,648 **17.** 60.903 **19.** 0.0612 **21.** 0.273(400), 2.73(40), 27.3(4), 273(0.4) **23.** 0.14(63)(5), 1.4(63)(0.5), 14(6.3)(0.5), 1.4(6.3)(5) **25.** $462.50

Pages 82–83
1. 20 **3.** 48 **5.** 800 **7.** 0.27 **9.** 540 **11.** 2 **13.** 0.06 **15.** 0.08 **17.** 0.03 **19.** 32 **21.** 1.8 **23.** 0.144 **25.** Answers will vary. Samples are 0.0043, 0.00415, 0.0035, 0.0039 **27.** About $40 **29.** About $3.50

Pages 84–85
1. 6.5 **3.** 0.75 **5.** 0.53 **7.** 0.006 **9.** 3.64 **11.** 0.35 **13.** 43.76 **15.** 63.2 **17.** 0.024 **19.** 0.00425 **21.** 0.012 **23.** 0.056 **25.** 0.08 **27.** 5.003 **29.** No **31.** No **33.** Yes **35.** $37.50

Pages 86–87
1. 45,600 **3.** 61 **5.** 24 **7.** 3 **9.** 51.9 **11.** 0.00006 **13.** 0.003417 **15.** 5 **17.** 34 **19.** 3,400 **21.** 340,000 **23.** 0.034 **25.** 0.00034 **27.** 9,700 **29.** 0.564 **31.** $4.28

Pages 88–89
1. 35 **3.** 0.8 **5.** 5.8 **7.** 0.05 **9.** 300 **11.** 800 **13.** 716.7 **15.** 12.0 **17.** 0.3 **19.** 85.33 **21.** 14.44 **23.** 0.61 **25.** 13.8 years **27.** $615

Pages 90–91
1. 1 **3.** 3 **5.** 4.32 **7.** 30 **9.** 100 **11.** 0.056 **13.** 7.48 **15.** 10 **17.** 41.958 **19.** 0.373 **21.** 0.5876 **23.** 0.008 **25.** 294.76 **27.** 0.6786 **29.** $414.50 **31.** 167 hairs **33.** 0.025 mm

Pages 92–93
1. $x = 3.1$ **3.** $n = 10.6$ **5.** $m = 9.3$ **7.** $y = 4.6$ **9.** $z = 6.2$ **11.** $b = 39.4$ **13.** $x = 2.3$ **15.** $y = 31.11$ **17.** $x = 331.2$ **19.** $t = 54.621$ **21.** $m = 7$ **23.** 3.5 extra hours

Pages 94–95
1. $2.6t = 1.82$ or $t = \frac{1.82}{2.6}$ $t = 0.7$ **3.** $0.141p = 8.46$ or $p = \frac{8.46}{0.141}$ 60 packages **5.** $g - 4.5 = 1.2$ or $g = 1.2 + 4.5$ 5.7 gal. **7.** $48s = 5.76$ or $s = \frac{5.76}{48}$ $0.12

Chapter 4

Pages 102–103
1. 16 **3.** 63 **5.** 7 **7.** 12 **9.** 0 **11.** 105 **13.** 3 **15.** 125 **17.** 6 30 40 **19.** $\frac{2}{7}$ **21.** $\frac{15}{16}$ **23.** $\frac{11}{16}$ **25.** $\frac{3}{5}$ **27.** $\frac{2}{5}$ **29.** $\frac{1}{2}$ **31.** $\frac{1}{5}$ **33.** $\frac{4}{5}$ **35.** $\frac{1}{2}$ in.

Pages 104–105
1. > **3.** = **5.** > **7.** < **9.** > **11.** > **13.** < **15.** > **17.** $\frac{1}{4}$ $\frac{3}{10}$ $\frac{2}{5}$ **19.** $\frac{6}{15}$ $\frac{4}{5}$ $\frac{13}{15}$ **21.** $\frac{2}{3}$ $\frac{7}{10}$ $\frac{4}{5}$ **23.** $\frac{7}{12}$ $\frac{7}{10}$ $\frac{7}{8}$ **25.** $\frac{11}{16}$ in.

Pages 106–107
1. $\frac{3}{10}$ **3.** $\frac{6}{125}$ **5.** $\frac{12}{25}$ **7.** 0.5 **9.** 0.16 **11.** 0.1875 **13.** $0.\overline{4}$ **15.** $0.41\overline{6}$ **17.** 0.175 **19.** $0.0\overline{675}$ **21.** $0.4\overline{09}$ **23.** $\frac{4}{125}$ **25.** $\frac{3}{64}$ in. bit

Pages 158–159
1. 50 **3.** 10.4 **5.** 130 **7.** 120 **9.** 95 **11.** 48 **13.** 864 **15.** 45 **17.** 0.2 **19.** 5.4 **21.** $90,000

Pages 160–161
1. $15 **3.** $48 **5.** $285 **7.** $3,687.50 **9.** $150 **11.** 4 yr. **13.** $700 **15.** 8.5%

Pages 162–163
1. $x = 36$ **3.** $t = 2.8$ **5.** $a = 2.7$ **7.** 6% **9.** 50%
11. 250% **13.** 70% **15.** $66\frac{2}{3}$% **17.** 250% **19.** $\frac{3}{4}$ **21.** $\frac{1}{3}$
23. $1\frac{1}{2}$ **25.** 0.3 **27.** 0.125 **29.** 2 **31.** 4 **33.** 60 **35.** 25
37. 4.9 **39.** 40% **41.** 128 **43.** 56.25 **45.** 150% **47.** 2.5
49. 2 **51.** 3,900 loans **53.** 195 Es **55.** 65%

Pages 164–165
1. $414.80 **3.** $67.50 **5.** $600.64 **7.** $292.53 **9.** 12%

Chapter 6

Pages 170–171
1. gram **3.** meter **5.** meter **7.** liter **9.** liter **11.** gram
13. hectoliter **15.** kilogram **17.** 100 **19.** 0.01 **21.** 0.001
23. 0.001 **25.** 100 **27.** 0.1 **29.** 100 **31.** 10
33. 1,000,000 **35.** 0.1

Pages 172–173
1. 1 mm **3.** 150 mm **5.** 1.8 m **7.** 9.24 **9.** 3,000
11. 864.3 **13.** 0.00421 **15.** 90 **17.** 32 **19.** 12.5 cm wide and 50 cm long

Pages 174–175
1. 12 m² **3.** 475 cm² **5.** 6 m³ **7.** 400 **9.** 0.00000004
11. 0.0000003 **13.** 7,000,000,000 **15.** 0.007
17. 0.000005 **19.** 6 m² **21.** Area is measured in square meters.

Pages 176–177
1. 1.8 kg **3.** 5 mL **5.** 0.768 **7.** 65,300 **9.** 14,000
11. 0.309 **13.** 0.013892 **15.** 1,000 L

Pages 178–179
1. 250 m³ **3.** 375-meter **5.** 2-meter **7.** 1,500 m²
9. $37.50 **11.** 170 cm **13.** 555-A-P-E-S

Pages 180–181
1. 12 kg **3.** 110 kg **5.** 1,950 km **7.** 4 L **9.** 15 m²
11. 2.7 m **13.** 3,000 cm³ **15.** 6,000 **17.** 23,400
19. 5,600 **21.** 45,600 **23.** 10 **25.** 9 **27.** 4.836 **29.** 5
31. 0.707 **33.** 8.9 **35.** 4.2 **37.** 30,000 **39.** 35,000 g
41. Square kilometers **43.** Yes

Pages 182–183
1. 15 ft. **3.** 45 cu. yd. **5.** 24 **7.** 432 **9.** 5 5 **11.** $3\frac{5}{6}$
13. 9 **15.** 3 2 **17.** 3,960 **19.** 96 **21.** 32 **23.** 1,760
25. 24 in. by 24 in. by 24 in. **27.** 600 sq. ft.

Pages 184–185
1. 1 oz. **3.** 6 qt. **5.** 5 **7.** 25 **9.** 16 1 **11.** $4\frac{1}{2}$ **13.** 4,020
15. 3 6 **17.** 4 lb. 10 oz.

Pages 186–187
1. 10 ft. 10 in. **3.** 13 gal. 1 qt. **5.** 23 lb. **7.** 2 ft. 2 in.
9. 8 qt. 1 pt. **11.** 3 lb. 13 oz. **13.** 7 yd. 2 in.
15. 10 lb. 11 oz. **17.** 3 yd. 1 ft. 3 in. **19.** 19 ft.
21. 9 gal. 2 t. **23.** $2\frac{2}{3}$ ft. or 2 ft. 8 in. **25.** 3 ft. 5 in.
27. 9 ft. 2 in.

Pages 188–189
1. 3 hr. 27 min. **3.** 1 hr. 50 min. **5.** 7:36 P.M. **7.** 2:50 P.M.
9. 1 min. 28 sec. **11.** 5 days **13.** 43 min. 56 sec.

Pages 190–191
1. About 2,025 mi. **3.** About 6.7 hr. **5.** 51.1 min.

Pages 192–193
1. inch, $\frac{1}{2}$ inch **3.** $\frac{1}{2}$ yard, $\frac{1}{4}$ yard **5.** quart, $\frac{1}{2}$ quart
7. 0.1 meter, 0.05 meter **9.** 0.01 kilometer, 0.005 kilometer
11. 0.01 gram, 0.005 gram **13.** $3\frac{1}{2}$ ft. **15.** 14.15 sec.
17. 37.1 mm **19.** 14 in. **21.** 4.4 kg **23.** 7.1 min.
25. 6.1 sec.

Chapter 7

Pages 200–201
1. Line **3.** Ray
5. Answers may vary. A sample is given.

7. Answers may vary. A sample is given.

9. Answers may vary. A sample is given.

11. Answers may vary. A sample is given.

13. Answers may vary. A sample is given.

15. $\overrightarrow{XJ}$, $\overrightarrow{XK}$, $\overrightarrow{XL}$, $\overrightarrow{XM}$
17–19. Answers may vary. A sample is given.

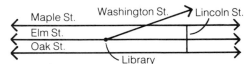

Pages 202–203
1. 68° Acute **3.** 90° Right **5.** 24° Acute **7.** Acute
9. Acute **11.** Obtuse

7. 42°   **9.** 78°   **11.** 171°

13. *Q* **15.** Answers may vary. A sample is given. ∠*TVN*
17. Answers may vary. A sample is given.

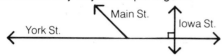

York St.   Main St.   Iowa St.

19. 90° each

Pages 204–205
1. ∠*ABD* and ∠*DBE*, ∠*EBF* and ∠*FBC* **3.** $\overrightarrow{AC}$ *and* $\overleftrightarrow{EG}$
5. 122° **7.** 144° **9.** 45° **11.** 17° **13.** Answers may vary. A
sample is given.

45°
45°

Pages 206–207
1. Alt. int. **3.** Vertical **5.** Vertical **7.** Vertical **9.** Vertical
11. 110°
13.

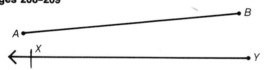
135°
45°   45°
135°

Pages 208–209
1.

A   B
X   Y

3.

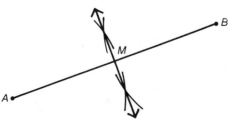
E   R

5.

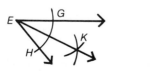
B
M
A

7.
E   G
H   K

9.

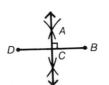
A
D   C   B

11.

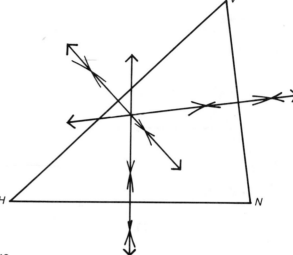
V
H   N

13.

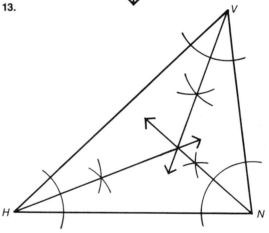
V
H   N

Pages 210–211
1.
Z
X   Y

3.

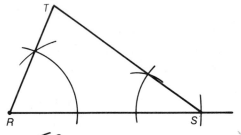

5.

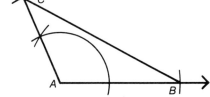

7.

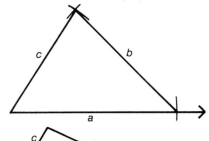

9.

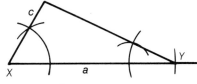

11.

Pages 212–213
1. 3 cm **3.** 2 cm **5.** Answers may vary. Samples are given.
7 cm and 4 cm, 8 cm and 5 cm, 6 cm and 7 cm
7. $a + b - 1$

Pages 214–215
1. b **3.** d **5.** 70° **7.** 90° **9.** 90°, 45°, 45°
11. Scalene, right **13.** Isosceles, acute

Pages 216–217
1. Square, rectangle, rhombus, parallelogram
3. Rhombus, parallelogram **5.** Answers may vary. A sample
is given.

7. Answers may vary. A sample is given.

9. 1,080 **11.** 108° **13.** Octagon, regular
15. Pentagon, not regular

Pages 218–219
1. No **3.** Yes
5.

Corres. vertices	Corres. sides	Corres. angles
F and P	$\overline{CF} \cong \overline{QP}$	$\angle F \cong \angle P$
C and Q	$\overline{CD} \cong \overline{QR}$	$\angle C \cong \angle Q$
D and R	$\overline{DE} \cong \overline{RS}$	$\angle D \cong \angle R$
E and S	$\overline{EF} \cong \overline{SP}$	$\angle E \cong \angle S$

7. 27 mm **9.** 25 mm **11.** 68° **13.** 4.8 cm **15.** 2 cm
17. 30 ° **19.** Yes

Pages 220–221
1. No **3.** Yes **5.** $w = 13$ **7.** $a = 50$ **9.** $x = 30$
11. 22.5 cm, 15 cm, 30 cm

Pages 222–223
1. a, c, d, l, n, p **3.** c, d **5.** e **7.** b, e, k **9.** c, d, l, n
11. f **13.** d **15.** d, e, f, h
17. Answers may vary. A sample is given.

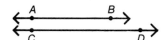

19. Answers may vary. A sample is given.

21. Answers may vary. A sample is given.

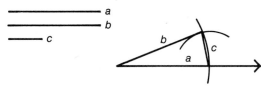

23. Answers may vary. A sample is given.

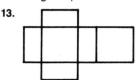

Pages 224–225
1. $\overline{KS}$, $\overline{KT}$, $\overline{KU}$, $\overline{KV}$ **3.** $\overline{PQ}$, $\overline{PS}$, $\overline{QR}$, $\overline{QS}$, $\overline{RS}$ **5.** $\angle PQR$,
$\angle PQS$, $\angle RQS$, $\angle PSR$, $\angle PSQ$, $\angle RSQ$, $\angle QRS$, $\angle QPS$
7. $\angle STU$ **9.** $m\angle JLK = 85°$, $m\angle NLK = m\angle JLM = 95°$
11. All the angles have the same measure

Pages 226–227
1. Rectangular prism **3.** Cylinder **5.** Cone
7. Pentagonal prism **9.** Rectangular **11.** 9
13.

15. Cylinder **17.** Cone

Pages 228–229
1. 6 **3.** 11 **5.** 8 **7.** 14 **9.** 10 **11.** 17 **13.** 16 **15.** 26
17. 200 **19.** 302 **21.** $3n$ **23.** $n + 2$ **25.** 2 **27.** 4
29. 8 **31.** 8 **33.** 5 **35.** 2 **37.** 6 **39.** 12 **41.** 16
43. 9 **45.** 2 **47.** 101 **49.** 202 **51.** $2n$ **53.** $n + 1$
55. 2

Chapter 8

Pages 234–235
1. 114 ft.   **3.** 48 in.   **5.** 182 units   **7.** 8.6 m   **9.** 26 cm
11. 36 ft.

Pages 236–237
1. 594 sq. in.   **3.** 70 sq. yd.   **5.** 3.52 sq. units
7. 54 sq. units   **9.** 60 sq. ft.   **11.** 432 sq. ft.   **13.** 432 tiles

Pages 238–239
1. 37.5 sq. ft.   **3.** 433.1 m²   **5.** 234 sq. units   **7.** 3.8 m²
9. 48 sq. ft.

Pages 240–241
1. About 63 or $62\frac{6}{7}$ in.   **3.** About 50 or $50\frac{2}{7}$ units
5. About 6 or $6\frac{2}{7}$ mi.   **7.** About 8 or $7\frac{6}{7}$ cm
9. About 82 or $81\frac{5}{7}$ units   **11.** About 20 or $20\frac{3}{7}$ yd.
13. About $2\frac{1}{5}$ mi.   **15.** About $942\frac{6}{7}$ ft.

Pages 242–243
1. About 12.6 or $12\frac{4}{7}$ cm²   **3.** About 7.1 or $7\frac{1}{14}$ sq. yd.
5. About 38.5 or $38\frac{1}{2}$ sq. ft.   **7.** About 153.9 or
154 sq. in.   **9.** About 45.3 or $45\frac{67}{175}$ sq. yd.
11. About 615.4 or 616 sq. units   **13.** About 530.7 or
$531\frac{1}{7}$ sq. units   **15.** About 21.2 or $21\frac{43}{175}$ m²
17. About 157 sq. in.   **19.** About 113 sq. ft.
21. About 285 sq. ft.

Pages 244–245
1. $19.98   **3.** 11,380 sq. ft.   **5.** About 36.77 sq. ft.
7. 0 ft., because the two perimeters are equal

Pages 246–247
1. 376 cm²   **3.** 110 cm²   **5.** 2.6 sq. units   **7.** $138\frac{1}{2}$ sq. ft.

Pages 248–249
1. About $578\frac{2}{7}$ sq. units   **3.** About 650 sq. in.
5. About 152.6 sq. units   **7.** About 1,584 sq. in.

Pages 250–251
1. About 4 qt.   **3.** About 3 gal.   **5.** About 11 gal.

Pages 252–253
1. 192 m³   **3.** About 1,526 or $1,527\frac{3}{7}$ cu. units
5. About 251 or $251\frac{3}{7}$ cu. in.   **7.** About 249 or $249\frac{12}{25}$ m³
9. About 1,780 or 1,782 cu. in.   **11.** 228 cm³   **13.** About
384.7 cm³   **15.** About 296.7 cm²

Pages 254–255
1. 126 m³   **3.** 120 cu. in.   **5.** About 377 or
$377\frac{1}{7}$ cu. units   **7.** 40 cu. ft.   **9.** $106\frac{2}{3}$ cu. in.
11. About 8 or $8\frac{8}{21}$ cu. ft.   **13.** About 262.2 cu. in.
15. The square pyramid in Problem 14

Pages 256–257
1. 34 in.   **3.** 21.3 m   **5.** 48 sq. in.   **7.** 21 m²
9. About 1,036 cm²   **11.** 90 sq. ft.   **13.** About 2,093 cm³
15. 39 cu. ft.   **17.** About 117 in.   **19.** About 707 cm³
21. About 173 cm²   **23.** 8,325 sq. ft.

Pages 258–259
1. 20 km   **3.** 9 km   **5.** 54 km²   **7.** 40 km   **9.** Doubled
11. Quadrupled   **13.** Quadrupled   **15.** Multiplied by 16
17. 4 ft.   **19.** 8 ft.   **21.** 192 cu. ft.   **23.** 9 ft.   **25.** 468 sq.
ft.   **27.** 8 ft.   **29.** 16 ft.   **31.** 1,536 cu. ft.   **33.** Multiplied
by 9   **35.** Multiplied by 25   **37.** Multiplied by 27
39. Multiplied by 125

Chapter 9

Pages 264–265
1. 80 books   **3.** 30 books   **5.** 35 books
7. Mon., Wed., Fri.   **9.** 55

Pages 266–267
1. 1972   **3.** 1976   **5.** 62,500,000   **7.** 61,900,000
9. 61,000,000   **11.** 1973, 1976, 1977, 1978, 1979
13. 1,500,000   **15.** 1980   **17.** 10,000   **19.** 1979
21. 26,000   **23.** Increasing

Pages 268–269
1. 18 /s   **3.** 305 consonants   **5.** $450,000   **7.** $96,000
9. 135°

Pages 270–271
1. 8.1   **3.** 5, 8   **5.** 4.2   **7.** 23.6   **9.** 16, 24   **11.** 251
13. 85.7   **15.** C   **17.** 95

Pages 272–273
1. 435 students   **3.** 1982   **5.** 105 students   **7.** 108°

9.

Test Score	Tally	Frequency
A	𝗜𝗜𝗜𝗜 𝗜𝗜	7
B	𝗜𝗜𝗜𝗜 𝗜𝗜	7
C	𝗜𝗜𝗜𝗜 𝗜𝗜𝗜𝗜 𝗜	11
D	𝗜𝗜𝗜𝗜	4
F	𝗜𝗜	2

11. 800

13.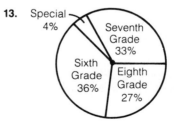

15. 82   **17.** 100   **19.** 64.7 in.   **21.** 66 in., 59 in.

Pages 274–275
1. Mean: 301, median: 141.5, mode: 117   mean
3. Increasing rapidly   **5.** Increasing slowly   **7.** Median or mode

9.

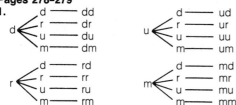

Pages 276–277
1. 1960   **3.** 1948, 1956, 1960, 1964   **5.** 81 in.

Pages 278–279
1.

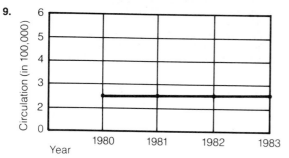

16 codes
3. 30,240 codes   **5.** 10,000,000 numbers
7. 12 combinations

Pages 280–281
1. $\frac{1}{10}$ **3.** $\frac{5}{10}$ or $\frac{1}{2}$ **5.** $\frac{1}{26}$ **7.** $\frac{3}{26}$ **9.** $\frac{1}{2}$ **11.** 1   **13.** $\frac{28}{60}$ or $\frac{7}{15}$
15. $\frac{16}{60}$ or $\frac{4}{15}$ **17.** $\frac{35}{60}$ or $\frac{7}{12}$ **19.** $\frac{5}{8}$

Pages 282–283
1. $\frac{1}{12}$ **3.** $\frac{1}{4}$ **5.** $\frac{4}{12}$ or $\frac{1}{3}$ **7.** $\frac{1}{100}$ **9.** $\frac{1}{216}$

Pages 284–285
1. $\frac{20}{90}$ or $\frac{2}{9}$ **3.** $\frac{1}{90}$ **5.** $\frac{60}{720}$ or $\frac{1}{12}$ **7.** 0   **9.** $\frac{552}{1,560}$ or $\frac{23}{65}$
11. $\frac{384}{1,560}$ or $\frac{16}{65}$

Pages 286–287
1. $\frac{65}{1,000}$ or $\frac{13}{200}$ **3.** $\frac{576}{1,000}$ or $\frac{72}{125}$ **5.** $\frac{170}{500}$ or $\frac{17}{50}$ **7.** $\frac{302}{500}$ or $\frac{151}{250}$
9. $\frac{5}{500}$ or $\frac{1}{100}$ **11.** $\frac{140}{500}$ or $\frac{7}{25}$ **13.** $\frac{2,640}{10,000}$ or $\frac{33}{125}$

Pages 228–289
1. About 50 students   **3.** About 45 students   **5.** About 620 students   **7.** About 150 defective tires   **9.** About 72 cars

Chapter 10

Pages 296–297
1. A withdrawal of $22   **3.** 455 mi. north   **5.** 60   **7.** −456
9. 4,058   **11.** 123   **13.** −14   **15.** −100   **17.** 74   **19.** −45
21. −14, no

Pages 298–299
1. >   **3.** >   **5.** <   **7.** >   **9.** <   **11.** <   **13.** <   **15.** >
17. −8 −3 8   **19.** −9 −2 3 5   **21.** −12 −9 0 8
23. Evening   **25.** Evening low, morning low, morning high, evening high

Pages 300–301
1. −10   **3.** 11   **5.** −3   **7.** 7   **9.** 0   **11.** −8   **13.** −22
15. 11   **17.** 15   **19.** −3   **21.** −10   **23.** 3 seats   **25.** 1 seat

Pages 302–303
1. −8   **3.** −1   **5.** −5   **7.** 2   **9.** 0   **11.** 38   **13.** 32   **15.** 34
17. −30   **19.** 8   **21.** −70   **23.** 15   **25.** 31   **27.** −4
29. 4 min.   **31.** 13 min.

33.

Day	Flight Time
Mon.	113 min.
Tue.	99 min.
Wed.	86 min.
Thur.	117 min.
Fri.	79 min.
Sat.	89 min.
Sun.	91 min.

Pages 304–305
1. −6   **3.** −12   **5.** 0   **7.** −5   **9.** 3   **11.** 5   **13.** 0   **15.** 11
17. 17   **19.** 12   **21.** 28   **23.** 645 mph   **25.** 560 mph

Pages 306–307
1. 24   **3.** −27   **5.** 24   **7.** −90   **9.** −144   **11.** 0   **13.** 64
15. 126   **17.** −6,400   **19.** 9   **21.** 125   **23.** 16   **25.** 192
27. 30   **29.** 10,368   **31.** −11   **33.** 8   **35.** $600

Pages 308–309
1. −6   **3.** 11   **5.** 3   **7.** −2   **9.** 0   **11.** −20   **13.** −7   **15.** 0
17. 4   **19.** −5   **21.** 33   **23.** −17   **25.** 900   **27.** −6
29. $3,000   **31.** $16.67 profit

Pages 310–311
1. 490 ft. above sea level   **3.** 30 degrees below zero
5. −14   **7.** 3,788   **9.** −49   **11.** −84   **13.** 11   **15.** 8   **17.** 5
19. −40   **21.** 68   **23.** 0   **25.** 38   **27.** 36   **29.** −13
31. −7   **33.** −72   **35.** 0   **37.** 11   **39.** −10 −3 0 9   **41.** 4
43. 8   **45.** $3,200 profit   **47.** 5 ft. below flood stage

Pages 312–313
1. −24   **3.** 2   **5.** 13   **7.** −4   **9.** 5   **11.** −35   **13.** −9
15. 21   **17.** 2   **19.** 8   **21.** −219   **23.** −25   **25.** 51
27. −20   **29.** 23

Pages 360–361
1. $c = -10$ **3.** $r = -1$ **5.** $x = 16$ **7.** $a = 2$ **9.** $x = 5$
11. $c = -10$ **13.** $m = -13.5$ **15.** $z = 8.1$ **17.** $x = 3.3$
19. $q = -10.1$ **21.** $d = -\frac{1}{4}$ **23.** $t = \frac{5}{6}$ **25.** $m = -\frac{3}{8}$
27. $x = 12\frac{43}{45}$ **29.** $-35°C$ **31.** $25°C$

Pages 362–363
1. $x = -12$ **3.** $y = 4\frac{2}{3}$ **5.** $a = -7$ **7.** $n = \frac{3}{4}$ **9.** $a = 12$
11. $x = 1\frac{1}{2}$ **13.** $m = -27$ **15.** $x = 2\frac{1}{3}$ **17.** $x = 2$
19. $t = -3$ **21.** $x = \frac{1}{2}$ **23.** $n = 1.5$ **25.** $y = 13.75$
27. 8 hr.

Pages 364–365

1. 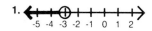 **3.**

5. 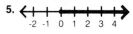 **7.**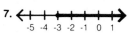

9.

11. $x \le -4$ **13.** $x = -3$ **15.** $x > -1$

17.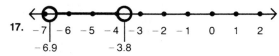

Pages 366–367
1. $1 < 5$ **3.** $0 \le 1\frac{1}{4}$ **5.** $1.1 < 2$ **7.** $x < 2$ **9.** $z > 24$
11. $c \le 4$ **13.** $d > -3$ **15.** $9 < q$ **17.** $3.1 \le x$
19. $r < 0.9$ **21.** $3.7 \le t$ **23.** $a > 4.1$ **25.** $12.5 < n$
27. $r \le -2.3$ **29.** $-5.9 \ge x$ **31.** $-9,000 < -7,000$
33. $-11,000 < -9,000$

Pages 368–369
1. $10 < 14$ **3.** $0 \ge -24$ **5.** $10 \ge -30$ **7.** $10 > -4$
9. $n < 6$ **11.** $x > -2$ **13.** $a \le -5$ **15.** $q \ge 4$ **17.** $c \ge 6$
19. $s \ge -6$ **21.** $x \le 20$ **23.** $m < 40$
25. More than 2.5 ft. per sec.

Pages 370–371
1. $x = 6$ **3.** $x = 4$ **5.** $x = -4$ **7.** $x = -5$ **9.** $x = 4.3$
11. $x = -7$ **13.** $x = -1$ **15.** $x = 3$ **17.** $x = 1\frac{1}{3}$
19. $x = -1\frac{1}{3}$ **21.** $x = 7$

23. 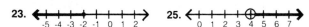 **25.**

27. $y \ge 2$ **29.** $q < 15$ **31.** $w \ge 0.2$ **33.** $s < -\frac{5}{8}$
35. $m \le 10\frac{2}{3}$ **37.** 4.4°F above normal
39. 11.6°F below normal

Pages 372–373
1. Pegasus, QII **3.** Ophiuchus, x-axis **5.** Cetus, QI
7. Cancer, QIV **9.** Leo, y-axis **11.** Cygnus, QII
13. Taurus, QI **15.** Ursa Major, QIII **17.** (6, 1)
19. $(-5, -7)$ **21.** $(-4.5, -4)$ **23.** $(-5.5, 4.5)$

25-34.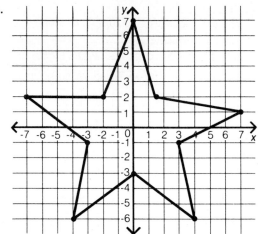

Pages 374–375

1.

x	-4	-2	0	2	4
y	-4	-2	0	2	4

3.

x	-4	-2	0	2	4
y	-7	-5	-3	-1	1

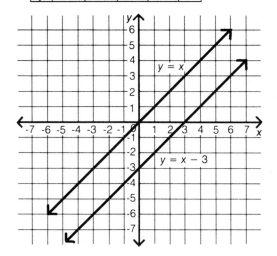

5.

x	−4	−2	0	2	4
y	4	2	0	−2	−4

7.

x	−5	−4	−2	0	1
y	1	0	−2	−4	−5

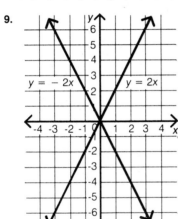

9.

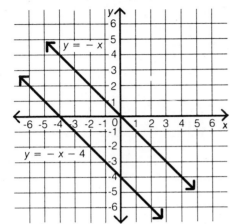

11.

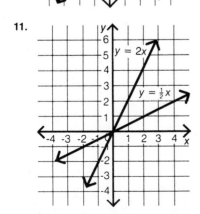

13. Parallel, rising to right **15.** Both pass through the origin **17.** Both pass through the origin **19.** $y = kx$, where k is positive **21.** About 300 cm^3

Pages 376–377
1. At 4 hr.
3. Less than 4 hr.

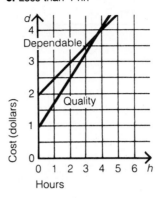

5. More than 250 mi.

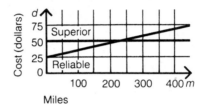

7. At 500 mi.
9. Less than 500 mi.

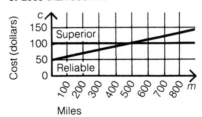

Pages 378–379
1.

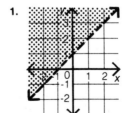

3.

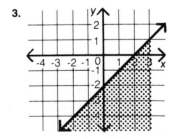

5.

7.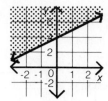

9.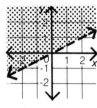

11.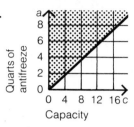

Squares and Square Roots

n	n^2	$\sqrt{n}$	n	n^2	$\sqrt{n}$	n	n^2	$\sqrt{n}$	n	n^2	$\sqrt{n}$
1	1	1.000	51	2,601	7.141	101	10,201	10.050	151	22,801	12.288
2	4	1.414	52	2,704	7.211	102	10,404	10.100	152	23,104	12.329
3	9	1.732	53	2,809	7.280	103	10,609	10.149	153	23,409	12.369
4	16	2.000	54	2,916	7.348	104	10,816	10.198	154	23,716	12.410
5	25	2.236	55	3,025	7.416	105	11,025	10.247	155	24,025	12.450
6	36	2.449	56	3,136	7.483	106	11,236	10.296	156	24,336	12.490
7	49	2.646	57	3,249	7.550	107	11,449	10.344	157	24,649	12.530
8	64	2.828	58	3,364	7.616	108	11,664	10.392	158	24,964	12.570
9	81	3.000	59	3,481	7.681	109	11,881	10.440	159	25,281	12.610
10	100	3.162	60	3,600	7.746	110	12,100	10.488	160	25,600	12.649
11	121	3.317	61	3,721	7.810	111	12,321	10.536	161	25,921	12.689
12	144	3.464	62	3,844	7.874	112	12,544	10.583	162	26,244	12.728
13	169	3.606	63	3,969	7.937	113	12,769	10.630	163	26,569	12.767
14	196	3.742	64	4,096	8.000	114	12,996	10.677	164	26,896	12.806
15	225	3.873	65	4,225	8.062	115	13,225	10.724	165	27,225	12.845
16	256	4.000	66	4,356	8.124	116	13,456	10.770	166	27,556	12.884
17	289	4.123	67	4,489	8.185	117	13,689	10.817	167	27,889	12.923
18	324	4.243	68	4,624	8.246	118	13,924	10.863	168	28,224	12.961
19	361	4.359	69	4,761	8.307	119	14,161	10.909	169	28,561	13.000
20	400	4.472	70	4,900	8.367	120	14,400	10.954	170	28,900	13.038
21	441	4.583	71	5,041	8.426	121	14,641	11.000	171	29,241	13.077
22	484	4.690	72	5,184	8.485	122	14,884	11.045	172	29,584	13.115
23	529	4.796	73	5,329	8.544	123	15,129	11.091	173	29,929	13.153
24	576	4.899	74	5,476	8.602	124	15,376	11.136	174	30,276	13.191
25	625	5.000	75	5,625	8.660	125	15,625	11.180	175	30,625	13.229
26	676	5.099	76	5,776	8.718	126	15,876	11.225	176	30,976	13.266
27	729	5.196	77	5,929	8.775	127	16,129	11.269	177	31,329	13.304
28	784	5.292	78	6,084	8.832	128	16,384	11.314	178	31,684	13.342
29	841	5.385	79	6,241	8.888	129	16,641	11.358	179	32,041	13.379
30	900	5.477	80	6,400	8.944	130	16,900	11.402	180	32,400	13.416
31	961	5.568	81	6,561	9.000	131	17,161	11.446	181	32,761	13.454
32	1,024	5.657	82	6,724	9.055	132	17,424	11.489	182	33,124	13.491
33	1,089	5.745	83	6,889	9.110	133	17,689	11.533	183	33,489	13.528
34	1,156	5.831	84	7,056	9.165	134	17,956	11.576	184	33,856	13.565
35	1,225	5.916	85	7,225	9.220	135	18,225	11.619	185	34,225	13.601
36	1,296	6.000	86	7,396	9.274	136	18,496	11.662	186	34,596	13.638
37	1,369	6.083	87	7,569	9.327	137	18,769	11.705	187	34,969	13.675
38	1,444	6.164	88	7,744	9.381	138	19,044	11.747	188	35,344	13.711
39	1,521	6.245	89	7,921	9.434	139	19,321	11.790	189	35,721	13.748
40	1,600	6.325	90	8,100	9.487	140	19,600	11.832	190	36,100	13.784
41	1,681	6.403	91	8,281	9.539	141	19,881	11.874	191	36,481	13.820
42	1,764	6.481	92	8,464	9.592	142	20,164	11.916	192	36,864	13.856
43	1,849	6.557	93	8,649	9.644	143	20,449	11.958	193	37,249	13.892
44	1,936	6.633	94	8,836	9.695	144	20,736	12.000	194	37,636	13.928
45	2,025	6.708	95	9,025	9.747	145	21,025	12.042	195	38,025	13.964
46	2,116	6.782	96	9,216	9.798	146	21,316	12.083	196	38,416	14.000
47	2,209	6.856	97	9,409	9.849	147	21,609	12.124	197	38,809	14.036
48	2,304	6.928	98	9,604	9.899	148	21,904	12.166	198	39,204	14.071
49	2,401	7.000	99	9,801	9.950	149	22,201	12.207	199	39,601	14.107
50	2,500	7.071	100	10,000	10.000	150	22,500	12.247	200	40,000	14.142

Trigonometric Ratios

Measure of angle	tan	sin	cos	Measure of angle	tan	sin	cos
1°	0.017	0.017	1.000	46°	1.036	0.719	0.695
2°	0.035	0.035	0.999	47°	1.072	0.731	0.682
3°	0.052	0.052	0.999	48°	1.111	0.743	0.669
4°	0.070	0.070	0.998	49°	1.150	0.755	0.656
5°	0.087	0.087	0.996	50°	1.192	0.766	0.643
6°	0.105	0.105	0.995	51°	1.235	0.777	0.629
7°	0.123	0.122	0.993	52°	1.280	0.788	0.616
8°	0.141	0.139	0.990	53°	1.327	0.799	0.602
9°	0.158	0.156	0.988	54°	1.376	0.809	0.588
10°	0.176	0.174	0.985	55°	1.428	0.819	0.574
11°	0.194	0.191	0.982	56°	1.483	0.829	0.559
12°	0.213	0.208	0.978	57°	1.540	0.839	0.545
13°	0.231	0.225	0.974	58°	1.600	0.848	0.530
14°	0.249	0.242	0.970	59°	1.664	0.857	0.515
15°	0.268	0.259	0.966	60°	1.732	0.866	0.500
16°	0.287	0.276	0.961	61°	1.804	0.875	0.485
17°	0.306	0.292	0.956	62°	1.881	0.883	0.469
18°	0.325	0.309	0.951	63°	1.963	0.891	0.454
19°	0.344	0.326	0.946	64°	2.050	0.899	0.438
20°	0.364	0.342	0.940	65°	2.145	0.906	0.423
21°	0.384	0.358	0.934	66°	2.246	0.914	0.407
22°	0.404	0.375	0.927	67°	2.356	0.921	0.391
23°	0.424	0.391	0.921	68°	2.475	0.927	0.375
24°	0.445	0.407	0.914	69°	2.605	0.934	0.358
25°	0.466	0.423	0.906	70°	2.748	0.940	0.342
26°	0.488	0.438	0.899	71°	2.904	0.946	0.326
27°	0.510	0.454	0.891	72°	3.078	0.951	0.309
28°	0.532	0.469	0.883	73°	3.271	0.956	0.292
29°	0.554	0.485	0.875	74°	3.487	0.961	0.276
30°	0.577	0.500	0.866	75°	3.732	0.966	0.259
31°	0.601	0.515	0.857	76°	4.011	0.970	0.242
32°	0.625	0.530	0.848	77°	4.332	0.974	0.225
33°	0.649	0.545	0.839	78°	4.705	0.978	0.208
34°	0.675	0.559	0.829	79°	5.145	0.982	0.191
35°	0.700	0.574	0.819	80°	5.671	0.985	0.174
36°	0.727	0.588	0.809	81°	6.314	0.988	0.156
37°	0.754	0.602	0.799	82°	7.115	0.990	0.139
38°	0.781	0.616	0.788	83°	8.144	0.993	0.122
39°	0.810	0.629	0.777	84°	9.514	0.995	0.105
40°	0.839	0.643	0.766	85°	11.430	0.996	0.087
41°	0.869	0.656	0.755	86°	14.301	0.998	0.070
42°	0.900	0.669	0.743	87°	19.081	0.999	0.052
43°	0.933	0.682	0.731	88°	28.636	0.999	0.035
44°	0.966	0.695	0.719	89°	57.290	1.000	0.017
45°	1.000	0.707	0.707				

Tangent

length of opposite side
length of adjacent side

Sine

length of opposite side
length of hypotenuse

Cosine

length of adjacent side
length of hypotenuse

Tables

Metric System

Length
$$10 \text{ millimeters (mm)} = 1 \text{ centimeter (cm)}$$
$$\left.\begin{array}{c} 10 \text{ centimeters} \\ 100 \text{ millimeters} \end{array}\right\} = 1 \text{ decimeter (dm)}$$
$$\left.\begin{array}{c} 10 \text{ decimeters} \\ 100 \text{ centimeters} \end{array}\right\} = 1 \text{ meter (m)}$$
$$1,000 \text{ meters} = 1 \text{ kilometer (km)}$$

Area
$$100 \text{ square millimeters (mm}^2) = 1 \text{ square centimeter (cm}^2)$$
$$10,000 \text{ square centimeters} = 1 \text{ square meter (m}^2)$$
$$100 \text{ square meters} = 1 \text{ are (a)}$$
$$10,000 \text{ square meters} = 1 \text{ hectare (ha)}$$

Volume
$$1,000 \text{ cubic millimeters (mm}^3) = 1 \text{ cubic centimeter (cm}^3)$$
$$1,000 \text{ cubic centimeters} = 1 \text{ cubic decimeter (dm}^3)$$
$$1,000,000 \text{ cubic centimeters} = 1 \text{ cubic meter (m}^3)$$

Mass (weight)
$$1,000 \text{ milligrams (mg)} = 1 \text{ gram (g)}$$
$$1,000 \text{ grams} = 1 \text{ kilogram (kg)}$$
$$1,000 \text{ kilograms} = 1 \text{ metric ton (t)}$$

Capacity
$$1,000 \text{ milliliters (mL)} = 1 \text{ liter (L)}$$

Customary System

Length
$$12 \text{ inches (in.)} = 1 \text{ foot (ft.)}$$
$$\left.\begin{array}{c} 3 \text{ feet} \\ 36 \text{ inches} \end{array}\right\} = 1 \text{ yard (yd.)}$$
$$\left.\begin{array}{c} 1,760 \text{ yards} \\ 5,280 \text{ feet} \end{array}\right\} = 1 \text{ mile (mi.)}$$
$$6,076 \text{ feet} = 1 \text{ nautical mile}$$

Area
$$144 \text{ square inches (sq. in.)} = 1 \text{ square foot (sq. ft.)}$$
$$9 \text{ square feet} = 1 \text{ square yard (sq. yd.)}$$
$$4,840 \text{ square yards} = 1 \text{ acre (A.)}$$

Volume
$$1,728 \text{ cubic inches (cu. in.)} = 1 \text{ cubic foot (cu. ft.)}$$
$$27 \text{ cubic feet} = 1 \text{ cubic yard (cu. yd.)}$$

Weight
$$16 \text{ ounces (oz.)} = 1 \text{ pound (lb.)}$$
$$2,000 \text{ pounds} = 1 \text{ ton (T.)}$$

Capacity
$$8 \text{ fluid ounces (fl. oz.)} = 1 \text{ cup (c.)}$$
$$2 \text{ cups} = 1 \text{ pint (pt.)}$$
$$2 \text{ pints} = 1 \text{ quart (qt.)}$$
$$4 \text{ quarts} = 1 \text{ gallon (gal.)}$$

Time

$$60 \text{ seconds} = 1 \text{ minute}$$
$$60 \text{ minutes} = 1 \text{ hour}$$
$$24 \text{ hours} = 1 \text{ day}$$
$$7 \text{ days} = 1 \text{ week}$$
$$\left.\begin{array}{c} 365 \text{ days} \\ 52 \text{ weeks} \\ 12 \text{ months} \end{array}\right\} = 1 \text{ year}$$
$$366 \text{ days} = 1 \text{ leap year}$$

Geometric Formulas

Area

rectangle	$A = \ell w$
parallelogram	$A = bh$
triangle	$A = \frac{1}{2}bh$
circle	$A = \pi r^2$

Surface Area

cylinder	$A = 2\pi r^2 + 2\pi rh$

Circumference

circle	$C = \pi d$ or
	$C = 2\pi r$

Perimeter

rectangle	$P = 2\ell + 2w$

Volume

rectangular prism	$V = \ell wh$
prism	$V = Bh$
cylinder	$V = \pi r^2 h$

Glossary

Acute angle An angle that has a measure less than 90°.

Addition property of zero The sum of zero and a number is that number.

Adjacent angles Angles *ABC* and *CBD* are adjacent.

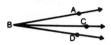

Alternate interior angles See transversal.

Altitude of a triangle A segment that extends from one vertex of the triangle to the opposite side and is perpendicular to that side.

Angle (∠) The figure formed by two rays with the same endpoint.

Arc Part of a circle

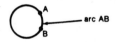

Area A number indicating the size of the inside of a plane figure.

Associative property of addition The way in which addends are grouped does not affect the sum. For example,
$(7 + 2) + 5 = 7 + (2 + 5)$

Associative property of multiplication The way in which factors are grouped does not affect the product. For example,
$(7 \times 2) \times 5 = 7 \times (2 \times 5)$

Average A number obtained by dividing the sum of two or more addends by the number of addends.

BASIC A simple language used to give instructions to computers.

Binary numbers Base two numbers which are used to store numbers in a computer.

Central angle An angle with its vertex at the center of a circle.

Chord A segment whose endpoints are on a circle. A diameter is a special chord.

Circle A plane figure with all of its points the same distance from a given point called the center.

Circumference The distance around a circle.

Common denominator A common multiple of two or more denominators. A common denominator for $\frac{1}{6}$ and $\frac{3}{8}$ is 48.

Common factor A number that is a factor of two or more numbers. A common factor of 6 and 12 is 3.

Common multiple A number that is a multiple of two or more numbers. A common multiple of 4 and 6 is 12.

Commutative property of addition The order in which numbers are added does not affect the sum. For example,
$4 + 6 = 6 + 4$.

Commutative property of multiplication The order in which numbers are multiplied does not affect the product. For example,
$4 \times 6 = 6 \times 4$.

Composite number A whole number, greater than 0, that has more than two factors.

Computer program A set of instructions that tells the computer how to do a certain job.

Concentric circles Circles in the same plane that have the same center but different radii.

Cone A space figure formed by connecting a circle to a point not in the plane of the circle.

Congruent Having the same size and the same shape.

Consecutive angles In this quadrilateral, angles *J* and *K* are consecutive.

Cosine For a given acute angle in a right triangle, the ratio:
$$\frac{\text{length of adjacent side}}{\text{length of hypotenuse}}$$

Cross-products For the ratios $\frac{3}{4}$ and $\frac{9}{12}$, the cross-products are 3×12 and 4×9.

Cube A prism with all square faces.

Cylinder A space figure shaped like this.

Degree (of an angle) A unit for measuring angles.

Diagonal In a polygon, a segment that connects one vertex to another vertex but is not a side of the polygon.

Diameter In a circle, a segment that passes through the center and has its endpoints on the circle.

Distributive property The general pattern of numbers of which the following is an example.
$4 \times (7 + 3) = (4 \times 7) + (4 \times 3)$

Dividend   A number that is divided by another number. In 48 ÷ 6 = 8, the dividend is 48.

Divisor   A number that divides another number. In 48 ÷ 6 = 8, the divisor is 6.

Edge   In a space figure, a segment where two faces meet.

END   The last line in a BASIC computer program.

Endpoint   The point at the end of a segment or ray.

Equation   A mathematical sentence that uses the = symbol.
    $14 - 7 = 7$.

Equilateral triangle   A triangle with all three sides congruent.

Even number   A whole number with a factor of 2.

Exponent   In 4^3, the exponent is 3. It tells that 4 is to be used as a factor three times.
    $4^3 = 4 \times 4 \times 4$

Exponential form   The form that the computer uses to print very large or very small numbers.

Face   A flat surface that is part of a polyhedron.

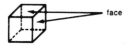

Factor   (1) A number to be multiplied. (2) A number that divides evenly into a given second number is a factor of that number.

Factorial   The product of a whole number and every whole number less than itself.
    $4! = 4 \times 3 \times 2 \times 1 = 24$.

Flow chart   A diagram illustrating the steps used to solve a problem.

FOR . . . NEXT   BASIC statements in a computer program that tell the computer to do something a certain number of times.

FORWARD (FD)   A LOGO command that tells the turtle to move forward a certain number of steps.

Fraction   A number written in the form $\frac{a}{b}$, such as $\frac{2}{3}$, or $\frac{11}{5}$, or $\frac{4}{1}$.

Frequency table   In statistics, a listing of the data and how many times each item of data occurred.

GO TO   A BASIC statement in a computer program that tells the computer to go to another line in the program.

Greatest common factor   The greatest number that is a factor of two or more numbers. The greatest common factor of 8 and 12 is 4.

Hexadecimal numbers   Base sixteen numbers used for storage in a computer.

Hexagon   A six-sided polygon.

Hypotenuse   In a right triangle, the side opposite the right angle.

IF . . . THEN   A BASIC statement used to test certain conditions and act on the results of the test.

Improper fraction   A fraction, such as $\frac{15}{2}$ or $\frac{2}{1}$, that can be written as a mixed number or as a whole number greater than zero.

INPUT   A BASIC statement in a computer program that allows information to be entered into the program by the program user.

Inscribed angle   An angle whose vertex is on a circle and whose sides cut off an arc of the circle.

Inscribed polygon   A polygon inside a circle with its vertices on the circle.

INT (N)   A BASIC function used on the computer to find the greatest integer less than or equal to N.

Integers   The whole numbers and their opposites. Some integers are +2, −2, +75, and −75.

Intersecting lines   Two lines that meet at exactly one point.

Isosceles triangle   A triangle with at least two sides congruent.

Least common multiple   The smallest number that is a common multiple of two given numbers. The least common multiple for 6 and 8 is 24.

LET   A BASIC statement that allows a value to be assigned to a memory location named by a letter.

LOGO   A simple language used to give instructions to a computer.

Loop   A set of instructions that a computer carries out more than once.

Lowest terms   A fraction is in lowest terms if 1 is the only number that will divide both the numerator and the denominator.

Mean   Another name for "average." The mean of the set 2, 4, 5, 6, 6 is 23 ÷ 5, or 4.6.

Median   The middle number in a set of numbers when the numbers are in order. The median of the set 2, 4, 5, 6, 6 is 5.

Midpoint   The point in a segment that divides it into two equal parts.

Mixed number   A number that has a whole number part and a fraction part, such as $3\frac{1}{4}$ and $6\frac{7}{8}$.

Mode   The number that occurs most often in a set of numbers. The mode of 2, 4, 5, 6, 6 is 6.

Multiple A multiple of a number is the product of that number and a whole number. Some multiples of 3 are 3, 6, and 9.

Multiplication property of one The product of a number and one is that number.

Negative integer An integer less than 0, such as −1, −5, −7, or −10.

Obtuse angle An angle that has a measure greater than 90° and less than 180°.

Octagon An eight-sided polygon.

Odd number A whole number that does not have 2 as a factor.

Opposite angles In this quadrilateral, angles J and L are opposite angles.

opposite angles

Opposites Two numbers whose sum is 0. +5 and −5 are opposites because +5 + (−5) = 0.

Ordered pair A number pair, such as (3, 5), in which 3 is the first number and 5 is the second number.

Origin On a coordinate grid, the point, (0, 0), where the two number lines, or axes, intersect.

Output Any information that is produced by a computer.

Parallel lines Lines in the same plane that do not meet.

Parallelogram A quadrilateral with opposite sides parallel and equal.

Pentagon A five-sided polygon.

Percent (%) A word indicating "hundredths" or "out of 100." 45 percent (45%) means 0.45 or $\frac{45}{100}$.

Perimeter The sum of the lengths of the sides of a polygon.

Permutations The ordered arrangements of a set of objects or numbers. The permutations of the set A, B, C are:

ABC BAC CAB
ACB BCA CBA

Perpendicular lines Two intersecting lines that form right angles.

Pi (π) The number obtained by dividing the circumference of any circle by its diameter. A common approximation for π is 3.14.

Polygon A plane figure made up of segments called its *sides*, each side intersecting two other sides, one at each of its endpoints.

Polyhedron A space figure with all flat surfaces. The outline of each surface is a polygon.

Positive integer An integer greater than 0, such as +1, +2, +10, or +35.

Power 3^4 is read "3 to the fourth power." $3^4 = 3 \times 3 \times 3 \times 3 = 81$. The fourth power of 3 is 81. 4^2 is read "4 to the second power" or "4 squared." *See* Exponent.

Precision A property of measurement that depends upon the size of the unit of measure. The smaller the unit, the more precise the measurement.

Prime factor A factor that is a prime number. The prime factors of 10 are 2 and 5.

Prime number A whole number, greater than 1, that has exactly two factors: itself and 1. 17 is a prime number.

PRINT An instruction to the computer to give certain output on the screen.

Prism A polyhedron with two parallel, congruent faces, called *bases*. All other faces are parallelograms.

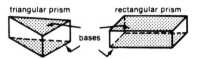

Probability A number that tells how likely it is that a certain event will happen.

Program *See* Computer program

Proportion A statement that two ratios are equal.
$$\frac{2}{5} = \frac{12}{30}$$

Pyramid The space figure formed by connecting points of a polygon to a point not in the plane of the polygon. The polygon and its interior is the *base*.

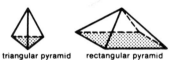

Quadrant One of the four parts into which a plane is divided by two perpendicular lines.

Quadrilateral A four-sided polygon.

Quotient The answer to a division problem. In 48 ÷ 6 = 8, the quotient is 8.

Radius (1) In a circle, a segment that connects the center of the circle with a point on the circle. (2) In a circle, the distance from the center to a point of the circle.

Ratio A pair of numbers that expresses a rate or a comparison.

Rational number Any number that can be expressed as either a terminating decimal or a repeating decimal.
$4\frac{3}{4} = 4.75$ $\frac{1}{3} = 0.333\ldots$

Ray Part of a line that has one endpoint and goes on and on in one direction.

READ . . . DATA Statements that go together in a computer program to assign values to memory locations.

Reciprocals Two numbers whose product is 1. $\frac{3}{4}$ and $\frac{4}{3}$ are reciprocals because $\frac{3}{4} \times \frac{4}{3} = 1$.

Rectangle A parallelogram with four right angles.

Rectangular prism See Prism.

Rectangular pyramid See Pyramid.

Regular polygon A polygon with all sides congruent and all angles congruent.

REM A remark in a program that is intended to be read by someone who lists the program, but it does not affect the logic of the program.

REPEAT A LOGO command that causes a list of commands to be done many times.

Repeating decimal A decimal in which one or more digits keep repeating. 0.518181818 . . .

Rhombus A parallelogram whose sides are congruent.

RIGHT (RT) A LOGO command that directs the turtle to turn right a specified number of turtle turns.

Right angle An angle that has a measure of 90°.

Right triangle A triangle with one right angle.

Scalene triangle A triangle with no two sides congruent.

Scientific notation A method of expressing a number as a product so that:
- the first factor is a number greater than or equal to 1, and less than 10, and
- the second factor is a power of 10.

Segment Part of a line, including the two endpoints.

Semicircle An arc that is one half of a circle.

Significant digits The number of digits in a measurement that have meaning in the measure and are not just estimates. The measurement 7.60 meters has three significant digits: 7, 6, and 0.

Similar figures Figures with the same shape but not necessarily the same size.

Sine For a given acute angle in a right triangle, the ratio:
$$\frac{\text{length of opposite side}}{\text{length of hypotenuse}}$$

Sphere A space figure with all of its points the same distance from a given point called the *center*.

Square A rectangle with all four sides congruent.

Square root A number a is the square root of a number b if $a \times a = b$. 3 is the square root of 9.

Surface area The sum of the areas of all the surfaces of a space figure.

TAB (N) A BASIC function that is used with PRINT to place output at column N on the screen.

Tangent For a given acute angle in a right triangle, the ratio:
$$\frac{\text{length of opposite side}}{\text{length of adjacent side}}$$

Terminating decimal A decimal with a limited number of nonzero digits. Examples are 0.5 and 0.0082.

Transversal A line that intersects two or more other lines in the same plane. In the drawing below, *t* is a transversal and angles 4 and 6 are alternate interior angles.

Trapezoid A quadrilateral with one pair of parallel sides.

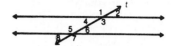

Triangle A three-sided polygon.

Triangular prism See Prism.

Triangular pyramid See Pyramid.

Trigonometric ratios See Cosine, Sine, and Tangent.

Variable In an expression or an equation, a letter that represents a number.

Vertex (1) The common endpoint of two rays that form an angle. (2) The point of intersection of two sides of a polygon. (3) The point of intersection of the edges of a polyhedron.

Volume A number, measured in cubic units, indicating the size of the inside of a space figure.

Index